General's Jottings

National Security, Conflicts & Strategies

General's Jottings

National Security, Conflicts & Strategies

Lt Gen KJ Singh

Title: General's Jottings:
National Security, Conflicts & Strategies
Author: Lt Gen KJ Singh

ISBN: 978-93-92210-91-4

Published by:
JGS Enterprises Pvt Ltd
Imprint: The Browser

Publisher's Address:
SCO 14-15, FF, Sector 8-C, Chandigarh 160 009

Website: thebrowser.org
Email: service@thebrowser.in

Printed in India

© Layout and Cover Design by 99 beagles
99beagles.com

Publishers & Booksellers | Oral History and Military Publishing

Contents

About General's Jottings

Intellectual March in Columns

General's Jottings is an updated and distilled collection of columns and articles published in newspapers and journals, including the ones published online. It is not a lazy compilation of articles but a reordered, updated and organized presentation. After re-attirement I decided to try my hand at writing articles. I wrote for papers like Tribune, Indian Express and online publications like Bharat Shakti. The idea of writing a column on national security in the Times of India's (TOI) regional edition of Chandigarh was proposed by author to Mr Robin David in Sept 2016. He not only liked the proposal but also launched the weekly column titled 'Generals Jottings' in April 2017. More importantly, he also mentored it in its formative stages. When he left on posting to Hyderabad, he passed the baton to Ms Sarju Kaul, who continues mentoring the column with her own value additions. Another big help has been Deputy Editor, Mr Ajay Sura.

Writing columns is an interesting yet challenging task. While there is an assured medium available to columnists, obviating disheartening editorial rejection slips (now emails) while maintaining reliability and addressing contemporary issues is the prime requisite. After an initial struggle, the process becomes addictive, and it is reassuring to hear from readers about missing the column when it is not published. **For me, it is another form of marching, an 'intellectual' one and in 'columns' but articulated in print instead of physically in marching contingents, in uniform.**

The weekly Sunday column series started with two columnists alternating every week. For me, it was a fortnightly column in this shared space. In this journey, starting in April 2017, I have had two very eminent partners: initially, Lieutenant General HS Panag till September 2018 and Lieutenant General DS Hooda, replacing him till August 2020. As we went along, both had other commitments and had to discontinue, so it became a fortnightly column instead of a weekly one from September 2020. **In sum, it has helped me to learn, reflect, and hone my analytical and articulation skills spread over 175 odd columns and 50 other articles.**

These columns helped to re-discover a latent skill of writing articles. My first organized foray after trying my hand in few professional journals was running columns as part of information operations in Nagaland-Manipur in 2002-2004, These were very regular during my two years tenure and continued sporadically till 2009. They were printed under 'Santa-Banta' series under pseudonym and were very popular.

The columns, limited to 900–925 words, are an interesting way to address contemporary issues. Unlike longer format articles, there is hardly any latitude. **Ideally, a column has to be direct, sharp, incisive, and brief yet cover all important aspects of the subject.** The oft-quoted analogy regarding the length of the skirt also applies to columns. Newspaper columns are based on an honorarium system, and payment remains nominal except for a few acclaimed columnists.

This compilation includes longer articles published in Year Books of the United Service Institution of India (USI), Centre for Land Warfare Studies (CLAWS), and compilations by Gyan Chakra and other authors in the form of books. These range from 1,500 to 3,500 words and have been utilised for theme setting and as consolidation papers for various subjects. Important issues have been highlighted, and key takeaway points have been duly flagged. Necessary updates to articles have also been done, along with an indication of the time of writing for better referencing. **Please browse through the Navigation hints to get a better understanding.**

NAGALAND POST

SANTA BANTA'S SALUTE & 'JAI HO' FOR NAGA WOMEN

Santa-Banta are overwhelmed by response of our Naga friends to their last article –"Return of Santa-Banta – Here They Come Calling Again". These reactions mirrored wide range of emotions, mostly full of praise but a few tinged with ridicule, overall of a feeling of acceptance. Let us just share three of these with you – Asenla Jamir mailed to say, "Good you are back, why were you gone? More power to your pen, Nagas need friends like you". Timika said, "Nice reading, good humour, I wish you good luck and God speed". Phunthing's remarks, "Naga struggle in long drawn one, endeavors like your's are unlikely to succeed, others have tried and failed" Please, let your e-mails keep coming on nagasantabanta@gmail.com. There is just one request, please do not direct your lottery related mails to us. Santa-Banta's mail box has been flooded with a flurry of such mails. We wonder if those sending them are indeed our friends or are they our foes or better still friendly foes. We are on a mission for peace and making money is certainly not on our agenda. You know even if we are lucky and make some, promptly tax notices and "Azhas" will follow, so please spare us. No lottery and no taxes and no Azhas please. The bitter reality is that Santa – Banta's better halves Jeeto and Preeto have been shopping away to glory in the hope that the 'Lady Luck' will smile on good old Santa and Banta. Can our groups please send one Azha to Jeeto and Preeto to stop shopping for no lady smiles at old Santa-Banta any more.

Santa Banta would like to salute the real woman of substance and epitome of Nagas courage, compassion and goodness, our very own Icon, Zapatuou u Angami. Those of you who want to heal their souls, forget reading 'Chicken Soup for Soul' but just visit the 30 year old institution, Mother's Orphanage at Kohima. Please meet those lovely 80 children including few from Myanmar besides our North Eastern States, their smiles will captivate you. You will come back feeling healed and closer to the Lord Jesus. Our brave Zapatuou was awarded the 'Real Heroes' award by CNN – IBN. She is the only one from the Eastern India to be given this recognition. We salute her and the courage and sacrifice of all Naga Mothers.

By some strange coincidence we came across some other younger women of substance, the first one was Khegoli Aomi of Dimapur. This 40 something brave President of Dimapur Business Organisation, is a taxation expert of sorts. She is a skilful negotiator with specialization in resolving disputes with our national workers. Besides serving delicious fare in her eating places, she runs a few restaurants, Khegoli has been mediating with factions on taxation. She has helped to secure release of many abducted business men and got tax demands rationalised. Her frank assessment is most heartening, " it takes a lot of time to improve things here but I will carry on for the sake of Nagaland's image". Bravo Khegoli, we wish more Naga women get inspired by you and even some men should learn from you. Another brave woman, just 28 is T Amongla Aier, ASP of Indore East in MP. She is a role model of sorts and her father Toshipa Aier a police officer must indeed be very proud. In Central India, Police men talk of Nagas with respect, they refer to a IRB as 'Daring Nine'. Imagine while our factions are fighting for independence, 'Daring Nine' is doing all to keep India together. We see many young, articulate smart Naga news readers and anchors like Bano Haralu, Iracy Shishi etc etc. There are many more in service sector with a endearing smiles, positive attitude and efficient business like manner.

Santa – Banta made it a point to chat with a few of them, like Rosy in a City Mall at Gurgaon, Jasmina on a Jet flight and Chumismo in book shop at Delhi.

All of them have aspirations but their dreams are more practical and unlike the dreams that our leaders are chasing under "one dream, one future". Their dreams are basically a good secure job, loyal husband, good house and nice car. Surprisingly many would want a house in Banglore, Pune, Chandigarh and even Gurgaon but not in Dimapur and Kohima.

This generation of Non Resident Nagas dismiss sovereignty and Nagalim as pipe dreams and feel that dreams should be realistic and practical. Santa and Banta call this lot as 'practical dreams' people. This generation will define our future and destiny. These folks are on the move, a bit uneasy, but highly practical and they want to net work and globalize. For them, these meaningless squabbles between Nagas, Meities and Kukis are futile like quarrels between Preeto and Jeeto, where Santa – Banta have to play the role of Cease Fire Monitoring Group or CMFG. Only thing like CFMG, no body takes them seriously not even Preeto and Jeeto. So Santa – Banta are tired and want to take a break but before they go away, here is one for the Naga women. This one is with a hope that they will take lead and help Nagas to have realistic dreams. One is reminded of an old lady of Kalanmei, who once told Santa-Banta that women are like neck and men like head, neck decides where head is to move.

Will our Naga sisters and mothers put some sense into heads that are chasing utopian dream. To sign off, here is 'JAY HO' for our ladies -

Shy smiling energetic Naga girls;

Full of practical dreams and on the go.

Shouldering bravely family burdens;Our

dear Naga mothers, mama-mia-mo.

Lead by grand old Zapatou –u;

For all of you, Santa Banta sing "Jay ho".

Enclosure-

NAGALAND POST DT 05 MAR 09

Return of Santa – Banta: Here they come calling again

Santa - Banta are back for those who have a funny bone and this is one thing that all Nagas certainly have it in common for they can laugh on themselves! Although Jury may still be due on exact number of Naga tribes and who all are Nagas yet nobody can deny that we have an amazing sense of humour and capability to see the lighter side of life.

Those with a sense of humour and good memory will recall the 'Santa – Banta' series of articles that became an instant hit in 2003 – 2004. There were nearly 20 of them and they evoked a good response going by feed back in letters to Editors and even on e-mail. Well the first news is that 'Santa – Banta' have a new mail ID, nagasantabanta@gmail.com, so please up-date your address books and let your mails keep coming as they help us to improve and refine. Even your criticism is worth it and very welcome, so dip your pen in acid and let it loose!

The first question from readers could be, where have you been and why this prolonged silence? Well, there can be large number of excuses and reasons like our politicians give, but the short answer is that they have been out, where most 'Sardars' go. Yes, in Canada and they just got back. In this period of five years they realised that they not only have a Naga funny bone but besides they have a Naga muscle connected to heart the aches and pains when they miss Nagaland for its people, Madhu, Japfü and music. While net kept them connected specially Geoffrey Yaden's Nagaland Post, Nagaland Page and Eastern Mirror but seeing is believing. So, the first thing was to visit Nagaland. Santa – Banta came back, saw and felt motivated to again put pen to paper but their nib is dipped in love, affection, care and concern.

There are a large number of issues but they require detailed analysis so more will follow soon. For this time it is a simple issue and one contemporary one at that. Santa- Banta were overwhelmed by the Awards fever, starting with the Horn bill till early March, it is the awards seasons with Republic Day awards, Personality of the Year awards by various media houses Grammy's' and now the Oscars, where "Slumdog Millionaire" made India's day. Do we have Naga content in these national awards? Unfortunately the answer is - very little. RD Civilian awards list had the lone Naga entry with K. Asungba Sangtam winning the coveted. Padma Shri Award. RD awards had couple of deserving entries in form of Lt General RK Loomba, GOC of Rangapahar Corps and Maj General JP Nehra, IGAR (N) winning AVSM. At national level, the famed Naga gate made it to the "wonders list" of the North East.

Please vote for our own gate to push it into the national finalists list, if we can pull it up the hilly slopes, let us not falter in the SMS contest, and just push it.

Nagaland state won the honours as the best State for growth in tourism. We in the Nagaland had our share of other recognition and honours. RS Pandey our ex-chief secretary, received the coveted UN Public Service award for community participation in Schools, hospitals, water supply and tourism. Pandey, who can qualify to be a non-resident Naga, is doing wonders as the Petroleum Secretary. He has earned a reputation for unflappability in most severe crisis; of course no one deny that when you handled the routine crisis in Nagaland all problems appear trivial. We have crisis brewing every day and every hour. In fact it may be a good idea to groom potential high ranking civil servants in Mon, Tuensang, Longleng, Phek, Peren and Zunheoto, etc.

Getting back to our core competence, Nagas once again had a large number of festivals, beauty contests and music extravaganzas. So, who were the winners? Well, Naga Idol for year 2008 was Toshinaro of Kohima with 1, 66,294 votes but more importantly a brand new car and Rs 1 Lakh for shopping. Inatoli of Dimapur with 1,41,017 votes was close on heels, literally on heels, for he got 1 lakh but no car, behind them were Kevin, Sheneita and Mathung. Hornbill festivals once again rocked with the tunes of ultimate national winners 'The Verbs" of Meghalaya and the real 'adverbs', close behind were our very own Naga bands Diatribe and Eximions. Of course the ultimate tunes that every one rocked were provided by Airtel, who sponsored the contest with winners pocketing Rs 5 lakh and a lot of goodies.

Once again Miss Nagaland contest got a stupendous response at Hornbill with coveted honours, going to Abin of Peren as winner, Nyeie Leinak Phom from Longleng and Chumlano Kikon of Wokha were close behind. We hardly had a "women of substance" recognised this year, the only notable being, Jasmina Zeliang, honoured by FICCI for her entrepreneurship.

Getting on to the serious note, what was our Event of the year, well, without doubt that was the Assembly elections and success of Neiphu Rio and DAN. But more important is that once again the event we waited for so eagerly just did not happen. Nagaland broke all records and even surpassed Kashmir in number of civilians killed. Who killed them - it was neither security forces nor Assam Rifles not even IRB or Nagaland Police; well it was our groups engaged in the turf battle. As per independent and verified estimates 144 innocent Nagas made the ultimate sacrifice. Santa- Banta have their own limerick on daily stand-offs that occur at Shiroi and Seitheikema.

By the blue streams of Nagaland;
Ten years of cross fire and still waiting, hey ho!
Buzz was to their agreed camps;
Cadres of all the groups will go!!
They discussed, argued but agreed;
Naga Hoho and both groups said so!
Many dead lines gone by, trust belied;
Broken promises, going no where, Brother Joe?
Guns still blaze, cadres at large;
Will blood of innocent Nagas continue to flow??
Even Slumdogs become winners, Jai ho?
When will Nagas sing-'Jai Ho'??

For those who have got used to these sense-less killings and regular reconciliation meets like the recent one, just consider these facts. The figure of 144 is a 50% jump on 108 killings in 2007 and 91 in 2006. It is also the highest since 1998, the so called golden years were 2002 to 2005, when this ghastly count was down to less than 50. Santa-Banta has picked up their pen once again to roll back these figures and to zero if possible. Their pen was active in this period, this time they add their prayers to pen and hope for that elusive peace.

While we have our share of achievers this year – Issac Chishi completed 50 years of Public life, Justice Sema retired from the Supreme Court, SC Jamir continues to make headlines as an effective Governor in Maharastra, one of the most important states, Neiphiu Rio led DAN back to power, yet the Naga of the year award goes to 144 innocent Nagas, who laid down their lives. We pray for peace to their departed souls and hope that next year, we all be able to sing our own version of 'Jai Ho', in a peaceful Nagaland.

Harpal Singh,
Commandant (Retd)

Navigation Hints for Making Sense of Jottings

Jottings guide you into a journey of making sense of National Security and Defence Studies. Readers have to delve into the study of the 'Strategic' domain connected with National Security. The first question that arises could be, 'But why should we get into this domain reserved for soldiers or military professionals?' Well, this is no longer valid with the COVID-19 pandemic shock. **The revised paradigm is that National security entails a 'whole of nation' approach. Even if you pretend to be not interested, national security includes you and affects you. Everyone has to be 'Nagrik Yodha' (Citizen Warrior) in the mode of a vigilant or 'Jagruk' Hindustani.** So put your thinking cap on, and don't hesitate to have your jotting pad handy. Making notes and highlighting helps. The subject is invariably geo-centric,with 'geo' as the prefix, making it geo-political and geo-economic within the ambit of geo-strategic.

All subjects and issues are anchored on the following factors:

- **Location: The first requirement is to geographically situate the issue by understanding its location and proximity.** This involves looking at neighbours and weighing their inter se importance geographically (locational, resource-wise, demographics, and other connected factors) in global and regional contexts. Just to illustrate, the Suez Canal and Malacca Straits can be leveraged as choking leverages, even in vast open maritime environments. It will be relevant to take a careful look at the maps included in this explainer. It will be most pertinent to quote, 'while nations can choose friends, they cannot change their neighbours' in this context. India is saddled with two inimical ones, Pakistan and China, with both acting in collusive mode, posing major challenges for us. An interesting exercise could be to acquire maritime orientation. **Turn India's map around and assimilate peninsular India's maritime domination. It is relevant as**

approximately 80% of cargo and energy is transported on sea lanes.

- Economics: **the second key parameter is geo-economics, which entails the mapping of resources, trading linkages, and supply lines.** Resource mapping entails natural, derived (manufacturing and services), and human resources. As an example, Qatar, having the largest proven gas reserves, has a considerable out-of-proportion geo-economic clout, notwithstanding her size.
- Demographics: **the third factor is population including size, distribution (geriatric profile-youth dividend), more importantly-religion and sects. It is equally important to consider intra religion divides like Sunni-Shia.**
- Past or History: **It is invariably the past that drives the present and complicates it.** It is imperative to consider the historical context, specially track record of populace, allies, adversaries or parties to conflict and leaders.
- Alliances: **The next important parameter is alliances and partnerships.** These vary from global ones like the North Atlantic Treaty Organization (NATO) to regional ones like the Association of South East Asian Nations (ASEAN). It is important to understand their objectives (stated and unstated/covert) and membership. Some, like NATO, have a security orientation, whereas others, like ASEAN, may have purely economic cooperation as the focus. Some, like the Shanghai Cooperation Organisation (SCO), are formalised with proper structure, whereas others, like G-20 and the Quad, have rotational staffing. It is also relevant to reiterate that there are no permanent friends (allies), increasingly referred to as partners, but only permanent interests.
- Leadership: **The fourth factor is government and leaders at the helm, as often ineptitude and sometimes arrogance have not only created challenges and conflicts but also prevented their**

resolution. Just to name a few, leaders like Hitler, Stalin, Saddam Hussain, and Fidel Castro have had defining influences.

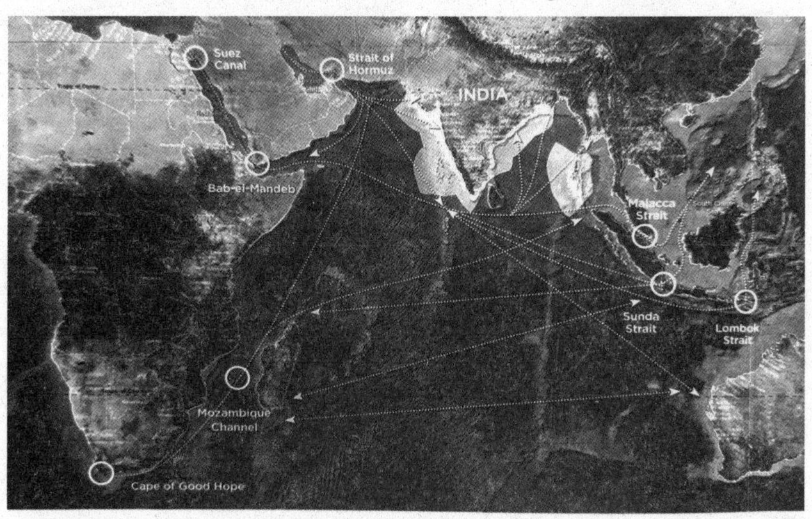

(Map-source-www.sirjournal.org/research/2018/7/5/indias-indo-pacific-strategy-understanding/ indias-spheres-of-influence)

To sum-up and as a ready reckoner, it may be easy to remember an acronym—LED-PAL—for location, economics, demographics, past, alliances and leaders. However, the **list is only indicative, and more factors relevant to the subject should be considered and factored in for comprehensive analysis. There can be no standard to discern likely trends, scenarios, and outcomes.**

L – Location

E – Economics

D – Demographics

P – Past

A – Alliances

L – Leaders

FIG: IMP. STRAITS & ISTHMUS IN SEA LANES

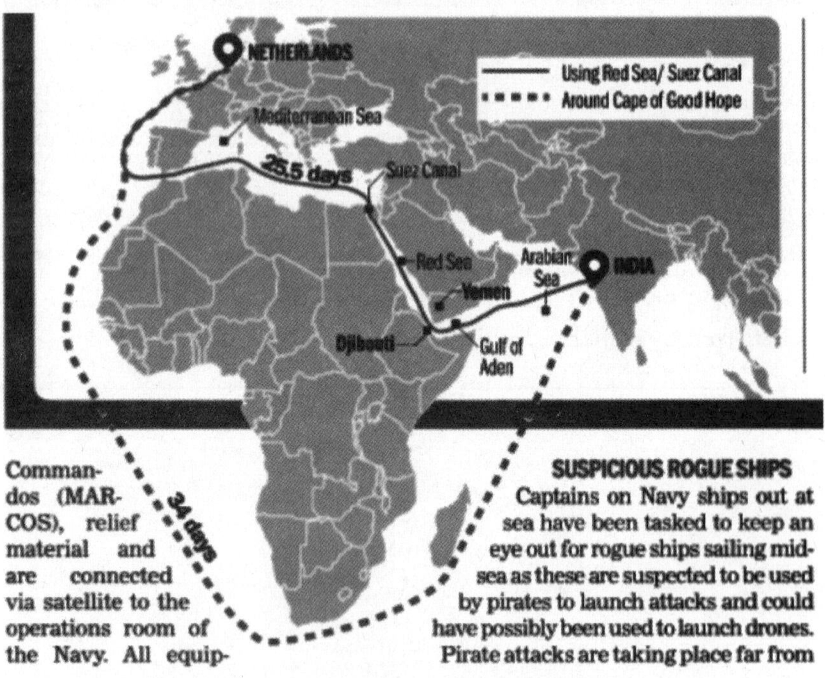

(Map credit-www.tribuneindia.com/news/features/guarding-the-sea-indian-navy-has-fielded-12-anti-pirate-patrolling-ships-in-the-arabian-sea-581035)

Opening Perspectives

Analytical Mapping of Trends in Unending Conflicts

The world is witnessing new forms of conflict. These occur in even otherwise stable areas where traditional rivals were seemingly headed towards a historic rapprochement. Conflicts have acquired non-kinetic dimensions, like the coercive stand-off in Ladakh along the Line of Actual Control (LAC). They are proliferating to newer domains—cyber, information, cognitive, energy, and economics. It appears that between the Belt and Road Initiative (BRI) and the India-Middle East-Europe Economic Corridor (IMEC), the world is moving towards a clash of connectivities and corridors. While it may be risky and premature to draw lessons, trends need to be not only deciphered but analysed, as these will drive future geo-strategic exchanges.

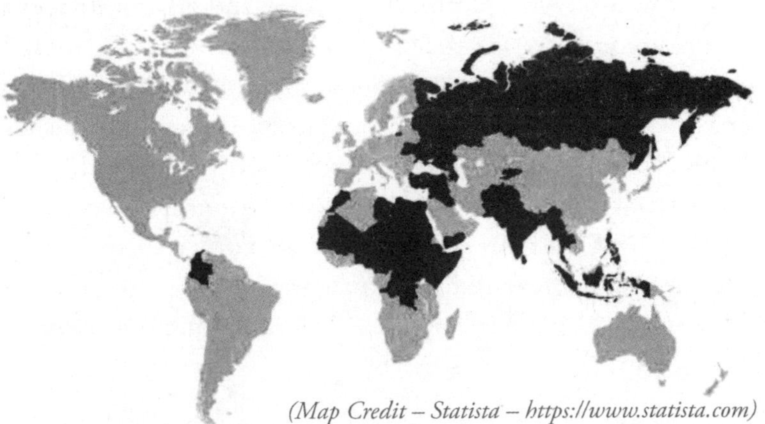

(Map Credit – Statista – https://www.statista.com)

Every year, strategic experts and renowned think tanks publish projected 'conflict-risk' indices, with likely global conflict hot spots for the year. These listings are invariably accompanied by maps and graphics. One such representative graphic is included.

An analysis of these lists reveals that they naturally draw inferences from the established and well-known geo-strategic theories like Halford Mackinder's 'Heartland theory', Nicholas Spykman's 'Rimland theory', and Alfred Mahan's 'Sea Power' theories. These are contextualised with contemporary geo-political realities. Analysis of these reveals that most projections conform to Greek analyst Dimitri Kitsikis' postulates. **He had opined that besides Mackinder's Eurasian heartland, the intermediate region of the Middle East and North Africa (MENA) will also remain the crucible of conflicts.** In effect, Kitsikis added a geo-civilisational dimension to an otherwise geo-political construct. MENA is the arena of competing civilisations, exemplifying Samuel Huntington's 'Clash of Civilizations'.

The major ongoing conflicts include Azerbaijan-Nagano Karabakh (since 2020), Ukraine (since 2020), and Gaza (since October 2023). It will be pertinent to mention that all these conflicts have been festering for decades, and the timelines indicated are only for the current round of hostilities. The world concurrently continues to be bedeviled with a low order of brewing conflicts/insurgencies unleashed by Houthis, Kurds, Islamic State in Syria/Levant (ISIS), Hezbollah, Hamas, and other militants and even private militias like the Wagner Army. This arc of instability currently extends from Mali-Sudan-Syria-Lebanon to Yemen. It may be a little early to add Venezuelan-Guyana skirmishes to this mix, as the situation seems to be getting defused, at least currently. In addition, more importantly, grey zone coercive posturing by China on the Sino-Indian border since 2020 and aggressive deployment and aerial/maritime manoeuvres of Chinese in the South China Sea targeting Taiwan need to be monitored very carefully.

Template for Analysis

It is indeed risky and somewhat premature to draw lessons from unresolved wars and conflicts, yet some important trends and pointers need to be deciphered. **In these unending, long, drawn-out conflicts, new paradigms of warfighting are emerging along with possible countermeasures. These may solidify into principles and define postulates in the future.** The most obvious case in point is the premature sounding of the death knell for tanks, consequent to disruptive top-attack effects unleashed by Turkish Bayraktar-TB2 drones and Switchblade 'Kamikaze' loitering munitions. Russian-origin tanks in Armenia and Ukraine bore the brunt of reverses, which was magnified by the Western media. Notwithstanding the hasty obituaries, Russian tanks duly fortified are back in Ukraine and modified Israeli Merkavas have been fielded in Gaza.

Emerging inferences in an uncertain, dynamic flux of ongoing conflicts need to be not only validated but also customised to the local environment. In our context, in Ladakh, drones are likely to have very limited efficacy due to high altitude and environmental factors. Israeli attacks into Gaza are being led by fortified Merkava-4. However, India never uses tanks in urban warfare. In contrast, India prefers to secure populated areas with combined arms teams. India is not really in the conflict crucible of MENA, yet we have existing challenges from aggressive China and Pakistan-fostered proxy wars.

More importantly, our adversaries are increasingly collusive. The conflicts seem to be ever-present, though latent and lurking in the shadows. They get triggered by surprise and isolated events like the Hamas raid in Gaza on 7 October, even when the region was headed for an impending re-rapprochement between Israel and Saudi Arabia. In a recent interaction, two of our former chiefs flagged internal challenges as our main threats; hence, there is a need to keep our guard up and be vigilant against both external threats and internal fault lines. The subject is analysed in the context of the relevance of mapped attributes in our environment.

Mapping Emerging Trends

The first defining trend is that the application of kinetic force has limited effect and utility. It is certainly not adequate for a decisive end-state. Putin's so-called special operations, designed to capture Kyiv and effect regime change in the garb of de-Nazification, ensure neutrality or keep away Western powers, planned to be achieved in two weeks, have entered the third year. This is even after the annexation of Crimea and areas in the Donbas region by Russia, starting in 2014. Even the planned counter-offensives by both sides are stalemated with negligible progress. Similarly, Israeli Defence Force (IDF) operations in Gaza are already going on for more that nine months and are likely to linger. Resource control, huge technical asymmetry, and relentless operations have yet to get IDF the desired objectives and the end state. The resolute stand adopted by India in Ladakh has certainly derailed the People's Liberation Army (PLA) game plan of forcing India into capitulation and scoring an uncontested grey zone victory.

As a complementary inference, it will be pragmatic for nations to avoid belligerence and application of kinetic force. **Even if forced into it, it will be prudent to stipulate realistic goals with a clearly defined end-state. It is also axiomatic to build interim exit options for conflict termination and face-saving.** Both Putin and Zelinsky seem to be caught in a never-ending logjam and ego trap on this account. Even in Gaza, Hamas's objective of getting the focus back on Palestine and Gaza seems more likely to be achieved rather than the IDF mission of destroying Hamas. Even securing the release of hostages may need more time, hostage rescue operations and even more concessions.

The next major corollary is the debunking of the long-held belief that wars are likely to be short, swift, and decisive. In the India-Pakistan context, the 14-day operational cycle was being used as a template. Consequently, stocking and war reserves were planned for 21 days of combat. **Long, drawn-out conflicts with indeterminate objectives are more likely to be the new normal in future. In addition, conflicts are likely to degenerate into extended hybrid**

wars/insurgencies, especially in Palestine, where Hamas may get temporarily marginalised, albeit only till a more dangerous variant of Hamas sprouts in its place. Wanton destruction of population centres is becoming the new normal, with Aleppo, Grozny, Mariupol, and Gaza razed to the ground. It is invariably accompanied by humanitarian crises with large-scale civilian casualties and displacement of refugees.

These festering conflicts are straining available combat power in terms of human resources; hence, **private militias, mercenaries and contractors are becoming an important element.** Russian Army in Ukrainian conflict has hired soldiers from India, Nepal, Sri Lanka and many other African countries. Wagner Group is reportedly state funded or aided private military company, which has fought in Ukrainian conflict and many African trouble spots. Similar volunteers are assisting Ukrainian forces.

Another major trend is the validation of the seminal maxim that no defence line is impregnable, especially in the face of determined fedayeen like Hamas. The famed Gaza Barrier has been added to compromised ones like the French Maginot and German Siegfried Lines (World War II), the Berlin Wall (Cold War), and the Barlev Line (1973 Arab-Israeli War). While breaching of defence lines is inevitable, the immediate response is the key imperative. IDF slipped up badly on this account during the audacious Hamas raid. It has been repeatedly seen that information, though available and in plenty, is not collated and analysed to convert it into operational and actionable intelligence. Hence, timely analysis of information and surveillance are the most important. We certainly need to revamp our analytics of surveillance and intelligence structures/mechanisms, as we have been repeatedly surprised in Kargil (1999) and again in Ladakh (2020).

For long conflicts, nations need to build resilience in the logistics chain and spurt capabilities to ramp up inventories rapidly. **We are witnessing Russia, famed for its depots and military-industrial complex, now scouting for spares and munitions from N Korea.** Countries like Pakistan have become suppliers to their own Original Equipment Manufacturers (OEMs)—Ukraine.

At one time, we were planning to stock only for a 21-day conflict. It is time to adopt a **'whole-of-nation' approach with civil-military fusion**, enabling dual-use technologies and applications. **An apt example is the fielding of Elon Musk's commercial-off-the-shelf (COTS) satellite communications, Starlink terminals, by Ukrainians to circumvent Russian electronics warfare.** Another interesting aspect is the use of crowdfunding to field low-end drones, such as the employment of ham operators in yesteryears. Fielding of such dual-use devices is the obvious way forward. These conflicts have literally become trial and testing grounds for armaments. Large manufacturers are exhausting munitions, nearing the end of their shelf-life. In a no-victor, no-vanquished scenario, the only winner seems to be the military-industrial complex with bulging order books. We also need to boost our defence industry ecosystem and infuse dual-use stakes.

The quest for the elusive silver bullet or game-changer weapon is never-ending and unlikely to yield a result. No single weapon like tanks or even the current favourite—drones—can win a battle on their own. It is seen that disruptive effects like drones give an initial advantage, but it is only temporary till mitigating defensive and counter-offensive measures are devised. Tanks are already being retrofitted with cage-like structures as part of Tank Top-Attack Survival Kits. In addition, high-end Active Protection Systems like Trophy and Shtora are being fitted, and tanks are being fielded within Air Defence envelopes and umbrellas. In essence, it will be a synergistic application of combined all arms teams duly backed up by smart logistics.

Nations strive for technological asymmetry, yet a determined adversary doesn't allow it to acquire debilitating character by closing the gap. Human elements and operators (men/women) behind machines (guns) remain very much relevant. This is especially relevant at high altitudes, where environmental factors degrade equipment performance.

The correct training and application of tactical concepts like dispersion, convoy discipline, and intelligent use of ground would have drastically reduced Russian casualties in Ukraine. **In this context, it is relevant to recall Indian crews exploiting their improvisation**

(jugaad) in antiquated Centurion tanks to defeat much superior and modern Patton (M-48) in the 1965 war. Another example is the audacious employment of helicopters along with the floatation of tanks in the 1971 war to bounce the formidable Meghna River and effect a siege on Dhakka from the most unexpected direction. In essence, well-trained and motivated human capital can offset technical asymmetry.

The most worrying aspect has been that nuclear installations are getting targeted in combat. In the Ukrainian conflict, the Zaporizhzhia nuclear power plant was damaged, wherein actions of Russian forces were questionable, notwithstanding it being a nuclear power plant. **More recently, the Israeli Sdot Micha base, housing Jericho missiles, was attacked by Hamas rockets, probably accidentally.** It underscores the need to ring-fence such facilities as the danger of radiation fall-out and proliferation is very real. Any attempt to reduce or surrender nuclear stockpile is unlikely to find traction in the light of the Ukrainian experience. It had surrendered its arsenal in 1994 in return for a Russian nuclear umbrella and guarantees. If it had retained its weapons, the same would have deterred Russians. It was predicted by John Mearsheimer that without nuclear weapons, Ukraine would be subjected to war. Consequently, the quest for nuclear weapons and retaining them is likely to increase. Iran seems to be the next serious contender and is on the verge of threshold limits in this quest.

Security alliances like NATO or less formalised ones like the Quad as a hedging strategy are unable to ensure requisite deterrence. **Ukraine is caught in such a pincer as its partners are most reluctant to put boots on the ground, and fatigue is creeping in on the issue of material support.** Such linkages have severe limitations and at best, support can come in the form of resources, but operating crews need re-orientation.

Fielding of such externally supplied armaments like American F-16 and German Leopard tanks has drawbacks in terms of training and complexities of integration in the existing combat architecture, surveillance, communication, and command grids of the beneficiary. For Ukraine, it's a transition from Russian to Western mode. We are going to face similar challenges as we are reducing dependence on Russian equipment. In the power play, China has opted to remain in the background in physical involvement even in United Nations force deployment. The only departure is China taking a pro-Palestine stance in the recent Gaza conflict at the cost of her traditional ties with Israel. **It bears reiteration that the performance of the PLA in Sudan and Chinese drones in Syria have been sub-optimal.** It's a moot question if leading powers like China can avoid responsibility and for how long. In our context and in a larger context, nations have to build smart partnerships, integral capabilities, and self-reliance (Atmanirbhar).

The basic paradigm of national interests being enduring and long-term is undergoing a radical shift in polarised, binary flip-flops at the apex level of security management, especially in the United States of America (USA). This is starkly evident in the transition from President Obama's 'Pivot to Pacific' to President Trump's 'Fortress America' and Make America Great Again (MAGA). Now, we are witnessing President Biden's Quad and Build Back Better World (B3W). Concurrently, the focus on NATO dealing with Russia and China has drastically changed between Democratic and Republican dispensations. Even in China, the transition from Deng's 'Hide your Shine-Bide your Time' to Xi's Wolf-Warrior aggressive China surprised many, like India. **The lesson for us is to endeavour to forge bipartisan consensus on key security challenges and promulgate a clearly defined national security strategy.**

Conflicts are characterised by relentless narrative wars on social media and electronic and print mediums, which were highlighted in the Ukrainian conflict. Now, in Israel, it is a concurrent clash of two narratives—Terrorist Hamas vis-à-vis genocide in Gaza. **Cognitive Warfare is only going to escalate and proliferate. It's important to be suitably prepared for it with policy, organisations (like PLA's Strategic Support Force, since re-organised as Information Support Force) and training.** Competition and contests, including conflicts, are proliferating in emerging domains like Cyber, Space, Artificial Intelligence (AI), Robotics, and Autonomous Weapons backed by quantum computing. It will be pragmatic if certain basic global norms and protocols are devised for these domains like the Chemical, Biological, Radiological and Nuclear (CBRN) protocols. In our context, concerted research and development (R&D) in AI, autonomous platforms, and quantum computing, as well as upgrading organisations in the cyber and space domains, is recommended.

Geo-strategy is yielding ground to geo-economics. Hence, there are conflicts in the economic domain, like energy supply, through the application of sanctions. In addition, the sabotage of the Nord Stream pipeline disrupted the energy supply to Europe from Russia. However, these have limited utility, as has been the effect of sanctions on Russian energy supplies.

Connectivity is another new frontier for power projection, which was flagged by Mike Pompeo, former US Secretary of State, when he dubbed Chinese connectivity corridors like the BRI as more geo-strategic than economics driven. The American counter strategy is routed through the IMEC; however, it is currently under a shadow due to the conflict in Gaza. The United States (US) establishment has claimed that the Hamas raid was an attempt to disrupt the IMEC initiative. Chinese Maritime Silk Route, including the Kra Canal project, is an attempt to overcome the Malacca dilemma and build energy security. India has to remain vigilant about these challenges and stay invested in relevant connectivity corridors like the International North-South Transport Corridor (INSTC), Chabahar, Kaladan, and the IMEC to build redundancies.

Summarised Listing of Trends

It is important to reiterate the trends:

a) **The application of kinetic force has limited utility in objectives and effects.**

b) **Realistic, clearly defined objectives and end state, along with exit options, must be devised when force application is unavoidable.**

c) The new normal is long, festering conflicts with indeterminate outcomes, often tapering off into hybrid war/insurgencies.

d) No defence line is impregnable; quick response and resilience are the key.

e) Timely analysis of information and surveillance to convert it into opportune, actionable intelligence is extremely important.

f) Resilience in logistics mandates a 'whole of nation approach' and civil-military fusion with dual-use technologies.

g) Private militias, contractors and soldiers recruited from non-warring parties is on the rise.

h) There can be no silver bullet; synergistic application of combined arms, backed by smart logistics, is mandated.

i) Technological asymmetry is temporary and contested, and human capital still has relevance, especially in high-altitude warfare.

j) Isolation of nuclear installations in battle space requires immediate attention.

k) The quest to acquire nuclear weapons is likely to amplify.

l) Security alliances have limited hedging value.

m) There is a need to evolve a national consensus on key security challenges and promulgate a national security strategy.

n) Narrative warfare and cognitive shaping are emerging trends. They require structures and organisation.

o) Conflicts are imminent in newer domains like cyber, space, and autonomous warfare, which incorporate AI.

p) Sanctions have limited utility, yet they are a growing ingredient in geo-economic contestations.

q) Geo-economic contests are evident in energy and connectivity corridors.

Uncertain Future

Power play is acquiring non-kinetic dimensions and a grey zone character like the coercive stand-offs in Ladakh and Taiwan (South China Sea). Even in the kinetic genre, conflicts are festering and, instead of finding resolution, are degenerating into insurgencies. Conflict is proliferating into newer domains like cyber, space, cognitive, and autonomous platforms. Geo-economics is being leveraged through sanctions, especially in energy security. **It also appears that between BRI and IMEC, the world is moving literally towards a clash of corridors.**

Alliances are unable to ensure deterrence. Hence, nations have to build integral capabilities and smart partnerships. The most worrying trend is that the United Nations Organisation (UNO) and other dispute-resolving bodies have been rendered ineffective. The key challenge is not only to discern and map emerging trends but to stay ahead of disruptive trends. **It is imperative that nations build survivability, resilience, and redundancies in their response mechanisms, infrastructure, manufacturing ecosystems, and supply chains.**

Indian Context

India, notwithstanding, her professed themes of non-alignment, peaceful co-existence, based on non-aggression has been at the receiving end of multiple wars and festering conflicts. These wars have left unresolved borders in the shape of Line of Control (LoC) and Actual Ground Position Line (AGPL) with Pakistan and Line of Actual Control (LAC) with China. This apart both neighbours are operating in collusion and Pakistan has gifted large tract of territory in Shaksgam Valley to China. India has also faced insurgencies and separatist movements in hinterland (Left Wing Extremism) and in border states in Northeast, Punjab and J&K. These have been aided and abetted by Pakistan and China, giving them proxy war character. Consequently, the focus shifted to counterterrorism with conventional war as unlikely possibility, which is now being reviewed for more balanced approach. Capacities are being ramped up to face longer conflicts instead of previous template of short and swift wars of 10-14 days duration. **Pakistan front has been receiving skewed and disproportionate attention till Ladakh face-off, which forced designation of China as primary adversary.**

Emerging trends need to be validated and customized against the backdrop of historical context, objective Strength-Challenges-Opportunities-Threats (SCOT) analysis, to draw appropriate lessons for incorporating them in doctrines and training methodologies. Taking heed from emerging trends, India has embarked on multiple measures to cope up with multi-spectral challenges. **The major initiatives include, first is rebalancing deployment to boost force level on Northern Front opposite China. Second, accelerating push towards theatrisation and transformation. Third, expedite building of border infrastructure. Fourth, push for Atam-Nirbharata (self-reliance) and modernisation. Fifth, revise ammunition stocking level and opening armament and ammunition manufacturing to private entities.** It is appropriate to quote Winston Churchill, "those that fail to learn from history are doomed to repeat it."

National Security at the 75th Republic Day

(February-2024, with minor updating)

Republic Day parade this year focused on two key themes: Viksit Bharat (Developed India) and Bharat-Loktanra ki Matruka (Bharat-The Mother of Democracy). It was a women-centric event with all women tri-services contingent participating for the first time. One hundred women playing traditional instruments led it. Women were all over—15 pilots in fly-past, all-women Central Armed Police Forces (CAPF) contingent, and so much more. Yet, even if it sounds discordant, the need is to take it beyond symbolism and displays.

Will it show in the ticket distribution in impending elections? The equipment displayed highlighted commitment to Atmanirbhar. Once again, we have a lot of ground to cover in this challenging mission. The primacy of citizens was emphasised in the parade in enhanced participation and invitations to unsung achievers. With so many things changing, traditional and much-loved ceremonial, heritage Presidential Buggy reappeared after a gap of four decades. The cultural extravaganza and displays were indeed awe-inspiring. The euphoric fervour and resolve were all too evident and palpable.

The 75th Republic Day is also an appropriate milestone to go beyond the atmospherics and take a reality check of the state of national security. This **macro review focuses on the four key parameters—environment in immediate and extended neighbourhood, strategy and structures, modernisation and capability building, and finally, HR and training.**

Firstly, the national security environment has become complex, with frozen and unresolved conflicts initiated by China on our northern borders. The next year, in all likelihood, will be challenging, as it is the 75th year of the formation of the People's Republic of China (PRC). The Chinese have a dubious reputation for setting targets around such milestones. Taiwan and Tibet, increasingly referred to as Xijang, are on their unification wishlist. There is an increasing push to settle the Sino-Bhutan border, albeit on their terms. Recounting Mao's analogy of five fingers, Ladakh, Nepal, Sikkim, and Bhutan seem to be under control. Is Arunachal (Southern Xinjiang) the next frontier?

We have ramped up our deployment, but two unintentionally revealed skirmishes (in January and November 2022) during a recent investiture ceremony, and PLA's failed Yangtse foray in December 2022 indicate the need to remain vigilant even in areas where a semblance of disengagement has been achieved. **Our current deployment is barely dissuasive, and we need to remain focused on modernisation, infrastructure development, and, above all, honing quid pro quo (QPQ) options, like the occupation of Kailash Heights, to graduate to credible dissuasive deterrence.** It was heartening to hear (in the same investiture ceremony) about audacious patrols and covert actions to thwart PLA and refine QPQ contingencies.

Turning westward, Pakistan is imploding and facing multifarious problems—fiscal, Baluchi, and Pashtun separatism, Tehrik-e-Taliban Pakistan (TTP) on rampage, and turbulence on borders with Iran and Afghanistan. Notwithstanding these crises, **Pakistan can sustain the proxy war in Jammu and Kashmir (J&K), shifting focus currently to the Rajouri-Poonch belt. An emerging threat is the Drugs-Drones combo aptly referred to as D-2 threat, in a diabolic bid to revive K-2 (Kashmir-Khalistan) fault lines.** As a contrarian trend, sections of *Awaam (*populace) in Pakistan are advocating rapprochement, yet no real traction on this account can take place till elections in both countries. On balance, fringe extremist groups, vectored by the Inter-Services Intelligence (ISI), are likely to remain permanent thorns. **Conflict resolution remains an area of concern with nominal gains like a ceasefire between the Meitei and ULFA factions. Early elections and restoration of statehood in J&K remain key objectives.** Similarly, Manipur requires a change of approach before it unleashes chain reactions in Mizoram and Nagaland. We need to build resilience and redundancies as part of buffers to combat threats in emerging frontiers—cyber, cognitive, and space.

The dangers lurk in the form of China playing a 'zero-sum' game in our neighbourhood to stymie even legitimate strategic reach. Maldives is the latest manifestation. While we are forging loose alliances with the USA and the Quad (referred to as partnerships), net gains remain marginal. **The new forms of engagement must remain nimble, agile, and even episodic within an overall format of plurilateralism, balancing and being the voice of the Global South.**

The next parameter for review is national security strategy and structures. While we have displayed commendable capability and capacity to execute surgical raids in Balakot and evacuate the diaspora from Ukraine, structures remain ad-hoc. The work on the promulgation of the National Security Strategy (NSS) remains to be expedited. It is only likely to figure, once again in election manifestos, as a promise.

We should risk putting out NSS-1.0 and refine it with iterations. Our structures are characterised by the centralisation of power and skewed staffing by intelligence experts. While we currently have extremely competent people at the helm, succession planning dictates de-centralisation and balanced staffing. The progress on theatre commands and joint structures remains stymied due to turf-centric fixation.

There is a fair degree of visible progress on infrastructure development and acquisition of 'effect-generating' force multipliers like Rafael, Predators, Apache, and Chinook helicopters. In addition, indigenous developments like Tejas, Vikrant, K2 Vajra guns, and Zorawar light tanks are noteworthy. **After elections, there would be a need to enhance budgetary allocations and get back to planned capability building instead of emergency procurements and a few inter-government deals,** described as strategic acquisitions. Revamping of the Defence Research and Development Organisation (DRDO) and Ordnance Factories needs urgent push.

Security Forces are undergoing transformation and optimisation or right-sizing. The scope needs to include CAPFs. The Agniveer scheme has to be put through objective trials and, if successful, should be extended to CAPFs. It would be a good idea if, after an initial nudge, services were allowed to pace these reforms, and even courts stepped back. **Finally, there is talk of revamping the promotion policy. It bears reiteration that wars were won by non-compliant generals—Sam, Sagat, and Harbaksh. Hope the new policy will breed such winners.**

Agenda for National Security @ Modi 3.0

(Written in June 24)

National Security architecture for Modi 3.0 is in place and message is of continuity and stability. Notwithstanding, the apprehensions generated due to extension to outgoing incumbent, the first decision on appointment of Army Chief, reflects respect for seniority. Yet, challenges in form of multiple, coordinated terror strikes in Jammu region are fuelling demands for another surgical strike. Concurrently, critical observations by RSS Chief have increased pressure for precipitate action, on priority, to resolve continuing Manipur imbroglio.

National Security During Modi 1.0

On inception, the Government proclaimed National Security as its overriding imperative. Modi 1.0, started with an ailing and over-worked Arun Jaitley, grappling with Defence as secondary charge, along with Finance. In less than six months, seemingly reluctant Manohar Parikar was persuaded to take over. He promised transformation but after two years and four months, headed back to Goa. The baton was back with ailing, Arun Jaitley for just six months. Finally, Nirmala Sithraman stepped-in, as the first woman RM, for the balance period of twenty-one months.

PM invested considerable personal effort to improve macro environment by engaging with Pakistan and China. His surprise, unscheduled visit to Pakistan was very bold attempt. Unfortunately, Pathankot terror strike scuttled, this well-intentioned initiative. Multiple summit level engagements-Sabarmati, Wuhan and Mahabalipuram, floundered in face of Chinese obduracy. The signature events were Doklam stand-off, post-Uri coordinated raids and Balakot surgical strikes. The **first term, at best can be summed-up as mixed-visible and effective operational response matrix, high on promise but with sub-optimal results on transformation and modernisation. Slowing down of raising of Mountain Strike Corps and festering OROP crisis, till belated partial resolution, blotted overall scorecard.**

Security Matrix – Modi 2.0

There seemed to be shift in gear, reflected in announcement of much awaited reform of CDS by PM. It was accompanied by launch of slew of reforms with focus on Atam-Nirbharata (self-reliance) and ramping-up border infrastructure. Rajnath Singh as RM, provided stability, yet agenda seemed to be steered by PMO and NSA. Diabolic Chinese coercive manoeuvres in Ladakh, in May 2020, even when world was grappling with COVID-19, put the entire system in reactive and coping-up mode. **It will be fair to conclude that after being initially surprised, response was creditable, particularly, QPQ manoeuvre of pre-emptive deployment on Kailash heights.** Crisis in Manipur rekindled festering insurgency in Northeast. **While revocation of Article 370 in J&K was laudable, accompanied by marked improvement in security environment, yet terrorism has found traction, South of Pir-Panjal. Much publicised and top-driven Agniveer scheme has drawn considerable adverse reactions. The progress on theatrisation and even modernization remains sketchy and at best, incremental.**

Agenda for Modi 3.0

PM, while accepting the verdict called for striving for Sarvamat (national consensus) rather than Bahumat (majoritarian view). **While switch to collegiate approach is the key challenge but it can indeed be the much-cherished, transformational catalyst.** It is only appropriate to attempt this seemingly difficult initiative in the national security domain. In the current vitiated political discourse, the most important requirement would be to enhance transparency and participation, on critical issues by putting out white papers on current challenges. These could include-Unresolved stand-off with China, Proxy war in J&K, Left Wing Extremism, Modernisation and Border infrastructure. **Concurrently, much belated exercise to formulate National Security Strategy needs to be finalized.** The document could serve, as an agenda and reference document for building accountability through watch-dog bodies like CAG, Parliamentary Standing Committee (Defence) and peer-review by think-tanks. Ambiguity, on establishing NDU vis-a-vis current indication of RRU taking-over the mantle, needs to be resolved.

Comprehensive National Power (CNP) is derived through synergistic 'whole of nation' approach. At functional level, it requires nimble diplomacy, unified approach on border defence, internal security and building multi-domain capabilities of defence forces, supported by adequate and imaginative funding. It mandates an out-of-box approach and revolutionary initiatives. Most importantly, consider separating pensions into a separate head as national obligation to veterans. India has faced unparalleled challenges: four-and-half acknowledged wars besides Op-Pawan, Nathu-La (1967), Galwan, Siachen, UN, and other conflicts. These and multiple insurgencies and proxy wars have meant that our Armed Forces are forever in war. It does not behove India to resort to penny-pinching, cutting pensions to fund modernization when subsidies continue to spiral and there are no matching fiscal cuts in other departments. **It is time that funding for defence modernization is liberated from the self-defeating 2% GDP ceiling.** Ongoing reforms in DRDO and corporatisation of Ordnance Factories should be fast-tracked. The present system of acquisition through strategic acquisitions like FMS and emergency powers needs to be replaced by long-term planning and acquisitions. There is urgent need for committed allocation for critical force-multipliers.

By virtue of seniority, the Home Minister is invariably No-2/3, saddled with political firefighting. It is time that focus on conflict resolution in disturbed areas is enhanced by appointing empowered interlocutors assisted by domain experts. The pending Kargil Review and Prakash Singh Committee reforms should be expedited. Recently, the NSA recommended inter-operability in CAPFs, which runs contrary to the concept of One Border-One Force and specialization. Skillset for internal security (CRPF) is different from border defence on contested LAC and LoC (BSF and ITBP) and border-guarding on settled borders (SSB). **This apart, each border is unique, and it will be pragmatic to group all forces, including CAPFs and agencies in theatre, under a designated theatre commander. The unique eco-system of Services needs to be respected and tinkering in name of transformation is avoidable. Clear directions with ample delegation should be the recommended way forward.**

Codified NSS-defining Paradigm for National Security

(Written in June 24)

The CDS, in a recent book-release function, made an interesting comment about formulation of National Security Strategy (NSS). As per media reports, he stated that, "when we talk about the national security strategy, I believe it consists of policy, processes, and practices to succeed. In our country, probably all three are addressed. The only thing missing is a written policy. I don't know why people insist on that". This statement, signaling major shift in policy, merits analysis and debate. **The obvious questions are-why we have been engaged in this exercise, with multiple drafts for the last two decades? More importantly, an apex-level Defence Planning Committee, chaired by the National Security Advisor was set up in 2018 to formulate the NSS and National Defence Strategy.** However, the status and progress of much publicised exercise, is not known. Currently, we are managing with very cryptic and inadequate RM's Operational Directive.

One is tempted to even ask, if it is just the CDS's personal opinion or official policy articulation, as it was in academic environment? In this context, it bears reiteration Mr Manohar Parikar, former RM, first announced major shift in nuclear policy-jettisoning 'No First Use' doctrine and later retracted, by describing it, as only his personal opinion in seminar. The lengthy explanation by the CDS and listing of recent successes like Balakote, indicate a desire to scuttle the ongoing endeavour to codify NSS into a written document. He even cited example of Israel, which doesn't have a written document. It is well known fact that most relevant nations, including otherwise opaque China, not only promulgate NSS but also publish periodic white papers. Even Pakistan, has promulgated her first National Security Policy (2022-26). **Neither Israel nor Pakistan can set the template for us, as our challenges are different and require customised approach. Hence, it is important that the issue of written NSS is clarified post-haste.**

It is also appropriate that in unfolding coalition-era, Sarvamat (consensus) as described by PM is built on this critical catalyst for National Security. It is interesting that in recent elections, all parties went overboard in swearing allegiance to written constitution. Ironically, in the domain of security, we seem to be content with ambiguity and ambivalence. Resultantly, we are hesitant to commit ourselves to much-needed codified, written document. There is an apprehension that in coalition era, reforms will take backseat as government will be tied down in routine management. We can take heart from Chief Economic Advisor's statement. He has opined that, "this actually makes some of the difficult reforms more feasible incrementally because it opens space for dialogue." Even alliance partners are calling for review of signature scheme like 'Agniveer'. Inclusive debate and consensus building seems to be the new normal. Opposition has been lamenting about opacity on recent security challenges, both external and internal like Ladakh face-off and Manipur imbroglio. **It may be ambitious but in interest of national security, it is logical to get opposition and partners on board and in the planning or at least in consultation loop.**

Merits of a Documented NSS

A well-crafted NSS would serve to foster 'whole of nation' approach and build synergy for harnessing Comprehensive National Power' (CNP). It would also enable setting milestones for capability-building for modernization, infrastructure and Atam-Nirbharata mission. The current status of Defence Planning is indeed worrying and in transition as Defence Plans (5 years) and Long-Term Perspective Plans (15 years) have been discontinued. The new format of Integrated Capability Plan (10 years) and Defence Capability Acquisition Plan (5 years) is yet to stabilize. At the same time, it will be objective to commend the Government for enhanced traction, as also visibility in defence modernization. However, without NSS specifying objectives, on-going well-meaning initiatives, remind of

Stephen Cohen and Sunil Dasgupta's book-Arming Without Aiming: India's Military Modernisation. The present system of reviews by Parliamentary Standing Committee and Chief Auditor General are sub-optimal. **These need to be backed up with net-assessment and statistical tools both for periodic audit but more importantly for predictive and dynamic goal setting. NSS, as reference for peer-review by think-tanks, hopefully will reduce ambiguity and build meaningful accountability.**

The most critical issue is related to operational clarity and ease of decision making. NSS is relevant in a system, where Army Commanders don't even do handing-taking over and for other commanders, process is brief and primarily, ceremonial. As per informed opinion, while theatre responses during Doklam crisis were commendable but strategic guidance was sketchy. The status was same for Ladakh face-off, as revealed, in released portions of, yet to published autobiography of former Chief. The current model has delivered but largely due to competence of present hierarchy. It suffers from over centralization and in the long term needs to be replaced by de-centralized Directive Style of Command (DSOC). NSS would spell out clear cut ends, ways and means, yet bank on delegation, synergy and operational freedom. At cutting edge level, it will foster initiative, innovation and improvisation. NSS is also a pre-requisite for operationalisation of theatre commands and transformation. Clearly spelt out NSS will certainly breed audacious commanders like Field Marshal 'Sam' Manekshaw, Lt Gen Harbaksh and Lt Gen Sagat Singh.

As India moves into Amrit-kaal, it is time to discard hesitation and ambiguity. **Every NSS has classified portion and that can certainly take care of confidentiality. If required, targeted ambiguity can be retained for messaging within documented NSS.** Concurrently, it is necessary to move to informed debates based on NSS rather than daily rabble-rousing Twitter campaigns to regain POK and Aksai Chin.

Securing Borders

Understanding Security of Our Borders

(Written in 2017 and updated in July 2024)

Key Takeaways

- **Before reading this article, please take a self-quiz.** With which country do we have the longest land borders? Most people answer-Pakistan or China, but the correct answer is Bangladesh. Name six states that have no land or maritime boundaries. What is your score? Answer-Haryana, Delhi, MP, Chatisgarh, Jharkhand and Telangana.
- **Despite numerous studies, including the Kargil Review Committee Report, we have been unable to achieve the agreed 'one border, one force'.** The same complexity prevails even for internal security. In Manipur, we have Assam Rifles (AR), BSF, Central Reserve Police Force (CRPF), ITBP, and SSB, as well as the state police.

Introduction

Securing and managing a 15,106 km long and tough land border and 7,516 km long coastal boundary is a major challenge for the country and also one of the topmost national priorities. The Ministry of Defence (MOD) and the Department of Border Management, part of the MHA, are tasked with securing most of India's borders, with some of their key objectives being to prevent infiltrations and drug smuggling as well as facilitate transit, trade, and safe movement of people. While doing so, forces deployed are confronted with challenges of infiltration, transgression, border raids, smuggling of weapons, drugs and goods, human trafficking, counterfeit, and cattle smuggling.

The western borders have witnessed three full-scale wars in 1947, 1965, and 1971, one limited war in Kargil in 1999 and an ongoing proxy war with Pakistan since 1989. On the eastern borders, besides the war in 1971 with erstwhile East Pakistan, the Chinese launched an all-out war in 1962, followed by skirmishes in 1967. **The main cause of these ongoing challenges is the unresolved status of our borders with China and Pakistan.**

Preview

The article is laid out in the following parts:

a) Analysis of Borders
b) Responsibilities and Manning Pattern
c) Challenges and Options
d) Recommendations

Scope

The scope of this article is limited to land borders.

Analysis of Borders

Land Borders: India shares land borders with the following six sovereign states:

a) **Afghanistan:** 106 kilometres (66 miles) – The border is currently included in an illegal part of PoK and is referred to as the **Wakhan Corridor; hence, it cannot be manned by India. It is de jure claimed but not de facto.**

b) **Bhutan:** 578 kilometres (359 miles) – This is a relatively **open border** manned by Sashastra Seema Bal (SSB).

c) **Myanmar:** 1,643 kilometres (1,021 miles) – The border has a **Free Movement Regime (FMR) based on traditional tribal laws permitting transit with head loads to ethnic stock up to 16 km and stay up to two weeks without a visa.** This border is manned largely by Assam Rifles, with an oversight by the Indian Army. FMR is currently under review.

d) **Nepal:** 1,752 kilometres (1,089 miles) – This is an **open border** manned by Sahastra Seema Bal (SSB).

e) **Pakistan:** 3,310 kilometres (2,060 miles) – This is the **most complex border with a settled IB, disputed Maritime Border (MB), LC, and AGPL. The IB and MB stretches of border are manned by the Border Security Force and balanced by the Indian Army assisted by the BSF.**

f) **China:** 3,380 kilometres (2,100 miles) – **This is an unmarked, disputed border referred to as the LAC and has trilateral dimensions with certain areas with Bhutan, Nepal, Myanmar, and even Pakistan if the illegally ceded Shaksgam Valley is included.** This border is manned by the Indian Army and Indo-Tibetan Border Police. It is covered in detail in separate section.

g) **Bangladesh:** 4,096 kilometres (2,545 miles) – **This border is the longest and is manned by the Border Security Force.** Recently, the complexity of this border was reduced by a mutually agreed exchange of enclaves.

h) **Sri Lanka:** 30 kilometres (19 miles) – This border is on the Ram Setu sand dune, manned by the Indian Coast Guard (ICG).

Maritime Borders

India has maritime borders with seven countries: Pakistan, Maldives, Sri Lanka, Thailand, Indonesia, Myanmar, and Bangladesh. Unconventional intrusion by Pakistan-backed terrorists through the Arabian Sea leading to the dastardly 26/11 Mumbai attacks has indeed opened the possibility of 'Samundri Jihad' (terror from sea) and, consequently, the need for enhanced maritime security. Coastal boundary of peninsular India is 5,422 km and islands have coastline of 2.094 km. **Island territories Andaman, Nicobar and Lakshadweep give us great maritime leverage and domination on sea lanes, yet open vulnerabilities.**

Indo-Pak Land Border

Growing Complexity and Disputes: After partition in 1947, the border was based on the hurriedly drafted Radcliffe Line. The border, which divides Pakistan and India from each other, traverses a variety of terrains, including inhospitable stretches, viz. swampy Rann, deserts, riverine, hilly, and glaciated areas. Since independence, the border has been contested and has witnessed numerous conflicts and wars. It is one of the most complex, contested, and dangerous borders in the world. The border's total length is 2,900 km (1,800 miles). It can be seen from space at night due to the 1,50,000 flood lights installed by India on about 50 thousand poles. **While the mutually agreed International Border is well marked, patrolled, and has joint mechanisms, there are issues connected with illegal infiltration, smuggling, and difficulties associated with the management of agriculture, which extends right up to the very zero line and beyond the boundary fence, which is on the Indian side.**

Disputed Portions: Immediately after partition, Pakistan launched war in Kashmir and annexed portions of Indian territory. The redefined status quo was mandated by the Karachi Agreement in 1949, and this temporary arrangement that arrived under the UN's supervision was called the CFL. Despite the 1965 war leading to the Tashkent Agreement, the status quo of the CFL was maintained. India squandered the major leverage of 93,000 prisoners in the 1971 war, and the only concession obtained in the Shimla Agreement was that while the border south of J&K was sanctified as the IB, the portion of J&K was accepted as the LC.

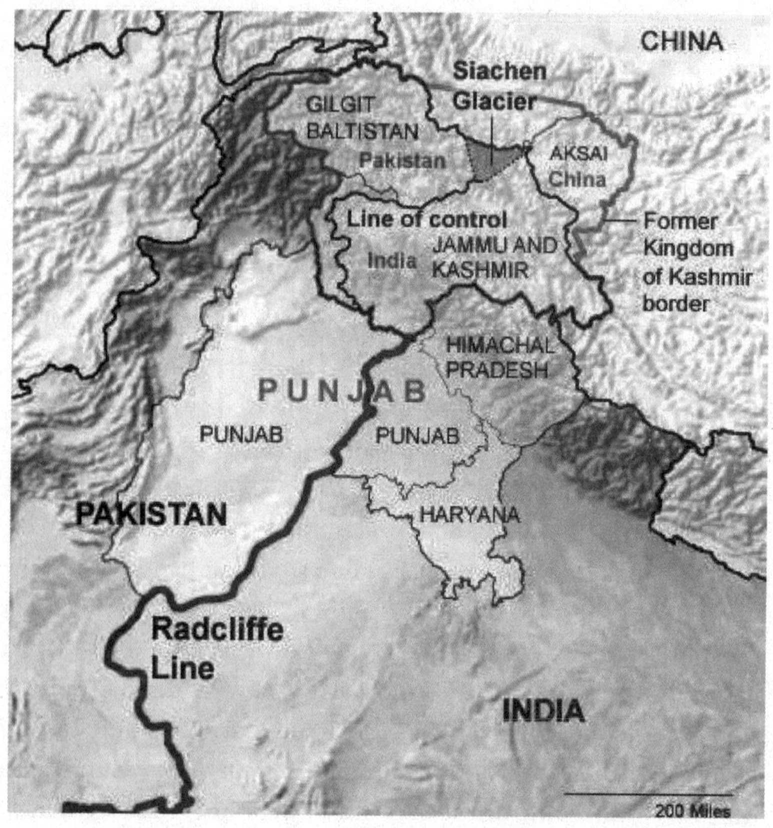

(Map source-https://www.pmfias.com/current-affairs-august-18-2016/)

The contested portions of this border include the following:

LoC: Line of Control is also referred to as LC in military parlance. LC fencing is also technically termed as Anti Infiltration Obstacle System (AIOS). It is a 550 km (340 miles) barrier along the 740 km (460 miles) disputed 1972 Line of Control (or modified version of the Cease Fire Line). **The fence, constructed by India, generally remains about 150 yards on the Indian-controlled side. Its stated purpose is to exclude arms smuggling and infiltration by Pakistani-based separatist militants.** The barrier itself consists of a double row of fencing and concertina wire eight to twelve feet (2.4–3.7 m) in height and is electrified and connected to a network of motion sensors, thermal imaging devices, lighting systems, and alarms. They act as 'fast alert signals' to the Indian troops, who can be alerted and ambush the infiltrators trying to sneak in. The small stretch of land between the rows of fencing is mined with thousands of landmines. The construction of the barrier began in the 1990s but slowed in the early 2000s as hostilities between India and Pakistan increased. After a November 2003 ceasefire agreement, the construction resumed and was completed in late 2004. The LC fencing was completed in the Kashmir Valley and the Jammu region on 30 September 2004. According to Indian military sources, the fence has reduced the number of militants who routinely cross into the Indian side of the disputed state to attack soldiers by 80%.

Working Boundary (WkB): Despite agreement and proper IB fencing to a point North of Jammu, covering districts of Jammu, Samba, and Kathua, Pak has resurrected the bogey of the whole of J&K being unresolved. Hence, this stretch is called WB by Pak. This 198.4 km of the border, as per Pak, is WB because while on one side, Sialkot is settled on the other side, J&K is still disputed. **From the Indian perspective, we should continue to use IB and avoid using WkB, at least in official formal documents.**

Actual Ground Position Line (AGPL): The Actual Ground Position Line (AGPL) is the line that divides the current positions of Indian and Pakistani troops in the Siachen Glacier region. The line extends from the northernmost point of the LC, also referred to as NJ 9842, to Indira Col. The AGPL is approximately 110 kilometres (68 miles) long and was created to surreptitious efforts of Pak to grab this glaciated but strategically vital territory.

Maritime Boundary (MB): This 96 km tidal estuary of Sir Creek is adjoining Rann of Kutch and includes a disputed portion of Sir Creek. Please see the accompanying graphic.

(Map source-https://images.app.goo.gl/xga4hwYrNmeJ2SBLA)

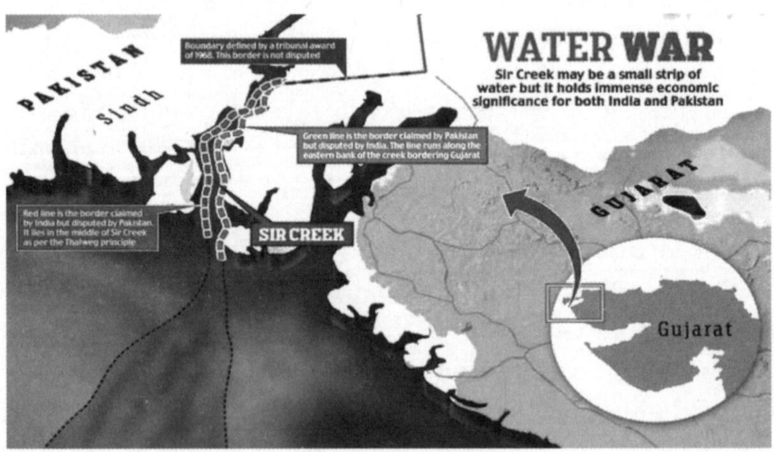

(Map source-https://images.app.goo.fl/eZSRHjEaHWKdBLV)

Responsibilities and Manning Pattern

Maritime Defence: The primary responsibility for the defence of the maritime border is with the Indian Coast Guard, assisted by the

Indian Navy and Coastal Police under respective state governments. This layered mechanism has coastal radars and a plethora of surveillance mechanisms, many of which are still to be operationalised. The major problem is the creation of an empowered and dedicated Maritime Security Agency. The subject requires a separate and detailed analysis.

Land Borders: The manning on land borders is ideally to be governed by 'One Force One Border'. However, the same is not fully achieved, and currently, responsibilities are divided as follows:

- Indo-Pak Border: Currently manned by the **BSF, although in the LC portion, the primary responsibility is with the Indian Army.** While operational control in such areas is with the army, administrative control is retained by the respective CAPF. It is dealt with in the section on Pakistan.
- Sino-Indian Border: **The designated CAPF is ITBP, but this is an unfenced disputed border, also referred to as the LAC, and the de facto responsibility is with the Indian Army.** This aspect has been covered in greater detail in the section on LAC.
- Bangladesh: **The fencing on the Bangladesh border has been completed for 3180.65 km out of 4096.7 km. The main challenge is human and cattle smuggling. Tidal areas are another challenge, and the BSF is creating a marine wing for tidal stretches.** A graphic of this border is included.
- Other Borders: **SSB has the mandate for Bhutan and Nepal, but there is no clarity on Myanmar, where there are reports of a move to transfer responsibility from Assam Rifles to BSF/ITBP.** A separate article on securing the Indo-Myanmar Border is included in this section. The relevant aspects of the border with Bhutan are included in the section on the Sino-Bhutan border. A graphical snapshot of the contested portions of the Indo-Nepal border is included.

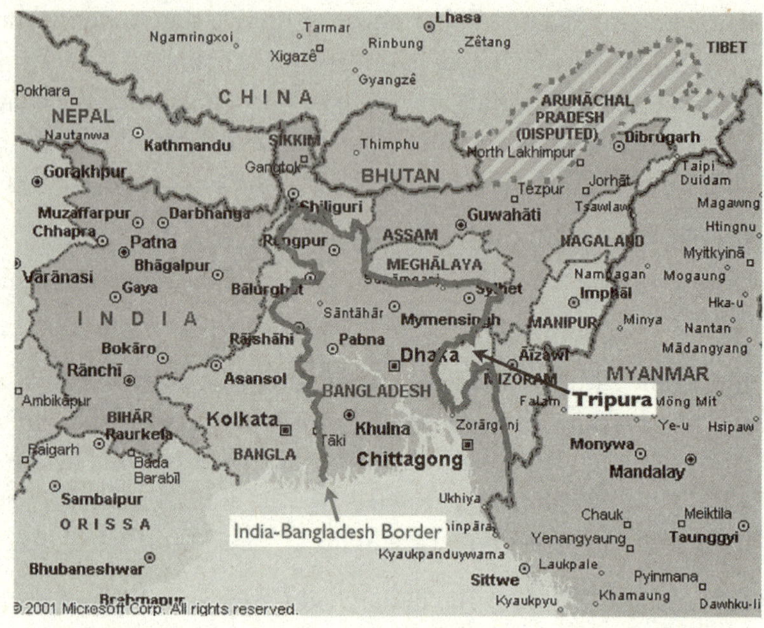

(Map source-https://images.app.goo.gl/gVqixbHqsfgwtkJK6)

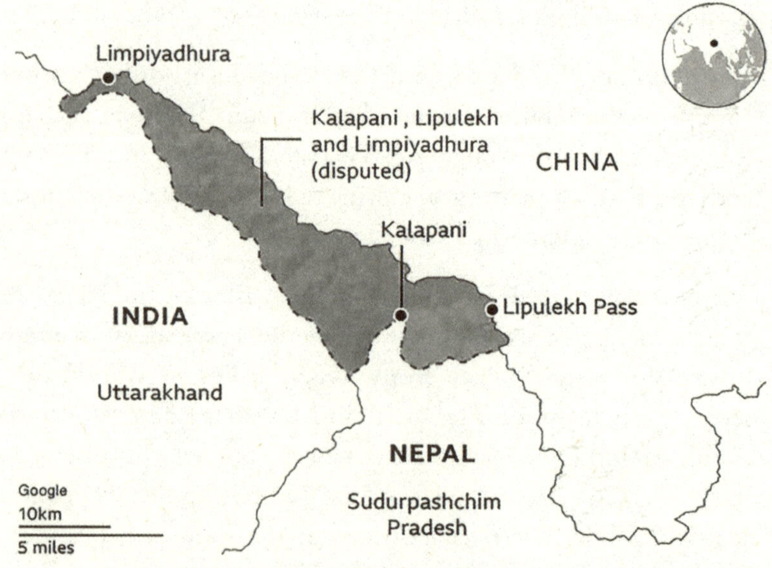

(Map source-https://images.app.g.gl/9t8WHbMXqVzH3uEi8)

Varying Charters

However, by and large, there is a need to bring uniformity in the charters of CAPFs to make them interoperable. A careful and detailed reading of charters will bring out variations that simply cannot be glossed over, even if they are termed as mere semantics.

Table–Tasks of Border Guarding Forces

S. No.	Assam Rifles	BSF	ITBP	SSB
1.	Safeguard the security of the borders of India and promote a sense of security among the people living in the border areas.	Promote a sense of security among the people living in the border areas.	Safeguard the security of the borders of India and promote a sense of security among the people living in the border areas.	Safeguard the security of assigned borders of India and promote a sense of security among the people living in the border area.
2.	Prevent trans-border crimes, smuggling, unauthorised entry or exit from the territory of India, and any other illegal activity.	Prevent trans-border crimes, smuggling, and unauthorised entry or exit from the territory of India.	Prevent trans-border crimes, smuggling, unauthorised entry or exit from the territory of India, and any other illegal activity.	Prevent trans-border crimes, smuggling, and illegal activities.
3.	Provide security to sensitive installations, banks, and persons of security risk.	Prevent smuggling and other illegal activities.	Provide security to sensitive installations, banks, and persons of security risk.	Prevent unauthorised entry into or exit from the territory of India.
4.	Restore and preserve order in any area in the event of disturbance therein.		Restore and preserve order in any area in the event of disturbance therein.	Carry out civic action programmes in the area of responsibility.
5.				Perform any assigned duty by the central government.

Challenges and Options

Transgressions: Sino-Indian Border: There are **large numbers of areas where PLA troops periodically transgress to keep alive their claim. China has also leveraged ambiguity associated particularly with tri-junctions** like Mt Gipmochi in Doklam with Bhutan, Lipulekh Pass with Nepal, and Diphu Pass near Walong with Myanmar. Please read the chapter 'LAC-Unresolved Stand-off' for more details.

Limited Infrastructure: There is a lack of infrastructure in border areas compared to Chinese state-of-the-art railroad connectivity, which has created a huge asymmetry in response timings.

Sparse Population: The border belt is dotted with ghost and deserted villages. Even where settlements exist, they are sparse and lack basic amenities and connectivity. **India has started the Vibrant Village Programme to develop border villages to counter Chinese project of Xiaokang, dual use border villages.**

Demographics: Many **border areas adjoining Bangladesh have seen an influx of certain segments of the population, who are more susceptible to exploitation by elements across.**

Options

Technological Solutions: World over, the trend is to seek technological solutions based on **smart fences, intrusion alarms, radar arrays, drones, unattended sensors, etc. India is making somewhat tardy progress in this discipline, which needs to be expedited.**

Manpower: No defence line can be protected merely by gizmos; hence, deployment of troops is inevitable. However, in our context, the burgeoning strength of the CAPF is being propelled by a turf-centric approach and is also justified as a means of additional employment avenues. However, the need is to use the right size CAPFs and invest in quality rather than in quantity.

Automated Decision Making: The plethora of agencies on the ground and technical ones generate a vast volume of data that needs to be processed on a real-time basis on an automated decision support system.

Recommendations

Border Resolution: There is a need to **expedite border resolution talks with a view to arrive at an early solution, as good fences make good neighbours. In the interim, better confidence-building mechanisms and protocols** like lines, border meeting points, and flag meetings should be factored in.

Unified Mandate: **In areas where the mandate is border defence, relevant CAPFs should be placed under the army's control, operational and administrative, with mutually agreed career protection measures.**

One Border One Force: Early resolution of designated force for the Myanmar border should be attempted. **Ideally, all security forces and agencies in a designated theatre should report and controlled by one commander.**

CAPF Cadres: The current CAPF cadres are headed at the apex by IPS officers who lack ground experience in a force culture. It is described as para-dropping by cadres and builds resentment. **It would be a good idea to have totally home-grown cadres with strong force affiliation like the coast guard.**

Expediting and Upgrading Fencing: Efforts should be made to complete pending fencing work and **upgrade these with automated smart fences.**

Special Cadre for Border Areas: The **old model of Frontier Areas Administrative Service duly upgraded to contemporary requirements should be applied in border areas.** This issue was also highlighted by former Governor Mr NN Vohra in his report.

Rightsizing: Like the Indian Army, CAPFs should also carry out an **optimisation study and cut down the increasing flab specially at the top in HQs.**

Conclusion

For a country of India's size, terrain complexity, and an array of neighbours, border management will remain a major and complex challenge, requiring a 'whole of nation' dynamic approach. **Newer challenges like drones and tunnelling to gain access will manifest and require a dynamic approach.**

Governing and Securing Critical Strategic Corridors

(Written in November 2020)

The title of Robert D Kaplan's famous book, 'The Revenge of Geography', readily comes to mind when we take stock of our critical strategic spaces. The challenges have been magnified by our two diabolic neighbours: China, bent upon asserting its coercive dominance, and Pakistan, whose existential raison d'etre is to create new criticalities for us. Compounding matters is their much-touted collusion, manifesting in the China-Pakistan Economic Corridor (CPEC).

While each space has its relevance, the three most critical corridors are – the Siliguri Corridor, Pathankot-Jammu link, and Darbuk-Shyok-Daulat Beg Oldie (DSDBO), touted as 'casus belli' by the Chinese for the current stand-off. Critical spaces are characterised by three main factors: firstly, the fragility of communications; secondly, inefficient governance and a lack of development; and thirdly, demographic challenges, especially ethnic balance. These factors generate centrifugal forces, creating ripe conditions for secessionist tendencies.

The sarpanch (village head) in the remote Pin Valley, while handing over a representation citing lack of basic facilities to the army commander, cheekily mentioned that if sent across, the Chinese would certainly oblige. Despite 70 years of the republic, surface connectivity in bordering states remains tenuous, with a misplaced focus on building statues, temples, and spiritual connectivity projects. Many states are barely beginning to get some semblance of rail connectivity, and it may take another decade for them to be on the rail map.

The Pathankot-Jammu link, with just 10-odd km of depth (in stretches), has not only witnessed skirmishes in operations, but Pakistan has also made multiple attempts to spread the arc of terrorism from the valley to the Kathua-Samba region.

The half-hearted attempts to build redundancy on the alternative Dhar-Udhampur link in depth have not found traction despite the army pushing it. The pressure of lobbies is such that the proposed Katra Expressway project doesn't mitigate vulnerabilities, as pilgrims will remain easy and high TRP targets. A better option would be to upgrade the Dhar-Udhampur link and construct a spur to Jammu, like the one linking Amritsar.

It is reassuring to witness some concerted action, though much belated, to ramp up communications in border areas. Besides the BRO, there is a plethora of agencies constructing and maintaining roads. They are classified as national/state highways, PWD, BRO, China Study Group, Border Area Development Project, CAPF, and PMGSY (rural) roads.

The unfortunate part is that there is very little coordination and a near-complete disregard for uniformity in specifications. Funding norms are such that the ITBP can outsource roads to civilian firms, getting better results. Even the BRO excels across in Bhutan due to liberal allocations. Recent media reports highlighted repairs of the Kaza-Gramphu road by the BRO, linking strategically important Lahaul and Spiti valleys.

The disturbing question is a lack of accountability of the PWD, responsible for deterioration, under its charge. There is marked reluctance on the part of states for capacity building. The overall sense is that states want central funding and want to retain the escape clause of passing on the blame to the BRO in the event of road closures.

Tunnelling to ensure all-weather connectivity is a welcome new feature, but most projects entail expansive foreign consultancy, banking on imported machinery. The Rohtang project was stuck due to seepage through Seri Nullah for nearly four years. Foreign consultants recommended alternate alignment, entailing massive additional expenditure, but some calculated risk-taking and alleviating "jugaad" measures enabled completion. It is hoped that designated institutions and IITs are incorporated to build domain knowledge and competence, including research.

Demography in border areas remains a challenge characterised by sparse population in ghost villages. In many states, there are serious theological challenges. Moderate strands are being radicalised by migrant Wahhabi clergy. While we can't emulate the Chinese model of Hanisation, allowing the Sufi culture and Kashmiryat to be completely marginalised amounts to socio-cultural harakiri. Theological filters need to be applied in sensitive areas to protect traditionally moderate communities – the Shias of Kargil, the Gujjars, and the Paharis. Attempts to alter demographic balance by settling outsiders like Rohangiyas need to be guarded against.

Representative local bodies and responsive administration can generate binding centripetal forces to negate aberrant centrifugal ones. Unfortunately, experience suggests that the best in bureaucracy and agencies avoid remote areas. A random check of DCs and SPs in bordering areas after the Pathankot incident revealed that most, like SP Salwinder, were from state services, enjoying nexus with local political mafias. The recent apprehension of Devinder, who was entrusted with the security of Srinagar Airport, is another such example. **These areas deserve better governance and vigilant monitoring agencies by committed administration with a unique 'hands-on' skill set.**

Governance has to be anchored by officers like Captain Bob Khathing, to whom the nation owes a deep debt of gratitude for planting the Tricolour in Tawang. **The suggestion of ex-Governor NN**

Vohra for a specialised cadre like the Indian Frontier Administrative Service needs to be implemented.

While it may sound a bit revolutionary, like Ladakh, the Siliguri Corridor needs to be reorganised into a UT. It has a complicated demography with just 20-odd km width and is the only terrestrial link to seven states of NE, Sikkim, and Bhutan. It borders four countries and has seen Gorkhaland and Kamatapur separatist movements. The recent elections in Bihar have highlighted the worrying rise of left-wing extremists in the Seemanchal region bordering the Siliguri Corridor.

Areas like Kaliachak have acquired a dubious reputation in crime. The federal structure is fraying, with states like Bengal on the warpath with the centre. Even within the state, the Gorkhaland council is at loggerheads, holding everyone to ransom by frequent blockades. Chinese intentions after Doklam appear ominous. Can we allow external forces to exploit our fault lines? **The possible solution, though seemingly radical, lies in central rule in this sensitive territory by creating Seemant UT", with the Gorkha and Duars councils enjoying limited autonomy.**

Development Model for Challenging Areas

(Written in October 2018)

Some very interesting inferences were highlighted in the recent national seminar on 'Transforming Backward Areas'. Ministries run 13 different schemes for focused development in backward areas, and nearly 90% of districts have managed to get enlisted in these. **It seems that everyone loves being classified 'backward', particularly when it is a question of getting additional funds.** When people of different castes are clamouring to hop on the 'Me too OBC' bandwagon, why should districts lag behind? A few schemes allocate paltry sums, but the idea is that all funds from the centre are welcome.

The second interesting inference was that the bureaucracy is leveraging its skill in wordcraft by substituting 'aspirational' for 'backward' and 'transformation' for 'change'. All this just to show renewed focus. While we wait for another innovative acronym, the question that arises is, can we treat livelihood issues in such a cavalier manner by resorting to crafty semantics?

The Niti Aayog has identified 30 districts in the aspirational category, MHA has added 35, and 52 more want to join the party, which brings the total to 117 out of 718 districts. Another aspect of such a scenario is the unchecked creation of new districts on political considerations.

While security forces are struggling to roll back the dreaded 'Red Corridor', states still want their districts to be included in the category of those affected by Left Wing Extremism (LWE) since funds for modernization are lucrative. This only proves that everyone is comfortable with simmering insurgency as it sustains many profitable enterprises. No one cares for the perspective of the security forces, which actually bear the brunt of the bloodshed.

Meaningful engagement with the uniformed fraternity makes us realize that it is of the utmost importance to deal with the most serious threat to national security, which is an inadequate and lackadaisical delivery mechanism. Despite automation and better tracking, the previous estimate that only 15 paise of development funds reach its intended target may have been enhanced to only 25 paise. Also, unabated extortion or 'levy' milking a significant chunk of development funds into the coffers of extremists remains a matter of serious concern. This provides financial sustenance to militancy.

The perspective of the security forces can be understood as the management of centrifugal forces, exacerbated mainly by a lack of development with contributory socio-political and theological influences. Our development or delivery model is 'one size fits all', which does not always work. Officers on punishment posting are assigned to these areas, and their angst is transferred to the suffering population, magnifying their alienation even more.

A check of DCs and SSPs in Punjab after the Pathankot attack revealed that most border districts were manned by state cadres, with the clairvoyant Salwinder being just one example. As Army Commander, I received a representation from a village head in a remote village on the Chinese border, asking whether he should approach Chinese authorities since the Indian administration was not responding to his repeated requests.

It is time we give these areas focused attention by **first classifying them in the de novo category as 'Challenging Districts'. These should include select border, insurgency, and left-wing extremism-affected districts.** It will be important to stipulate criteria. One possible parameter can be those under the Disturbed Area Act and managed by central security forces, including the army and the Central Armed Police Forces (CAPFs).

The funding model should build disincentives for the 'status quo' approach and promote conflict resolution by appropriating proportionate costs for the deployment of central forces and administrative structures. This should be factored into the design of the evolving distribution of the GST regime, wherein progress in achieving development-induced normalcy should be incentivized.

The only specialized administrative model applied was the Indian Frontier Administrative Service (IFAS), which was in existence from 1953 to 1968 and covered primarily the tribal areas of the North East Frontier Agency (NEFA), Sikkim, Tibet, and Bhutan.

The Indian administration at Tawang was established in 1951 by Captain 'Bob' Khathing of the Assam Rifles, who deserves to be designated as an all-time role model for administrators. While it may not be possible to replicate the IFAS, we can attempt to design a customized cadre with UPSC-mandated guidelines and link compliance to these stipulations for the release of central funds. Assignments in notified challenging areas should follow the criteria appointment system of the army and tenanted by volunteers on fixed tenures. They should have built-in financial and career rewards like additional allowances, fellowships in foreign universities and foreign/choice postings after a successful tenure.

The basic thrust should be like 'Super 30 for IIT' to have the very best as DCs and SSPs in these challenging areas. They cannot be greenhorns learning on the job but experienced ones like captains of aircraft carriers, who, despite seniority, volunteer and even forego higher rank, dropping from commodore to captain. Of course, the bureaucracy will surely be able to devise rules and procedures to get past such issues. The administrative structure at the top has to be supported by competent and dedicated supporting cadres like Block Development Officers and tehsildars. Matching upgrades of teachers, health workers, and patwaris will be required as they are the cutting edge of the delivery mechanism.

In the interim, the need is to institutionalize the role of security forces in military-civic action and to back it up with funds, training, and structures as the army fills the administrative vacuum in the so-called liberated areas till they become governable. It will be a good idea to post young administrators at SF headquarters, particularly Rashtriya Rifles and Assam Rifles. It is high time the army and civil administration call a truce in the 'turf war' and synergize delivery mechanisms.

It's Time India Focusses on Managing Its Borders

(Written in April 2019)

All major political parties have placed in the public domain the much-awaited manifestos just before the first round of electoral 'dangal'. The Congress adopted a de novo approach to national security by hiring a respected general to prepare its road map. The BJP devoted a full chapter on security in its Sankalp Patra. In keeping with our electoral DNA, articulations remain diffused, skipping and skirting some critical issues. The relevance of these documents is diluted as debate has been overtaken by fake news, echo-chamber cacophony, and the high voltage, orchestrated melodrama to milk a 'security cow' for votes.

Both parties, despite viable multiple tenures in running the government, are unwilling to explain why promises made after the Kargil Review Committee, like combined defence services (CDS), revamping intelligence, and border management still remain on paper and are once again being touted as lofty objectives. One can't help but recall the late defence minister's assertions that CDS and joint commands are just around the corner. Did he even realise that corners on the Raisina Hill are indeed fortresses guarded by status-quo-oriented satraps? The question that is being posed on WhatsApp groups is simple – will the rulers have it in them (genuine commitment and, more importantly, the skill set) to get past the bureaucratic dilatory tactics?

Border management is one critical issue that has been glossed over despite its overriding relevance in the current context. India shares approximately 15,000 km of land borders and 7,500 km of maritime boundaries with 11 countries. Only five Indian states do not have any borders. Yet, our basic knowledge about them is abysmally poor. I state this with conviction after running 'Seema Khoj', an initiative to enhance awareness about borders. Sceptics may like to try a simple self-quiz: Which country has the longest border with India? Where is the Wakhan Corridor? Name all border management forces. Well, answers may indeed surprise many – Bangladesh, the narrow stretch between Gilgit and Afghanistan, BSF, ITBP, SSB, and Assam Rifles. One contributory reason is that geography is losing relevance as a subject. On the other hand, China continues with imaginative cartography. **Knowing our borders is part of 'Hosh with Josh'. Unfortunately, currently, it is more of Josh without focus or genuine commitment.**

At the macro level, the genesis of our woes lies in the generalist approach and lack of specialisation. The hierarchy at the apex refuses to differentiate between border management and other policing functions. Consequently, Central Armed Police Forces (CAPFs) continue to be headed by parachuted DGPs, and the top hierarchy is staffed by IPS officers. Turf protection and HR interests of IPS override functional realities. The army has to share some part of the blame for the Assam Rifles cadre. All our neighbours have border guarding forces headed by generals and firmly under their army's control. Interestingly, China re-emphasised this aspect in its latest paper on reforms in the **People's Liberation Army. Recently, the parliamentary standing committee also observed that CAPFs are akin to the army in their functioning and should get more leadership content from the Armed Forces.**

The solution lies in elevating border management as a specialist function in a shared common domain. Induction in officer cadres in army and border management CAPFs could be through a common induction scheme. All inductees should serve with active battalions on borders for the first three years and, thereafter, join assigned cadres. This would breed desired ethos and competencies (flagged by Parliament), address unit-level deficiencies, and alleviate cadre management issues in the army by boosting support cadres. Above all, expenditure on multiple training academies will be curtailed. To ensure objectivity, the entire exercise can be supervised by the UPSC. Incidentally, this recommendation was approved by former Prime Minister IK Gujral in 1997 but ambushed on a tenuous road between the South and North blocks. Like the Coast Guard, all CAPFs, including Assam Rifles, should be allowed to develop their own cadres and achieve specialisation.

Even within border management, there is a need to further differentiate between border guarding and border defence. Guarding applies to settled boundaries, like International Borders and open borders. This would include approximately 2,000 km of International Border with Pakistan, open borders with Nepal and Bhutan, and large stretches of Indo-Myanmar borders. **Border defence, on the other hand, is applicable for sensitive and contested borders like the Line of Control with Pak and the Line of Actual Control** with China, 193km of the Jammu-Kathua-Samba stretch of international border described by Pakistan as a working boundary, and sensitive stretches on the Myanmar border. While the former can be managed entirely by the CAPFs, the latter requires a synergised combination of the army and the CAPFs. **The current model of silo-based, notional cooperation needs to be replaced with meaningful, functional unity of command.**

While the Armed Forces are engaged in transformation, below the horizon and out of public debate, CAPFs continue to multiply. Some estimates put the strength of this burgeoning force at 11 lakhs plus, leaving you wondering if the rightsizing is even applicable to them. The first reaction of affected forces to the recent court direction for rationalisation of variance in retirement ages is the demand for additional battalions.

Smart fencing and surveillance systems are replacing antiquated infrastructure as part of a comprehensive, integrated border management system and border electronically dominated QRT interception technique. **It is axiomatic that the technical threshold is raised and matching savings are effected through the rationalisation of manpower. In remote areas, the commonality of equipment with the army facilitates logistics, boosting interoperability.** Administration in border areas mandates a 'best hands on deck' approach with specialised sub-cadres like the erstwhile Indian Frontier Administrative Service to manage centrifugal forces and development challenges. This sub-cadre should be highly incentivised and utilised for staff security-related appointments at higher levels.

Securing the Indo-Myanmar Border

India's border with Myanmar, remote and largely excluded from public concern, is in the news with two important recent announcements. The MHA has announced the suspension of the Free Movement Regime (FMR) with immediate effect. The government has also

decided to fence a 1643-km-long border. The suspension of FMR, which allowed transit up to 16 km on either side (with headloads) and stay for 14 days, was in the offing in the wake of unrest in Myanmar, resulting in a large influx of Chin refugees in Mizoram and even Manipur. The implementation of both measures poses tremendous challenges and has evoked widespread opposition. Yet, regulation is required in view of the smuggling of narcotics, arms, timber, wildlife products, and, more importantly, fear of demographic inversion.

Understanding Border

The unfenced open border starts in the North, in the vicinity of the Diphu Pass, from the un-demarcated tripoint of India, Myanmar, and China. It runs down south and west to another tripoint of India, Myanmar, and Bangladesh. It passes through Arunachal Pradesh (520 km), Nagaland (215 km), Manipur (398 km), and Mizoram (510 km). The large stretch is hilly, traversing Mishmi, Patkai, and Chin hills, comprising the Arakan range. In addition, it is covered by thick jungles and devoid of communications. The challenges are magnified by adverse climate, the presence of wildlife, and the near total absence of local resources. The writ of the Myanmar state is rather notional in bordering Kachin, Sagaing, and Chin regions and even the neighbouring Rakhine state, enabling sanctuary and unbridled access for terrorist groups. The Arakan Army recently gained control of Paletwa, a critical node on the proposed Kaladan multi-modal project.

Unlike the old maxim 'good fences make good neighbours', this imaginary division runs through tribal settlements. **Derived from the Pemberton Line, it is like other boundaries crafted by the British colonial power, which left festering complexities. It has illogically divided tribes like Konyaks, Khieumengan, Kukis, and Zomis in the bordering areas of Nagaland, Manipur, and Mizoram.** The iconic house of Angh (ruler) of Longwa bears special mention, where the line runs literally through his house. Mercifully, his writ runs over the entire village, spread on both sides of the border. Eastern districts in Nagaland have been demanding the creation of separate administrative entities like the autonomous council for Eastern Naga People's Organisation (ENPO) on the lines of the erstwhile Tuensang Frontier Division.

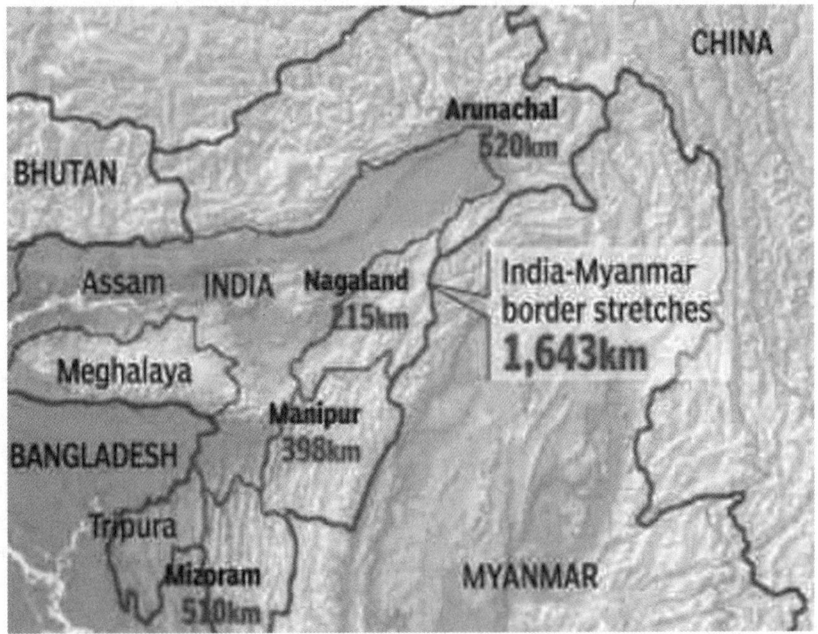

(Map source-https://insightsonindia.com/international-relations/india-and-its-neighborhood/india-myanmar-relations/introduction/)

Challenges and Complexities

The biggest challenge is to overcome resistance and win over tribal society, to build a shared stake for them in regulating access. In any case, land ownership being a collective tribal convent, their partnership is imperative. Ironically, Pakistan is facing similar challenges in fencing the border between Baluchistan and Sistan (Iran). The Pak-Afghan border along the Durand Line, which separates Afridis and Mehsuds, bound by common Pashtunwali code, is even more complicated.

The analysis of defence lines like Maginot, Siegfried, Barlev, and Berlin-Wall reinforces historical lessons: **no defence line is impregnable and determined intruders (like the fedayeens) will get**

through. Defying trends of globalisation and open borders, the desire to fortify borders has only increased. This is notwithstanding the recent breaching of the formidable Gaza Barrier, the so-called gold standard of defence lines. The requirement is for customised solutions based on an optimal mix of technology (smart fencing) backed up by human vigilance. **It would require considerable effort to get Myanmar on board and set up a joint monitoring mechanism. Equally important is to restore the credibility of our mandated force, the Assam Rifles.**

Way Forward

Securing entails fencing, manning, joint patrolling, and quick reaction. **Barrier systems need to be futuristic and have built-in redundancies, structured in layers, providing depth and reaction time.** While it is important to detect and deny access, the most critical imperative is a quick reaction system to rapidly localise the intrusion and deal with it. Tardy response and failure on this account led to not only high casualties but also Hamas escaping with hostages. It is important to bear in mind that while smartness has no limits, it entails a huge premium in cost. As physical barrier takes shape, new threats—drones and tunnels—are likely to manifest, as is being witnessed on the Punjab border. Both ends of the drug combo of Golden Crescent in Af-Pak and Golden Triangle in China-Myanmar are equally deadly, posing formidable challenges.

Currently, barely a stretch of 4 km near Moreh has rudimentary fencing. In addition, two hybrid surveillance-based pilot projects (1 km each) are being executed in Arunachal and Manipur. Fencing is demanded stridently by the Meitei groups but is opposed by the hill tribes. The valley-based population is rooting for a barrier, fearing demographic inversion, citing somewhat trumped-up fears of the Zomia tribal homeland. The government has given the go-ahead for fencing of an additional 20 km in Manipur. Building such systems entails a long gestation period, even in fast-track mode. As per the MHA report of October 2023, fencing on the Bangladesh border has been completed for 3180.65 km out of 4096.7 km. The ministry had projected a highly optimistic deadline of Mar 2024 for a balance of 916 km, which has since passed. The main stumbling block, as stated in the Supreme Court, has been the availability of land due to the reticence of the West Bengal government.

The project is likely to face multiple challenges, but given the firm resolve, ingenuity, and financial and technological back-up, it is certainly not an impossible objective. Planners will have to devise innovative solutions like local participation in the erecting and maintenance of fencing systems. The Vibrant Villages Programme can be harnessed to build incentives and imaginative solutions (tried in other borders), like bee farming and the cultivation of medicinal plants. **The Act-East policy mandates access and connectivity but regulated yet hassle-free transit can be built into it. It would be pragmatic to initially roll out pilot projects in Arunachal and Manipur and concurrently get other states on board.**

LAC – Claim Lines and Unresolved Standoff

Line of Actual Control, International Boundary, and Claim Lines: Getting Better Perspective on India's Northern Borders

Key Takeaways

- Chinese claims have been based on selective manipulation of imaginative cartography aided by lawfare-selective leveraging of favourable treaties and amnesia on those not supporting Chinese claims. Ten Dashes line, an expanded version of the Nine Dashes line in the South China Sea, exemplifies such revanchist trends.
- China prefers ambiguity as it has not provided any maps indicating her claims. It also wants to put the issue on the back burner and prefers the concept of buffer/no patrolling zones.
- China is altering the geography of borders by setting up model border villages—Xiaokangs—to solidify their claim lines.
- 1959 claim line propounded by Chinese Prime Minister Chou Enlai seems to be the current reality in Ladakh. India did miss a great opportunity to partially resolve the issue as China, till the '70s, was probably aggregable to a swap deal, giving up claims in Arunachal in return for Aksai Chin.
- After the standoff, partial disengagement with the designation of buffer zones has taken place in Galwan (PP-14), Gogra (PP17A)-Hot Springs (PP-15). Similarly, in Pangong Tso, the

area between Fingers 3 and 8 has become a buffer zone with no patrolling zones or demilitarised areas.

- **The focus remains on the unresolved standoff in Depsang and Demchok. Access to PP-10, 11, 12, 12A, and 13 in Depsang remains blocked due to PLA deployment.**
- **Only the first step- partial disengagement has taken place, in Depsang and Demchok is still pending. The next two steps—de-induction and de-escalation—are still being negotiated.**

Introduction

India's northern borders with aggressively rising China have remained unresolved despite prolonged and tortuous structured deliberations. The ambiguity on borders has resulted in the articulation of various conflicting claim lines and the 1962 war, the 1967 skirmish at Nathu La, other face-offs at Sumdrong Chu in 1986/87, Doklam in 2017, and the recent ongoing Chinese action in Ladakh. This complex situation is falling out of festering colonial legacy and covenants between Britain, Tibet, Bhutan, Nepal, Sikkim, and China. The current standoff on the Line of Actual Control (LAC) has once again raised sensitivities and makes a compelling case for early resolution. **Indian borders range from settled International Border (IB) to Line of Control (LC) and Maritime border (Rann of Kutch) with Pakistan and Actual Ground Position Line (AGPL) in Siachen, Unmanned Border (Shakasgam Valley), and Line of Actual Control (LAC), unfenced and unmarked with China.** The complex issue of the Sino-Indian border requires analysis structured on the following key parameters:

- Basics of Evolution of Borders
- Geo-strategic Context
- Chinese Border Policy and Agenda
- Claim Lines
- Way Forward

Basics of Evolution of Borders

The term 'border' is commonly understood as the boundary or geographic limits of a country or state. The historic idea of limits or the outer edge of a country included no man's land, buffer states, and frontiers. Buffer states like Nepal and Bhutan are relatively smaller and neutral countries that help to keep two major powers geographically apart. They serve to preclude skirmishes and standoffs and also provide time and space to resolve contentious issues. Frontiers like Federally Administered Tribal Areas (FATA) on the Pak-Afghan border were autonomous areas with limited suzerainty of governing powers. They were organised in the form of no man's land, which denoted a lack of institutional control. Tibet, till 1951, is a classic example of a frontier and buffer state. Unfortunately, both Tibet and FATA have been subsumed into China and Pakistan, respectively, thereby altering the geo-strategic template. Ideally, **Tibet should have remained as a buffer between India and China, with her genuine autonomous status.**

In keeping with the old proverb, 'Good fences make good neighbours', the quest is to physically demarcate boundaries. Borders have evolved into international boundaries after a structured process, including the following major stages:

- **Delimitation**
- **Delineation**
- **Demarcation**

Delimitation is the acceptance of broad principles for settling boundaries like watersheds, rivers, or ridgelines. This is followed by translating the delimited concept into an agreed line on the map. Such delineation has resulted in the Radcliffe Line and the Durand Line in the Indian subcontinent, though both got vitiated in finalisation, creating unresolved problems. The most difficult part is the physical demarcation of this line on the ground. In the Sino-Indian context, the McMahon Line is an attempt to delimit and resolve the borders based on the concept of a watershed. However, all three stages are pending.

Geostrategic Context

The unresolved Sino-Indian border has acquired significant strategic heft in the 'Thucydides Trap'-like situation developing between increasingly aggressive China and aspiring India. China would like to cement its hegemony and limit India to a compliant state. Indian quest for strategic autonomy and non-alignment has riled the Red-Dragon. India's recent leveraging of alliances like Quad is perceived by China as a conspiracy against her. China would like India to join her against the US.

India, on the other hand, has felt threatened by Chinese forays described as the 'String of Pearls'. India has also resisted Chinese invitations to join connectivity initiatives like the BRI and China-Pakistan Economic Corridor (CPEC). India's stand on CPEC is linked to the violation of Indian de-jure sovereignty due to its alignment through Gilgit-Baltistan (GB). The Sino-Indian border has a complex trilateral dimension with other neighbours like Pakistan, Nepal, Bhutan, and Myanmar. These areas are described as tri-junctions. They are most contentious and strategically important. The first one is with Pakistan in the Karakoram-Tortuk sector, complicated by Pakistan gifting away Shaksgam Valley to China in 1963. Similarly, the tri-junction with Nepal in the Lipulekh-Kali River sector is in focus, with Nepal claiming Limpiyadhura-Kalapani. Mount Gipmochi, a tri-junction with Bhutan, became the main issue for the Doklam crisis in 2017. Even the other truncation in the Sakteng Wildlife Sanctuary in the Trashigang district is now being disputed by China to forestall the development of the projected Guwahati-Tawang Road. In this tri-junction, Pakistan and Nepal have resolved their borders, albeit on Chinese-dictated terms, leaving Bhutan as the only exception.

Chinese Border Policy and Agenda

China has borders with 24 countries in both terrestrial and maritime domains. It has a land border with 14 countries and claims to have settled boundary issues with all except India and Bhutan. However, these claims have to be viewed realistically in the context that **most disputes have been either put on the back burner or settled on the terms laid down by Beijing.** It is also relevant to recount that the People's Republic of China (PRC) launched aggression against India in 1962, a 6-month-long border conflict with the Union of Soviet Socialist Republics (USSR) in 1969, and Vietnam in 1979. It is currently engaged in an unresolved standoff with India in Ladakh. Despite Chinese assertions, boundary issues with Nepal and Kazakhstan flare up intermittently. In the maritime domain, China is having serious issues with all its important neighbouring littorals due to its dynastic claims, which interfere with other nations' exclusive economic zones. It is engaged in serious issues with the Philippines, Taiwan, Vietnam, Brunei, and Malaysia in the South China Sea and Japan in the East China Sea.

Most experts opine that the Chinese use border disputes to put pressure on smaller neighbours. They have mastered the art of filibustering and endless parleys to tire out the other party. It is also relevant that the so-called historical claims based on grazing areas during imperial Chinese dynasties are not sacrosanct and are based on one-sided interpretation. Out of 23 territorial disputes settled since 1949, including 12 in the terrestrial domain, China has substantially retracted claims in 17 of them. China settled the 130-year-old dispute with Tajikistan in January 2011, accepting just 3.5 per cent (approximately 1,000 square kilometres) against the original claim of 28,000 square kilometres. The same trend was evident in the settlement with Kazakhstan and Kyrgyzstan, where it accepted just 22 and 32 per cent of original claims. China is also making use of imaginative cartography by articulating multiple claim lines backed up by the selective use of treaties in what is being termed as lawfare.

Historical Perspective

Claims on Tibet and Ladakh date back to the Dogra regime as part of the Sikh empire in 1834. Later, the Chinese defeated the Sikh Army in Ladakh, resulting in the Treaty of 1842, which stipulated mutual respect and non-aggression. In 1846, the British took control of Sikhs. In effect, areas like Karakoram Pass and Pangong Tso Lake were delineated, but the status of Aksai Chin remained vague. In the North-East, the British amalgamated Assam in 1826 and sanctified it with the Treaty of Yandabo. After the Anglo-Burmese wars, Burma (now Myanmar) was incorporated into the British Empire. Trilateral meetings in 1914 with Britain, China, and Tibet at Simla remained inconclusive as China rescinded after endorsing initials on the agreement. Britain and Tibet signed the convention with an appended map depicting the McMahon Line. This agreement conflicted with the Anglo-Chinese Agreement of 1907, which mandated the inclusion of China in all deliberations with Tibet. Chinese claimed to enjoy suzerainty over Tibet and insisted that the Lhasa regime was the largely temporal authority with the localised writ. They rejected Tibet's Declaration of Independence in 1913.

In the original conception, India and China were to have buffer states of Tibet, Nepal, Sikkim, and Bhutan. The Sino-Indian border has never been officially recognised or demarcated and is largely a fallout of the inherited colonial legacy of British rule. The claims are based on traditional control exercised and not backed up by agreed maps or documentation. It has been a complex construct based on exchanges between Tibet, Sikkim, Nepal, Imperial China, and British India. Chinese claims date back to the Manchu dynasty in 1910/11 when the pre-PRC regime staked territorial claims on parts of Tibet and other buffer states. These were reiterated by the Chinese Communist Party (CCP) in 1949 when the PRC was established. The theoretical construct was outlined in Mao Zedong's diktat and expounded in the party treatise 'The Chinese Revolution and the Communist Party' in 1939, 'the correct boundaries of China would include Burma, Bhutan, and Nepal.' This implied Tibet, including Arunachal and Sikkim, being parts of the Manchu empire.

Mao emphasised this concept in his expansionist **'Five Fingers of Tibet' policy. Citing Tibet as the palm, fingers included Ladakh, Nepal, Sikkim, Bhutan, and Arunachal**. In Chinese conception, all these are part of greater Tibet, annexed under unequal treaties. This claim was reinforced with imaginative cartography, including maps, as part of the publication *A Brief History of China*, published in 1959. Large portions of adjoining areas in territories of other countries were included within the ambit of Chinese claims. The **annexation of Tibet in 1950/51, followed by a 17-point agreement forced on the hapless Tibetan regime, resulted in the withdrawal of Indian and Bhutanese representatives from their missions in Lhasa. This was followed by the rebellion in Tibet in 1959, the flight of the Dalai Lama to India, and many refugees seeking asylum in India and Bhutan.** PLA occupied several adjoining Bhutanese exclaves in western Tibet in July 1959. These included Darchen, Gartok, and several other villages near Mount Kailas, which have been under Bhutanese since the seventeenth century for 300 years and had been given to Bhutan by Ngawang Namgyal in the seventeenth century.

Sectors and Disputed Areas

The Sino-Indian border is based on contested claim lines as these are conditioned on perceptions in the absence of even basic exchange of maps. These are-Indian perception, Chinese perception as also Chinese understanding of Indian perception and finally, Indian comprehension of Chinese claims.

However, generally well-known disputed areas are as follows:

a) **Western (Ladakh) Sector**: Claim lines include colonial (British) Johnson, Macartney-MacDonald, and Johnson-Ardagh lines. Chinese don't recognise them and have their own 1959 claim line, articulated by Zhou Enlai.

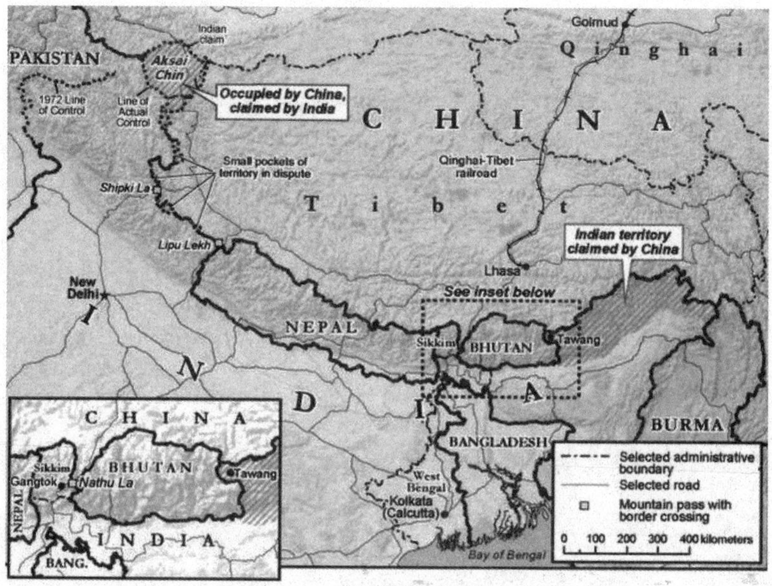

(Map source-https://images.app.goo.gl/PWcysVvMS45eNM)

b) **Middle Sector:** This sector includes stretches in Himachal Pradesh (HP) and Uttarakhand, with areas like Shipki La in Himachal Pradesh and Barahoti in Uttarakhand.

c) **Eastern Sector:** It includes Sikkim and Arunachal Pradesh (AP). China is referring to AP as Southern Tibet or Zangnan. The Indian claim line is based on the McMahon Line indexed on the watershed principle.

IDENTIFYING THE AREAS OF DISPUTE

IN JWG TALKS (1990S)

- WESTERN: Trig Heights, Demchok
- MIDDLE: Barahoti
- EASTERN: Namka Chu, Sumdorong Chu, Yangtse, Asaphila, Longju-Bisa

MAP EXCHANGE (2000)

- MIDDLE: Kaurik, Mumri Dogri, Shipki La

MAP COMPARISON (2002)

- WESTERN: North Samar Lungpa, east of Point 6556, north of Kugrang river, area of Kongka La, Spanggur Gap, east of Mount Sajum opposite Dumchele

BY PLA ACTION

- WESTERN: North bank of Pangong Tso, south bank of Pangong Tso, Chumar, Galwan, Hot Springs
- EASTERN: Dichu area, Dibang Valley (Fish Tail I & II), Lamang

d) **Disputed/Contested Areas:** The main contested areas are Aksai Chin (Depsang, Demchok, Pangong Tso, and Hot Springs), Doklam, and Tawang (Yangtse). China claims that Aksai Chin is part of the Xinjiang Autonomous Region (XAR) and AP, as their claim belongs to Southern Tibet. There is a listing of disputed areas, which is given in Wikipedia and other literature, but it is not official or agreed upon by both parties. To complicate the issue, the PLA has maintained ambiguity and activated new areas in randomised sequence to basically keep India unsettled. These are tabulated; however, list is at best indicative.

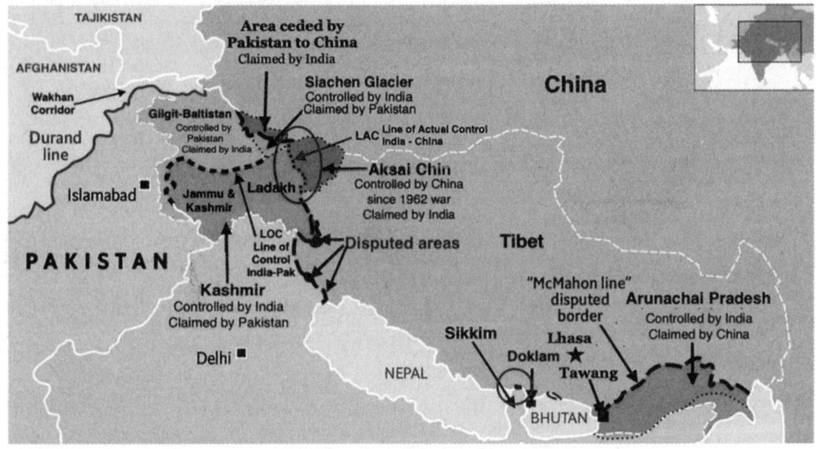

(Source-https://images.app.goo.gl/Yocagog757oDnuFVJ9)

Claim Lines

- **Line of Actual Control (LAC):** It is a notional, unresolved, loosely defined line that separates Indian and Chinese-controlled territories in the Sino-Indian border dispute. The term was first used by the Chinese Premier Zhou Enlai in a letter addressed to the then Indian Prime Minister Jawaharlal Nehru. The evolution can be traced to various claim lines.

- **Johnson Line:** The line was proposed in 1865 by the Survey of India (SOI) official. It was a maximal projection, incorporating Aksai Chin in Jammu and Kashmir. The line sought territory up to and even beyond the Kunlun range, including areas of Shahidulla (currently called Xaidulla). A fortified staging post to monitor caravans was maintained by Dogra rulers in Shahidulla for some period, but later, the control of these areas and the Karakoram passed to imperial China in 1892. Accordingly, Sir John Ardagh proposed a more realistic and defendable line aligned along the crest of the Kunlun range and the Yarkund River. This was termed as the Johnson-Ardagh line.

- **Macartney-MacDonald Line:** This Line was proposed in 1899 and generally ran along the natural frontier of the Karakoram Mountain, south of the Laktsang range. Broadly, it left the Tarim River basin and Aksai Chin for China, retaining the Indus basin for British India. The foreign office line was another correction on the line, ceding control on more areas in Lingzi Tang plains.

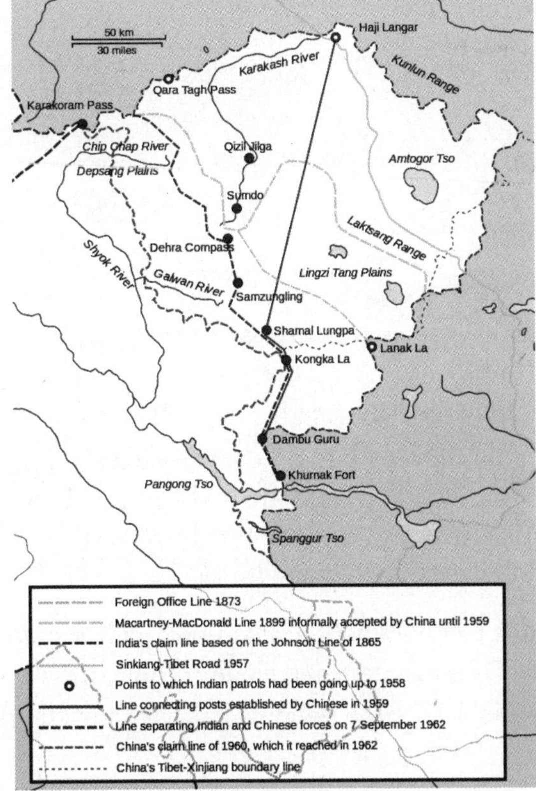

(Source-https://images.app.goo.gl/qWgcWuhmuQBYFMxP7)

- **McMahon Line:** The line was devised by Sir Henry McMahon, Surveyor General, and is based on the concept of watershed. It utilised the Himalayan range to define watershed, yet contentious areas like Tawang remained unresolved due to the concept of traditional claims dating back to imperial dynasties like Qing and Manchus. Chinese claims conform to the watershed in approximately 90 per cent of the border (Map 3).

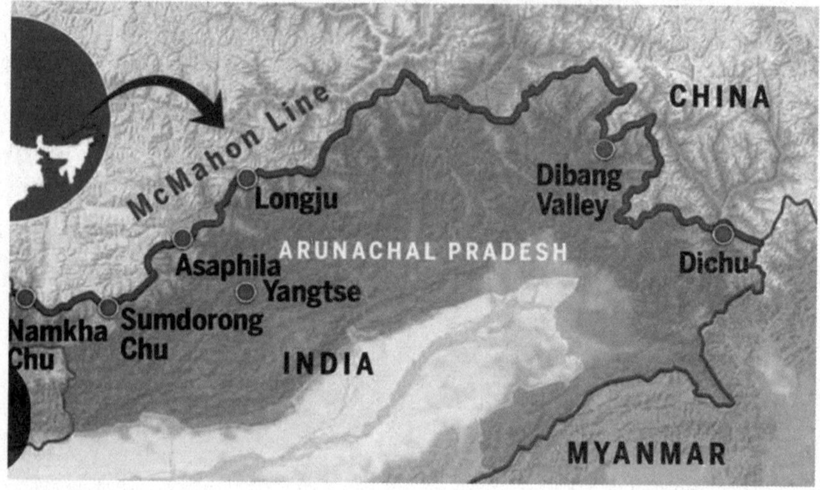

(https://currentaffairs.adda247.com/india-china-troops-clash-along-lac-in-twang-region-arunachal-pradesh/)

- **Chinese Claims:** Chinese articulation and designs became clear with the surreptitious construction of Aksai Chin Road in the 1950s. This spurred India to adopt a 'Forward Policy', in essence establishing presence up to the claim line. Then, the Chinese Prime Minister projected the 1959 claim line and reportedly indicated a desire for a package deal. This offer reportedly included giving up a claim in Arunachal in exchange for Aksai Chin. This was followed by the 1962 war and unilateral withdrawal by the PLA.

- **Sikkim Border:** China had boundary-related issues with Sikkim, a protectorate of India. This manifested in bloody clashes in Nathu La and Cho La passes in 1967. The standoff at Jalep La pass was averted due to Indian withdrawal. The merger of Sikkim after a referendum in 1975 was initially rejected by the PRC. However, it was later accepted through a Memorandum of Understanding (MOU) signed in 2003. Notwithstanding MOU, issues on the Finger area in Kerang plateau, Naku La, and most importantly, Doklam fester up occasionally. The most recent happened in 2017, and though supposedly resolved, China continues salami-slicing and building border villages in disputed areas.

- **Dolam Issue:** Strategic heft and the edge are imparted to the Dolam (referred by Chinese as Doklam) issue due to the relative location of Chumbi Valley vis-à-vis Siliguri Corridor, gateway to the North-Eastern states, also called seven sisters and one brother. The corridor, which is 22 kilometres at its narrowest, is also described as the 'chicken' s neck' or 'North-eastern jugular'. It can also act as a springboard for forays in Nepal and Bangladesh. This is covered in detail in separate chapter on Sino-Bhutan border.

- **Chumbi Valley:** It is a dagger-shaped narrowing wedge between India and Bhutan. The southern narrow portion of the valley, the Dolam plateau, with its strategic significance, has the potential to pose a threat to the tenuous Siliguri Corridor, termed as jugular, connecting the North-East with the mainland. The Chinese quest is to widen the extremely narrow base of the valley. The dispute is indexed to the location of Mount Gipmochi and the correct interpretation of the watershed of rivers like Amo Chu. It is a complex bevvy of crest lines and heights—Gamochen, Batangla, and Sinchela. The most sought-after is Zompelri (Jampheri) Ridge, providing a launchpad for reaching the Siliguri Corridor. The balanced view is that while it is indeed a threat, but logistics and terrain make it a tortuous and slow exercise requiring extensive logistics build-up. This is covered in detail in separate chapter on Sino-Bhutan border.

Unresolved Status

The trend of standoffs is marked by Sumdrong Chu (1987/88), which festered for nearly a year. Prolonged parleys resulted in multiple agreements in 1993, 1996, 2005, 2006, 2012, and 2013, outlining protocols and confidence-building measures (CBMs) to maintain peace and tranquillity on the LAC. China Study Group (CSG) devised a concept of limit patrolling with designated Patrolling Points (PPs). Some of these, like PP 14, 15, 16, and 17, have been in focus during the ongoing Ladakh face-off. **PPs as cartographic aids were stipulated by the CSG in the 1970s and followed by Indian patrols to stake our claims. In Ladakh, they start from PP-1 in the west near Daulat Beg Oldie, and there are 65 odd such points stretching onto PP-60 towards the east. As per paper research paper in DG's conference in Jan 23, India has lost access to 26 PPs.** Multiple mechanisms like the Joint Working Group (JWG), Special Representative (SR), and Working Mechanism for Consultation and Coordination (WMCC) have been set up without much headway. In the interim, the frequency of standoffs at Depsang, Chumar, Demchok, and Pangong Tso has increased from 2013 onwards, leading up to the recent Chinese aggression in Ladakh from 2020 onwards.

The current resolution round involves a three-step process: disengagement, de-escalation, and de-induction. The first step of disengaging has been achieved in Pangong-Tso, Galwan, Hot Springs, and Gogra, but in two areas of Depsang and Demchok, even the disengagement has not been achieved yet despite multiple rounds of negotiations. **The PLA has introduced the concept of buffer/no patrolling zones in resolved areas, wherein Indian patrols are not able to go up to claim lines.** After the standoff, partial disengagement with the designation of buffer zones has taken place in Galwan (PP-14), Hot Springs (PP-15), and Gogra (PP-17A). Similarly, in Pangong Tso, the area between Fingers 3 and 8 has become a buffer zone with no patrolling zones or demilitarised area. **The focus remains on the unresolved standoff in Depsang and Demchok. Access to PP-**

10, 11, 12, 12A, and 13 in Depsang remains blocked due to PLA deployment.

Disputed Areas – Sikkim and Arunachal

There are a number of disputed areas in Sikkim and Arunachal Pradesh. However, the PLA has been activating new areas like the Naku La pass in the Muguthang sector of Sikkim apart from the agreed list. The patrols on both sides attempt to patrol up to their perceived claim lines. These are mostly temporary to stake claims and are termed in media as violations/incursions/intrusions/encroachments but are officially described as transgressions or border incidents.

Way Forward

Unresolved borders between two powerful neighbours, both armed with nuclear weapons and in aspirational trajectory, have the potential for conflict, given their acrimonious history. It is axiomatic that both settle the boundary dispute on priority. The CBMs and protocols have become meaningless due to the unilateral actions of the PLA. It will be pragmatic if interim protocols are worked out and, in the interim, China tones down its 'wolf warrior' approach, respecting LAC to restore the status-quo-ante of January 2020.

References

1. Mihir Bose, Understanding Sino-Indian Border Issues: An Analysis of Incidents Reported. Available at https://www.orfonline.org/research/understanding-sino-indian-border-issues-an-analysis-of-incidents-reported-in-the-indian-media/?amp
2. Chervin Reed, Cartographic Aggression: Media Politics, Propaganda, and the Sino-Indian Border Dispute. *Journal of Cold War Studies*,

2020. Jianli Yang, Bhutan China Border Negotiations in Context. *The Diplomat,* 18 November 2021

3. Harsh V Pant and Aditya Gowdara Shivamurthy, Himalaya: The Complexity of Bhutan. Available at www.orfonline.org, *The Economic Times*

4. Manoj Joshi, The China Bhutan Deal Should Worry India. Available at www.orfonline.org, *Hindustan Times*

5. Lieutenant General KJ Singh, Dynamics of Security of Siliguri Corridor: Way Forward. *USI Strategic Year Book, 2018*

6. Lieutenant General KJ Singh, Siliguri Corridor and Gorkhaland: Generals Jottings. Available at https://timesofindia.indiatimes.com/blogs/generals-jottings/siliguri corridor-and-gorkhaland/

7. Lieutenant General KJ Singh, Threats to Siliguri Corridor Wargamed. *Tribune,* available at https://m.tribuneindia.com/news/archive/features/india-ready-theoretically%E2%80%98threats%E2%80%99-to-siliguri-corridor-war-gamed-43378

Debunking Myths of China' Geostrategic Moves

(Written after Galwan Clashes – June 2020)

While remaining focused on time-bound infrastructure development, it will be pragmatic to reduce the hype attached to the construction and inauguration of infrastructure in sensitive areas. The concurrent requirement is to fast-track China-centric, joint theatre commands. To deter the Red Dragon, we must discard myths, accept new realities, and reduce asymmetries.

A spate of recent border standoffs at two ends of the unsettled Sino-Indian border in Naku La (Sikkim), followed by multiple incursions in Ladakh-Galwan and Pangong Tso, is another manifestation of coercive salami-slicing by China. For a more informed analysis, the requirement is to debunk prevalent myths and formulate a realistic template.

It is appropriate to start this process with an 'unsettled-settled' border. The then Chinese Premier Wen Jiabao said in 2005, 'Sikkim is no longer a problem between China and India.' In recent discussions, the Chinese Ambassador alluded to Sikkim as a low-hanging fruit, disregarding the prolonged standoff at Doklam. It is indeed comical that Chinese patrols regularly resort to childish pranks of disassembling cairns (stone heaps) on the Kerang plateau. The transgression at Naku La, in the desolate and sparsely populated Muguthang valley, was activated, most surprisingly, for the first time in 2017. Galwan, the current flashpoint in Ladakh, is an apt example of 'creeping claim lines' by the Chinese. In contrast, our approach has been fuelled by optimism, conditioned by false notions.

- **Myth 1:** The Sino-Indian border is largely settled with just a few recorded and identified flashpoints. **The harsh reality is that the PLA activates different areas, in keeping with their grand design, often as diversionary tactics. In this case, Naku La was a distraction for Galwan.** We draw comfort by nuancing incursions as transgressions, but the unmistakable bottom line is that nothing is settled till it is delimited, delineated, and demarcated on the ground. We must be prepared for the long haul with more surprises, as China is in no hurry to resolve issues.

- **Myth 2:** The standoffs are due to overreaction by local commanders. This is another false notion, a convenient excuse to pass the buck. Most standoffs are recorded by PLA patrols with considerable play acting, giving an impression that they are vectored by higher headquarters (HQs). It will be prudent to surmise that the **Chinese are masters in centrally planned but locally orchestrated events.** In any case, the Chinese Western Command controls the entire Tibet border against four different commands of India, micromanaged by the Army HQ, adding to the confusion. **Indian patrols have displayed remarkable restraint and maturity in face-offs. It throws up a disturbing possibility that 'strategic guidance' (agreed to at the summit level) is being flouted by the PLA with tacit blessings, while we are following it.**

- Myth 3: The Chinese are superior to us. This myth needs to be junked. **Objective comparison proves that our troops are more than a match for their counterparts.** The 1962 syndrome was discarded in a resolute standoff at Nathu La and Cho La in 1967. Unfortunately, we have downplayed this heroic action as a skirmish to avoid embarrassing the PLA. In fact, most Chinese troops are a conscript variety with questionable domain competence. In Somdrong Chu and other standoffs over the years, as well as UN operations, Chinese vulnerability has been exposed repeatedly.

- Myth 4: Chinese technological asymmetry will cripple adversaries even before the battle is joined. **The much-hyped technology is yet to be operationalised and is severely degraded by high altitude and weather.** On balance, it is part of psychological warfare and can't be taken as a game changer at least in short term.

- Myth 5: By and large, peace prevails as no bullet has been fired since 1967. This needs to be moderated with the realisation that **China is already waging unrestricted warfare.** There is considerable evidence of Chinese-engineered cyber disruption in our power grid. Parechu floods are causing severe damage to power plants astride Sutlej, and the more recent devastating deluge in Assam, coupled with the denial of hydrological data, is a gross misuse of upper riparian leverages. Even in the current standoff, water flow has been blocked in the Galwan River. **Pacifism was rooted in Deng's maxim of economic consolidation, preceding precipitate military action, which has been discarded by Xi's aggressively rising China.**

- Myth 6: **In all situations, China will act responsibly, in accordance with stature requires revisiting. Will any responsible power misuse the pandemic for power play?** Conventional wisdom, propagated by experts, is that Pakistan will invariably exploit Sino-Indian hostilities and intervene. China, showing maturity as a global power, will desist from exploiting Indo-Pak hostilities. Chinese reticence in 1971 and Kargil are cited as examples. However, the degree of collusive linkages has strengthened manifold with the CPEC.

- Myth 7: China will show reciprocity and will respect our sensitivities. 17 Corps, which was initially designated as Mountain Strike Corps and later played down with the dropping of 'strike' and curtailing of budgetary allocation, has not resulted in any reduction in Chinese intransigence. **China simply doesn't care.**

The coping strategy in dealing with China must factor in existing asymmetry and should be confined within the bounds of realism. We have viable options, though limited, yet we must signal resolve. It may take considerable time, like Doklam, but our sensitivities in terms of security to the new Darbuk-DBO road and unfettered patrolling up to our claim lines, including the Pangong Tso area, should be ensured. In this age of 5G, nail-studded clubs, stoning, and wrestling bouts on the LAC need to be eliminated. While diplomats and commanders are resolving the situation, the electronic media should enable an honourable resolution by avoiding rabble-rousing debates.

Remaining focused on time-bound infrastructure development will be pragmatic to reduce the hype attached to the construction and inauguration of infrastructure in sensitive areas. The concurrent requirement is to fast-track China-centric, joint theatre commands. The Mountain Corps needs to be customised as an agile force and, most importantly, funded to generate multiple quid-pro-quo options. **To deter the Red Dragon, we must discard myths, accept new realities, and reduce asymmetries.**

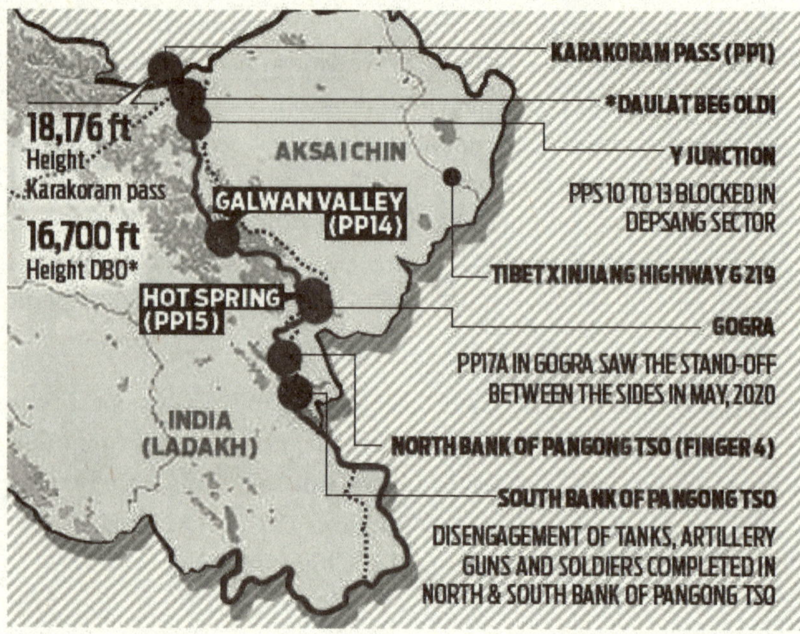

(Map source-https://www.drishtiias.com/daily-news-analysis/india-china-military-talks)

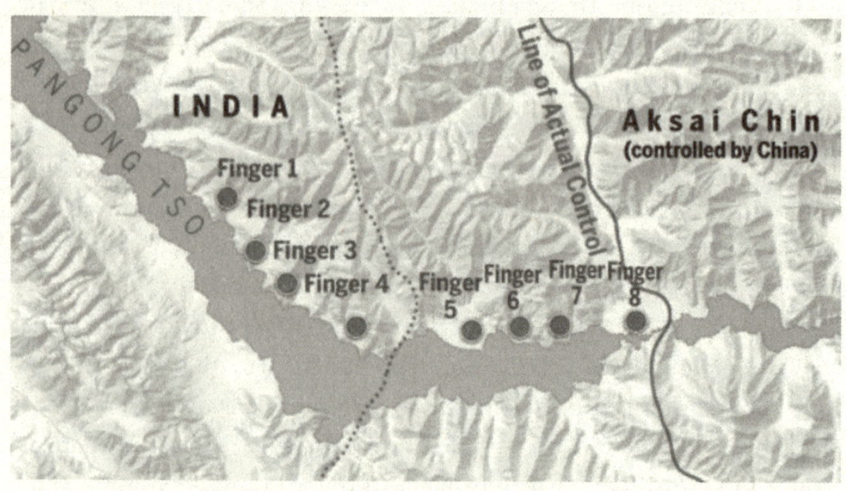

(Map source-https://www.ias4sure.com/wiliias/pangong-tso-upsc-prelims/)

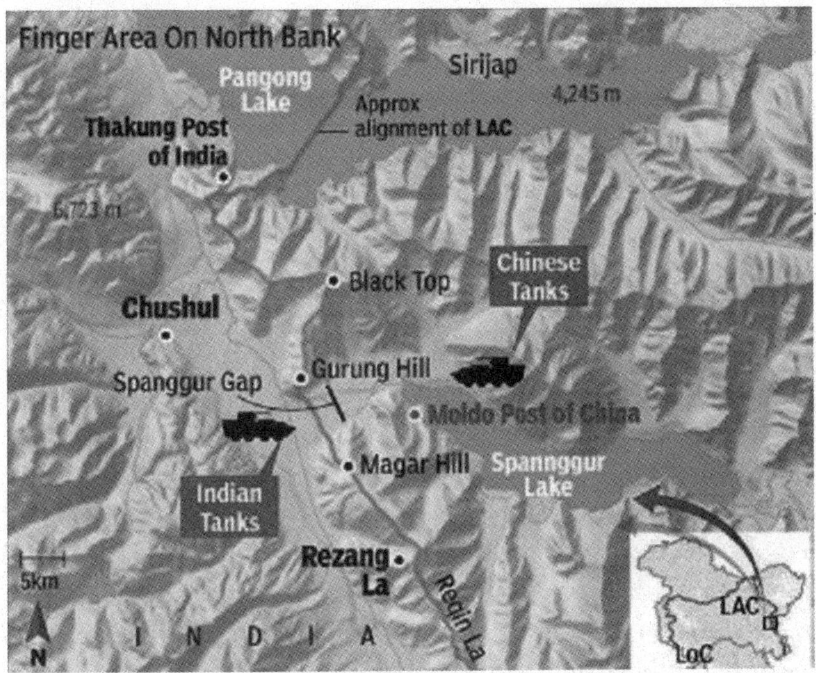

(Map source-https://imrmedia.in/india-china-agreement-on-disengagement-in-eastern-ladakh/l)

Strategic Review from Kargil to Kailash

(Written in February 2021)

VICENNIAL is a rarely used term, defined as 'occurring once every 20 years. The first two decades of the 21st century are over. Ravaged by Covid-19, India has skipped annual, let alone decadal or vicennial strategic reviews. In our context, the period from 2001 to 2020 is unique, meriting a special analysis. It triggered a slew of reforms in the aftermath of the Kargil shock in 1999 and ended with the attempted Ladakh grab by China, catalysing more reforms. On both occasions, the Armed Forces reacted admirably to restore the situation, notwithstanding our propensity to get surprised.

This century dawned with the spectre of the looming Y2K disaster. Twenty years down the line, the threat of disruptive technologies like armed drones threatens the very relevance of existing platforms like tanks and aircraft. The raging pandemic has made public health a key ingredient of Comprehensive National Power. **With the Dragon administering a rude shock on the LAC, there is the belated realisation that China is indeed the biggest adversary, and the only antidote is capability-building.**

This period started with the National Democratic Alliance (NDA) government till it was replaced by the United Progressive Alliance regime. The latter ruled for two successive terms, followed by the NDA, now in its second spell. In essence, both have had 10 years at the helm, yet there is an unabated tendency to pass the buck to escape accountability. **It is time our political parties consider national security in a bipartisan format and forge national consensus.**

Most advanced countries, including even opaque ones (like China), publish white papers and reviews. The US puts out a quadrennial review, which is both educative and prescriptive. We have an annual report of the Ministry of Defence, largely a bureaucratic compilation, lacking analysis. The aim of this review is basically to flag some key trends and promote greater transparency and accountability. It is anchored in five key parameters — policy, readiness, structures, force levels and logistics.

On the policy front, we continue to await the promulgation of the national security strategy, which seems to be a work in progress, albeit with no deadline. Secrecy and ambiguity seem to be the cornerstones of the current strategy. The Raksha Mantri had once even advocated ambiguity in the nuclear policy, which was later described as his opinion. Surprise, indeed, unnerves the enemy; credit on this score is due for the surgical strikes and pre-emptive occupation of the Kailash Range. **However, in the long term, clearly articulated red lines, especially among nuclear-armed nations with certainty of response, ensure stability and deterrence.** As per Clausewitz, 'a

successful commander, while leveraging deception, has to remain largely predictable to his command'.

Readiness is best measured by deterrence levels achieved and the responses to enemy action. It is a function of budgetary allocations, procurement, and training. Unfortunately, defence spending has remained low, leading to critical shortages. Post Kargil and during the current crisis, emergency procurement had to be invoked. Much-hyped but limited big-ticket purchases like those of Rafale, Apache, and S-400 have not been able to achieve the desired credible dissuasion. Our commendable response, especially in Ladakh, is largely due to the human factor honed by training and the unit ethos. It will be in order that desired deterrence levels are spelt out, backed by quantified net assessment parameters. **There is urgency on the part of the government to kick-start modernisation and Atmanirbharta initiatives, but the way forward is a functional procurement policy with committed, non-lapsable funds. Defence plans, which are known more for slippages, need to be put back on the rail.**

During the Kargil conflict, it required a reading of the riot act by America to control Pakistan's nuclear sabre-rattling. However, the Balakot airstrike called Pakistan's bluff conclusively. India needs to sharpen its punitive response backed by other leverages to shackle Pakistan's proxy war strategy.

The Kargil Review Committee's major recommendations included the establishment of the Chief of Defence Staff (CDS), theatre commands, intelligence structures, border management (one border, one force), and the National Defence University (NDU). After initial impetus, the reform process was put on the back burner by the UPA government. It goes to the credit of the current government that not only CDS but also the Department of Military Affairs (DMA) is in place, and theatre commands seem imminent.

It is high time the issues of operational control of ITBP and Assam Rifles are resolved. It is an enduring mystery why the NDU has not yet found traction. We need to critically appraise intelligence and surveillance structures to avoid being surprised time and again. A review of diplomacy is a crying need as Act East and Neighbourhood First policies have not yet found the desired traction.

The Kargil conflict resulted in the creation of the Ladakh Corps. The current crisis has kick-started belated rebalancing of the northern borders. The reassignment of corps-sized formations to Ladakh has created the second mountain strike corps. The first one, raised during the UPA regime on a standard, unwieldy format, is now exclusively assigned to NE. It is hoped that these formations will be customised and modernised. The desired fighter strength needs an empirical revisit to factor in drones, current capabilities, and costs. Concurrently, the maritime capability to heighten China's Malacca dilemma and neutralise the Gwadar advantage needs to be funded.

Critical logistics have improved with enhanced ammunition stocking levels, but quality control needs urgent improvement with built-in accountability. **The renewed focus on connectivity (roads, tunnels, and bridges) and, most importantly, the removal of hurdles of environmental clearance are indeed commendable. To sum up, it will be appropriate to quote Robert Frost, '...and miles to go before I sleep' Reviews it is hoped will certainly keep the journey focused.**

Key takeaways after one year are as follows:

- **First – at the tactical level, audacious initiative and spontaneous reactions at Galwan would have forced a caution and rethink in PLA.**

- **Second – at the operational level, pre-emptive and surprise occupation of Kailash Heights and subtle leveraging of the Tibetan (SFF) card was game changer of sorts.**

- **Third – strategically, induction and sustenance of dissuasive force levels. They, in effect, reined PLA's vaulting ambitions, forcing a stalemate of sorts.**

Time to Rebuild Protocols on LAC

(Written after the Yangtze Incident in December 2022)

The Yangtze incident was yet another reminder that PLA's diabolic game of altering realities on LAC continues unabated. The choice of location and timing of the next round of salami slicing adds a psychological dimension to retaining control of the escalation matrix. Every such round is followed by a meeting like the recently concluded 17th Corps Commanders parleys, with meaningless terms like stability, peace, and tranquillity. For soldiers on the ground, it translates to enhanced deployment and surveillance. A flurry of activity leads to avoidable collateral damage like the recent road accident. The present chaotic situation is most unfair for troops on the ground.

The Yangtze is the tactical prong, combined with a theological dimension of Tawang, defining the template in an evolving strategic game to further claim on Arunachal, described by the Chinese as Zang Nan (Southern Tibet). The Yangtze has great spiritual significance due to its proximity to Chumi-Gyatse, a holy waterfall. Chinese checkers has taken another twist from earlier Chinese articulated move of 'swap-settlement' entailing Aksai Chin for China in lieu of Arunachal for India. China has gained in asymmetry, and its revanchist desires have multiplied. Having achieved its claims in Ladakh, grabbing is now unfolding in Arunachal.

The loss of Yangtze in 1987–88 still rankles China as it is the potential launch pad to reclaim Tawang, having linkages with the Dalai Lama. Chinese have regularly staked their claim, but it was different this time. The strength of 300 plus, in mid-December at 3.00 am, indicates detailed planning and clearance at the highest level. It is to the credit of the Indian Army that they were vigilant and pushed back riot-clad PLA marauders equipped with spiked sticks, tasers, and barbaric contraptions.

As we lapse into the usual frustrating analysis of why and how of incidents, the only certainty is that it will happen again. It is appropriate to recall that we have not found any conclusive answers to the original question on the 1962 war.

Why did China go back if it wanted areas like Galwan and Tawang so badly? Noted Chinese affairs expert Vijay Gokhale, in his recent report, 'A Historical Evaluation of China's India Policy', has tackled many such issues. Like most analyses on China, the report, while partially answering many questions, throws open new ones.

The report's takeaway is a reality check on how Beijing perceives India in zhengzhijunshi-zhang (politico-military war).

- **First, as an unequal and unreliable neighbour. Unworthy of any standalone status or consideration.**
- **Second, relevant only in hyphenated mode tagged with great powers in the strategic trinity – USA, USSR, and China.**
- **Third, clear expectation that India should first understand Chinese objectives. To put it bluntly, India should play along.**
- **Fourth, China can afford to deal with India in episodic tactical mode within her own long-term trajectory. Consequently, the petty 'zero-sum' approach by China to stymie India in the Indian Ocean and neighbourhood continues.**

The natural corollary is **how we deal with China. It may sound incredulous, but without a coherent strategy, we are basically responding in reactive mode**. It is a strange mix of optimism and denial amongst decision makers (diplomats and experts) searching for the elusive peace and tranquillity, even when the wolf-warrior remains unrelenting. There have even been instances of conceding the benefit of the doubt and accepting the explanation of the local Commander going rogue. But the same so-called rogue is now in the apex hierarchy in Central Military Commission (CMC).

Even worse is the sense of bravado seen amongst social media warriors who are giving clarion calls to liberate Aksai Chin. As per a reliable opinion poll by an international think tank, 60% of Indians believe that we can simply put it across to the Chinese. At the same time, it is disheartening that we fail to honour the 1962 and 1967 heroes. The least we can do is to celebrate their valour and sacrifice every year by holding appropriate ceremonies at National War Memorial (NWM).

Galwan is indeed the defining marker, with Indians jettisoning the residual trust in the Chinese. The incident has been reconstructed by Manoj Joshi, a noted China expert, in his book, *Understanding the India-China Border: The Enduring Threat of War in the High Himalayas*. Considering the very high credibility of the author and the absence of a cogent official account, it is the only reliable source. The most telling detail is the role of unsparing General Winter, accounting for 17 Bravehearts due to hypothermia. It is most disheartening with our enviable record in high-altitude medicine. When the late Naik Hanumanthappa was hospitalized in Army R&R hospital, we reached out to leading hospitals globally for advice, and the reply across was that you have the best knowledge pool. The challenge is in deploying it forward and timely evacuation at such altitude during the night. It will be fair to assume that the PLA may have lost similar numbers due to hypothermia, but unlike us, it has excluded them from their list, restricting to four fatalities. **The Chinese game plan is based on underestimating Indian capability, appetite, and even willpower to impose costs on China. This could be indeed a fatal error.**

While this may be true in some measure in the politico-bureaucratic hierarchy, it will be fatal to miss out on the resolve at the tactical level. Even at a higher level, Op Snow-Leopard, in August 2022 indicated audacious resolve. China has destroyed the edifice of CBMs and border management protocols with Galwan, Yangte, spiked clubs, and tasers. While Indian troops have shown remarkable restraint, yet under provocation, incidents can spin out of control, leading to serious escalation. **Buffer zones with the PLA in grab mode will only be sub-optimal and temporary solution, as probing is part of defensive surveillance. Localised salami-slicing cannot be ruled out. Two nuclear nations wrestling across undefined lines with Stone Age weapons should spur leaders and diplomats on both sides to resolve at least interim border management protocols.**

PLA Organisation and Coping Strategy

Emerging Politico-military Structure in China

Key Takeaways

- President Xi Jinping has subsumed the roles of President and Chairman of the Central Military Commission (CMC) besides the all-powerful General Secretary of the CCP. In addition, like an emperor, he has waived off tenure limitations.
- The PLA has added Rocket Force (erstwhile Second Artillery) and Strategic Support Force (SSF) as full-fledged verticals, in addition to Army, Navy, and Air Force. SSF has been now again reorganised into three separate Arms-Cyber, Aerospace and Information Support.
- Western Theatre Command synergies operations across Tibet, combining forces from Chengdu, Lanzhou, and even Guangzhou region, in some contingencies.
- Update: Notwithstanding reforms and a concerted drive for weeding out corruption, in October 2023, members of apex decision-making structures like Defence Minister-Li Shangfu, Foreign Minister-Qin Gang and several top generals of Rocket Force were sacked.

Introduction

China is at a critical threshold of its rise and ascent on the global power matrix. It has already established its place in the top league, and there is an informed body of opinion within China that feels that institutions that steered China's peaceful rise need to shed their defensive, status-quo orientation to become more proactive, dynamic, and assertive. **This is, indeed, a major departure from Deng Xiaoping's maxim. 'Hide your brightness, bide your time.' The crux was to have a long stick but hide the capabilities, which was described as the 'peaceful rise of China'.** There was limited knowledge of the structures and organisation to execute this policy, and they all maintained a low profile and stayed out of the media glare. Most of it is still shrouded in considerable opacity, with very little known about the nitty-gritty of the functioning and organisation of the politico-military decision-making process and structures.

The shift from a peaceful to an assertive rise was signalled by the recent Chinese aggressive behaviour, especially in the South China Sea, characterised by the conversion of the Fiery Cross Reef into a full-fledged air base, disregarding international opinion and the concerns and sensitivities of the other littoral states. This change has been accompanied by a review of the apex structures and, accordingly, the alignment of subordinate organisations to the newly evolved organisation. China is also beginning to showcase its systems as a model for others to follow for economic progress. An interesting case study cited in support of the **success of the Chinese model is the lifting of 700 million poor citizens above the poverty line in three decades.** A review of the structure and organisation at the apex of the politico-military decision matrix in China is to enable better comprehension of the changes and their likely implications, along with a brief recapitulation of the history, leading to the evolution of the current structures.

Preview

The subject is analysed in the following parts:

- Evolution of Decision-Making Structures
- Current Structure and Leadership

- Major Military Reforms
- Likely Implications at the Macro Level

Evolution of Decision-Making Structures

First and Second Generation – Absolutism: The two milestones in the history of Communist China are the formation of the CCP on 1 July 1921 and the PLA in the aftermath of the Nanchang Uprising on 27 August, beginning with the establishment of the PRC in 1949 and characterised by the era of the Long March and the Cultural Revolution, till the demise of Deng Xiaoping in 1992, covering the first and second generations of leadership. **The defining characteristics of the Chinese politico-military decision-making were the unparalleled authority of the supreme leader and complete subservience of all decision-making to the CCP. It will be pertinent to recall Mao's statement at the 9th CPC meeting in 1929, 'The role of the military is chiefly to serve the political ends.'** The two doyens of this period were Mao Zedong (1949–76) and Deng Xiaoping (1978–92). While this facilitated rapid decision-making and unity of purpose, this arrangement was probably inevitable due to a lack of mature leadership. Hence, key strategic articulations like joining the Korean War and exporting Communism abroad had the unmistakable stamp of the so-called Great Helmsman, Mao. Many of these decisions, in hindsight, proved to be hurried, and some even turned out to be catastrophic, as evidenced by the unprecedented casualties in the Cultural Revolution. Mao had the unique distinction of being the father of the Chinese Communist movement and enjoyed a life tenure.

Break from the Mao Era and Deng's Reforms: A subtle and gradual transition to the maxim of 'Collective Leadership' was approved in 1978 after the Mao era in the Third Plenary Session of the much-heralded 11th Party Congress or CPC. 'Absolutism' or unquestioned authority was diluted, and more collective leadership was gradually introduced. Yet, key strategic decisions regarding Taiwan,

Hong Kong, and the island territories in the East and South China Seas continued to have the influence of Deng right till his demise. This was facilitated also by the fact that the new generation of leaders lacked the prestige and legitimacy that was enjoyed by the generation of Mao and Deng. **Deng also instituted a two-term limit and age criteria; the latter, though not clearly specified, has been understood to be 68 years.** The aim of these reforms was to essentially weed out the deadwood and the staunch loyalists of Mao. **Deng Xiaoping ushered in a series of reforms under the 'Four Modernisations', even opening up the economy in line with his famous remark, 'It doesn't matter whether a cat is black or white, as long as it catches mice.'**

Third and Fourth Generation – Shift to Collectivism: Reinforcement of collective leadership was more notable during the reign of the third and fourth generations of leadership, with Jiang Zemin (1993–2002) and Hu Jintao (2002–2012). This transition, in its application, may seem well short of the Western norms, yet it was significant with the initiation of 'democratic centralism'. **The overall opacity of the Chinese system hides a complex, nuanced, and subtle interplay of factions and interest groups like the core elitists or princelings, also referred to *as 'taizidangs'* and populists known as *'tuanpai'*.** Besides these well-known groupings, there have been formulations like the Gang of Four, the Shanghai Group, etc.

Current Structure and Leadership

Apex Structure: The basic structures of the CPC include the National People's Congress (NPC), which comprises delegates representing all the regions. The NPC, being a very large body with currently 2,970 Deputies, elects a Politburo, which is the de-facto decision-making body, as the NPC remains largely a rubber-stamping body. In this matrix, the most powerful appointments are of the General Secretary of the CPC and President of the Central Military Commission (CMC). The CMC is the apex military decision-making structure, which is staffed predominantly by military officers. The process of control over the PLA by the party in the earlier era was facilitated by Mao and Deng, who had their roots in the PLA itself.

Fifth Generation Under Xi: Xi Jinping heralded the ushering in of the fifth generation of leadership in the 18th Party Congress in November 2012 by taking over as President with a five-year term lasting till 2017. **Xi engineered a major constitutional amendment on 11 March 2017, duly ratified by the NPC, wherein the two-term limit introduced by Deng Xiaoping in the 1990s was dropped. As a result, when Xi was elected for a second term on March 17, it really implied an indefinite life-long term, a rare privilege, which was the exclusive preserve of Chairman Mao. Without this amendment, which makes 64-year-old President Xi virtually an emperor, he would have otherwise ruled till 2023 only.** This move did generate its usual share of controversy, yet informed analysts opined that the earlier two-year term had its own complications, such as the exit of Jiang Zemin after two terms despite being groomed as Deng's successor. As a result, Hu came to the fore, but his term did cause certain imbalances and latent crises, which manifested during the Xi era.

Along with Xi, his trusted loyalist and close aide, 69-year-old Wang Quishan, was also elected as Vice-President for a life-long stint. Here again, the age criteria of 68 years, in vogue for nearly three decades, was waived. Wang is the most dreaded official, as he steered the anti-corruption purge in the first five-year term of Xi, which saw the sacking of 1.5 million bureaucrats and party functionaries, including nearly 100 ministers and top generals, in the biggest crackdown in the history of China. While working under the overall direction of Xi, he is likely to steer global outreach, including relations with the USA, vitiated by Trumpism.

Premier Li Keqiang, who was appointed to a second five-year term, is virtually No. 2 in the hierarchy and handles economic affairs, but he has been reduced to a truncated role as Xi has taken over some of the key economic charters under his direct control. Xi intends to continue with his anti-corruption agenda through a newly instituted National Supervisory Commission (NSC) headed by Yang Xiadu. This body will also serve to enforce the party's control over a burgeoning bureaucracy and society. It has been given draconian powers of detention of suspects for up to six months without due court permission. Yang has some sort of India connection as he was China's Special Representative for the Sino-Indian boundary talks in his capacity as state councillor, the top diplomatic post. Wang Yi, erstwhile foreign minister, steps into this job and will now handle boundary negotiations with India.

Wang Fenghe, a former commander of the Second Artillery and a noted missile expert, was appointed as the new defence minister. He was later sacked as part of the anti-corruption purge. It is an astute choice as he is likely to bring his experience to mentor the separation of the Missile Force into the recently reconfigured Rocket Force and Strategic Support Force, besides overseeing the infusion of cutting-edge technologies in surveillance, drones, artificial intelligence, radars, submarines, aircraft carriers, and the whole range of weapon systems Xi has entrusted the NPC to his erstwhile Chief of Staff Li Zhanshu. Chen Wenquing has been retained to manage internal security, which includes the troubled and insurgency-affected region of Xinjiang. Chen's other functions are counterterrorism, internal security, espionage, and counter-espionage. While many top-ranking appointments are retained, the system is likely to induct many new faces when lower-level appointments are finalised in what are officially described as elections but are really guided by the top hierarchy.

Major Military Reforms

While Mao was a legendary leader, objective analysis suggests that his approach was 'attrition oriented', which is borne out by the over half a million casualties in the Korean War between 1950 and 1953. The PLA also suffered a considerable loss of face in the Vietnam War in 1979. The process of reforms in the PLA was triggered as part of

Deng's 'Four Modernisations', which included reforms in the Armed Forces. However, the process remained diffused. Learning from the RMA initiated by the USA in the Gulf War in 1992, President Jiang decided to orient the PLA to prepare for its own version of RMA in what was dubbed as winning 'local wars under modern conditions'. The process crystallised into '*Linaggezhuanbian*', which, in essence, was a 'twin transformation' encompassing a shift from 'Quantity to Quality' and 'winning local wars under high-tech conditions'. President Hu Jintao gave enhanced clarity and refined the mission to 'win local wars under informationalised conditions', thereby highlighting the overarching importance of information operations. Hu's vision, which was contained in the famous White Paper titled 'New Historic Missions', was promulgated in 2004. The process of reforms in China, starting with the Deng era, is well thought out, deep-rooted, and reflects long-term commitment, though it is tweaked to keep it in sync with contemporary realities.

The installation of Xi and the fifth-generation leadership initially focussed on two key issues: firstly, preparing the PLA for the emerging global and enhanced roles, and secondly, getting the PLA under the party apparatus firmly under party control. As a follow-up to the 18th Party Congress, it was decided in 2013 to set up an NSC headed by the president. To reiterate the party's hold over the PLA, President Xi Jinping addressed a conference of party workers at Gutian, where Mao had outlined the philosophy in 1929, stating that the PLA is the party's army. Xi's remarks were: 'The PLA still remains the party's army and must maintain absolute loyalty to the political masters.' President Xi has also given additional impetus to the ongoing reforms, like a reduction in strength by three lakh troops to downsize the PLA strength to two million overall from the earlier 2.3 million. As has been outlined earlier, rightsizing has been part of a trend; the PLA was 4.5 million till 1980, resized to three million in 1985, and now to two million. The optimisation also includes cutting down the army and enhancing the strength, equipment, capabilities, and role of the maritime forces. The prime example is the induction of aircraft carriers and deployment of a naval task force for counter-piracy in the Gulf of Aden from 2009 onwards. China has also acquired a number of bases and operating/surveillance facilities in ports like Djibouti, Gwadar, Hambantota, Maldives, Coco Island, and Fiery Cross Reef, in what is described as the 'string of pearls' or more benignly as the Maritime Silk Corridor.

Xi has also chosen to address the issue of corruption and other malpractices in the PLA head-on. In a somewhat risky and bold move, as many as 3,000 personnel, including over 50 top generals, were removed, and some meted out serious punishment. This has also served to build a loyal stream of the PLA, duly vetted by him. Despite his non-PLA background, he has established a firm grip over the Armed Forces and is also seen donning combat gear to identify with them. Notwithstanding reforms and a concerted drive for weeding out corruption, in October 2023, members of apex decision-making structures like Defence Minister Li Shangfu, his predecessor Wei Fenghe, and Foreign Minister Qin Gang were sacked. Besides, nine PLA generals, including five top generals of Rocket Force, the former Air Force Chief, and the Fleet Commander of the South China Sea, were removed from the National People's Congress (NPC). More importantly, the chairmen of China Aerospace Science and Technology Corporation and major manufacturing entity Norinco Group were also sacked. **It raises very serious concerns about – firstly, scale and degree of corruption; secondly, the process of selection and appointment; and most importantly, the very quality of products made in such a compromised system. It has also raised questions on the competence of Xi as all top appointments are cleared by him.**

Structurally, the PLA was reorganised in 2015 as the Ground Force Command (erstwhile army), PLA Navy (PLAN), and PLA Air Force (PLAAF) with two new service HQs: Rocket Force and Strategic Support Force. The Rocket Force is essentially an upgrade of the Second Artillery, which will operate strategic and conventional missiles. The Strategic Support Force was tasked with the emerging disciplines of cyber, space, and political (psy-ops). These reforms

reflected an enhanced role for the maritime forces, missiles, cyber, space, and technology, at some cost to the army. These five and five theatres were considered theatre grade appointments. Joint Logistics Force were sub-theatre (corps level) appointments.

However, in Apr 2024, Strategic Support Force was re-organised into three separate Arms- Aerospace Force, Cyberspace Force and Information Support Force. This would lead to four Services and four Arms, including Joint Logistics Force. The latter are sub-theatre level and are required to report directly to CMC.

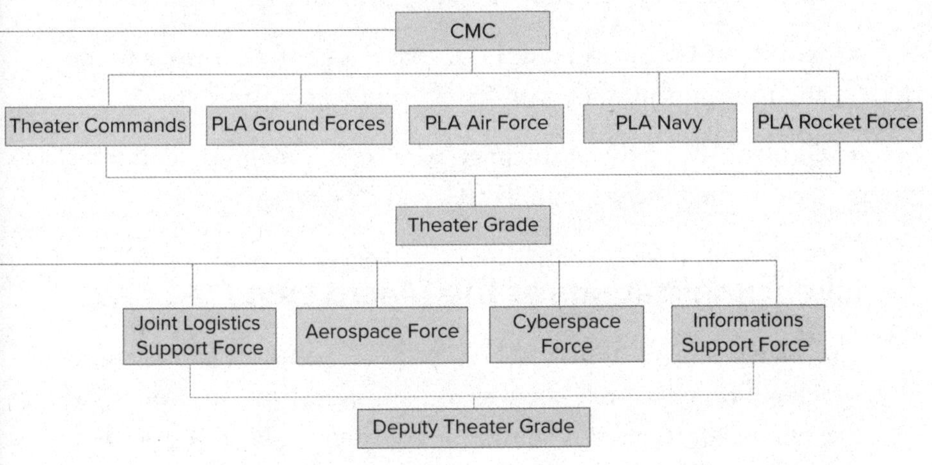

(Graphic source-https://www.claws.in)

These reforms have been followed through at the operational level with the **reorganisation of 17 unwieldy commands into just five theatre commands. The net result is that the Tibet border is now managed by one theatre command—the Western Command—instead of the forces of the Chengdu and Lanzhou Military Regions, with some reserves from Guangzhou in certain contingencies.** All resources, including ground, air, maritime, missile, cyber, space, and logistics, are now seamlessly integrated at the command level, ensuring synergy. These reforms have been followed through at the operational level with the creation of 84 Corps-level organisations, including 13 operational ones. A matching review of training, repair, and logistics structures has also been carried out.

The outline organisation of theatre commands (TCs) with their responsibilities is as follows:

- **Eastern TC:** HQ at Nanjing with responsibilities for Taiwan and the East China Sea, comprising 71, 72, and 73 Corps.
- **Southern TC:** HQ at Guangzhou, with the charter of Vietnam and the South China Sea, including 74 and 75 Corps.
- **Western TC:** HQ at Chengdu, with responsibilities of Tibet and internal security, primarily Xinjiang, including 76 and 77 Corps.
- **Northern TC:** Shenyang as HQ, with charge of the Russian border and Korean peninsula, with 78, 79, and 80 Corps.
- **Central TC:** HQ at Beijing, with responsibilities of internal security and reserves with 81, 82, and 83 Corps.

Likely Implications at the Macro Level

The changes have functional as well as political ramifications, which are of special relevance to us. An assured life term does give the system great stability, ensuring continuity, yet it also leads to absolutism and sycophancy. It can lead to a vacuum and even a power struggle in the event of the untimely demise or removal of the president. It also removes all pretensions of democracy and collectivism, which the Chinese emphasise very stridently. It will endow Xi with an enhanced international stature and larger-than-life image as such unparalleled authority has been enjoyed only by a very few like Mao, Fidel Castro, Saddam, and Gaddafi, but, unfortunately, all of them earned considerable notoriety for being autocratic and despotic.

Functional changes, especially in the PLA, notably of rightsizing reorganisation, like the TCs, an enhanced role for the maritime forces, reliance on technology, and eradication of corruption are all path-breaking, commendable, and will set the stage for continued transformation. China's modernisation of the PLA is reflected in the increasing footprint of the Chinese in the South China Sea, Indo-Pacific, and even Africa. China has also enhanced its participation and funding in the United Nations (UN) peacekeeping missions. It has also engaged the African countries in a concerted drive and even pledged $100 million for a Standby Force for the African Union, as well as resources for a disaster management force. The PLA has achieved considerable capability to produce armaments and munitions and has emerged as the largest exporter of small arms and light weapons as per the latest Stockholm International Peace Research Institute (SIPRI) projections.

Conclusion

China, under its fifth-generation leadership, and the PLA, after its transformation, has started muscle flexing, causing considerable discomfort and concern amongst the neighbours. While China continues to downplay these concerns, it will be in order if China walks the talk and settles the maritime and other border disputes. For India, all these changes have a direct implication, and it is axiomatic that these are analysed and carefully watched.

References

1. CPC Report to the 18th CPC
2. CPC Report to the 19th CPC
3. Nalin Surie, Past 19th Party Congress: China's Strategic Direction and Behaviour. *USI Strategic Yearbook, 2018*
4. Major General GG Dwivedi, China's Revolutionary Military Reforms; Salient Imperatives: Strategic Implications. *USI Strategic Yearbook, 2018*
5. Major General Deepak K Mehta, Xi Set to Rule For Life. *IMR*, April 2018

Coping with Chinese Techno-psy War

(Written in January 2021)

Key Takeaways

- **Drones have emerged as potent weapon systems and sort of a game changer.**
- **The myth of Chinese technical asymmetry being decisive is largely debunked. Indian forces have been able to execute their missions effectively. However, complacency on this account cannot be allowed in future, and efforts must remain focused on technical modernisation.**

As we crystal gaze security challenges likely in 2021, it is appropriate to recall the major trends of last year. Despite the Covid pandemic, **China blatantly altered the tenuous status quo on the LAC in utter disregard of agreed protocols. It also instigated a barbaric standoff in Galwan using stone-age weapons. Yet, the year finished with a stalemate, with Indians in control of dominating features on the Kailash range. It is a settled principle that unresolved stalemate implies defeat for the aggressor.** The moot question remains – will the Chinese accept it? Before any face-saving exit, will the PLA attempt another foray, leveraging its much-trumpeted technological prowess? Is asymmetry hyped up?

Another trend was the phenomenal success of drones in Nagorno-Karabakh (NGK). Headlines exclaimed, 'Azerbaijan's drones owned the battlefield and defined the future of warfare'. The total decimation of platforms by armed drones has prompted relevant posers.

- First, is it the death knell for tanks and costly platforms? After all, nearly 250 AFVs and 200 other platforms were destroyed/degraded.

- Second, most of these engagements were recorded and beamed on Twitter, acting as the exponential multiplier in the psychological domain, forcing Armenian capitulation.
- Third, the cost-effectiveness of aircraft is under scrutiny. Drones are achieving the same and more, at a fraction of the cost, without risk to pilots, though Azerbaijan dished out 69 million petrodollars for six systems. The pricing debate is best summed up in the words of Michael Korean, Director of Russian Studies, "Drones offer small countries very cheap access to tactical aviation and Precision Guided Weapons, enabling them to destroy an opponent's much costlier equipment such as tanks and AD system, across the board due to local factors." But on balance, the so-called aviators, Top guns and Tankers have certainly lost a bit of swagger due to enhanced vulnerability as also cheaper and more flexible options.
- Fourth, it has raised serious questions on the efficacy of counter-drone systems like Armenia's air defense systems, such as Pantsir-A1 and electronic warfare system, Krusukha, sourced from Russia.
- Fifth, at the macro level, it has highlighted asymmetrical advantages to the attacker in the offense-defense matrix. The traditional belief that wars are unlikely, as the cost of defending outweighs that of attacking, is under challenge.

Objective analysts counter this hype with the argument that the success of drones seen in NGK and other skirmishes (Syria, Libya, and Yemen) cannot be applied universally as a template. These conflicts were characterised by near-total air dominance against irregular militia-like forces. The abject surrender by Armenia was primarily due to antiquated AD armaments and, more importantly, a lack of coordinated AD control and reporting system. Azerbaijan employed slow AN-2 agricultural planes (converted as drones) as baits, luring Armenians to disclose their electronic AD profile. This enabled Israeli Kamikaze loitering munitions to literally demolish the entire Armenian AD network. Concurrently, Turkish Bayraktar TB2 destroyed undefended platforms, arrayed in laagers (harbours), seen only in historical movies.

Tanks leverage dispersion and damage template of conventional 20 KT strike predicts losses of less than a squadron of tanks, with standard distances. Mechanised columns have integrated tracked AD platforms. Modern tanks incorporate Active Protection Systems (APSs) like Shtora and Trophy despite their high costs. Franz-Stefan Gady of the American think tank IISS says, 'Platforms, including tanks, will not become obsolete'. The USA is already working on Next Generation Combat Vehicle (Optionally Manned Tank)-2030. However, platforms will have to incorporate better electronic signature suppression techniques and decoys and operate in defended envelopes. The Chinese are leveraging psychological warfare to paint a scary scenario of overwhelming technological ascendancy.

Notable examples have been stories of the positioning of microwave oven type of devices, to literally vaporising troops on the Kailash range. Another fable has been swarms of drones flying noodles to the PLA troops with the capability to deliver munitions. The more recent one is the supply of 50 Wing Loong II armed drones to Pakistan. These may have been provided with conditions to enhance the security envelope of CPEC installations. The accompanying hype in Chinese media predicts that Indian troops will be sitting ducks. It will be prudent to debunk such attempts aimed at cognitive manipulation as part of the three-warfare strategy. The aim is to trigger another psychological collapse like the one witnessed in Armenia.

The Chinese technology, especially in aerial weapons, though cheap and widely proliferated, has its share of serious hiccups. In 2011, China unleashed a kind of 'supply shock', selling drones to many countries. Michael Horowitz of the University of Pennsylvania described this proliferation as a 'pursuit of status synonymous with tech innovation'.

Algeria has had a series of accidents in the last six years with CH-4 UCAVs. Jordan had to put on sale the Chinese-supplied UAVs after they failed on all parameters. In the recent war in NGK, the only Chinese equipment was WM-80 MLRS on the losing side. Chinese UAVs are yet to prove their efficacy and reliability in contested environments. This appraisal notwithstanding, we should prepare for this inevitably promising weapon of the future, as both our adversaries are building potent capabilities.

Preparations must be in both offensive and defensive domains. We have a functional AD control and reporting system, which should be tweaked. Indigenous initiatives on RF guns to distract incoming drones and the anti-drone radar system developed by BEL need fast tracking. In the offensive domain, our limited stock of Israeli Harop (Harpy-2) requires an urgent boost with the induction of munitions currently under order. The project of arming Herons needs to be expedited. After the conclusion of BECA, negotiations for armed MQ-9 drones from the USA should find greater traction.

With the induction of drones, forces need technological upgrades, along with a review of inventories of aircraft and costly platforms. **Drones should be the key focus of the Atmanirbhar initiative. The biggest takeaway is that front-line entities require better and organic air defense envelopes.**

Chinese Conundrum – Conflict or Reconciliation

Two contrasting trends have emerged in the four-year-old and still unresolved Sino-Indian imbroglio. The first – the Directorate of National Intelligence, in its report released in March 2024, warns of the distinct possibility of Sino-Indian conflict. It reiterates that continued large-scale deployments by both sides on contested and undefined LAC can lead to miscalculation and escalation. **The obvious questions are – will PLA attempt another foray to realise its Tibet objective? Does integration of Xijang (Chinese term for**

Tibet) take precedence over Taiwan? Chinese are known for utilizing historic milestones, will the window between 2024 (75th anniversary of PRC) and 2027 (centenary of PLA) turn out to be ominous leading to another bigger and bloodier conflagration?

The second, **somewhat reassuring sign was the recent interview of PM Narendra Modi to US magazine, indicating possibility of initiative at political level for resolving the crisis.** It is important that statement is in direct contrast to his articulation on other adversary, Pakistan, ruling-out possibility of rapprochement. Global strategic community was waiting anxiously to decipher these trends, especially those pertaining to reconciliation, albeit after the elections. **However, early trends after mixed mandate in elections indicate cautious approach and status-quo.**

Chinese Core Interests

China has emerged as the pivotal manufacturing hub in the global supply chain, with ambition to leverage BRI connectivity's as radiating spokes, to reinforce influence and dependencies. China has surplus of funds and infrastructure creation capability, which it wants to leverage through BRI. It is important to reiterate that India is the most prominent nation to oppose BRI, justifiably so, because CPEC violates her sovereignty, it runs through parts of Pak Occupied Kashmir (POK) and Gilgit-Baltistan (GB), both are contested and de-jure Indian territories.

China has catapulted herself as the second largest economy and competing pole to USA, in bi-polar global power matrix. Ultimately, it seeks to be at the very helm. It is aggressively pushing for unipolar Asia and orchestrates petty 'zero-sum' game, to stymie even the modest Indian outreach, with string of pearls and multiple connectivity projects in extended neighbourhood. It is simply unwilling to accommodate Indian aspirations and contemptuously rejects formulations like 'Indo-Pacific' and 'Indian Century'.

Chinese Perception of India

Noted Chinese affairs expert, Vijay Gokhale has outlined Chinese beliefs and perceptions about India. While we may find them diabolic, yet they merit consideration, as they shape Chinese policies till, we can force narrative correction. **First, China views India as unequal, and unreliable neighbour, unworthy of any stand-alone status or consideration. Second, India is relevant only in hyphenated mode, tagged with great powers in strategic trinity of USA, USSR and China. Third, clear expectation that India should first understand Chinese objectives and play along. Fourth, China can afford to deal with India in episodic tactical mode, within her own long-term trajectory.**

It is important to remember that **Chinese think of time in centuries. Their aim is to wear out the opponent by building overwhelming asymmetry**. Chinese assertion to push resolution of Sino-Indian border to back-burner, coupled with salami-slicing, setting-up Xiokangs (border villages) and no patrolling zones are all part of plan to create new and altered fait-accompli realities for us, to simply fall in line. With the kind of dependencies, especially in primary sector and adverse trade balance, India is on back-foot economically. This has even been acknowledged by Indian FM.

Bharat Narrative – Push Back

Chinese pre-emptive deployment in Ladakh in May 2020, accompanied by hype on technical asymmetry are manifestations of grey-zone warfare. China had literally applied its old maxim, "loot the house on fire" by launching co-ordinated salami-slicing in Apr 2020, even when COVID-19 was raging. However, India has managed to push-back China with display of resilience in Galwan, Yangtze (Dec 2022) and most importantly, quid-pro-quo deployment on Kailash heights in Sept 2020. **India has not only rebalanced her forces but also deployed dissuasive grid, backed by adequate reserves.**

As per media reports, raising of another division for Mountain Corps and operationalisation of Area HQ into Corps HQ, are under advanced consideration. There is relentless focus on border infrastructure like the recently inaugurated Sela Tunnel and road over Saser-La to Daulat Beg Oldie (DBO). It has also added maritime dimension with successful anti-piracy operations in Indian Ocean, announcements of setting-up Jatayu base in Lakshdweep Island chain and plans to expand Andaman-Nicobar bases. Technological dimension is evident in trials of Agni-V, MIRV and MaRV tests. All these, add to **unfolding Bharat Narrative, which is now being acknowledged even in Chinese media, Weibo and think-tanks**. The moot question is how much more is required to check the Dragon?

Geostrategic Flux

In ever evolving geo-strategic flux, two critical "known-unknown" challenges are evolving. First, it is now known that Russia is in resurgent mode but its quantum and inter-se influence in Russia-China-India trinity is unknown. Indian concern would be to ring-fence and strengthen Indo-Russian commitment on strategic co-operation, regardless of growing Sino-Russian ties. President Putin not only chose to visit China, soon after swearing-in but also displayed visible bon-homie. The second imponderable is that while USA has forged bipartisan consensus on check-mating China but its character, especially in likely Trump regime is difficult to predict. The recent visit of Secretary, Blinkin raises even more questions on US commitment. **We must be cognizant that heavy lifting is our burden and external assistance from groupings like QUAD would be limited.** QUAD, itself is creating complementary groupings like AUKUS and I-5. There is growing parallel engagement with Japan and South Korea with India being pushed to periphery.

Way Forward – Narrowing Asymmetry

Pre-mature and ill-advised Chinese foray in Tibet has exposed limitations of application of coercive deployment. The recent conflicts in Ukraine and Gaza have further reinforced, the very futility of application of kinetic force. Most importantly, it has jolted us out of our Pak-centric fixation and skewed focus on counterinsurgency. Our strategy was based on traditional beliefs that conventional operations are unlikely, and Xi will continue to follow Deng's policies of subdued rise. Irrational, wolf-warrior approach of China under Xi Jinping has foxed the global community. On positive note, it has also busted the very myth and hype of Chinese asymmetry, which is certainly not debilitating and is being managed well. However, **the next arenas in grey-zone warfare are likely to extend into cyber and cognitive domains, besides maritime. Yet, we simply cannot afford to let our guard down in terrestrial domain on LAC, notwithstanding, huge fiscal burden.**

For India, while Pak remains permanent irritant, China is the primary challenge. Threat is further accentuated by growing collusive linkages between the two. We are making steady progress but have decades to go before we narrow the existing asymmetry for stable and credible deterrence against the Dragon. The terms of reconciliation, when it materializes, will be influenced by levels of asymmetry. While Ladakh foray, in all probability was one-off irrationality, yet we cannot let our guard down, notwithstanding, financial costs and other challenges. In short and medium term, it is imperative to maintain vigilance and readiness. **Focused preparations and narrowing asymmetry, hopefully will bolster dissuasive coefficient in Sino-Indian matrix.**

Guard Rails of Reconciliation

It is creditable that India has maintained her stance of primacy and focus on resolution of border and not fallen into Chinese ploy of pushing the issue to background. The way PLA has destroyed set of comprehensive and agreed protocols in Doklam, Depsang, Demchok, Galwan and Yangtze will indeed now make it very difficult to rebuild trust. **Yet, two rising powers with large unresolved borders, both equipped with nuclear weapons, make it imperative for both countries to seek meaningful reconciliation.** Dependency of Indian primary sector like pharmaceuticals, solar energy, electronic appliances, power generation and electric vehicles would compel us to seek interim solution, centred around maintaining the new, altered reality on borders with agreed tweaks and protocols. We may have to postpone the idea to restoring status-quo as existing before Chinese foray in 2019.

India will have to upgrade her intelligence and surveillance systems to preclude getting deceived by repeat of Ladakh-2020. **Even if the process of disengagement and de-escalation is completed, complete de-induction will be difficult. Adequate reserves and reactionary forces will have to be maintained in the theatre and well forward. The new regime of buffer (no-patrolling) zones may become fait-accompli and it may become necessary to build protocols around them to sanctify these.**

Sino-Bhutan Border, Siliguri Corridor, and Dolam (Chinese describe it as Doklam)

Bhutan-China Border Problems and Boundary Talks: Implications for India

Key Takeaways

- The annexation of the buffer state of Tibet by China in 1950 jolted Bhutan into the strategic shock of China as a neighbour.
- China has deliberately kept its land borders with India and Bhutan unresolved.
- The issue has a trilateral dimension with strategic implications for India due to Dolam posing a threat to the Siliguri corridor.
- Bhutan seems to have altered its long-held policy of conducting external affairs through India, yet it has reassured that it will keep India's interests in mind.

Introduction

China has an unresolved land border with just two countries—India and Bhutan—out of a total of 14 bordering nations. The Sino-Bhutan border in the Western (Dolam/Doklam) and Eastern (Sakteng) sectors has strategic significance for India as it not only includes tri-junction but also has far-reaching operational implications. Bilateral talks between Bhutan and China stalled since the Dolam crisis in 2017, notwithstanding the signing of the Memorandum of Understanding incorporating a three-point framework, were revived with the 25th round on 23 and 24 October in Beijing. In a move that has ominous portents for India, both sides signed another Cooperation

Agreement. It appears that Bhutan is willing to settle its boundaries, notwithstanding Indian reservations, although Bhutan has assured that it will consult India and keep her interests in mind.

Aim

The basic aim of this paper is to map various dimensions connected with the Sino-Bhutan border and analyse the issue in a trilateral format, factoring implications for India.

Preview

This paper is laid out in the following parts:

a) Chinese Border Disputes – Major Inferences
b) Geo-strategic Significance
c) Historical Context
d) Disputed Territories
e) Border/Boundary Resolution Process
f) Indian Concerns
g) Way Forward

Chinese Border Disputes – Major Inferences

China has borders with as many as 24 countries, including terrestrial (land) and maritime domains. It has a land border with 14 countries and claims to have settled boundaries with all her neighbours except India and Bhutan. However, these claims must be viewed realistically in the context that most disputes have been resolved on the terms stipulated by China. There are contentious claims in some sectors in countries like Kazakhstan and even Nepal. The PLA has a belligerent history, marked by aggression against India in 1962, a six-month-long border conflict with the USSR in 1969, and a brief armed conflict with Vietnam in 1979. It has been currently engaged in an unresolved standoff with India in Ladakh since 5 May 2020. Apart from this, there have been unilateral Chinese attempts at salami-slicing in the Eastern sector in Arunachal Pradesh and Sikkim. The recent instances include a 72-day-long standoff in Dolam/Doklam in June 2017 and in Yangtse on 9 December 2022.

In the maritime domain, China has serious issues with all its neighbouring littoral states. It is engaged in serious skirmishes/standoffs with the Philippines, Taiwan, Vietnam, Brunei, and Malaysia in the South China Sea and Japan in the East China Sea. China has unilaterally proclaimed its own claims in terms of ambiguous nine-dash and even eleven-dash lines. The layout of these has varied over the years, and claim lines are contested by other affected states. These have been misused to take control of tiny, uninhabited reefs and shoals and convert them into artificial islands for naval facilities. An arbitral tribunal in 2016 declared Chinese claims as violations of the United Nations Convention on the Laws of the Sea (UNCLOS). **International strategic experts opine that China uses border disputes to build pressure on smaller neighbours by bullying them. She has mastered the art of filibustering and endless parleys to tire out the other party. It is also described as an application of Mao Zedong's dictum, 'Tan, tan, da, da'—'talking, talking (but) preparing for war'. The [1]settlement, if any, has to be within the Chinese template, with time being of no consequence.** It also makes use of imaginative cartography by articulating multiple claim lines backed up by selective use of favourable treaties, which is being increasingly termed lawfare. These have acquired a dangerous overtone with China in 'wolf-warrior' mode, and the country is referred to as the Dragon, which is on the hegemonic overdrive.

Geostrategic Significance

Bhutan and China as two neighbours are very apt manifestations of the Biblical analogy of David and Goliath. Bhutan was envisaged as a

1. Srikant Kondapalli, Bhutan under China's Shadow, https://www.deccanherald.com/opinion/bhutan-under-chinas-shadow-2794475

buffer state between India and Tibet and had no border with China. The region was,confronted with geo-strategic shock when Tibet was annexed and amalgamated with China in 1951. Coupled with this is the unresolved border between India and China, further vitiating the imbroglio. It has acquired a strategic dimension in the 'Thucydides trap' type of situation developing between rising powers, China and India. With the Chinese proclivity to dominate India's immediate neighbourhood, it also affords opportunities to smaller states like Nepal, Maldives, and Bhutan to play the balancing game between two contestants, India and China. Bhutan, with an area of 38,000 sq. km, is a very sparsely populated, hilly, and landlocked state with just 750,000 people. For ease of comprehension, it is even smaller than Denmark in area but with one-seventh of its population. Its capacity to police and manage its disputed borders is very limited. Bhutan follows an insular and gateway approach to preserve its ecology. Even tourism is regulated through numbers under the 'minimum impact with maximum revenue' paradigm. Bhutan shot into prominence by topping Gross National Happiness (GNH) rankings.

Bhutan's border with China is bounded by two tri-junctions with China and India and extends 477 km or 295 miles. In the east, the border starts from Mount Gipmochi (the location of which is contested) and was highlighted during the Doklam crisis in 2017. The border, starting from the Western sector, extends northwards over the partially disputed Jomolhari (also known as Chomolhari) range, turning eastward near Mount Masang Gang, including a large unresolved stretch in the Northern sector and turning south-eastward, in proximity to Singye Dzong, the provincial capital, ending at tri-junction point. The eastern stretch, including the Sakteng Wildlife Sanctuary, was traditionally considered settled but has now been claimed by China, thereby expanding the scope of the dispute. Access from Bhutan to China is regulated through a road trail at Tremo-La, which connects Tsento Gewog and Phari.

Bhutan-India Border

India has a border of 699 km, spanning four Indian states (Sikkim, West Bengal, Assam, and AP). Most of the Indo-Bhutan border is open, and transit is channelised through Phunsetlong/Jaigaon, Gelephu, and Samdrup Jongkhar border towns. **Geo-strategic edge and sensitivity are imparted to the Sino-Bhutan-India border issue due to the relative location of the Chumbi Valley in the Western sector vis-à-vis the Siliguri Corridor. The corridor, which is just 22 km at its narrowest, is also described as the 'Chicken's Neck' or the 'North-Eastern Jugular'.** It is literally the gateway from the mainland to the North-Eastern states, also called 'seven sisters and one brother'. It can also act as a springboard for forays in neighbouring Nepal, Bhutan, and Bangladesh. Please refer to Map-1.

Historical Context

Bhutan's border with Tibet has never been officially recognised or demarcated and is largely a fall-out of the inherited, ambiguous colonial legacy of British rule. It has been a complex construct based on exchanges between Tibet, Sikkim, Nepal, and British India. Chinese claims date back to the pre-Peoples Republic China regime of the Manchu dynasty in 1910–11 when Zhao Erfeng staked territorial claims on parts of Bhutan and Tibet. These were reiterated by the Chinese Communist Party in 1949 on establishing the PRC. The theoretical construct was outlined in Mao Zedong's diktat expounded in the Communist Party treatise 'The Chinese Revolution and the Communist Party' in 1939: "The correct boundaries of China would include Burma, Bhutan, and Nepal".

Mao also emphasised this in his expansionist 'Five Fingers of Tibet' policy. Citing Tibet as the palm, fingers include Ladakh, Nepal, Sikkim, Bhutan, and Arunachal (referred to as South Tibet). In Chinese conception, all these are part of greater Tibet, annexed under unequal treaties by erstwhile colonial powers. This claim was reinforced with imaginative cartography, including maps forming part of the publication, 'A Brief History of China', published in 1959. Large portions of Bhutan, as well as territories of other countries, were included within the ambit of Chinese claims. The annexation of Tibet in 1950–51, followed by a 17-point agreement forced on the hapless Tibetan regime, resulted in the withdrawal of Indian and Bhutanese representatives from their missions in Lhasa. [2]This was followed by a rebellion in Tibet in 1959, the flight of the Dalai Lama to India, and approximately 6,000 refugees seeking asylum in Bhutan and many more in India. Consequently, Bhutan, fearing being swamped by migrants and refugees, closed its borders. The PLA occupied several adjoining Bhutanese exclaves in Western Tibet in July 1959. These included Darchen, Gartok, and several other villages near Mount Kailash, which have been under Bhutanese control since the seventeenth century for 300 years. These had been given to Bhutan by Ngawang Namgyal in the seventeenth century.[3]

Diplomatic Ties with India

Indo-Bhutanese ties are based on the Treaty of Perpetual Friendship, signed in 1949 and renewed in 2007. Fearing Chinese expansionist forays, which included repeated incursions and denial of traditional grazing rights, Bhutan established military relations with India. These included the Indian Military Training Team (IMTRAT), joint check posts for access, and joint defence contingencies. **In this situation of inequality with China, instead of a 'Balance of Power' for Bhutan, it is realistically a 'Balance of Terror' due to the aggressive salami-slicing by the PLA. Bhutan officially still maintains a neutral stance in order to retain an uneasy balance in the triangular matrix.** India represented and negotiated Bhutan's concerns in talks with China in

2. Harpreet-Bhutan-China Boundary Dispute: A Historical Perspective. https://www.cestmoizblog.com

3. Harsh V Pant & Aditya Gowdara Shivamurthy-Himalaya: The Complexity of Bhutan, The Economic Times. https://www.orfonline.org

Sino-Indian border conflict resolution parleys till 1970. India has been the largest export market for Bhutan, accounting for 93 per cent of its total exports and is also the largest aid provider. Bhutan also plays a vital, synergistic role in India's Neighbourhood First and Act East policies.

Bhutan – External Affairs

Bhutan has been dealing with the outside world through a reliable ally, India, and has allowed just three embassies in Thimphu to India, Bangladesh, and Kuwait, despite having diplomatic ties with 53 countries. Bhutan joined the UNO in 1971. Like India, Bhutan has followed the 'One China policy'. China is actively pushing to open a mission in Thimphu. India has discouraged unregulated diplomatic forays in Bhutan to shield the tiny state from avoidable great power games and manipulation. China has made huge inroads into Bhutan's economy, replacing India as Bhutan's largest trading partner, albeit in one way, traffic with mounting dependencies. The Chinese footprint has proliferated in infrastructure projects, including connectivity, power generation, and communications. All these are building up to tremendous economic coercive leverages.

Disputed Territories

Bhutan's perception of disputed areas was outlined in official statements in the National Assembly. These have listed four disputed areas between Bhutan and China (please see Maps 2 and 3) In the west, it includes approximately 89 sq. km in the Dolam (increasingly referred to as Doklam) plateau (please see Map-4). Sinchumlumpa and Giu (approximately 180 sq. km) make it 269 km of unresolved stretch bordering the Chumbi Valley in the Western sector. The Chumbi Valley is a dagger-shaped narrowing wedge between India and Bhutan. The southern narrow portion of the valley, the Dolam (Doklam) plateau, with its strategic significance, has the potential to pose a threat to the tenuous Siliguri corridor, termed as jugular, connecting the North-East with the mainland. **The Chinese quest is to widen the extremely narrow base of the valley. The dispute is indexed to the location of Mt Gipmochi and the correct interpretation of the watershed of rivers like the Amo Chu. It is a complex bevy of crest lines and the heights of Gamochen, Batangla, and Sinchela** (please see Map-5). The most sought-after is the Zompelri (Jampheri) ridge, providing a launch pad for reaching the Siliguri Corridor. The balanced view is that while it is indeed a threat, logistics and terrain make it a tortuous and slow exercise requiring extensive logistics build-up. However, it will remain a very potent threat in the future.

Unresolved areas in the Northern region are in two pockets of Jakarlung and Pasamlung, spanning approximately 495 sq. km. In June 2020, China sprung a surprise by bringing in unspecified areas in the Eastern region of the Sakteng Wildlife Sanctuary in the Tashigang district. This was surprisingly articulated in a virtual meeting of the Global Environment Facility (GEF), where they discussed a grant for Sakteng, which China termed a disputed region. It is opined that the claim may be just to increase leverage as a bargaining chip in the swap deal and also to preclude the development of joint infrastructure by Bhutan with India.

Border/Boundary Resolution Process

The first outreach to China by Bhutan was an invitation to the Chinese envoy in New Delhi for the coronation of K-5, Jimmy Singhe Wangchuk. The steering role of the present king's father, K-4, as an elder statesman is based on his domain knowledge. He remains the key enabler for Bhutan in boundary dispute resolution. Two Foreign ministers, Wu Xueqian and Dawa Tsering, held parleys in New York to formulate a mechanism for bilateral ties. Some reports state that these talks happened without taking India into confidence, taking her by surprise. This resulted in annual direct boundary talks starting in 1984. Both countries signed a bilateral agreement for maintaining peace on the border, broadly based on the five principles of Panchsheel. Peaceful co-existence is to be based on mutual respect for sovereignty and territorial integrity. After 14 years, both sides signed a memorandum on Guiding Principles on the Settlement of Boundry Issues in 1988.

China proposed a 'package proposal' in 1990 in the seventh round of talks. It proposed to concede its Northern claims (495 sq. km) in exchange for Bhutan agreeing to China's Western claims, including 89 sq. km of Dolam. China has already renounced its claim on the 154 sq. mile area in Kula Khari in the North, explaining it as a cartographic error. This is in line with the Chinese quest for strategic reach through the Chumbi Valley. Bhutan, in the tenth round (1995), appeared willing to accept the package deal.[4] However, Bhutan retracted in 1996, allegedly under Indian influence. China and Bhutan signed an Agreement on the Maintenance of Peace and Tranquillity along the Border Areas. However, China's building of roads on Bhutanese territory, allegedly in violation of the informal 1998 stand-still agreement, provoked tensions again. In a 2002 round of parleys, China presented purported 'evidence', asserting ownership of disputed tracts of land; after negotiations, an interim agreement was reached. Foreign Minister Damochi Dorji visited Beijing in August 2016 for the twenty-fourth round of boundary talks with Chinese Vice President Li Yuanchao. Both sides indicated a willingness to settle the boundary issues. The entire process hit a major roadblock with the Doklam standoff in 2017 when India objected to the PLA attempting to build a road to the Zompelri (Jampheri) ridge, passing through contested Bhutanese territory in close proximity to Indian deployment on unresolved LAC. The issue was resolved after a 72-day-long standoff between Indian and Chinese troops.

The Bhutan-China MOU of October 2021, signed in a video conference, is based on the three-step road map for a settlement. The

---

4. Suhasini Haider, Bhutan, China want deal on boundaries 'soon' https://www.thehindu.com/news/international/bhutan-china-want-deal-on-boundaries-soon/article67455065.ece

stages are likely to be: first, establishing framework; second, confirming and focusing on identified disputes, including the exchange of maps; and finally, the resolution stage. Ironically, disputed territory, especially in the Western region, is already under PLA control, making it a 'fait-accompli' situation.[5] **Bhutanese Foreign Minister Tandi Dorji held the twenty-fifth delegation-level talks on 23 and 24 October 2023 with his Chinese counterpart during his maiden official visit to Beijing. They signed the Cooperation Agreement – Responsibilities and Functions of the Joint Technical Team (JTT) on the Delimitation and Demarcation of the Bhutan-China Boundary.** These talks came after the first joint Delimitation meeting, earlier in August 2023, held as part of the thirteenth Experts Group Meeting. Both sides exuded confidence for the early conclusion of talks. The Chinese side also expressed hopes for setting up a diplomatic mission in Thimphu. While Bhutan has not commented on the Chinese optimism, it has not ruled out this possibility.

Indian Concerns

The Bhutanese side has assured that no agreement will be made 'against India's interests' and clarified that any talks about the 'tri-junction' at Dolam will only be held trilaterally between India, Bhutan, and China. Major concessions by China, especially in the Western sector of the Chumbi Valley, are unlikely. China, when asked to be considerate to the smaller neighbour, reportedly responded that China has two dozen bordering states and cannot give such concessions. In this context, China, with its aim to establish its hegemony by keeping India under check, wants to expand its hold on the Chumbi Valley to pose a threat to the Siliguri Corridor. Physical salami-slicing combined with economic dependencies will eventually build coercive leverage on Bhutan. It appears that the

5. Jianli Yang- Bhutan China Border Negotiations in Context- The Diplomat- 18 Nov 2021.8

Chinese strategy is to finally force Bhutan to accept the terms being set by the Dragon.[6]

Soon after the resolution of the Doklam crisis, China intensified efforts to build Xiaokang, a dual-purpose so-called model (moderately prosperous) village, on the Mochu River with military and logistics infrastructure, including habitation, helipads, ammunition dumps, and communications. Robert Barnett and his team of China experts claim that, since 2015, the PLA has been building military infrastructure, habitation, and communications in disputed areas of Northern Bhutan as well. Satellite imagery experts have mapped Gyalaphug as one of the five established villages.[7] They have deciphered approximately 105 km (66 miles) of new roads/tracks, a small hydropower generating station, two CCP administrative complexes, a communications centre, a disaster relief storage, five military/police outposts, and suspected major installations like communications tower, satellite receiving station, military base, and potentially up to six security sites and satellite outposts. China claims that these constructions are in parts of Lhodrak in the Tibet Autonomous Region (TAR), but in reality, they are located in Northern Bhutan. This infrastructure with distinct military character can be utilised to build up threats and operations against the Siliguri Corridor and India.

Update

The recent elections in January 2024 resulted in the voting out of Lotay Tshering, who was seen to be pushing for the resolution of the Sino-Bhutan border dispute. **The new PM, Tshering Topgay and his party, People's Democratic Party (PDP), are likely to be more sensitive to Indian concerns. The Bhutanese king visited India and**

6. Manoj Joshi- The China Bhutan Deal Should Worry India. and Hindustan Times and https://www.orfonline.org

7. Arushi Gupta, China-Bhutan Border Talks- Indian Stakes Under Discussion, https://www.vifindia.org/article/2023/november/17/china-bhutan-border-talks-indian-stakes-in-the-discussions

discussed the biggest connectivity and mega city project anchored on Gelephu Mindfulness City.

Way Forward

Bhutan is faced with the challenge of walking a tightrope between increasingly aggressive China in 'wolf-warrior' diplomacy mode and time-tested ally India. While India would like to safeguard its interest, Bhutan may, at some stage, yield to a Chinese package deal offer. India needs to balance its core interests with the desire of Bhutan's compulsions. It will be appropriate to guide Bhutan in seeking the best deal, especially in limiting Chinese ambitions in the Doklam plateau. India should also remain invested in capacity building in Bhutan, especially in the security domain, to limit the Chinese footprint in economy and communications. It would be ideal if India is able to maintain joint defence capabilities and joint border check posts, even enlarging their scope. However, scaling down these after the border resolutions is a very distinct possibility.

Autonomy and balancing are sensitive issues and can be built by long-term trust and a healthy respect for mutual interests, eschewing a 'big brother' attitude. In this context, it bears reiteration that the ill-advised embargo on LPG and Kerosene in 2013 is still quoted and lamented by the Bhutanese populace. **India stood to cater for the contingency of Bhutan yielding to Chinese pressure and strengthen its hedging strategy. This would entail reinforcing the security grid and response matrix to safeguard the Siliguri Corridor. It is axiomatic that the Indian endeavour to build alternate connectivity in the North-East and resilience through strategic stocking is given enhanced impetus to cope with the growing Chinese threat.**

References

1. Srikant Kondapalli, Bhutan under China's Shadow. https://www.deccanherald.com/opinion/bhutan-under-chinas-shadow-2794475

2. Harpeet, Bhutan-China Boundary Dispute: A Historical Perspective. https://www.cestmoizblog.com

3. Harsh V Pant & Aditya Gowdara Shivamurthy, Himalaya: The Complexity of Bhutan. *The Economic Times,* https://www.orfonline.org

4. Suhasini Haider, Bhutan, China Want Deal on Boundaries 'Soon'. https://www.thehindu.com/news/international/bhutan-china-want-deal-on-boundaries-soon/article67455065.ece

5. Jianli Yang, Bhutan China Border Negotiations in Context. *The Diplomat*, 18 Nov 2021

6. Manoj Joshi, The China Bhutan Deal Should Worry India. *Hindustan Times* and https://www.orfonline.org

7. Aarushi Gupta, China-Bhutan Border Talks—Indian Stakes Under Discussion, https://www.vifindia.org/article/2023/november/17/china-bhutan-border-talks-indian-stakes-in-the-discussions

Map-1- (https://nitinagokhale.com/chine-crafts-new-dispute-in-bhutan-wildlife sanctuary-bordering-india/)

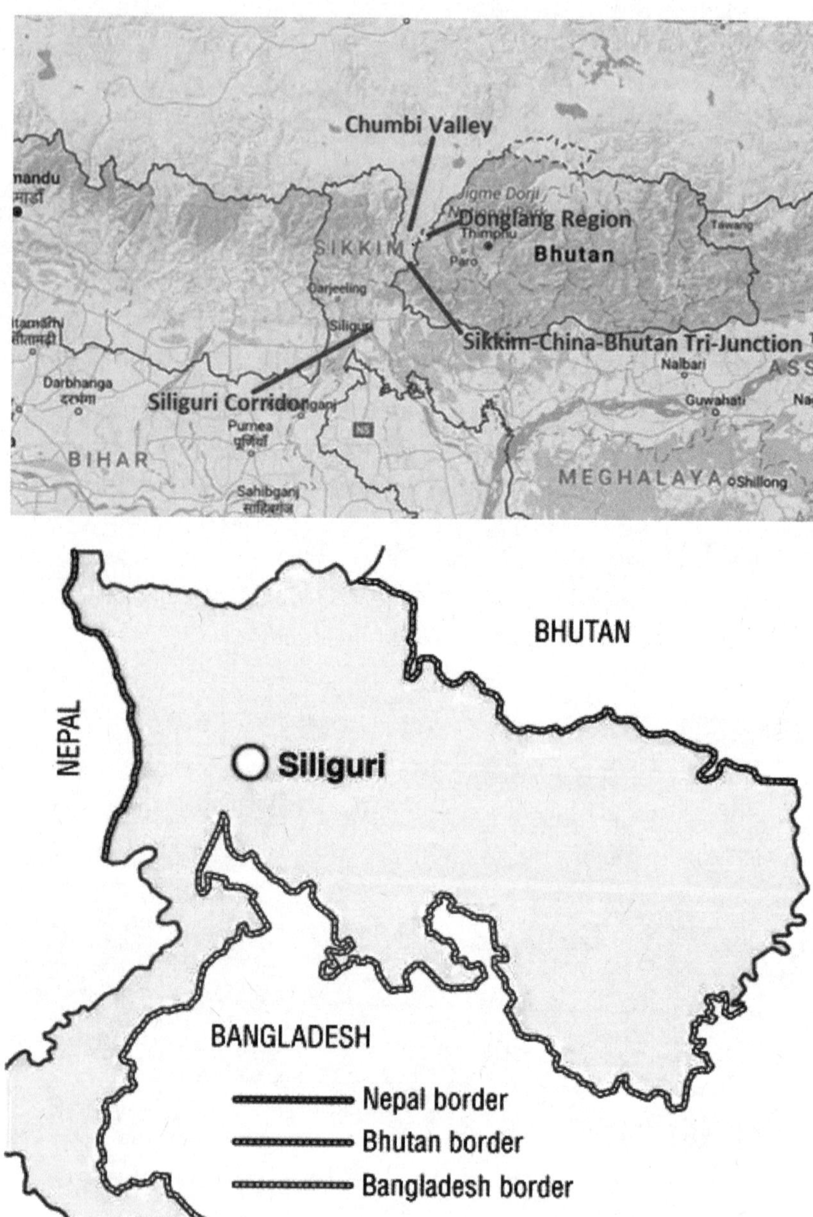

Map-2 (htttps://www.scribd.com document/391964464/Doklam-Crisis)

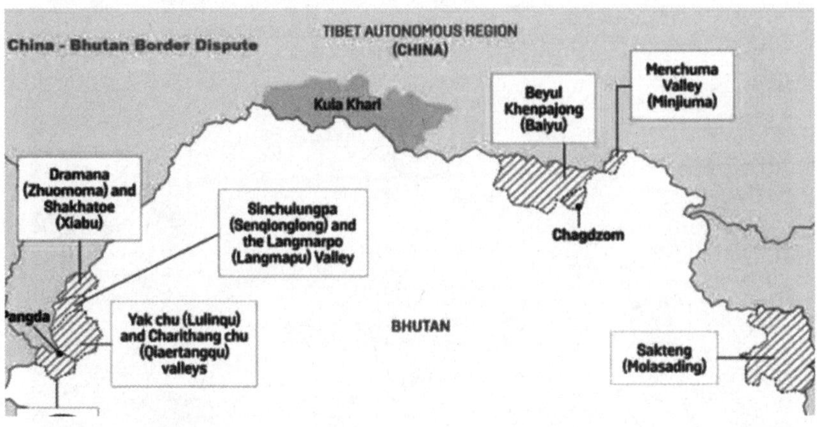

Map-3 (https://optimizeas.com/china-bhutan-boundary-talks/)

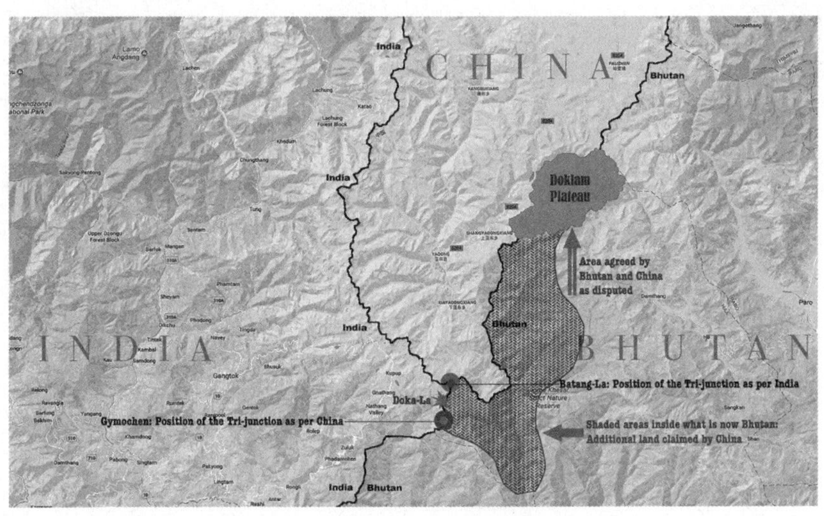

Map-4 (https://chellaney.net/2018/06/12/doklam-exemplifies-chinas-broader-recidivism-in-himalayas)

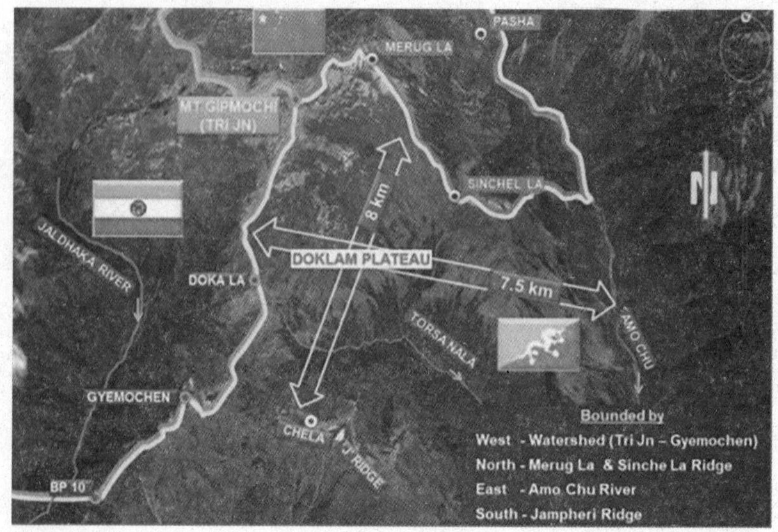

Map-5 (CENJOWS Handout)

Dynamics of Security of the Siliguri Corridor: The Way Forward

Key Takeaways

- The Siliguri Corridor has a border with four countries and is a gateway to the North-East – Seven Sisters and Brother.
- Multiple fault lines include the Gorkhaland and Kamatapur movements.
- Mitigating measures in surveillance, strategic reserves, and alternative connectivity need to be accorded priority.

Abstract

The Siliguri Corridor, a tenuous link with eight North-East states and a gateway for citizens of the North-East, is a strategic space of national salience. Vital surface communication and logistics links to the North-East are routed through this narrow corridor. It also has a large number of important security and other establishments besides being a commercial and trading hub extending into neighbouring countries. **The corridor has a border with four neighbouring countries; however, besides these benign neighbours, the Chumbi Valley is pointed at the corridor like a dragon's dagger.** *The jostling at Doklam was a controlled Indian reaction to help hapless Bhutan in the face of China-concerted unilateral move to extend its surface communication through the unresolved border with Bhutan. Its significance and vulnerability came as a wakeup call during the 73-day standoff in 2017 at Doklam (also referred to as Dolam or Donglang), which, though currently diffused, has the potential to escalate again. The corridor has some unresolved internal fault lines like Gorkhaland, Kamalapur/ Rajbongshi agitations and is also utilised by other Insurgent and terrorist groups for transit. This was evidenced during Operation 'All Clear' in Southern Bhutan in 2003–2004. Sensitivities involved call for an imaginative road map incorporating both internal leverages and regional cooperation to build up redundancies to achieve risk mitigation.*

Introduction

Geography, in terms of neighbours and boundaries, throws up myriad challenges, which are classified as cartographic anxieties. These concerns and challenges, if not managed well, magnify into strategic vulnerabilities. The Siliguri Corridor, a tenuous link with eight North-East mates and gateway for more than 50 million Northeasterners, is indeed one such critical national vulnerability. This situation can be attributed to many geo-strategic and geo-economic factors accentuated in the recent past by aggressive activities of the Chinese in the Doklam or Dolam plateau. Apart from this, centrifugal forces manifesting in unresolved insurgencies and separatist movements in the North-East further accentuate these concerns.

Besides the external drivers, sensitivity is exacerbated by the mismanagement of lines, most notably Gorkhaland problems combined with other problems like the Kamatapur and Rajbongshi movements, which, though currently subdued, can spin out of control. This issue provides an opportunity for external elements to fish in troubled waters and keep the region on a boil. The corridor has a multitude of external and internal challenges like illegal migration, counterfeit, narcotics, and cross-border smuggling of animals and wildlife products.

Dynamics of the Siliguri Corridor

The Siliguri Corridor is approximately a 200-km stretch in length with the width varying from 17 to 60 km. It is also aptly referred to as Chicken's Neck and measures approximately 12,203 sq. km. The eastern part of the corridor is wider and borders Bhutan and Bangladesh. The Chumbi Valley tapering into the Dolam/Doklam plateau is barely 50 to 100 km away, depending on contrasting boundary claims. While it is approximately 50 km as the crow flies, in such hilly and wooded terrain, large-scale movement is restricted and is confined along beaten paths/tracks. Mapping the corridor is a challenge as its limits are a matter of interpretation. The corridor is criss-crossed by streams like Teesta, Rangeet, Mahananda, Torsa, and a large number of *nallahs* and rivulets. Please refer to the maps at the end of this article. The corridor has a large number of reserve forests and plenty of wildlife, like elephants, and it also serves as a migration corridor for them. The corridor is defined by low hills, jungles, and broken ground dotted with numerous rivers, streams, and *nallahs,* thereby posing multiple obstacles and formidable defence lines.

Terrestrial communication from the mainland to the North-East is based on a double-line broad gauge rail link. That is complemented by two National highways, which also provide a gateway to Bhutan through the twin townships of Jalgaon and Phuntsholing. In addition, vital hydrocarbon pipelines pass through this stretch along with communication links based on Optical Fibre

Communication (OFC). The corridor has two major airbases—Bagdogra and Hashimara. In addition, the army aviation base at Shaugaon is also planned to be operationalised. A large number of army and CAPF installations and their HQs, including a Corps HQ, are located in this narrow stretch. In keeping with the 'one border, one force' policy, the responsibility of borders is divided between the army and the ITBP for China, the Sashastra Seema Bal (SSB) for Nepal and Bhutan, and Bangladesh with the BSF. The multiplicity of forces and agencies requires an effective and tailor-made coordination mechanism. Most of the border, except for Bangladesh, is unfenced and porous with treacherous riverine stretches. Tea, timber, and tourism are the main drivers of economic activity, controlled from Siliguri, which is the de facto capital of North Bengal with regional headquarters and associated offices. The booming city is also becoming a trading and medical tourism hub for neighbouring countries, as well as a skill provider based on education centres located in hill towns in the vicinity.

Kaliachak in Malda, in proximity, notorious for criminal activities, is the hub of counterfeit trafficking, narco-terrorism, and bomb-making. Uncontrolled migration from Bangladesh has complicated demographics, and radical Islamist groups and madrasas have proliferated with the tacit support of government agencies. Adding to the complexity are non-indigenous Meitei and Bodo settlements, which provide shelter to cadres, in addition to the United Liberation Front of Assam and Kamtapur Liberation Organisation (KLO) utilising it for transit as was highlighted in Operation 'All Clear' in South Bhutan in December 2003. Simmering the Gorkhaland problem coupled with the Kamatapur insurgency has made this region a potential target for hybrid warfare. Insurgency in Cooch Bihar is of low order and follows twin tracks of demand for Kamatapur and Rajbongshi causes. These movements are sustained due to the support of other groups, who often seek shelter in parts of Southern Bhutan in collusion with KLO and other such splinter groups. These groups have also maintained linkages with Bhupalese

(Nepali origin) elements settled in Southern Bhutan. However, Gorkhaland is a much more serious issue. The obvious question is, why should we allow it to become an Achilles heel in our geo-strategic calculus and this critical space? More of the Gorkhaland problem is discussed in the next part.

Parameters of the Gorkhaland Problem

Gorkhas, early settlers from Nepal, migrated in the seventeenth century as part of the expansion of the Nepali kingdom and made the hills their homeland. In 1777, Nepal appropriated Sikkim, including the Darjeeling district. Settlers leveraged their entrepreneurial skills and took over Sikkim and adjoining Darjeeling, marginalising native Lepchas and Bhutias. The treaty of Sugali in 1816 brought these areas under the British rule.

Gorkhas first articulated the demand for a separate administrative unit in 1907 through the Hillmen Association. However, it didn't find critical traction. The Gorkha National Liberation Front (GNLF), under an ex-soldier, Subash Ghising, gave the movement a new lease in the 80s. This led to the establishment of the Darjeeling Gorkha Hill Council in 1988 after a violent phase from 1986 to 1988, which claimed 1,200 lives. The GNLF ruled for 20 years with a say in economic development, tourism, and culture. Following in the mould of militant turned failed leaders like Laldengs, Ghising got virtually booted out in 2008 and was a non-entity till his demise. His legacy was appropriated by Bimal Gurung and Roshan Giri under the Gorkha Janmukti Morcha (GJM), surprisingly riding the popularity wave for Indian Idol candidate Prakash Tamang. After the second wave of agitation lasting three years, a modified council, the Gorkha Territorial Administration (GTA), was established in August 2012 with an enhanced mandate and an additional five mouzas (revenue units corresponding to different villages), notionally enlarging the geographical scope into Dooars. Gorkhaland, demanded by the protagonists, combines hill tracts of Darjeeling, Kalimpong, and Mirik with Dooars, which is a relatively plain area with low rolling hills.

The dilution from the original demand of 398 mouzas to just five and the non-inclusion of tea revenue indicated that the problem is likely to fester. Notwithstanding the fact that the number of departments under the GTA has increased from 19 to 59, real delegation never happened. The ruling party in Bengal decided to utilise the British trick of divide and rule by instituting councils and boards for Lepchas, Sherpas, Bhutias, Tamangs, and other communities. Buoyed by the recent success of Trinamool Congress (TMC) in Mirik municipal elections and on the verge of GTA elections due in July, Chief Minister Mamta made the ill-advised move of declaring Bangla as an additional language in the hills. The motive behind this move was revealed in the immediate rescinding of the decision, but it gave the GJM an escape route as it was starting at a possible Ghising moment due to its failure on all fronts. However, a large share of the blame lies with the state government. Currently, there is an uneasy truce with Bimal Gurung going into hiding consequent to being declared a proclaimed offender. The dissenting faction is running an interim arrangement till elections, which have been delayed indefinitely.

Gorkhas deserve our gratitude and understanding for their loyalty as they have made unparalleled sacrifices in many wars, starting from the legendary Maharaja Ranjit Singh, but more importantly, they need committed leaders. The state that they want is hardly economically viable but can find negative resonance and cause economic disruption in neighbouring states like Sikkim and even Bhutan, where the Bhupalese (Nepalese settled in Bhutan) issue has caused its own share of problems. The governance and development of such a sensitive strip **is a national responsibility and obligation; however, it has been conspicuous by near total absence. It is high time the state government, aided by the Centre, calms down frayed tempers in the hills and establishes a genuine and functional autonomous administration, as they have made unparalleled sacrifices in various campaigns.**

Update – North Bengal

There is an emergence of a demand for the division of West Bengal into North and South Bengal provinces. This **demand, though politically motivated, has the potential for better security management if a union territory is carved out around the Siliguri Corridor and borders. It needs to be taken cognizance of for the possibility of consideration in the future.** Similarly, for political reasons again, Lepcha and Bhutia councils were being recommended in the ambit of GTA to dilute the Gorkhaland movement. **Any new measure needs to be carefully deliberated and executed after due consensus building.**

Chumbi Valley and Doklam

Chumbi is a dagger-shaped valley, broad at the top and narrowing down to barely 15 to 20 km at the southern tip in the TAR, China. The valley is on the south side of the Himalayan drainage divide, near the Chinese border sandwiched between Sikkim (India) and Bhutan. The Chumbi Valley is connected to Sikkim to the southwest via the mountain passes of Cho La, Nathu La, Jelep La, Batang La, and Doka La from north to south. While Jalep La is controlled by the Chinese, Nathu La is managed jointly by both countries. Three passes of Cho La, Batang La, and Doka La are controlled exclusively by India. The valley is at an altitude of 3,000 m (9,800 ft) and, being on the south side of the Himalayas, enjoys a wetter and more temperate climate than most of Tibet. It is on one of the primary routes between India and Tibet; hence, the Chumbi Valley has been at the forefront of several military expeditions like the Young Husband expedition. The British military expedition of 1904 occupied the Chumbi Valley for about three years after the hostilities to secure Tibetan payment of indemnity. Contemporary documents show that the British continued the occupation of the Chumbi Valley until February 1908, after having received payment from China. Since the valley is dominated on both flanks, the Chinese endeavour has been to increase its width with unilateral claims, as a narrow valley restricts manoeuvre and deployment. China has already unilaterally extended its control in the east up to its claim line. Towards the south, the Chinese quest is being mounted through the Doklam tri-junction to gain a foothold on Jampheri ridge as a launch pad.

Dolam

Dolam, as referred to by India and Bhutan, is called Dolam/Donglang by the Chinese and Zhoglam in Standard Tibetan. It is an area with a plateau and a valley, sandwiched between Tibet's Chumbi Valley to the north, Bhutan's Ha Valley to the east, and India's Sikkim State to the west. While traditionally, it has been depicted as part of Bhutan in the Bhutanese and other maps since 1961, it is also claimed by China. To date, the dispute has not been resolved despite several rounds of border negotiations between Bhutan and China. The area is of strategic importance to all three countries due to its proximity to the Siliguri Corridor and because it also provides launch pads into Sikkim and Bhutan.

Humphrey Hawksley's *Dragon Fire* and *The Assassin's Mace* by Brigadier Bob Butalia outline a scenario of the Dragon using the Chumbi Valley through Doklam and Jaldhaka to cut off the corridor. The recent 73-day standoff at the Doklam (also referred to as Dolam) plateau was a stark projection of the Chinese desire to build a road from the Chumbi Valley across Torsa Nallah to the Bhutanese Chela post to gain a foothold on Jampheri ridge with a view to threaten the Siliguri Corridor (please refer to maps in the previous article on Sino-Bhutan border dispute).

Way Forward – Siliguri Corridor: Reducing Vulnerability

Defence of the Corridor: The Siliguri Corridor, with low hills, jungles, and broken ground dotted with numerous rivers, provides multiple formidable defence lines. **Various possible scenarios with associated forms of threats like airborne raids have been war-gamed many times with the devil given more than its due, but in every such exercise and simulation, the Dragon is not only stymied short of the corridor but the stage is set for quid pro quo options. While India certainly does not want war for such an eventuality, troops, including mechanised forces, are not only earmarked but are regularly rehearsed.**

Managing Internal Fault Lines: It is absolutely important to deal with internal fault lines, most notably Gorkhaland, and to some extent, Kamatapur and Rajabongshi in the corridor on priority and not allow this to be exploited by external players and intelligence agencies. It is also important to follow a zero-tolerance policy towards narcotics, counterfeit, and other illegal activities. State governments should rise above narrow interests, like in the case of sharing Teesta water in lean season through the Farakka barrage, to accommodate the interests of Bangladesh and forge better ties, which can open possibilities for transit corridors.

Inter-Agency and Force Coordination: There is a need to have a clear-cut division of responsibilities between security, intelligence agencies, and Border Guarding Forces to set up efficient coordination mechanisms. Problems of illegal migration, cattle smuggling, narco-terrorism, and trafficking of counterfeit wildlife products need to be managed efficiently.

Theatre Dynamics: In the Eastern theatre, India is likely to engage in three separate sub-theatre battles in respective Corps Zones due to terrain configuration. The primary defensive architecture with inbuilt reserves is already in place. Newly raised Mountain Corps can be applied to further stabilise and even create limited quid pro quo options. Strategic airlift capability can be utilised to induct additional reserves. Even with attrition on communication links, at worst, there can be partial degradation but certainly not disruption, for a lot has been changing since 1962 in terms of building of infrastructure and force levels by India and also a will to stand up to the bullying China, which was displayed in ample measure at Doklam. The requirement is to boost this dissuasive capability with additional surveillance, mechanised forces, air defence, and surveillance resources. There is also a requirement to have a separate designated HQ for the defence of the corridor with multi-agency coordination.

Building Redundancies: Risk mitigation dictates focused investment in strategic storage for critical commodities like hydrocarbons and munitions to boost the sustenance capability of Eastern theatre to reduce dependence on the corridor. The overall thrust should be to reduce the salience of the corridor.

Alternative Connectivities: There is a need to invest in the 'Act East' policy to link North-East to the ASEAN, thereby reducing dependence on the mainland. The success of this policy is predicated on maintaining amicable relations with neighbours, especially Bhutan, Bangladesh, and Myanmar. There is also a need to invest in alternative connectivities, such as the Sittwe-Kaladan multi-modal project, which has been inordinately delayed, like the much-touted tri-lateral friendship highway connecting India, Myanmar, and Thailand.

Bangladesh Corridor: A very viable project is the transit corridor through Bangladesh, as sustenance on aerial bridges, even in emergencies, has limited potential. **Contagious to the corridor is a long-pending project of Tetuliya Hink (4 km) through Bangladesh, which has the potential to reduce vulnerability and transit distance.** The security of the region is linked to partnerships with neighbours, particularly Bangladesh, for which early resolution of the Farakka/Teesta dispute is mandatory. All these factors, cumulatively applied, have the potential to reduce the salience of the corridor.

Operationalising 'Act East' Policy: India is showing increasing focus and interest in regional groupings oriented towards the east, like BBIN (Bangladesh, Bhutan, India, and Nepal), BIMSTEC (Bay of Bengal Initiative for Multi-Sectoral Technical and Economic Cooperation), and now ASEAN. India needs to build on the diplomatic coup of getting ten ASEAN heads of state as chief guests for Republic Day by graduating from symbolism to concrete measures like the swift conclusion of the Regional Comprehensive Economic Partnership (RCEP).

Indo-Pacific Switch: India needs to partner with Pacific countries by joining the Asia Pacific Economic Cooperation (APEC) and further strengthening the Quad grouping forged with the USA, Japan, and Australia.

Conclusion

The Siliguri Corridor is an important strategic space; in fact, it is critical. If handled well and leveraged with our resilience and capabilities, it can ensure that it does not become our Achilles heel or critical vulnerability. Since aggressively rising China is showing interest in this space and region, we need to apply a range of measures to build up our strategic deterrence from persuasive to credible deterrence. It is axiomatic that we build our capabilities and infrastructure and also forge regional linkages to reduce dependence on the corridor.

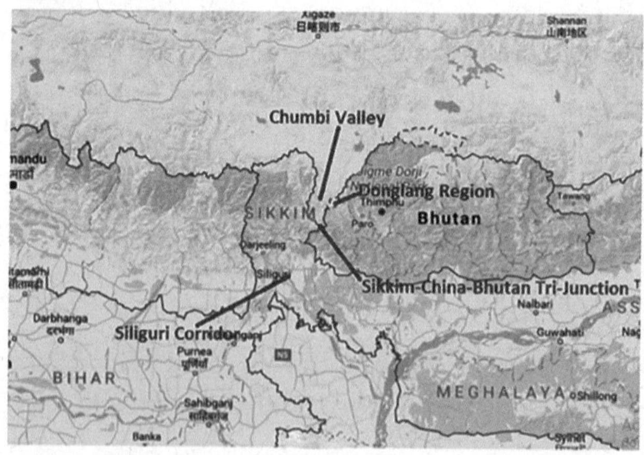

(Credits- Wiki maps and The Telegraph, Kolkata)

Relevance of Mechanised Warfare-countering Drones and Chinese Tanks in High Altitude

Drones-Top Attack and Armoured Warfare: Relevant or Outdated?

Abstract

Tanks and armoured platforms have suffered very high attrition in the recent conflicts in Ukraine, Azerbaijan, and Syria, which have been amplified in the media. Consequently, this has triggered serious debate on the very relevance of armoured warfare. **Tanks have traditionally been described and viewed as a sort of silver bullet; however, their limitations have been exposed by low-cost, armed drones attacking in 'top attack' mode. Defying the sceptics, Israel has recently fielded Merkava-Mk 4-Barak, duly fortified, against drone attacks.** Hence, it may be premature to write the obituary of tank and armoured warfare itself. It is imperative to carry out an objective appraisal of the efficacy of Armoured Fighting Vehicles (AFVs) as fighting platforms and examine the continued relevance of armoured warfare. Concurrently, relevant improvements in operational philosophy, employment, training, and design to prosecute armoured warfare more effectively in contemporary battlefield environments need to be identified. It is also imperative to examine their relevance and applicability in our environment. **While most experts anchor the debate on demise of tank, but drones pose similar threat to all mounted platforms, hence it may be relevant to look at demise of all mechanised platforms like self-propelled guns, air-defence systems and combat support platforms.**

Introduction

Hybrid warfare, with its growing relevance and largely being contested in urban environments, has exposed the limited efficacy of Armoured Fighting Vehicles AFVs in this genre of warfare. It has even prompted a few experts to opine that tank, like the Walkman (discarded audio device of yore), have become obsolete. This concern has been amplified due to statistics of inordinately high tank casualties in recent conflicts like Ukraine, Nagorno-Karabakh (Azerbaijan), Syria, and Libya. **The success of armed drones has exposed the vulnerability of tanks against munitions in top-attack mode. The relative cost differential of tanks compared to considerably cheaper drones and even anti-tank missiles has magnified concerns amongst the strategic community.** It has become possible to saturate battle space, especially restricted urban ones, with drones and portable anti-tank weapons. Various conflicts have witnessed the fielding of disruptive technologies in the form of anti-tank missiles, remotely delivered mines, attack helicopters and armed drones, and loitering munitions, which seek to challenge the conventional hierarchy and invincibility of established weapon platforms in the new paradigm of asymmetric warfare.

It will be pragmatic to carry out an empirical analysis of the relevance of armoured warfare and AFVs, as the premature sounding of the death knell will put ongoing research and development on hold. In our context, we have large, armoured formations deployed on Western borders. In addition, recently, many tanks were deployed in Ladakh and Sikkim at high altitudes. They were even applied in the vanguard of the pre-emptive occupation of the Kailash ranges. India and her potential adversaries (China and Pakistan) have very large fleets of AFVs and have shown no inclination to discard them. India has also recently launched a project to develop a light tank, Zorawar, in response to the fielding of a light tank, ZTQ-15, by PLA opposite us in Ladakh in a high-altitude environment, indicating our continued commitment to armoured warfare.

Preview

The subject is discussed in the following parts:

a) Armoured Warfare – Early Trends
b) Anti-Tank – Emergence of Challenges
c) Performance Appraisal in Recent Conflicts
d) Specific Issues Relevant to Our Environment
e) Recommended Way Forward

Armoured Warfare – Early Trends

Quest for Silver Bullet: Starting with spears, shields, bow-arrows, gun-powder, and chariots, the quest for super weapons has been shaped along movement (manoeuvre), firepower for lethality, and protection for survivability as the three key determinants for designing and development of weapons. Armed Forces propelled by innovations, industrial revolutions, and military-industrial complexes tend to strive for the magical 'silver bullet' to secure decisive results on the battlefield. In the terrestrial domain, the quest started with elephants, horses, and chariots, progressing to mechanical locomotion coupled with protected, armoured platforms. Tank was described as the game-changer in its appearance on the battlefield of Somme in 1916. Armoured warfare in great world wars was introduced as the answer to static trench warfare designed around the Maginot and Siegfried lines. Armoured battles have often been hyped up in war movies in Rambo-type imagery of the tank being the ultimate terminator.

Design Parameters: Tanks combine three key elements of mobility (agility), firepower (lethality), and protection (survivability) in varying proportions, reflecting the warfighting and design philosophy of stakeholders. The stress is to design a lighter (more agile) platform carrying a big calibre gun and missiles, with all-round protection. **Yet, it finally turns out to be an optimised, compromised product, balancing conflicting macro determinants and even**

adjustments within each key design attribute. This explains the current vulnerability of tanks against top-attack munitions due to the emphasis on protecting the frontal arc, leaving the top portion of the platform (turret) relatively vulnerable. Different countries accord varying importance to design parameters. Germans advocate agile platforms, citing mobility (agility) aids survivability as the governing paradigm. In contrast, Israel, with a premium on human resources, gives protection overriding importance, fielding much heavier tanks, even putting engines in front, for additional protection.

Russian Tank-Design Philosophy: Russia follows an **evolutionary design** concept with incremental improvements. Chinese have cloned this approach. These tanks have lower and rounded silhouettes. In order to curtail weight, they have opted for auto-loader and ammunition stowage in the crew compartments. This has caused horrific incidents of turrets getting yanked off and ammunition infernos in fighting compartments. In contrast, Western nations have ammunition stored in special compartments/pods, with blow-off panels shielding crews.

Combined Arms and Joint Operations Concept: Tanks were designed to be utilised as part of an integrated warfighting matrix, referred to as a combined arms team or integrated battle groups (IBGs), in a joint operations regime. Combined Arms, as a term, is all-inclusive and incorporates combat support and logistics elements. They are certainly not stand-alone weapon platforms. Hence, it is more appropriate to use 'AFV' instead of 'tank' as a term. Even where the term tank is used in this paper, it includes relevant implications to the connected AFV family. Over the years and driven by combat experience, the family of AFVs has grown with the spawning of newer complementary variants like infantry fighting vehicles (IFVs), reconnaissance/amphibious variants, combat support (firepower, Air Defence (AD), combat engineering, and network management) platforms, duly supported by logistics carriers. The bottom line and defining paradigm for armoured warfare has been fighting as part of a well-integrated matrix in combined arms and joint operations template, duly supported by timely and responsive logistics. Matching mobility, complimentary firepower, and shared protection have been key drivers, reflected in variants like self-propelled (SP) tracked guns, mounted AD carriers, half-tracked and even high mobility wheeled vehicles like Stryker's, currently on offer by the USA. Unlike India, many modern armies invariably have a complement of AFVs with infantry, especially those deployed in plains and deserts. Israeli Merkava can carry up to eight infantry soldiers, making it a unique combo platform.

Operating Paradigms: In armoured warfare, the emphasis is on manoeuvre to **generate surprise and shock action.** It is ideally prosecuted in open terrain to leverage attributes of mobility and long ranges. Combined Arms Teams, dispersion, and inexorable manoeuvre have been the overriding parameters. The complexity of multiple platforms over large, dispersed battle space has resulted in the incorporation of battlefield management and situational awareness systems. These are based on optronics (optics and electronic sensors), making it the fourth key design ingredient. Despite multiple lethal and long-range vectors, **AFVs have the unique capability to manoeuvre and close in with the target, projecting protected, vectored firepower to directly deliver shock and awe, triggering psychological dislocation.** Over the years, the large fleets of AFVs—Russia (12,000), the USA (6,300), China (5,900), Pakistan (2,500), and India (4,300)—provide ample proof of the proliferation of this concept. Even Bangladesh recently acquired Chinese VT5 medium tanks. This large global inventory is backed by a proven combat track record and performance, albeit peppered with some recent reverses.

Anti-Tank – Emergence of Challenges

Yom-Kippur War (1973): The Sinai War of 1973 was one of the largest deployments of mechanised formations after World War

II (WW2). IDF fielded approximately a thousand Israeli armoured vehicles against 2,400 AFVs of Arab forces. **This war witnessed the introduction of wire-guided, first-generation Russian Malyutka (AT-3 Sagger) missiles as cost-effective anti-tank weapon systems.** It also highlighted Israeli crew proficiency, enabling them to hold off superior Russian T-62s and T-55s with their older Centurions and M-48 tanks in Golan Heights. **Israelis also displayed commendable skills in retrofitting and recovery during combat to resuscitate damaged tanks, sometimes fielding 60 to 70 per cent repaired AFVs in a 24-hour cycle.** This was based on classifying AFVs as, firstly, M-kills (only locomotion impaired but utilised as pill-boxes); secondly, F-kills (armament non-functional but capable of movement), and very few K (complete) kills. Even K-kills were scrounged to source functional components for cannibalisation. Conflict also highlighted the efficacy of the integration of weapons as part of combined arms and joint operations, including aircraft, AD, tanks, missiles, and artillery. The relative dominance of AFVs was challenged by a decisive reiteration of relatively economical 'anti-tank' in the form of anti-tank missiles, munitions, and mines.

Gulf War 1 (1991): Coalition forces, in 1991, in Gulf War-1 (Operation Desert Storm), a multi-nation offensive anchored by the USA, employed as many as 3,000 tanks, including 1772 Abrams (594 with heavy armour). This fleet also included 180 Challengers, M-60, AMX-30, and lighter Sheridan tanks clad with aluminium. Asymmetry created by multiple force multipliers like the Patriot AD system and bypassing manoeuvre in desert terrain rendered Iraqi defences completely ineffective. **Defining manoeuvres enabled columns to advance 350 km in 97 hours.** As per reliable accounts, Iraq lost 3,300 AFVs against just 31 of the Coalition forces. This war highlighted the relevance of IBGs, led by mechanised forces, especially in open desert terrain.

Gulf War 2 (2003 to 2011): In stark contrast, Gulf War 2 in 2003, **after initial success catalysed by technical asymmetry with**

force multipliers, including AFVs, degenerated into slogging hybrid war for eight years till 2011. It underscored the limited efficacy of AFVs in counter-insurgency and urban fighting. Skilful use of anti-tank weapons contributed to negating asymmetry and conflict, degenerating into a prolonged unresolved stalemate, where multi-national forces and Americans were forced to seek face-saving exits. Success in Gulf War 1 and the initial phase of Gulf War 2 spurred a debate on Revolution in Military Affairs (RMA); however, it got eroded to a considerable extent in Gulf War 2, particularly due to forces getting bogged into a quagmire in slogging hybrid war.

Lebanon Conflict (2006): Anti-tank tactics were successfully employed by Hezbollah against the mighty Merkava 4M tanks in 2006 in Southern Lebanon. **Fifty-two such platforms, each costing $2.5 million, were hit and disabled by Kornet missiles and even basic rockets, costing just $900 per piece.** This was despite Israel adopting the revolutionary concept of putting engines in front to bolster protection. Out of this array, missiles and rockets made it difficult for tanks to operate in urban milieu, where tanks lost their stand-off leverage due to restricted fields of fire. Consequently, the ill-fated Operation Change of Direction was called off mid-way due to heavy casualties and dented the famed invincibility of IDF, particularly its signature platform, Merkava 4M. Over-reliance on Merkava tanks proved suicidal for the IDF. The lessons of this conflict were reinforced in the concurrent unresolved Gulf War 2 due to the similarity of terrain, weapons, and tactics.

Tank and Anti-Tank: Anti-tank warfare arrays have seen the introduction of 'top-attack' by long-range vectors like artillery-delivered Krasnopol, guided bombs, and remotely delivered mines. Attack helicopters and armed drones have boosted this capability. The modern tank costs Rs 75–80 crores, whereas drones cost approximately Rs 40 lakhs, and missiles cost just a fraction. This also gives a bit of David vs Goliath characterisation to this contestation. **Low-cost and versatile anti-tank weapons can be used to saturate**

the confined urban battle space. In urban milieu, tanks lose their advantages of manoeuvre and long ranges. AFVs have sought to boost their protection by improvising the Tank Urban Survival Kit (TUSK) and Built-up Area Survival Kit (BUSK). Kits incorporate cage-like structures comprising spaced slat claddings and flails. AFVs also incorporated Explosive Reactive Armour (ERA) panels and grenade launchers, which disrupt penetrative jets of High Explosive Anti-Tank (HEAT) attacks. Automated Active Protection Systems (APSs) like ARENA, Shtora, and Trophy, though expensive, are also being incorporated to detect and degrade threats to AFVs. It would be seen that, like a cat and mouse game, every new disruptive effect or weapon triggers an antidote. At best, asymmetrical advantage like the current one in favour of armed drones is only temporary till it is offset by an effective antidote.

Performance Appraisal in Recent Conflicts

Nagorno-Karabakh (2021). Inordinately heavy casualties suffered by Armenian tanks fuelled concerns about the vulnerability of Russian tanks, particularly against Byraktar TB2, Turkish-supplied drones. It was reported that Armenia lost as many as 255 tanks. 146 (approximately 57 per cent) were completely destroyed as K-kills. Of these 146 K-kill tanks, 83 (nearly 57 per cent) were destroyed by Bayraktar TB2, operated by Azerbaijan forces. Others were partially damaged (F or M-kills) by a combination of TB2 strikes, artillery shelling, and anti-tank guided missiles. It bears reiteration that most targets were located by aerial and drone surveillance. Some other Armenian tanks were also destroyed by loitering munitions. The stage for unprecedented destruction was set by the creation of asymmetry in the opening gambit by Azerbaijan in the very first hour, destroying approximately 60 per cent of AD and 40 per cent of artillery. The **resultant air superiority gave armed drones a virtually free run against tank columns, which were bunched up, ignoring basic tactics of dispersion, camouflage, and concealment.** While acknowledging the efficacy of armed drones, it is pragmatic to place on record that Armenia's AD system was inadequate to defend its AFVs and artillery guns from Azerbaijan's airpower, including drones.

Important Trends – Ukrainian Conflict. While it may be a bit premature to draw conclusive inferences/lessons from the ongoing and unresolved Ukrainian imbroglio, a few indicative trends need to be examined. Mandatory caution is also necessitated due to the absence of impartial, objective reporting and info-war characterised by narrative shaping. Inferences applicable to armoured warfare are as follows:

a) The **operation described as a special operation by Russia was planned in utmost secrecy and lacked consultative planning.** In mechanised operations, instructions in the form of briefings have to be disseminated to junior leaders.

b) The **objectives of the operation were not only highly optimistic but also rigid, lacking any fallback options.**

c) The Russian offensive defied the key terrain parameter of the **bogging effect of 'Rasputista', also described as General Mud or Marshal Mud.** The thawing snow combined with mud prevented manoeuvres and forced movement on linear road axes.

d) The **Russian movement was designed along too many linear axes, widely separated and without mutual support.** These long linear columns had no dispersion, providing easy bunched-up targets, much like Nagorno-Karabakh.

e) **Russian crews lacked motivation and abandoned their platforms.** Even senior leadership was found wanting, leading to the sacking of many senior commanders.

f) The Russian offensive relied too heavily on mechanised columns, **ignoring the seminal reality of the combined arms concept.** Most notable was the lack of infantry to secure and clear areas.

g) The Russian offensive had **inadequate logistics backup** as it was based on the hope of capitulation by the Ukrainians. An apt example was the abandonment of a large number of functional T-80 tanks with gas turbine engines due to a temporary shortfall in special fuel replenishment.

h) In sum, it appears that large platforms, fighter aircraft, tanks, and ships didn't deliver, leading to these being described even as obsolescent. **In the domain of mechanised operations, drones, anti-tank missiles (Javelins), and artillery barrages emerged as effective anti-tank shields.**

Objective Evaluation of High Russian Tank Losses. An objective comparative analysis of losses has to wait, but an indicative (preliminary) one reveals few trends. As per estimates of Mossad and Oryx blog, Russia suffered 994 tank losses. These included 334 AFVs (approximately 34 per cent) simply abandoned. This implies that abandoned AFVs were partially functional and were only M or F-kills and not K-kills. In the first month of the offensive itself, 53 per cent of losses were abandoned platforms by demotivated crews. Many platforms were first abandoned and later destroyed by Ukrainians and often by the civil populace. It would be fair to surmise that approximately 50 per cent of Russian tank losses can be ascribed to crews abandoning them, much unlike Israeli crews, who fought with partially damaged tanks and carried out amazing repairs and resuscitation during operations. In Chechnya in 1999–2000, the Russian Army lost 122 out of 146 tanks and infantry fighting vehicles due to a similar lack of motivation and ignoring basic tactics. Concurrently, it is estimated that Ukraine may have lost approximately 6,320 AFVs again due to confusion, capitulation, and Russian fire assaults. **Notwithstanding losses, the continued relevance of AFVs is being reiterated on both sides by seeking and fielding more platforms, like Leopard tanks and T-90s. However, drones seem to hold an upper edge.**

Specific Issues Relevant in Our Context

The large stretch of open terrain in the form of desert, plains, and plateaus in high altitudes provide an ideal template for the employment of AFVs. Unlike many other countries, India doesn't routinely employ tanks in counter-insurgency warfare. Starting with the 1947 operations, Stuart tanks were hauled across Zoji La pass by intrepid crews after stripping and re-assembling turrets across the formidable pass. They proved to be game-changers, exploiting legendary 'jugaad' (improvisation), resourcefulness, and dedication of Indian crews to their weapons and platforms. In the 1965 war, Pakistan based its plan on the stratagem of fielding an otherwise hidden second armoured division (6 Armoured Division), raised in secrecy and utilised the latest American M48 (Patton) tanks against old Indian tanks—Centurions, Shermans, and AMXs. Once again, our crews devised a simple yet effective three-round technique to create a graveyard of Patton tanks, appropriately christened Patton Nagar. While Indian crews improvised, Pakistanis fumbled with optical coincidence range finders. In 1971, operations again took place on both fronts. Mechanised columns were in the vanguard, duly supported by all arms columns. Indian crews overcame boggy terrain and optimised even medium tanks, T-55s. In the final push, the audacious utilisation of amphibious PT-76 tanks across the Meghna River and heli-lift of troops, coupled with para-drops, enabled the capture of Dacca.

Indian sub-continent boasts of approximately 13,000 AFVs with PLA, leading with 5,900 and in collusion with 2,500 of Pakistan against 4,300 Indian AFVs. Pakistan, Bangladesh, Myanmar, and Sri Lanka have Chinese-supplied equipment. This provides China with a base for life-cycle support and modernisation in India's neighbourhood. Pakistan's Heavy Industry Plant, Taxilla, and Ordnance Factory, Wah, have a very large Chinese presence. China plays a significant role in the production and modernisation of Al-Zarar and Al-Khalid tanks and other Pak AFVs. Notwithstanding disquiet and erosion of confidence in AFVs, their relevance in the Indian subcontinent is likely to endure due to large inventories and ongoing modernisation programmes. **It bears reiteration that the life spans and efficacy of AFVs need to be enhanced by following the Israeli model of retrofitting and upgradation.**

India has also made a switch from large mechanised columns aiming for deep thrusts to IBGs with shallow objectives. These objectives are below the nuclear threshold. PLA has recently fielded their version of the light tank, ZTQ-15, optimised for high altitude operations, thereby triggering the Indian light tank programme for Zorawar. In the recent pre-emptive securing of Kailash ranges, medium tanks were in the vanguard, with our skilled crews even defying conventional power-to-weight ratio ceilings in audacious QPQ operations. It is also important to take into account the fact that the performance of drones is degraded due to environmental challenges at high altitudes. APS is being incorporated into modernisation programmes to minimise top-attack threats by drones. Hence, AFVs, albeit modernised (to combat contemporary challenges), are likely to remain relevant in our battle space.

Recommended Way Forward

Armoured warfare is already witnessing an introspective churning in the organisation, employment, and design of platforms. The USA has already opted for lighter Stryker brigades. Marine Corps has de-activated tank battalions and transferred assets to the army. The UK Army has rolled back the Chieftain modernisation programme. Major shortcomings of Russian tanks, such as ammunition fires and turrets getting detached, are being addressed. **Russian Armata tanks have been drawn from the Swedish design of turret-less S-tanks, which involves putting crew in protected armoured capsules (pods) and incorporating unmanned turrets.** This design is also being refined in the US development proramme—Next Generation Combat Programme—and Decisive Lethality Platform. AbramX is experimenting with a much more agile tank powered by hybrid-electric diesel power plants, incorporating Artificial Intelligence (AI) technologies besides crew in the safe pod in the hull. Indicative trends identified in recent conflicts are already being incorporated into the design philosophy of AFV development. The same are also finding resonance in organisation, employment, and training. Even objectives are limited to shallow, attainable, and realistic ones

Conclusion

AFVs, in general, and tanks, in particular, have been utilised as main platforms in major battles and have witnessed periodic improvements and design changes. The recent conflicts have thrown up interesting trends, which should be validated and applied in our environment. These need to be utilised to refine our organisation's armoured warfare operational philosophy and as inputs in AFV development programmes. **In sum, armoured warfare and tanks may lose their salience but are likely to remain important platforms, more so if applied as part of combined arms teams and in joint operations format. The seminal paradigm is that all asymmetry is temporary and can be countered with resilience and countermeasures.** Armoured warfare is redefining itself with the incorporation of better surveillance and protection systems as part of battlefield management systems. It also is likely to see the introduction of autonomous platforms incorporating AI.

References

1. Sébastien Roblin, The Yom Kippur War Gave the World a Horrifying Glimpse of What a Modern Mechanized Warfare Would Look Like. *National Interest*, 1973, https://nationalinterest.org

2. Dave Roos, How Tanks Played a Critical Role in Persian Gulf War. *History*, 11 July 2022, https://www.history.com/news/tanks-abrams-persian-gulf

3. Rob Lee, The Tank is not Obsolete and other Observations about the Future of Combat. *War on the Rocks*, 6 September 2022, https://www.warontherocks.com

4. Lieutenant General AB Shivane, Eleven Big Lessons for the Employment of Tanks in Future Battlespace: The Russia-Ukraine Conflict. CLAWS Journal-Apr 2022

5. Lieutenant General KJ Singh, Have Light Tanks Become Irrelevant Like Walkman. Generals Jottings, TOI Chandigarh, https://timesofindia.indiatimes.com/blogs/generals-jottings/have-light-tanks-become-irrelevant-like-walkmans/

6. Lieutenant General KJ Singh, Relevance of Mechanised Forces and Tanks in Future Battle Space. Scholar Warrior-Autumn 2023, CLAWS New Delhi

7. Lieutenant General KJ Singh, Drone's Edge over Tanks only Temporary. *Tribune* Chandigarh

8. https://www.tribuneindia.com/news/features/drones-edge-over-tanks-only-temporary-568010

9. Lieutenant General KJ Singh, PLA Armour Offensive in Himalayas-

10. https://chanakyaforum.com/pla-armour-offensive-in-himalayas/

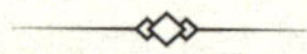

PLA Armour Offensive in Himalayas

(Written in May 2021)

Background

PLA executes its 'Three warfare' strategy spear-headed by an array of armoured formations in Ladakh. PLA exercises in the last few years have **included mechanised manoeuvres and heavy drops of armoured**

vehicles, as well as simulated the capture of passes and lightly held areas in high altitudes. It is widely reported that 6 Highland Mechanised Infantry Division and 4 Highland Motorised Infantry Division have deployed assorted AFVs—medium, light tanks, and heavy support equipment—across LAC in Ladakh to project their coercive messaging potential as part of psychological warfare.

At the very outset, it can be categorically stated that India has not only stalemated the situation but has also caused criticality for PLA by the pre-emptive occupation of dominating features on the Kailash Range. **The operation on the Kailash Range had mechanised elements in the vanguard and was in the face of massed PLA armour across the Spanggur gap.** According to informed experts' stalemate for initiators claiming to be global hegemony amounts to a loss.

Theme Setting

PLA has injected more versatility in their armoured fleet with the **introduction of the light tank ZTQ first fielded during the Doklam crisis.** Our BMP-2s, ICVs, duly integrated with medium tanks, can be adapted for some of the relevant tasks. The Chinese threat, though stemmed currently, could manifest again, and more such forays can't be ruled out. Hence, it was axiomatic that a review of the mechanised fleet was carried out to meet emerging challenges in the Himalayan sector. Consequently, a Request for Information (RFI) for 350 light tanks has been issued. Concurrently, customised modernisation of the existing fleet of medium tanks is also being fast-tracked.

PLA's Mechanised Profile in Tibet

6 Highland Mechanised Infantry Division and 4 Highland Motorised Infantry Divisions are orbatted with two Mechanised Infantry Regiments (Brigades) supported by an armoured regiment. Each Mechanised Infantry Regiment has four mechanised battalions. It has combat support elements – artillery, air defence regiments supported by engineers, EW, and CBRN Defence battalions. **The division has a reconnaissance battalion equipped with eighteen ZBD-04A infantry fighting vehicles armed with ATGMs.** Artillery and Air Defence and most other combat support equipment are tracked. Other associated equipment like helicopters, drones, and rocket artillery are grouped as per the envisaged tasking.

Comparative Evaluation – Medium Tanks

PLA medium tank battalions are equipped with **thirty-five ZTZ-99A (Type-99)** tanks or earlier versions like Type-96. Chinese tanks follow an evolutionary approach and are **reverse engineered** from original Russian models and cloned by China North Industries Corporation (NORINCO). **Their numbering has typical psychological hype attached. The T-54 clone is referred to as Type-59, and the T-90 equivalent as Type-99. The current lot of PLA medium tanks weigh around 55 tonnes, with 125-mm smooth bore guns and 1000 to 1200 HP engines.**

Our medium tanks, T-90s and T-72, in the right combination, are more than a match for these tanks. It is pertinent to highlight that numerically, four of our regiments can match five Chinese regiments, as our regiments have nearly 50 A vehicles. However, our mainstay, the T-72, needs to be equipped with an upgraded engine. **Additional power is required to compensate for the de-rating of engines by approximately 25% in high-altitude areas.** Russian tanks are customised to operate in extremely cold climates, but customised value additions like Auxiliary Power Units (APUs) have been identified as part of ongoing modernisation, including creating an ecosystem of heated garages and repair bays, which needs to be fast-tracked.

Comparison – Mechanised Infantry

PLA's mechanised infantry **is a mix of old tracked Type-86 ICVs, wheeled WZ-551 APCs (6×6) and a limited number of more**

contemporary VN-1 (8×8) ATGM carriers with Red Arrow missiles. Our BMP-2s are more than a match to PLA ICVs. **It is seen that the PLA infantry has got used to being transported and operates largely in motorised mode.** Although we enjoy a marginal edge in our ICVs, modernisation in terms of the **upgradation of the power pack** is a critical requirement for operation in high-altitude terrain to offset losses in engine power. While India follows the traditional philosophy of employment of infantry, largely without vehicles, the need is to give them some **protection and mobility in the form of mechanised/ motorised infantry**. It is indeed commendable that much-needed though belated correctives are underway with the induction of Kalyani M4, Mahindra ALSV, and TATA LAMV variants.

Appraisal – PLA Light Tank

China added considerable versatility to its mechanised fleet by fielding a light tank, **ZTQ-15, also referred to as Type-15 or Xinquingtan.** It is essentially a lighter medium tank with a weight of around 34 tonnes, amounting to a sort of hybrid between medium and light tanks. Classically, light tanks are generally in the sub-30 tonne class, ideally 25 tonnes, with a power-to-weight ratio (PWR) between 30 to 35. Type-15 has been fitted with extra wide tracks to offset additional weight and reduce Nominal Ground Pressure (NGP). PWR and NGP are key enablers for agility and trafficability in marginal terrain. To that extent, it is a compromise solution of sorts, especially in terms of protection, firepower, and mobility.

Type-15 has been utilised in heavy droppings, giving it an edge for utilisation in quick reaction forces. This tank was introduced in 2017, and 40 tanks have been supplied to Bangladesh, with 140 more in the pipeline. **The main features of this tank are 105-mm rifled guns and 1000 HP engine. Type-15, though hyped as a game changer, is neither really light nor a replacement for medium tanks, certainly not a panacea.** In keeping with Chinese reliance on incremental or evolutionary designs, this tank is a follow-up and replacement for antiquated Type-62 tanks.

History – Indian Light Tank: As is well known, we currently don't have a light tank in our inventory. Historically, light tanks had a defining and iconic role in 1947 operations when **Stuart tanks** were inducted across Zojila to stem raiders. AMX-13 was again utilised in Chusul in 1962. **We had Stuarts, Shermans, AMX-13, and assorted armoured cars in 1965 and earlier operations till the 70s. Russian PT-76 tanks, replacement of older light tanks, proved their mettle in the 1971 operations.** Light tanks have their utility in reconnaissance, scouting, and out-of-area contingencies, including peacekeeping operations. They can also be utilised in riverine, creeks/marshy backwaters, island territories, and coastal areas besides high-altitude terrain. **Light tanks, if applied audaciously and with imagination for reconnaissance in force, can open up the possibility for quid pro quo (QPQ) operations.**

Quest For Replacement Light Tank

After the de-induction of PT-76 tanks in 1989, half-hearted attempts to find a replacement were made, including trials of the Brazilian Urutu, the British Scorpion, and the French light tank in the late 80s. A formalised RFI for 200 wheeled and 100 tracked light tanks was promulgated again in 2009 as part of the build-up for Mountain Strike Corps. Major specifications were 22 tonnes with a gun calibre between 105 to 120 mm. A wheeled variant was to be an 8×8 or 6×6 configuration. However, this RFI was retracted. **Concurrently, DRDO has experimented with certain variants, utilising BMP chassis with a 105-mm gun as well as the French GIAT TS-90 chassis.** Even certain private manufacturers and DPSUs/Ordnance factories have produced prototypes in both wheeled and tracked versions. However, they have not found much traction.

Current RFI and Options

India has projected a requirement for **350 light tanks on a fast-track basis.** This would translate to six to seven regiments depending on equipping norms. It will be important to clarify that the requirement is for an 'Agile' tank with optimum balance between firepower and weight (light) yet with sufficient protection. Strategic mobility in terms of air portability is an added imperative enabling strategic mobility. The desired profile would be a tank of around 25 tonnes with a power-to-weight ratio of 30–35 and a gun calibre of 105–120 mm with missile firing and modern optronics. It is desirable to **have tracks with rubber shoes** to minimise damage to fragile communication arteries. Modernisation in terms of Active Protection System (APS), anti-drone measures and rubberised tracks could be incorporated later. **The overriding parameter is the ownership of not only TOT but also 'know-how' through co-development under the Atmanirbhar route.**

Options

A scan of global inventory generates a few options ranging from eight-wheeled Stryker variants, which were tried out in Yudh Abhyas series of joint exercises and even offered by the USA through the FMS route but not found suitable. Russia **has a 2S25 Sprut-SD light tank** weighing 18 tonnes, with a 125-mm SB gun and PWR of 28.3 hp/ton. These tanks have also been air-dropped in exercises. The **Israeli Sabrah tank** is in keeping with her protection-oriented philosophy, weighs 55 tonnes, and is only suited for desert terrain. Another viable line of development is to utilise expertise gained in the production of the **K-9 Vajra SP gun.** This is aligned with the South Korean **K21-105 Hanwaha tank.** This tank is a joint production endeavour with **Belgian John Cockerill Defence.** Prima facie, it can be tweaked to meet most RFI parameters, thereby adhering to stipulated deadlines. The details of this platform can be accessed on the web and company sites.

Recommendations

- **First and foremost, the requirement is to build a versatile family of 'A' vehicles with an optimum mix of medium and light tanks** with customised support equipment. Consequently, there is an urgent need to fast-track the development process for light tanks.

- Secondly, we need to find partners and achieve indigenisation and joint production.
- Thirdly, the existing fleet of medium tanks in high-altitude areas needs to be modernised, most importantly by upgrading their power packs.
- Fourthly, ageing ICVs should be given a much-needed upgrade package, including a power pack and a better protection system.
- Fifthly, an ecosystem for garages, training, and sustenance should be set up in these areas.
- Sixthly, infantry should be provided with protected high-mobility vehicles.
- Seventhly, the commonality of the platform should be attempted to reduce logistical challenges.

Zorawar – India's Light Tank: Is It Enough?

India has rolled-out Zorawar, described as Armoured Fighting Vehicle-Indian Light Tank (AFV-ILT) for trials and evaluation. The tank has been developed in fast-track mode in three odd years, after PLA fielded light tank and deployed them in Doklam in 2017 and in the ongoing unresolved imbroglio in Ladakh in 2020. Tank is named after the legendary, Dogra General, Zorawar Singh renowned for extending Sikh empire to Ladakh in 19th century. Implied in the name, is reiteration of Indian resolve as also confidence in growing defence manufacturing eco-system. The project has been mentored by DRDO and has utilised facilities and assembly line, developed by

L&T for K-9 Vajra Self-Propelled gun system at Hazira (Gujarat). Vajra has been developed in collaboration with South Korean, Hanwaha-Techwin. Zorawar (1.0) integrates available indigenous systems with Belgian, Cockerill turret with Cummins (750 HP) power-plants, sourced from USA. The original plan was for MTU engines (1,000 HP) from Germany, which are not available due to closing of German assembly line. The plan should be to graduate to various variants in series like-1.1; 1.2 and so on to make it both local (in content) and more potent with product improvement, to face ever growing contemporary challenges.

Appraisal – PLA Light Tank

It will be appropriate to take stock of the trigger, which has catalysed this development. China added considerable versatility to its mechanised fleet by fielding a light tank, ZTQ-15 also referred to as Type 15 or Xinquingtan. It is essentially, a lighter, medium tank with weight of around 34 tonnes, amounting to sort of hybrid between medium and light tanks. Classically, light tanks are generally in sub-30 tonne class, ideally 25 tonnes, with Power to weight ratio (PWR) between 30 to 35. German, Marder, weighing 28 tonnes had to use skirts to float. Type-15 has been fitted with extra wide tracks to offset additional weight and reduce Nominal Ground Pressure (NGP). **PWR and NGP are key enablers for agility and traffic-ability in marginal terrain. Most countries have utilised air-portability and floatation as key attributes.** To that extent, PLA tank is essentially sort of compromise solution, especially in terms of protection, fire power and mobility. Tank at best can wade or ford through but is not capable of floatation. However, it is relevant that most streams in Tibet can be negotiated without floatation.

Type 15 has been utilised in heavy droppings, giving it as an edge for utilisation in quick reaction forces. PLA has used it in multiple scenario-based exercises for capturing passes. This tank was introduced in 2017 and 40 tanks have been supplied to Bangladesh, with 140 more in pipeline. The main features of this tank are 105 mm rifled guns and 1000 HP engine. Type 15 though hyped as game changer is neither light nor replacement for medium tanks, certainly not panacea. In keeping with Chinese reliance on incremental or evolutionary designs, tank is follow-up and replacement for antiquated Type-62 tanks.

Brief History – Indian Light Tanks

As is well known, we currently don't have a light tank on our inventory. Historically, light tanks had defining and iconic role in 1947 operations, when Stuart tanks were inducted across Zojila to stem raiders. AMX-13 were again utilised in Chusul during 1962. We had Stuarts, Shermans, AMX-13 and assorted armoured cars in 1965 and earlier operations till 70s. Russian PT-76 tanks, replacement of older light tanks proved their mettle in 1971 operations. Light tanks have their utility in reconnaissance, scouting and out of area contingencies including peace keeping operations. They can also be utilised in riverine, creeks/marshy back waters, island territories and coastal areas besides high-altitude terrain. In our context, tank has utility in Ladakh, Sikkim, Siliguri Corridor, Rann of Kutch, amphibious, reconnaissance and peace-building roles. Light tanks, if applied audaciously and with imagination for reconnaissance in force, can open up possibility for Quid Pro Quo (QPQ) operations.

Quest For Replacement of Light Tank

After de-induction of PT-76 tanks in 1989, which I was privileged to crew, half-hearted attempts to find replacement were made including trials of Brazilian-Uruthu; British-Scorpion and French light tank in late 80s. Formalised RFI for 200 wheeled and 100 tracked light tanks was promulgated again in 2009 as part of build up for Mountain Strike Corps. Major specifications were 22 tons with gun calibre between 105 to 120 mm. Wheeled variant was to be 8×8 or 6×6 configuration. However, this RFI was retracted. Concurrently, DRDO has experimented with certain variants, utilising BMP chassis with 105 mm gun as also French GIAT TS-90 chassis. Even certain private manufacturers like TATA, Mahindra, Bharat Forge and DPSUs/ Ordnance factories have produced prototypes in both wheeled and tracked versions of protected platforms, finding limited but belated traction, like fielding of Bharat Forge-M-4 and Mahindra-LBPV.

Options and Current RFI

Scan of global inventory generated few options ranging from eight wheeled Stryker variants, which were tried out in Yudh-Abhyas series of joint exercises. These were pushed rather persistently by USA, for acquisition through FMS route, but not found suitable. Russia has 2S25 Sprut-SD light tank, weighing 18 tonnes, with 125 mm SB (low pressure) gun and PWR of 28.3 HP/Tonne. These tanks have also been air dropped in exercises; however, Russia has hesitated in fielding them in the ongoing Ukranian conflict. Israeli Sabrah tank is in keeping with her protection-oriented philosophy and weighs 55 tonnes and only suited for desert terrain. The most viable line of development is to utilise expertise gained in production of K-9 Vajra SP gun. **This is aligned with S Korean, K21-105 Hanwaha tank. This tank is joint production endeavour with Belgian, John Cockerill Defence. Prima-facie, it can be tweaked to meet most RFI parameters, thereby adhering to stipulated deadline.**

India has projected requirement for 364 light tanks on fast-track basis. This would translate to six to seven regiments depending on equipping norms. DRDO is slated to manufacture 59 tanks. The rest 295 will be manufactured under the Make-I category. Selection of development partner would be after competition, where Zorawar will also participate. It will have crew of three, implying fitment of auto loader. Besides main gun, platform will have machine guns to combat terrestrial and aerial threats. There is also stipulation for third generation ATGM, preferably fired from gun tube. The tank must be equipped with an active protection system (APS); explosive reactive armour (ERA); offensive and defensive electronic countermeasures (ECM); missile warning system; nuclear, biological, chemical (NBC) protection; 360° day-and-night cameras; a battle management system (BMS); and a hybrid navigation system. User is even looking for captive drone launching and counter-drone capability. Tank reportedly will have special tracks to minimize damage to fragile communication arteries, which are at a premium in such terrain.

Is Zorawar Enough?

The most important paradigm of mechanized warfare emphasised in recent conflicts is that tank is just a part, albeit an important one in combined arms and logistics system. It certainly is not the silver-bullet, it's vulnerability against top-attack delivered by drones, loitering munitions and ATGMs has even prompted many to question its continued utility. **Hence, it is important to reiterate that we need optimized mix of medium and light tanks supported by other platforms like ICVs, guns, AD for mitigating drone and aerial threats, combat support and logistics with matching mobility. Light Tank will have to fight as part of combined arms matrix.** Concurrently, there is imperative criticality to upgrade existing power-packs in T-72s and BMPs to compensate for de-rating of engine output, due to rarefied atmosphere. It is relevant to state that based on article and projections by author and few others in 2020-21, K9 SP gun has been fielded in Ladakh after high-altitude hardening.

Inevitably, in our development, there is worrying quest by the user to pitch for more features, leading to cascading delays, cost over-runs and design rebalancing. It will be prudent if user scales down aspirations and scales them at appropriate scale. Can drone launching capability limited to one AFV per squadron and structured on the support platform of Armoured Recovery Vehicle? Similarly, missile launchers can be scaled and optimized at suitable level. It is also recommended that developers should develop basic variant, with flexibility to strap-on customized add-ons. One such contraption could be cage like contraption with Slat and Spaced armour. Modernization, in terms of Active Protection System (APS), anti-drone measures and rubberized tracks could be incorporated later. The key challenges are developing indigenous engine of 1,000 HP and turret system. **Most importantly, overriding parameter is, ownership of not only TOT from foreign partners but also 'know-how' and 'know-why' through co-development under Atam-Nirbhar route.** Another challenge is to boost protection level as light tank has only basic protection and relies on agility, low signature and support by other accompanying platforms like medium tanks. One suggested line could be to develop composite armour with low density ceramics and metals/alloys, for optimising protection.

Two Front Threat

Dragon and the Tale

Key Takeaways

- **The proxy war by Pakistan, starting with the Kabayali raids in 1947, has been a persistent trend. Pak threat abetted by China is a challenge on the Western front.**
- **India has rebalanced its forces and created both defensive and limited counter-offensive capabilities against the Chinese threat.**

India in Amrit Kaal is gearing up to claim her rightful place on the global stage. This journey is marked by a multitude of challenges in the security domain. It is indeed appropriate to briefly map our conflicts to draw appropriate lessons. The 1947–48 war by the Pakistan Army masquerading as Kabayali raiders initially surprised the new nation. Analysts opine that the British were complicit in promoting the Pakistani plot to annex Jammu and Kashmir. It was also an attempt by Pakistan to gain salience to emerge as a compliant buffer state for colonial masters. India gained the upper hand due to resilience and innovative responses. The fielding of Stuart tanks across Zojila Pass by first stripping tanks and re-assembling them across the pass surprised the enemy and stemmed raiders. Similarly, daring air support missions by basic aircraft defined our operational jugaad. The 1962 war caught us completely unprepared, but we can draw some solace from the bravery of our soldiers at Rezang La. Five years later, in 1967, Indian troops imposed heavy casualties on the PLA in localised conflicts at Nathu La and Cho La.

The 1965 war was orchestrated by Pakistan, reportedly on the advice of the US Think Tanks to take advantage of their technical asymmetry based on modern American equipment. The latest Patton tanks and

Sabre jets were pitted against our obsolescent Centurion tanks and Gnats. Yet, our tank crews devised the 'three round' technique and air warriors and warded off superior Sabre jets. The 1971 war remains a high point in our operational history, characterised by the sequencing of a campaign to preclude Chinese intervention and the prioritisation of the Eastern front coupled with the bold application of air and naval forces. The Kargil War tested our capability to redeploy and marshal resources like the Bofors guns and retain control of the escalation matrix. The recent Balakot surgical strike and post-Uri coordinated surgical raids called off Pak's nuclear bluff and crafted space for conventional force application below the much-touted nuclear threshold. The most notable trend was the nuanced selection of targets and strategic messaging of Indian resolve to strike terror hubs beyond the LAC and even beyond Pakistan-occupied Kashmir (PoK).

Proxy War and the Two-Front Conundrum

The first seeds of proxy war were sown by Pakistan in the form of misplaced use of Kabayalis and instigation of revolt along religious lines in J&K State Forces in the 1947 war. The same diabolic plan was repeated in December 1963 with Moe-e-Muqaddas (holy hair relic of the Prophet) to promote an uprising in J&K as a precursor to the 1965 war. It bears reiteration that task forces named after Islamic fighters like Salauddin were deployed in the same war. The Mujahideen narrative in Kargil in 1999 was another attempt to leverage the same malfeasance. The list continues with the ISI-aided Khalistan separatist movement and the ongoing proxy war in Kashmir.

Unknown to most, East Pakistan became a sanctuary for Naga rebels as early as the 1950s. Naga leader Phizo escaped to London via East Pakistan in 1956. Mowu Angami and other rebels had concurrently trekked to China for weapons and assistance. In the same period, Naga rebels were ferried from the eastern to the western wing for commando training. Pakistan gifted the strategic Shaksgam Valley to China without de jure justification. Both countries agreed on a strategic alliance, and China issued an ultimatum to India during the 1965 war when the tide turned against Pakistan. Notwithstanding these and other signals, **there was a belief among the strategic community that China would stay out of Indo-Pak conflicts despite late Railway Minister George Fernandes flagging China as the main enemy in 1990. There was a feeling that we needed to focus on a hybrid war and deal with Pakistan in the short term.** The dominant belief was that China is unlikely to initiate any conflict as it is focused on economic development.

History of the Proxy War

- The first seeds of the proxy war were sown by Pakistan in the form of misplaced use of Kabayalis and instigation of revolt along religious lines in J&K State Forces in 1947 war.
- The same diabolic plan was repeated in December 1963 with Moe-e-Muqaddas (holy hair relic of the Prophet) to promote an uprising in J&K.
- The Mujahideen narrative in Kargil in 1999 was another attempt to leverage the same malfeasance.
- East Pakistan became a sanctuary for Naga rebels as early as the 1950s.
- Naga rebels had concurrently trekked to China for weapons and assistance.

Build-up on the LAC

- **After the Galwan incident, India has undertaken force-rebalancing to match the Chinese posture on the northern border.**
- **India has created dedicated corps-sized reserves dedicated to Ladakh and Arunachal sub-theatres.**
- **Connectivity to forward areas has substantially improved.**

- **Rafaels, drones, and surveillance systems have been inducted along the LAC.**
- **Long missile systems like Brahmos and Pralay missiles are being positioned to match the Chinese Rocket Force.**

Current Geostrategic Realities

India has been jolted by the Chinese coercive salami-slicing deployments and fisticuffs face-offs on the LAC, even while coping with COVID-19. A few defining trends have emerged. Firstly, the two-front threat is real. Secondly, the Chinese threat is the primary one, and the Northern Front is the main front. Thirdly, India has resilience, and if forced, it can successfully exercise QPQ options like the pre-emptive occupation of the Kailash Heights. Fourthly, coercive tactics have limits, and China simply cannot push its way through. Most importantly, we must remain focused on infrastructure development and force modernisation.

The pandemic in the form of COVID-19 reinforced the need for the nation's resolve and resilience, which was displayed in abundance. It also brought home the need to reduce dependence and adopt a smart Atmanirbhar approach. Consequently, considerable headway has been made in this direction. There is also a renewed thrust to develop infrastructure and eco-system in border areas.

Force Rebalancing

India has undertaken force-rebalancing to match the Chinese posture on the northern border. One Strike Corps and additional formations, along with weapon systems, have been redeployed on the northern borders. **With this, India has created corps-sized reserves dedicated to Ladakh and Arunachal sub-theatres. While retaining a defensive posture, the capability of QPQ and a timely and effective offensive-defence response, as witnessed in Yangtze and Doklam, is also in place.**

Update: The proposal to reorganise the Uttar Bharat Area into an operational corps with two infantry divisions and two to three independent infantry brigades is in the advanced stages.

Infrastructure development is on course, and connectivity to forward areas has substantially improved. The air force has also upgraded and developed new airfields in forward areas coupled with the deployment of the latest platforms like Rafael. Drones and surveillance systems are being inducted. Long missile systems like Brahmos and Pralay are being positioned to match the Chinese Rocket Force. The navy is also modernising to tackle increased Chinese forays in the Indian Ocean, consequent to the PLA acquiring the Djibouti naval base and the development of Gwadar as part of the CPEC. India has joined alliances like the QUAD and is trying to leverage others like SCO, Brazil, Russia, India, China, South Africa (BRICS), and BIMSTEC to build deterrence and dissuasive influences. India has also established an enviable reputation for peacebuilding, disaster relief, and multi-national exercises. However, alliances have limited utility, as partners are unlikely to get directly involved or intervene in our conflicts.

Bolstering the Naval Power

India continues to bolster its naval power amid growing Chinese hegemony in the region. The Indian Navy currently operates two aircraft carriers. In 2022, in a historical milestone, India commissioned its first-ever Indigenous Aircraft Carrier (IAC) Vikrant. The country already operates INS Vikramaditya. The navy operates two nuclear-powered ballistic missile submarines, and reportedly, it has launched the third Arihant-class nuclear-powered submarine. In June 2021, India cleared a project worth ₹43,000 crore to build six high-tech submarines. Indian Navy also operates 11 destroyers, 12 frigates, 16 conventionally powered attack submarines, 19 corvettes, eight Landing Craft Utilities (LCUs), and ten large offshore patrol vessels.

As the government has prepared a mega plan to spend $130 billion to bolster the combat capability of the Armed Forces in the next five to seven years, the navy has already finalised a plan to have 200 ships, 500 aircraft, and 24 attack submarines in the next few years.

Way Forward

China is looking to develop multi-domain warfare and has set up a Strategic Support Force (SSF). It is also embarking on a comprehensive civil-military fusion mission. In sum, we can match China in the conventional sphere and are on course to reduce asymmetry. Yet, we need to remain alive to tackle future threats in the cyber and space domains. **The three key recommendations are: firstly, expediting the formation of theatre commands; secondly, upgrading the cyber and space agencies; and thirdly, instituting no lapsable capital fund with enhanced budget allocation. It is important to remember that preparation is the best deterrence, and preparation is never complete.**

India's Strategic Gameplan vis-à-vis China-Pak Collusive Linkage

For China, Pakistan is a low-cost secondary deterrent to India while for Pakistan, China is a high-value guarantor of security against India.

—Husain Haqqani

Abstract

The basic approach of this article is to discuss and outline an optimum strategy or broad game plan to tackle collusive Sino-Pak threats. The detailed strategy and specific action plan are beyond the scope of this article. However, deliberations and inferences drawn in this article can help refine/validate the template for such formulation. It will be

appropriate to reiterate that clarity on threat parameters is an essential pre-requisite for planning levels of preparedness, force structures, equipment profile, modernisation, and budgetary allocations. Hence, these are discussed in brief. Reasonable assumptions have been factored in, where necessary, as detailed national security policies are yet to be promulgated.

Introduction

The ongoing Chinese aggressive deployment and prolonged face-off in Ladakh have rekindled the debate on collusive threats posed by two neighbours—China and Pakistan. The latter has maintained an aggressive and hostile posture with the calibrated proxy war in J&K, fire assaults on the LC, and hostile presence on the AGPL. It is heartening that the ceasefire inked in February 2021 has been holding for the last fourteen months. China has delayed the resolution of the border, coupled with the orchestration of transgressions and 'salami-slicing' at periodic intervals to stake her claim on shifting claim lines on the LAC. India and Bhutan are the only two neighbours, having the dubious distinction of unsettled land borders with China due to stonewalling and obduracy by Beijing. These coercive orchestrations are primarily designed to keep India in check and unsettled, thereby denying her development, progress, and stability. The recent strategic situation on the northern borders, coupled with the ongoing proxy war in J&K, has once again stoked concerns about the challenges of a two-and-a-half-front threat. It has thrown up a number of issues relating to the scope of collusion, likely manifestation scenarios, designation of primary and secondary threats, and, above all, the need for an effective response strategy. The scope of collusion between Pakistan and China transcends from geo-strategic to geo-economic and other domains like defence manufacturing, transportation, power generation, nuclear weapons, and space. The most notable multi-dimensional, collaborative project is the ongoing CPEC, which is described as a signature project for the BRI and sets a new benchmark in collusive collaboration.

Preview

The subject is analysed with a focus on the following major parameters:

a) Collusive Linkages – Definitions, Scope, and Manifestation
b) Historical Context
c) CPEC – New Collusive Paradigm
d) Construct and Catalysts for Collusion
e) Strategic Options to Counter Collusion
f) Summary of Recommendations

Collusive Linkages – Definitions, Scope, and Manifestation

Definitions

'Collusion' and its derivatives like 'collusive' are terms increasingly used in geo-strategic dialogue and have spawned another more commonly used, non-dictionary but colloquially popular variant, 'collusivity'. The word may soon get included in the dictionary, considering its extensive usage. Webster's dictionary defines collusion as a 'secret agreement or cooperation, especially for an illegal or deceitful purpose'. A more appropriate formulation in our context is outlined in Collins Dictionary as an adjective: 'Collusive behaviour involves secret or illegal cooperation between countries or organisations'. There are many other definitions, but a common strand in almost all is a threefold operation characterised by secrecy and deceit. **Collusion requires collaboration or working together, albeit in covert or secret mode combined with deceit. China and North Korea provide an apt example of such comprehensive collusive linkages. The Sino-Pak relationship is another such case study.** With China acting as the nucleus, relationships with North Korea and Pakistan are a complex web of concentric, collusive networks, including nuclear proliferation. As a concept, it is natural that alliances, especially in the security domain, facilitate or promote some degree and form of collusion.

Most security pacts invariably have classified/secret clauses and even classified annexures. An apt example was the leasing of the Shamsi air base by Pakistan to the UAE for hunting and, in turn, the base being sublet to the US forces for drone and missile operations against the Taliban. Tri-lateral collusion essentially was a clever ploy for bypassing regulations and pressure of domestic lobbies. However, the presence of American personnel on air bases like Shamsi and Jacobabad accorded Pakistan some degree of immunity during Operation Prakram in 2001–02. In all probability, India would have been constrained to omit these bases from possible target lists in the event of hostilities.

Scope

The scope of collusion is defined by geo-political and geo-strategic templates but transcends increasingly into geo-economic domains. Recently, Chinese President Xi Jinping, in a telephone chat with Imran Khan, hailed their ties as between 'iron brothers'. A commentary in the state-run Xinhua news agency in 2013 during the visit of the Chinese PM to Pakistan stated that 'China and Pakistan have shaped a paradigm of neighbour-to-neighbour relations. Their time-tested friendship, described by some as 'higher than the mountains and deeper than the oceans', is not just a bunch of empty words. The important and relevant details of the Sino-Pak collusion are mapped later in this paper in the section on historical context. It will be appropriate to emphasise the growing scope of collaborative linkages, which is now being referred to and alleged in secret bio-weapon labs in China and, more recently, in Ukraine, reportedly funded by the USA and Western pharmaceutical lobbies. The CPEC also has plans for vaccination projects.

Manifestation of Collusion

Collusive ties, as per conventional understanding, are described to be secretive, like the nuclear exchange between China, North Korea, and Pakistan. They even incorporate deniability, as was attempted by AQ Khan and his clique, in the proliferation of nuclear designs on Iran and Libya. Notwithstanding the emphasis on secrecy in basic definition, there are methods to project positive aspects and hide spin-offs with security pay-offs. It is axiomatic that in the age of enhanced transparency through satellite imagery and remote sensing techniques, collusion will be **couched and designated, invariably, for benign purposes like communication, connectivity, and economic development. CPEC, which is discussed later, is the most relevant example in this context.** In an era where wars are described as 'Special Operations', **collusion, rather than declared collaboration, is likely to become the new normal accompanied by deniability.**

Forms of Collusion

Collusion may adopt various shapes, such as ***synchronised or sequential/ deferred in timing.*** It may be ***planned or even impromptu*** to take advantage of a situation/opportunity or redress reverse/criticality. The deployment of the Seventh Fleet by the USA in the Bay of Bengal in the 1971 operations was deferred collusion to bail out East Pakistan in dire straits (criticality), though it failed to have the desired effect. In application, collusion may ***be in the same theatre, in proximity, or even in different theatres.*** The Gulf operations witnessed the application of multiple national forces in the same theatre and in synchronised mode. Collusion and collaboration may have a **deterrent effect, even when not actually applied, as a threat.** The fear of Chinese posturing in 1971 forced the deferring of operations to December during the pass-closure period to preclude two-front scenarios. Collusion can be ***short-term or even episodic, essentially tactical, long-term, or strategic*** collaboration/collusion. Sino-Pak collusion meets the criterion of the long-term and strategic one, having completed nearly 50 years. On the other hand, the US-Iran collusion in the Central Treaty Organisation (CENTO) era was broken off with the advent of the Ayatollah regime in Iran, making it a short-term engagement.

Historical Context

Setting the Stage

Pakistan was among the first to accord diplomatic recognition to the PRC in 1950. **The first signs of the China-Pak collusion manifested as early as the 1950s when erstwhile East Pakistan became a sanctuary for Naga rebels.** Phizo escaped to London via East Pakistan in December 1956. Mowu Angami and others trekked to China for training. Similarly, Naga rebels were ferried from the Eastern Wing to the Western one for specialised commando training in the late 1950s. **Pakistan gifted vast tracts of strategic territory of the Shaksgam Valley, measuring 5180 sq. km, in 1963**, enabling it to settle boundary issues with China. The treaty incorporates Section 6, which mandates that after the settlement of the Kashmir dispute, there will be another round between China and the treaty-designated sovereign state for final settlement. It actually was an abject surrender of territory, which de jure belonged to Kashmir and India. It was also a flagrant violation of standstill arrangements mandated in the UN resolution. Pakistan planned the 1965 operation to take advantage of the situation in India after the Chinese aggression in 1962. It was based on the assessment of Indian forces being demoralised and unprepared. As per some media reports, a US-based think tank had reportedly recommended 1965 as a now-or-never opportunity to put it across India. In the interim, the USA, as a reward for membership in military pacts, had armed Pakistan with modern weapons like Sabre jets and M-48 Patton tanks, emboldening it to undertake the 1965 aggression on India. Beijing, having warmed up to Pakistan in the early 1960s, issued an ultimatum to India during the Indo-Pak war of 1965. This was followed by the formalisation of military assistance in 1966, leading to the provision of assorted weapons worth $60 million. In the economic domain, there was an inkling of trade pacts in 1979, triggering growing economic cooperation.

Pak Propensity for Alliances

Unlike the Indian policy of nonalignment and stress on near-equal partnerships rather than alliances, **Pakistan has displayed commendable diplomatic manipulation and dexterity.** Pak has managed to leverage her geo-strategic location at the crossroads of civilisations to the hilt by forging concurrent collusive linkages across divergent spectrums. It first became part of the Southeast Asia Treaty Organisation (SEATO) in 1954, the Baghdad Pact in 1955, and CENTO in 1956. This, in effect, makes it an outpost for the USA in Central Asia. Surprisingly, it also cosied up to China in the 1960s, concurrently keeping OIC connections alive. **Pakistan became a surprising enabler between the USA and China. Henry Kissinger's visit to China in July 1971 was shrouded in secrecy and concealed as a diversion during his Pak visit.** After Bangladesh's operations and losing the Eastern wing, it established a strategic alliance with China in 1972, concurrently retaining active membership of US-led military alliances like CENTO. **Pakistan has shown compliance and even agreed to become a client state in unequal tie-ups.**

Indian Response and 1971 Operations

Trilateral linkages between Pakistan, China, and the USA **forced India to sign the Indo-Soviet friendship treaty in 1971, which acted as a restraining check on Chinese designs to provide aid to Pakistan during the Bangladesh Liberation War.** However, China extended flying rights and passage to Pakistan for operations in the Eastern wing. Pak's linkages with China impacted India's plans in responding to the refugee crisis in 1971 and deferring planned operations to December to preclude Chinese intervention. In the intervening period of six months, India had to cope with an unprecedented humanitarian crisis caused by the massive influx of refugees. Both in the 1965 and 1971 wars, despite choosing an appropriate period to preclude Chinese intervention, minimum forces and readiness posture had to be maintained on the Sino-Indian border, thereby restricting the availability of forces to be applied against Pakistan.

Proxy War and Insurgency

The sordid chapter of collusion between China and East Pakistan and later Bangladesh, though documented, is rarely discussed. Ironically, the ISI and Chinese managed to keep camps and sanctuaries active till the Sheikh Hasina regime. It was only the Awami League government that handed over fugitives like Anup Chetia and threw out others like Anthony Shimray after cracking down on insurgent camps. Ruili in Yunnan province reportedly still acts as the hub for procuring weapons and a sanctuary for fugitive insurgents of NE rebel groups. Pakistan employed the Kabayali narrative in the 1947–48 conflict and, later, infiltration task forces in the 1965 war. Having suffered humiliation in 1971, it adopted the 'Bleeding India with a Thousand Cuts' strategy. It fomented terrorism by funding and aiding Khalistanis in the 1980s and 1990s (1984 to 1995). Later, it initiated a proxy war in Kashmir in 1988, which is still simmering. Kargil raiders in 1999 were also described as Mujahideen despite clear evidence to the contrary. The challenges for India in terms of narco-terrorism, counterfeit smuggling, and arms trafficking remain. The ISI has also been toying with the idea of K2 (Khalistan and Kashmir) after the opening of the Kartarpur corridor.

Mujahideen and Taliban

Pakistan has the dubious distinction of setting up Mujahideen and Jihadi militias at the behest of the USA in the 1990s. Pakistan managed to calibrate her duplicity and perfidious behaviour to remain America's main interlocutor in Afghanistan. The first venture was training, arming, and aiding Mujahideen militias to overthrow the Russian-backed regime from 1979 to 1989. Since then, it remained a frontline state till the US withdrawal in September 2021. It still retains some degree of control and is now engaged in carving a role for China in Afghanistan. This turnaround comes at considerable cost to Indian interests, including investments of US$ 3 billion in development projects. **China and Pak are colluding to deny India a legitimate role in Afghan talks.**

Calibrated Chinese Collusion

China has taken a carefully calculated approach to supporting Pakistan. There has been undiluted support from international bodies like the UNO and the Financial Action Task Force (FATF). It put up the façade of responsible power during the Kargil operations in 1999 when it chose to maintain a restrained posture despite appeals by Pakistan. This has even spawned a strong belief that in a conflict initiated by Pakistan against India, China may not intervene. Indian strategic thinkers opined that historically, China had not made decisive interventions in 1965, 1971, and the Kargil conflicts and limited support to providing arms, issuing ultimatums and tying down troops deployed on the Sino-Indian border. Any intervention by Chinese troops is likely to generate signals of opportunism, fear, and awe amongst smaller neighbours. There was also a feeling that even in conflicts initiated by China, she may not like to be seen colluding and taking help from Pakistan. There are unverified reports of intelligence sharing and posturing in the recent Ladakh stand-off, but physical participation has not yet been proven. There is also a belief that **Pakistan will invariably try to take advantage of any conflict initiated by China against India.** It will be appropriate to place on record that Pakistan has acted in a restrained manner in the current stand-off with China in Ladakh, in all likelihood at the behest of her controlling partner, China.

CPEC – A New Collusive Paradigm

Defining the Treaty of 2005

A special bilateral China-Pakistan Treaty of Friendship, Cooperation, and Good Neighbourly Relations, ratified by both sides in 2005–06, is the most significant milestone in the China-Pakistan collusion and collaboration. It mandates the two nations to desist from '**joining any alliance or bloc which infringes upon the sovereignty, security, and territorial integrity of the other side**'. It also forbids both countries from concluding a similar treaty with a third country, thereby closing avenues for a strategic pact with the USA. **It set the stage for the CPEC. It has been pitched as a showpiece for the BRI, adding geo-economic heft to the collusion.** The project, with a projected investment of US$ 62 billion, is also being dubbed as the economic colonisation of Pak by China, thus adding an ironical twist to the acronym itself. Dependencies and debt traps are likely to lead to China getting the ownership of Gwadar and chunks of the transportation corridor on a long lease basis. Pakistan also figures prominently in maritime, digital, and health silk routes, also described as the 'String of Pearls'.

Strategic Drivers

CPEC is showcased as a benign economic collaboration in an open domain, yet behind this cloak of development, it conceals and down-plays collusive strategic drivers like warm-water port (Gwadar) connectivity for China to the Makran coast. The collateral benefits of enhanced interoperability between two Armed Forces, two additional divisions for the protection of the corridor, maritime cooperation, logistics, and optic fibre connectivity are all downplayed. The very alignment and execution of projects in GB and Pok, like the Kohala and Daimer-Basha dams, are altering the very status quo mandated in the UN resolution. **These projects challenge the de jure sovereignty of India and extend the legitimacy of Pakistani claims.** Pak has allowed access and deployment of the Chinese workforce along with security personnel in GB and PoK. This amounts to negating her territorial claims. **The Chinese presence in operational terms constrains targeting options to avoid escalation, resulting in collateral damage to Chinese personnel and assets.**

Construct and Catalysts for Collusion

Pak Objectives

Pakistan as a state is defined by the **self-professed raison d'etre for its creation, the need to be a separate theological state and anti-India in its orientation.** This urge and mindset acquired fanatic flavour when **Pak added ideological frontiers** as an add-on to its physical boundaries. Pakistan chose to name her capital Islamabad and even described her nuclear bomb as an 'Islamic bomb'. Most of her strategic missiles have been named after invaders like Babur, Ghaznavi, and Shaheen. Even infiltration task forces in 1965 were named similarly—Saladin, Khilji, etc. Kargil raiders were described as Ghazis and Mujahideen. This has **spurred a craving for 'parity fixation in strategic domain'**, a tendency of constant comparison with India, articulated recently by former Pak PM Imran Khan's recent comparisons of Pakistan's foreign policy with Indian neutrality, strategic autonomy, and heft in the international community. In blunt terms, it amounts to Pak's desire to punch much above her weight classification. The quest for parity has degenerated into multiple aggressions, proxy wars, and constant affliction to foment anti-India narratives. Pak, while aspiring to be a leader of the Islamic ummah, has displayed rank hypocrisy by maintaining a stoic silence on Chinese atrocities on the Uyghur community in Xinjiang.

Chinese Aspirations

China, on the other hand, wants to establish her hegemony and keep India hyphenated with Pakistan. It is a **diabolic 'push-pull' formulation of pushing down India to keep her embroiled in the sub-continent, denying her rightful place on the global stage.** This is concurrently accompanied by pulling up to artificially hoist Pak to drum up the notion of parity. The only glue in this collusive relationship is to deny India strategic salience. Chinese actions in denying India membership in the Security Council and Nuclear Security Group are reflective of this trend. Ironically, Beijing links Indian admission with Pak, being concurrently given membership of the Nuclear Suppliers Group (NSG), notwithstanding her dodgy record in nuclear proliferation. Double pincer collusion drives multi-spectral linkages like helping Pak to acquire nuclear weapons. China has aided and colluded with Pak to bypass the Missile Technology Control Regime (MTCR) and Nuclear Proliferation Treaty (NPT). Collusion between these two nations was predicted **by Samuel Huntington** in his famous book, *Clash of Civilizations*, **wherein he flagged congruence between Sinic and Islamic civilisations.**

Multi-spectral Collusion

China has emerged as the largest arms supplier to Pakistan, replacing America. Pakistan has allowed Chinese cloning experts to reverse engineer US-supplied equipment in flagrant violation of proprietary end-user clauses. China and Pakistan are also engaged in regular training exercises, manoeuvres, and exchange visits. All these weapons and expertise are likely to be focused against India, and some of them are being used in the proxy war. China allows Pak to piggyback on strategic projects like missiles, defence production, and space collaboration. North Industries Corporation (NORINCO) and other Chinese arms manufacturers have upgraded Heavy Industries Taxila (HIT), ordnance factories, Aviation Complex Kamra, and missile plant at Tarwanah, near Rawalpindi. It has enabled Pak to execute joint production of the JF-17 aircraft, Al-Khalid main battle tanks, howitzers, missiles, and a variety of munitions. China has announced joint projects in submarines and underwater vehicles. **The proliferation of Chinese-origin weapons in neighbouring countries enables Pak presence for servicing and repairs besides export orders.** Pak's reliance on Chinese equipment has its own glitches due to relative technological and serviceability levels. There have been reports on problems with Chinese-supplied equipment and its comparison with modern American platforms like Huey Cobra, Strykers, Chinooks, drones, and Javelin missiles.

Strategic Options to Counter Collusion

Strategic Baggage. Till the recent course correction on the designation of primary threat, Indian policymakers believed that China could be managed diplomatically. There was marked reluctance to discuss 'two-and-a-half-front' scenarios, with half denoting internal security threats like Left Wing Extremism (LWE). It was coupled with the **primary focus bordering on Pak threat as a sort of strategic affliction or even strategic historical baggage.** There was an over-reliance on dual task formations (DTFs) and inter-theatre switching of forces. This belief was based on three premises: first, the Chinese focus on internal economic consolidation and development. It was inferred that China would avoid distractions. Second, reliance on border treaties and protocols, especially on agreed CBMs. India rightly expected maturity on the part of China in keeping with her rising stature. This was bolstered by historical reticence on the part of China to decisively intervene in Indo-Pak conflicts. Third, the fact that the global coupling of supply chains and trade linkages, especially with the huge Indian market, will discourage such adventures. However, China seems to have leveraged Indian dependencies in critical sectors in a smart and coercive format.

Recalibration

However, the recent trend of **'aggressively rising China' and 'wolf warrior diplomacy'**, as well as flagrant violations of agreed CBMs, treaties, and protocols during the Ladakh face-off, have forced a complete rethink and recalibration of strategy. Discarding the sort of self-generated denial syndrome, there is the clear designation of China as the primary threat. Collusion has been accepted as a corollary and reality. Collusion in many facets like intelligence, info operations, cyber, surveillance, manufacturing, preparation, and many more disciplines has **acquired abiding permanency and seamless fusion between the two nations.** The two-front challenge refers to a simultaneous or synergised armed conflict (aggression) with both China and Pakistan engaging India. They could follow either a collaborative or a collusive approach, and the difference between these two terms has become mere semantic, as the collusion is permanent. Collaboration is declaratory and becoming rare, and it implies one country openly aiding the other militarily, whereas collusion involves covert cooperation between the two. **In this case, we are confronted with collusive collaboration.**

Response Matrix

Indian preparation levels against **Pakistan are reportedly pegged on parameters of 'credible deterrence' to be upgraded to 'punitive deterrence'. Against China, it has been indexed as 'dissuasive deterrence', to be upgraded to 'credible deterrence'.** Punitive deterrence entails building up asymmetrical capabilities in niche domains to deliver sharp and surgical responses. These, like the Balakot air strikes, can be pre-emptive, provided targets are carefully selected with due justification for international opinion. Execution has to be surgical, with minimum collateral damage and backed up by information operations to amplify the message. As a corollary, the initiator has to be prepared for a retaliatory response and retain control of the escalatory ladder. China's mandate is to graduate from defensive dissuasion to credible deterrence, which should at least ensure stalemate, as for an aggressor, unresolved stalemate amounts to a loss of face. This would require building and executing QPQ options like pre-emptive deployment on Kailash Heights, south of Pangong Tso. **Such QPQ responses predicate meticulousness and, more importantly, 'willpower' to act.** The application of riposte or counter-offensive in other theatres facilitates horizontal escalation. This can be applied in vertical mode by enlarging the conflict to maritime or nuclear/space domains. India is opposed to both as it believes in the peaceful use of space and also that there is adequate space below the nuclear threshold for conventional conflicts.

Rebalancing

There has been a **rebalancing of force levels and resources across frontiers in keeping with the reappraisal of threats.** The most notable change is the re-orientation of one strike corps from western to northern borders, primarily for the Ladakh theatre and its reconfiguration from mechanised to mountain. It enables two mountain strike corps to focus on their respective theatres. **The scope of rebalancing is holistic and extends to mechanised, firepower, surveillance, airpower, cyber, and communications domains.** There is also an enhanced focus on the development of infrastructure, logistics, and connectivity in border areas. This reorganisation has consequences on reduced force levels on the Western front. It can impact the notion of 'decisive victory', and emphasis has shifted to focused surgical capabilities and synergised integrated battle groups with limited objectives. It will be appropriate if integrated theatres are formed on priority to synergise and orchestrate a more coherent response. There have been concerns about ammunition stocking for two-front wars, especially with earlier decisions to prune stocking levels to cater for short war scenarios. The ongoing Ukrainian war has brought into question this premise, and it is axiomatic that the stocking policy and levels for collusive threat are reviewed. It is imperative to maintain an enhanced focus on internal security and need to expedite conflict resolution to tackle ubiquitous half-front threats and internal fault lines. India also needs to evaluate its 'No First Use and Massive Retaliation' nuclear policy to inject a certain degree of ambiguity for better deterrence vis-à-vis China. **In a scenario where all three players are armed with nuclear weapons, the need is to build genuine CBMs, more transparency, and reduce collusion.** Ramping up deliberations, interoperability exercises, other connected initiatives, and **alliances/partnerships are not silver bullets or panacea and have their inherent limitations.** It is unlikely that alliance partners will commit troops on the ground, especially as India is the only Quad nation to have land frontiers with China.

Strategic Autonomy

Countering collusive linkages requires strategic autonomy, which can be achieved by **Smart Atmanirbhar. The thrust should be on minimising dependence on strategic and critical technologies.** Some examples are power plants for aircraft and naval crafts; cyber, guidance, surveillance, and communications; autonomous and remote systems; rare earths; active pharmaceutical ingredients (API) for the pharmaceutical industry; and many more sectors. It bears reiterating that self-reliance is not self-isolation. A smart edge can be acquired by transitioning to the role of the lead integrator. It will be axiomatic to gain autonomy in strategic sectors coupled with acquiring leverage in niche areas. **This is a long-term agenda and predicates sustained focus backed up with budgetary allocations to acquire 'know why' besides 'know how'.** This will entail expenditure on R&D and building up domain competence.

Summary of Recommendations

In conclusion, the following need to be emphasised:

a) **Collusive collaboration between China and Pakistan is an abiding strategic reality.**

b) **Aggressively rising China has emerged as the primary challenge, yet Pakistan remains a permanent irritant.**

c) **Internal fault lines need to be addressed, and conflict resolution expedited to reduce the scope for collusive interference.**

d) **Alliances/strategic partnerships are certainly not enough, and reliance has to be on building our own capabilities.**

e) **The whole-of-nation approach to boosting Comprehensive National Power can make Pak irrelevant due to decisive asymmetry and reduce the gap with China.**

f) **Force rebalancing and theatrisation need to be expedited to synergise integrated responses.**

g) **Modernisation, capability building, and infrastructure require sustained focus, backed up by an adequate budget.**

h) **Terrestrial and maritime domains need to be concurrently developed.**

i) **Smart Atmanirbhar is the recommended way forward to gain salience in niche and disruptive technologies.**

j) **Realistic scenario-based war gaming and simulations backed up with net assessment should be carried out to improve responses and preparation levels.**

k) **Notwithstanding Chinese obduracy, India should continue efforts to resolve boundary disputes and also build credible CBMs to avoid border flash-points.**

A collusive two-and-a-half-front threat is the ultimate challenge and requires synergy at all levels and a 'whole-of-nation' approach. It will be appropriate to quote Clausewitz, 'War is nothing but the continuation of policy with other means.' Deft diplomacy is required to prevent and mitigate this threat. Intelligence and surveillance agencies should remain vigilant to generate appropriate warnings. Security agencies must rebalance and reorganise optimum force levels to generate appropriate responses. **Preparation is the best deterrent.**

References

1. https://www.merriam-webster.com

2. https://www.collinsdictionary.com

3. https://news.cgtn.com/news/2021-10-26/Xi-Jinping-holds-phone-conversation-with-Pakistani-PM-14FDxvhmJ4k/index.html

4. https://www.hindustantimes.com/world/china-pak-relations-higher-

thanmountain-deeper-than-ocean/story-22JIWjJtaqGWZJ6okMwzXK.html

5. https://m.economictimes.com/opinion/interviews/we-have-never-seenpeace-a-normal-lifeadinno-phizo-daughter-of-the-father-of-the-nagas/articleshow/48725756.cms?from=mdr

6. http://www.indiandefencereview.com/news/nagaland-the-beginning-ofinsurgency-i/5/

7. https://moderndiplomacy.eu/2018/09/27/chinas-role-in-1965-indo-pak-war/

8. Tapan Das, *Sino-Pak Collusion and US Policy* (Bangladesh: Asia Publishing House, 1972).

9. Hein G Kiessling, *Faith, Unity, Discipline*: The ISI of Pakistan (India, Harper Collins, 2016)

10. https://ciaotest.cc.columbia.edu/olj/sa/sa_99sis04.html

11. C Christine Fair, *Fighting To The End: The Pakistan Army's Way Of War* (Oxford University Press, 2014)

12. https://www.beyondintractability.org/bksum/huntington-clash

Pakistan Army – Ethos and Hierarchy

Evolution of Pakistan Army's Character and Ethos

There are armies that guard their nation's borders, there are those concerned with protecting their own position in society, and there are those that defend a cause or an idea. The Pakistan Army does all three.

—Stephen Cohen, renowned strategic expert

Key Takeaways

- The Pak Army has usurped the dominant role in governance and created a 'deep state' to retain control.
- Khaki Generals are driving the nation on an anti-India trajectory and are afflicted with parity syndrome.
- General Zia has put the army on the Islamist (jihadi) path.
- The army has also created an empire with tentacles in all profit-making ventures, wherein larger national interests have been relegated.

Introduction

The India and Pakistan armies were carved out of the British Indian Army consequent to the partition and were like identical twins for the first few years, but both have charted different trajectories in the 72 years since independence. In the case of Pakistan, a major slant came in 1956, with the Americans deputing the Military Assistance Advisory Group (MAAG) to shape Pakistan's integration into the CENTO and SEATO. The collapse of the Soviet regime in Afghanistan in the 1990s gave Pakistan an opportunity to emerge as America's proxy. The evolution of both armies has also been shaped by two contrasting systems of governance: **in Pakistan, military rule has given the army a pivotal and all-pervasive role. Apart from this, theological drivers have also conditioned the ideological dimension. General Zia-ul-Haq has the dubious distinction of giving the Pakistan Army fundamentalist overtones, with the open espousing of the 'Quranic concept of warfare'.** The Pakistan Army, unlike most other armies, has added defence of ideological frontiers, besides geographic borders, in its revised mandate. This slant was further cemented with Pakistan running the *fassadi* (mistakenly also referred to as jihadi) assembly line at the Western powers' and America's behest for employment in Afghanistan.

Moving from the colonial British legacy to the American slant, lurching onwards to the sinister *fassadi* makeover, and now the collusive Chinese embrace is, indeed, a major milestone in the evolution of the Pakistan Army. **Generals in khaki have shown amazing politico-diplomatic dexterity in balancing the Americans with the Chinese and Russians, to a limited extent, and Sunni Saudis with Shia Iranians to leverage their geo-strategic relevance due to the location at the confluence of cultures.** It is, indeed, ironical that despite the crushing defeat of 1971, leading to the loss of the larger wing of East Pakistan, the reverse in 1947, and the stalemate in 1965, major setbacks in Siachen and Kargil, the army continues to enjoy the patronage of the populace, sustained on the narrative of vilification and marginalisation of other legitimate instruments of the state, that are painted as corrupt and lackadaisical.

Scope

Despite a shared heritage, currently, the two armies of India and Pakistan, while retaining some commonalities, are poles apart, meriting a comparative analysis. The thrust of this article is to flag the macro trends in the evolution of the current character and ethos of the Pakistan Army. The scope of the analysis has been confined to the army, with only an outline discussion on connected issues relating to the army. The Pakistan Army has an overriding and dominant role, which was officially promulgated in March 1956, with Pakistan jettisoning the traditional order derived from colonial powers of Navy-Army-Air Force to Army-Navy-Air Force.

Politicisation of the Pakistan Army

Pakistan veered toward the concept of 'guided democracy', leading to military rule just a decade after independence, in October 1958, with Ayub Khan seizing power and promoting himself to Field Marshal's rank. An interesting fact is that **Ayub was not even on the panel of the three seniormost officers to be considered for appointment as the first chief, and, after his appointment, he engineered multiple extensions and two promotions. This trend has continued through Zia, Musharaff, Raheel, Bajwa, and even Asim Munir, wherein the appointing authority disregarded seniority in picking suitable and apparently pliable nominees. But, invariably, each of these incumbents outgrew their stature to assert their independence and even upstage those appointing them.** The unluckiest was the former Prime Minister Zulfikar Bhutto, who was hanged by his protégé, General Zia. Close on his heels is Nawaz Sharif, who was upstaged by all four chiefs appointed by him. Ayub's rule for more than a decade was followed by Yahya Khan till his defeat in 1971. The initial spell of military rule stretched to 13 years. After a break of seven years of civilian rule, there was another spell of military rule and a dubious Islamic decade under General Zia-ul-Haq from September 1978 to August 1988. The third spell of military rule lasted seven years under General Pervez Musharraf, from June 2001 to August 2008. In effect, Pakistan has been ruled by army generals either openly (through martial rule) or by proxy by having pliant puppet regimes. This is in sharp contrast to India, where the mere whiff of an unusual move of troops towards Delhi spooks the entire ruling elite on Raisina Hill, as it happened in 2014. **Another interesting indication is that soon after independence, the governor-general's residence in Delhi was taken over and converted into the prime minister's residence and is now a museum. In contrast, all four *fauji* presidents in Islamabad retained the Chief of Army Staff's appointment and continued to run the country from the Army House in Rawalpindi.**

The status of the character of governments till 2024 was as tabulated below.

Civilian Govt	Military Regime	Total
40 yrs	36 yrs	76 yrs

Types of Governments

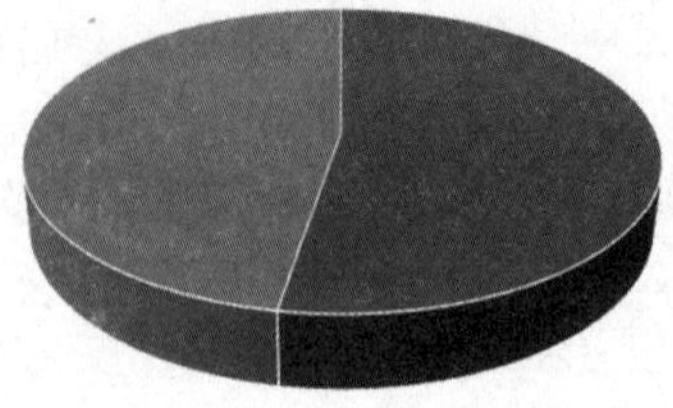

▪ Civilian Regime ▪ Military Rule

This excludes the proxy rule, which has been a constant factor.

In essence, the army enjoys an overriding say in defence (including the budget), sensitive issues of foreign policy like Kashmir and Afghanistan, and nuclear weapons (including their development and employment). In addition, intelligence organisations like the ISI and Inter-Services Public Relations (ISPR) continue to operate under the army with no civilian oversight. The army retains firm control of traditional homeland security subjects like internal security frontier areas and border management. The current Minister for Internal Security, Brigadier Ijaz Shah (Retd), like many of his predecessors, has an army and ISI background. The list of subjects and concerns is only indicative, as subjects can be added or deleted at the whims and fancies of the Pindi Generals. **The sheer range and scope of interference has resulted in independent analysts pointing out, 'While nations have armies, the Pakistan Army has the nation at its disposal.'** The installation of Imran Khan in what is dubbed as 'managed elections' and the army and ISI Chiefs accompanying Imran during his recent US visit are clear indicators of the control exercised by the army. The trend has continued, with Imran being eased out, an interim regime being installed in place, and controlled elections being planned.

Anti-India Bias

The Pakistan Army, in pursuance of the two-nation theory, chose to make the anti-India bias its raison d'être. This has manifested in multiple attempts to destabilise and even mount aggression on India. Immediately after the partition, Kashmir was taken up as an unfinished agenda, leading to raids in October 1947 by plundering tribal *lashkars* (militias), notably Mehsuds and Kabayalis, aided by the Pakistan Army's Chitral Scouts and regulars. This war lasted for 15 months till the one-sided ceasefire was applied by India, despite its ascendency at that juncture. Hein G Kiessling has pointed out in his book *Faith, Unity, Discipline: The ISI of Pakistan* that **Pakistan started aiding and training Naga rebels in the 1950s. After the 1962 war, Pakistan forged links with China despite being in American formal alliances like CENTO and SEATO, primarily in pursuit of its quest to marginalise India.** Sensing this opportunity, Pakistan again launched an attack on the Rann in April 1965, followed by full-scale operations in September 1965. It is also interesting that India mounted the Siachen operations in April 1984 to stymie Pakistan's plans to occupy the glacier. Pakistan aided Khalistani extremism in the 1980s and later the ongoing proxy war in J&K. The failed Kargil operation was another manifestation of this deviant tendency. An interesting explanation has been provided by Khalid Ahmed, a leading Pakistani columnist, 'Pakistani nationalism comprises 95 per cent India hatred. They call it Islam because that is how we learn to differentiate between ourselves and India.' This bias has fuelled tendencies like the parity syndrome despite the very basis of the two-nation theory becoming shaky with the liberation of Bangladesh.

Parity Syndrome

The Pakistan Army has always suffered from the parity syndrome, wherein it seeks to match its Indian counterpart. This has been sustained by false narratives, unfortunately, dressed up with religious metaphors, alluding that a single Pakistani soldier (*momin*) can defeat five Indians (*kafirs*) merely due to religious beliefs. It will be pertinent to quote ZA Bhutto," If India builds the bomb, we will eat grass or leaves, even go hungry, but we will get one of our own." Despite clear reverses, Pakistan has continued to prosecute ambitious policies of 'Bleeding India with a Thousand Cuts' and proxy war forays, first in the North-East, then in Punjab, and currently in J&K. This is combined with a tendency of provocation and nuanced irrationality, which will be discussed later. It will be relevant to recount the seminal wisdom of C Christine Fair in her landmark book *Fighting to The End: The Pakistan Army's Way of War.* Pakistan has to recognise that it simply cannot match India through whatever stratagem it chooses; it is bound to fail. **The sensible thing, then, is for Pakistan to reach the best possible accommodation with India now, while it still can, and shift gears toward a grand strategy centred on economic integration in South Asia, one that would help Pakistan climb out of its morass and allow the army to maintain some modicum of privileges, at least for a while. The alternative is to preside over an increasingly hollow state.**

Theological Template

The Pakistan Army, like the rest of the nation, jettisoned the secular ethos of the British Army and the vision of Jinnah to embark on the Quranic concept of war, as outlined by Brigadier SK Malik. This trend was fuelled by Zia, who made it a compulsory text in military courses. The book legitimises instruments of terror and gives a mischievous twist to the concepts of *jihad, fedayeen, and ghazi*. **Zia also discarded the original secular motto, '*ittehad, yaqeen, tanzeem*' implying 'unity, faith, discipline'. The new motto was '*Iman, taqwa, jihad fi sabilillah*', meaning 'faith, piety, holy war in the path of Allah'.** This has resulted in Pakistan describing its quest for a nuclear device as one for an Islamic bomb. It is ironic that in case Iran makes a separate 'Shia bomb', Pakistan's lofty idea may get stymied into just a 'Sunni bomb'. Pakistan has also given provocative names of invaders to its task forces and missiles, like Ghauri, Ghazni, Babur, etc. It is most ironic that due to this dangerous dalliance with terrorists, the Pakistan Army, espousing *jihad* in its very motto, named its anti-terror operation '*Raad-ul-Fasaad*', terming *jihadis as fassadis*. It will be once again appropriate to quote C Christine Fair, 'Pakistan's military journals frequently take as their subjects famous Quranic battles, such as the Battle of Badr. Ironically, the varied Quranic battles are discussed in more analytical detail in Pakistan's journals than are Pakistan's own wars with India.' This dangerous trend has proliferated in the air force, as seen in the assassination attempt on Musharraf and even in the navy, as evidenced during the raid on the PNS Mehran in 2011.

Notwithstanding its struggling economy, Pakistan has taken over the mantle of protecting the larger Islamic brotherhood (ummah), which led to the development of the so-called Islamic bomb. Former Army Chief General Raheel Sharif commands the Islamic Military Alliance, also referred to as the 'Sunni Force'. Pakistan Army troops and pilots operate and run training teams and maintenance facilities in many Sunni countries like Saudi Arabia, Jordan and other Gulf countries like the UAE, Qatar, and Bahrain. It is pertinent to recount that a Pakistan pilot flying a Syrian Air Force plane was shot down during the Yom Kippur War in 1973. However, none of these countries allowed its equipment, like aircraft (even when flown by Pakistani pilots), to be used in wars against India. Pakistan has made a substantial contribution to various UN peacekeeping missions and has earned an enviable reputation.

Deceit and Denial

The Pakistan Army has utilised theological narratives to incorporate infiltration as an instrument in its operations. Infiltration task forces were utilised in both the 1947 and 1965 operations and were named after Muslim raiders. Pakistan banked on these tribal militias, aided by the Chitral Scouts and regulars, but kept denying their presence till caught by the UN-mandated Dixon Commission. The 1965 operations were timed with the missing *Moi-e-Muqqadas* (holy hair of the Prophet) controversy, which was probably engineered to foment trouble. In addition, despite the aggression by Pakistan and the stalemate weighted in India's favour, Pakistan continued to celebrate the 1965 operations as a victory and ironically called it *Youm-e-Difa* (celebration of defence). The genocide and plunder in erstwhile East Pakistan were denied by the generals despite evidence presented by international observers and media. Pakistan used the Northern Light Infantry (NLI) troops in the Kargil operations, building the deniability clause, and even refused to accept the dead bodies of its soldiers.

Cultivated Nuanced Irrationality

Pakistan has tried to offset its asymmetry by cultivating a nuanced irrationality wherein it threatens to transition from hybrid war to the tactical nuclear domain with a declaratory policy, as described by C Christine Fair, 'Pakistan's nuclear weapons are India-specific.' **The nuclear threat is accentuated by vague red lines and tactical delivery means.** However, the Balakot strike and the American warning during the Kargil crisis seem to have resulted in the carving out of some discreet space below the nuclear threshold.

Quest for Strategic Depth

Pakistan's policy on its western borders is conditioned by a lack of strategic depth and realisation of the informality of the 2,600-km

Afghan border termed as the Durand Line. While Pakistan considers it a settled border, the Afghans demand a greater Pashtunistan. This border is neither demarcated nor properly fenced. In effect, the Pashtun population, steeped in the frontier culture, spills over onto both sides. Pakistan is now embarking on a project to fence selected stretches and demarcate crossing points after clashes with Afghan forces and reports of rampant narco-arms trafficking. Similarly, the Iranian border between Baluchistan and Sistan, spanning 959 km, has only a tattered fence, which is being replaced by a concrete wall fortified with steel by Iran due to its concern about the Sunni insurgency in the Sistan province. The fear of being swamped by India has spurred the Pakistani quest for strategic depth and nurturing of the Taliban. Noted author Ahmed Rashid describes the Pakistani policy in Afghanistan as '**Islamabad views its Afghan policy through the prism of denying India any advantage in Kabul.**' C Christine Fair has debunked the popular fallacy that Pakistan is caught up in the Afghan conflict due to its role in aiding the Western powers in the fight against their Soviets. She has reiterated that Bhutto set up the Afghan cell in the ISI much before this operation.

Tentacles of Milbus

The Pakistani Armed Forces have created a labyrinthine foundation comprising the Fauji Army Welfare Trust, the Shaheen for the Air Force and the Baharia for the navy to extend their tentacles into the military-business (Milbus). Apart from this, they have a controlling stake in major public sector corporations like the National Logistics Cell (NLC), Frontier Works Organisation (FWO) and Special Communications Organisation (SCO). Also, a critical utility provider, the Water and Power Development Authority (WAPDA), has been placed under the Armed Forces. This logistics framework has dual-use capability and is leveraged by the army and the other two services. Ayesha Siddiqa, in her book *Military Inc: Inside Pakistan's Military Economy*, has observed that 'Milbus is military capital that perpetuates the military's predatory style.' This mega financial empire, worth approximately $40 billion, gives the army fiscal autonomy and assured pre-eminence. It is both a manifestation of the feudalistic character of Pakistani society and a perpetuation of non-democratic forces. **Army-affiliated entities (SCO and FWO) also cornered a number of ancillary projects of the CPEC, especially when General Aseem Bajwa headed it in a rather controversial tenure. The latest ill-advised foray is the army taking over large tracts of land for contractual farming as part of the CPEC.**

Alliances and Collusion

Pakistan has shown amazing flexibility and dexterity in balancing alliances with America and China. The first alliance was with the USA through SEATO and CENTO in the 1950s. It resulted in the induction of frontline equipment like Sabre jets, Patton tanks, and guns, which, unfortunately, emboldened Pakistan to attack India in 1965, resulting in the American cooling off in the 1960s and 1970s. The Americans returned in the 1980s to use Pakistan as a firm base for their Afghanistan operations for two decades and then lost interest, only to return again. The USA has essentially used Pakistan intermittently, yet Pakistan got considerable largesse in funds and equipment like the F-16s. **Pakistan also opened a channel to China after the 1962 operations and even acted as a facilitator to set up Kissinger's forays to Beijing.** The Pakistan-China friendship is described metaphorically as 'stronger than steel and deeper than oceans', but China has been discreet enough to only posture this and not get embroiled physically in the 1965, 1971, and Kargil operations. China has helped Pakistan to build nuclear weapons and missiles, flouting the proliferation regime. It also has a significant footprint in armament complexes at the Heavy Industries Taxila, Ordnance Factories Wah, and aviation complexes, with the latest being the joint production of the JF-17. This collusion with China is getting further cemented through the CPEC, notably the development of the Gwadar port.

Conclusion

Notwithstanding these peculiar biases in the ethos of the Pakistan Army, specifically at the higher echelons, it is not a pushover but has a considerable professional framework. At the unit level, the army is cohesive and remains efficient. Hence, it will be pragmatic not to underestimate it. Independent and competent experts feel that in the long-term interest, it will be in order if the army yields the mandated space to other legitimate agencies of the state. **The recent domestic chaos unleashed post dismissal of Imran Khan, with the storming of the corps commander's residence in Lahore by angry crowds in May 2023, is indicative of developing angst, yet it may be premature to underestimate Pak Army's capability to regain control.** Though it may appear highly optimistic and unlikely, it is hoped that the army will embark on correctives to become a functional and professional army.

References

1. Syed Nur Ahmed, in Craig Baxter, ed., From *Martial Law to Martial Law* (Lahore: Vanguard, 1985)

2. Shuja Nawaz, *Crossed Swords* (Karachi: Oxford University Press, 2008).

3. Babar Ayaz, *What's Wrong with Pakistan?* (Faridabad: Hay House India, 2013).

4. Husain Haqqani, *Pakistan Between Mosque and Military* (New Delhi: Penguin Viking, 2005).

5. C Christine Fair, *Fighting to The End: The Pakistan Army's Way of War* (Oxford: Oxford University Press, 2014).

6. Christophe Jaffrelot, *Pakistan at The Crossroads: Domestic Dynamics and External Pressures* (Gurgaon: Random House India, 2016).

7. Kamal Davar, *Tryst with Perfidy: The Deep State of Pakistan* (Mumbai: Rupa, 2017)

Pak Army Chiefs – Interesting Facts

- Pak has **appointed 17 Chiefs** including Gen Syed Asim Munir. In comparison, Indian Army has 28 Chiefs, including Gen Manoj Pande. **Average tenures work out to 4.5 yrs for Pak vis a vis 2.85 yrs for Indian Army Chiefs.**

- Both Indian and Pak Armies started with Commander-in-Chief (Cs-in-C) at the apex, with British Generals as first two Chiefs. After, Gens- Lockhart and Bucher, India appointed Gen Cariappa as the first Indian COAS, on 15 Jan 1949 realizing British complicity in Kashmir conflict. India had only four Cs-in-C and transited in Apr 1955 (in less than eight yrs) to Chief of Army Staff (COAS) appointment, with Gen Maharaj Rajendrasinhji Jadeja being re-designated from C-in- C to COAS.

- Pak continued with British Cs-in-C (Frank Messervy and Douglas Gracey) till Jan 1951. It also persisted with Cs-in-C system till Mar 1972 (for nearly 25 yrs) but had only six incumbents. Leaving out, first two British incumbents and Gen Gul Hasan Khan (the last one), the other three- Gens- Ayub Khan, Muhammad Musa and Yahya Khan, enjoyed 5 to 7 yrs tenures.

- **Pak Chiefs grant themselves or organize extensions, some multiple ones like Gen Zia.** Amongst recent incumbents, cases of extension to Gen Pervez Kayani and Gen Qamar Javed Bajwa were even contested in courts. On the other hand, **extensions for Indian Army COAS are most rare.**

- Gen Raheel Sharif though denied extension, fixed a tenure for himself as Chief of Saudi anchored, International Task Force for conflict in Yemen.

- **Gen Gul Hassan was removed with less than three months** (74 **days) in appointment. Gen Zia-ul-Haq and Gen Asif Nawaz Janjua died in harness**, both deaths remain matter of speculation regarding engineered accident and poisoning respectively by external intelligence agency. **Gen Jehangir Karamat was eased out** and forced to resign by PM Nawaz Sharif after nuclear testing.

- **Three Pak Army COAS (Ayub Khan, Zia-ul-Haq and Pervez Musharraf) applied martial law, taking over the reins replacing civilian regimes. Gen Ayub promoted himself as Field Marshal.** Gen Yahya Khan replaced Ayub Khan becoming the fourth one to rule under martial law, concurrently as COAS for two yrs and nine months.
- **Pak Chiefs, who took over as Martial Law rulers (except Ayub), like Yahya, Zia and Musharraf carried on as Army Chiefs concurrently**, Gen Ayub had two surrogate Chiefs- Musa and Yahya. **Zia didn't risk any one as Chief for entire ten yrs span as Martial Law Administrator.** Gen Musharraf appointed Pervez Kayani, only after six yrs as concurrent COAS and in his contrived political avatar as President, which lasted less than one year.
- **Double-hatters like Zia-ul-Haq and Musharraf continued to even occupy Army House in Rawalpindi rather than Aiwan-e-Sadar, Presidential Palace.** Eviction of Pervez Musharraf by Gen Kayani from Pindi House in May 2009 (nine months after he ceased to be President) became an ugly spat and was covered in media also.
- **The longest tenure was of Gen Zia-ul-Haq (12 yrs) and the shortest was Gen Khawaja Ziauddin, less than six hours.** Even Gen Gul Hassan had less than three months tenure becoming casualty of post Bangladesh shake-up. In Indian Army, Gen Thimmaya had the longest, 4 yrs tenure.
- After Kargil fiasco, Nawaz Sharif tried to sack Gen Musharraf, returning from overseas trip and appoint Ziauddin as Chief. In a counter coup, Musharraf took over the reins and PM Nawaz Sharif was packed-off to exile.
- **Supersession has been the norm to build personal loyalty yet,**

ironically it has been transient and such appointees build their own coterie, often defeating the agenda of such appointments.

- **Nawaz Sharif had role in appointment of six including Waheed Kakkar, Musharraf, Ziauddin, Raheel Sharif, Qamar Jawed Bajwa and Munir. After shifting loyalty, they contributed in his removal.** Gen Kakkar in somewhat even-handed approach got both President (main supporter) and PM Nawaz to resign after constitutional face-off. Musharraf not only executed coup but forced Nawaz into exile in Saudi Arabia. Gen Bajwa acquiesced in court dictated resignation of Nawaz and subsequent exile to London. Bajwa hoisted Nawaz's bete-noir, Imran Khan as PM in fixed elections, only to get him unseated.
- **Most Chiefs have been from Infantry though Armoured Corps had three** – Gen Gul Hassan, Ziq-ul-Haq and Gen Jehangir Karamat. Coincidentally, all three had their tenures truncated, two were eased out. While Zia-ul-Haq, not only became the military ruler but also carried on till his death in air crash. **Artillery had two incumbents** -Tikka Khan and Pervez Musharraf- both became Martial law Administrators.
- **Baloch Regiment has maximum five on the coveted list**- Gen Yahya, Aslam Beg, Kayani, Bajwa and Aseem Munir.

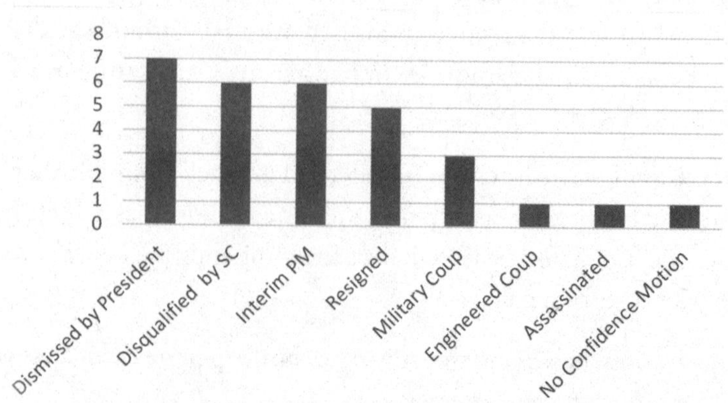

- **Only eight out of 17 Chiefs with combined tenures of 36 out of 77 yrs (47% till 2024) have been Punjabis (56% population).** Gen Tikka Khan in 1972 was first Punjabi Chief, 25 yrs after independence). Three (Tikka Khan, Asif Nawaz and Raheel Shariff are Rajputs from Pothwar in Punjab. Zia-ul-Haq (though Punjabi speaking but part Mohajir) was Chief for 12 yrs.

- Five (Ayub, Yahya, Gul Hasan, Waheed Kakkar, Jehangir Karamat) with combined tenures of 16 yrs (21%) have been Pushtuns (16 % population).

- Muhajirs (6% population) have contributed two - Musharraf and Aslam Beg, both Urdu speaking, accounting for 12 yrs (15%) **In essence, Pushtuns and Mohajirs have punched above their weight class. Trends may be changing as last three and current one (Aseem Munir) are all Punjabis.**

- **No Sindhi (17% population) or Baluchi (3%) have made it to be COAS, though Gen Muhammad Musa Khan was born in and resident of Baluchistan.** Gen Mohammed Musa, Hazara (miniscule population out of Shias and of Afghan descent) was C-in-C for eight yrs (10% tenure share).

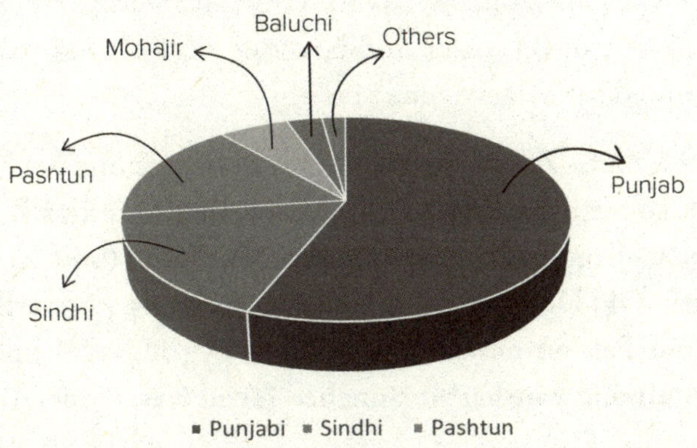

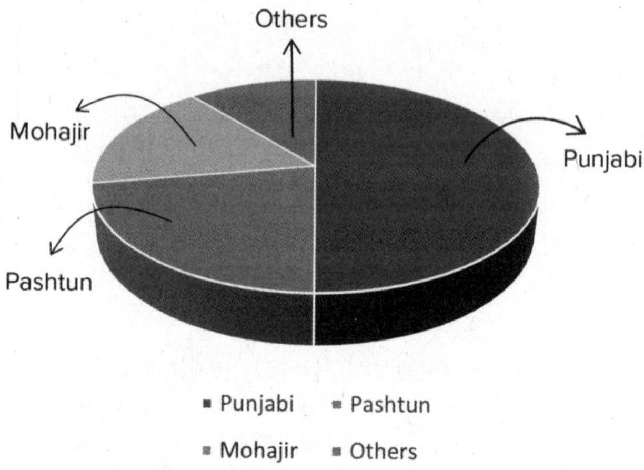

- **Musa, Yahya Khan and current incumbent, Aseem Munir belong to Shia community**, which make 17% population in Sunni (90%) dominated country with unending Sunni-Shia strife. Shias have been at the apex for 12 yrs (16% tenure share). Musa led Pak Army in 1965 operations and Yahya in ill-fated 1971 war. Gen Bajwa as per some reports was alleged to have distant familial links with Ahmediya community, now declared heretic.

- Ayub and Yahya were both Pushtuns and even ruled the country for 14 yrs. Non-Punjabis (Ayub, Yahya and Musharraf) at the helm for 25 out of 34 yrs of military rule. Zia-ul-Haq, part-Punjabi accounted for balance nine yrs.

- **Three Chiefs- Zia-ul-Haq (Jullundur born, St Stephen's educated, IMA commissioned); Mirza Aslam Beg (Azamgarh born and Shibli College graduate) and Pervez Musharraf (born in Neharwali Haveli, Old Delhi) had Indian roots dating to pre-partition days. Zia put Pak on radical path, Aslam Beg initiated proxy-war in Kashmir and Musharraf launched failed Kargil operation.**

- Pervez Musharraf lived and died in exile in Dubai. His successor

Pervez Kayani lives abroad in Australia. **Almost all former Chiefs have interests and assets abroad.**

Leveraging of Religious Diplomacy by Pakistan Army

Key Takeaways

- **Pakistan has ascribed to itself the role of the guardian of Islam.**
- **Islam within Pakistan has acquired extremist overtones, with the radicalised Pak Army driving the narrative.**
- **Islamic society in Pakistan is witnessing contestation and violence between Sunnis and Shias and even between various strands within Sunnis.**
- **Radicalisation triggers competitive radicalisation in non-radicalised societies and faiths.**
- **There is a need for inter-faith dialogue and forging a more moderate form of Islam.**

Introduction

Three terms—religion, faith, and theology—are used interchangeably but are seldom analysed for their nuances and subtle variations. The first two, religion (*dharma*) and faith, are frequently used as synonyms and relate to the practice of a particular religious order and cover outward expression and rituals. On the other hand, theology (*dharma shastra)* encompasses analytics and detailed reasoning. **Religion and faith have always been potent drivers in national politics and, increasingly, even in international diplomacy and power politics.** Despite articulations and pretensions of secularism and assertions of keeping politics insulated from religion, propelled by a wave of nationalism, religion has become a potent instrument in international diplomacy.

The tendency is more apparent in monotheistic or theocratic states like our neighbour Pakistan, which is an early proponent of this and, of late, has tried to leverage it for sinister purposes.

American and International Context

This trend further gained traction after the 9/11 terrorist attack, though the USA had created a special office designated an ambassador-at-large for 'International Religious Freedom' in 1999, consequent to the proliferation of Islamist extremism. Out of five incumbents, only one has been a non-Christian Jewish rabbi. An ex-ambassador, Senator Sam Brownback was appointed after the casting of a vote by the vice president, reflecting the ironic polarisation for an appointment mandated to promote consensus. He recently visited Dharamshala for parleys with the Dalai Lama. **The biggest current theological challenge is to evolve a more moderate form of Islam, containing the designs of caliphates and groups like Al Qaeda and ISIS. The king of Jordan and Saudi royalty are also engaged in this effort without much success.** It appears that outsourcing of the Wahhabism and Salafi strains to the extended neighbourhood, especially the Indian subcontinent, has run its course, and radicalism is already back in the Middle East. Hence, it is more of a compulsion to roll back radicalisation or at least keep it within manageable limits.

The American-prodded initiative for moderate Islam is not free from internal contradictions and has naturally led to the coalescing of radical states. Malaysia recently led an initiative outside the traditional body, the Organisation of Islamic States, as an alternative platform, with Indonesia, Turkey, and Qatar as prominent participants in the meeting. The platform has been seen as an alternative and challenge to the traditional Saudi-led theological Islamic block. Pakistan pulled out at the very last minute, forced by the relentless pressure of the Saudis and the Gulf nations. Imran's move to play a key role in forging the proposed alliance has annoyed Saudi Arabia, the UAE, and other Gulf nations. **The reticence of Gulf nations during the**

Pakistani fiscal emergency and refusal to get drawn into the Indo-Pak issues has raised pertinent questions about the 'ummah' (Islamic brotherhood) and its efficacy.

It is also pertinent to take note of the fact that radicalisation promotes competitive radicalisation in other societies and, consequently, it has spawned neo-conservative movements and hardening tendencies in other religions like Buddhism and now even Hinduism and Sikhism. All these malevolent strands are dangerous and need to be curbed.

Manifestations in Pakistan

India has been at the receiving end of the malevolent forays of Pakistan's religious diplomacy, which has acquired *fassadi* overtones. **The use of the term *fassad* in preference to the incorrectly used *jihad* is theologically validated. The Pakistan Army chose to call its anti-terror operations *Radd-ul-Fasaad*. Even American cultural education discourages the misuse of the term *jihad*.** It is hardly logical to have different terms for indigenous and exported versions of *fassad*. The Pakistan Army's hypocrisy was first exhibited in the early 1950s when it colluded with Naga militant groups despite these groups openly striving for a Christian regime and Nagaland for Christ. The army under Tikka Khan indulged in the rape and massacre of fellow Bengali Muslims, disregarding the concept of ummah (Islamic brotherhood), leading to East Pakistan breaking away. This, in effect, negated the very raison d'être for the two-nation theory and the rationale for a separate Islamic nation. Giving primacy to religion, it disregarded other equally relevant factors like lack of geographical connectivity and cultural and linguistic disparities between the two wings of Pakistan. Hypocrisy is currently seen in the silence of Pakistan and the ummah on the rampant persecution of Uyghurs in Xinjiang by the Han Chinese. Hence, Pakistan and other Islamic nations have misused theocracy as per their convenience and in conjunction with other drivers and interests.

Pakistan, created as a homeland for Muslims, got the initial thumbs down when 35 million Muslims chose to cast their lot with secular India despite the partition riots. Compared to this, Hindus and Sikhs deserted Pakistan in droves despite Jinnah's assurance that the new nation would be inclusive, allowing minorities their fair share. Soon after Jinnah's death, the Islamic nation, which had Karachi as the capital, chose to make Islamabad, a suburb of Rawalpindi, the new seat of power. With this naming, it also chose to carry the cross or (crescent) of Islam. Manifestations were seen in kabayali *lashkars* in Kashmir under Colonel Akbar (anointed as General Tariq) and *razakars* in Hyderabad, albeit the religious aspect was subdued. More sinister was the contrived misplacing of the *Moi-e-Muqqadas* (holy hair relic of the Prophet) to whip up emotions in the Kashmir Valley in 1963. Despite the failure to achieve its diabolic designs, Pakistan launched Operation Gibraltar in 1965. Infiltration by Mujahideen Task Forces, named after mostly infamous Muslim raiders Salahuddin, Ghaznavi, Tariq, Babur, Qasim, Khalid, Nusrat, and Khilji, was organised under General Musa. The provocative tendency of using Islamic symbolism, particularly for the raiders, continues in the naming of missiles as Ghaznavi, Babur, and Ghauri.

In this dangerous lurch from subcontinental Sufi/Barelvi to Deobandi, Wahhabi and Salafi forms of Islam, *Khuda Hafiz* has become *Allah Hafiz* and *Ramazan* replaced by the Arabic *Ramadan*. Pakistan seems to have linked its socio-cultural and theological moorings westwards, choosing Arabic influences over traditional linkages. Another major milestone was Bhutto's articulation of resolve to manufacture the Islamic bomb. Sadly, competitive radicalism under Zia-ul-Haq and later the Taliban accounted for the death of Zulifkar, his daughter Benazir, and probably even Zia. The very dream of an Islamic bomb is getting reduced to a Sunni bomb because Shia Iran doesn't trust the Sunnis. In Talibanised Pakistan, Jinnah's Shias and Nobel Physicist Abdus Salaam's Ahmadiyyas are being targeted and eliminated. Former Army Chief General Raheel is now leading a coalition of Sunni forces against the Shia Houthi rebels. Pakistan also provides troops to guard sheikhdoms and royalty in many Gulf countries like Saudi Arabia. It has also been training pilots and other specialists, including veterans, engaged in the maintenance of equipment. **Within Pakistan, various strands of the Islamic faith are at loggerheads, overtaken by competitive extremism. The first manifestation is to apply the label of blasphemy on other faiths like Hindus, Sikhs, and Christians, though in the minority. The next are Ahmadiyyas, dubbed as non-Islamic. The dominant Sunnis often target Shias, Bohras, and even Sufis, questioning their practices and beliefs. Sunni society has contestation amongst the Barelvi, Deobandi, Ahle-Hadith, Salafi, and Wahhabi sects.**

Mainstream Islamist activists in electoral politics and the army utilise these radical groups, like Qadri's Tehreek-e-Labbaik Pakistan (TeLP), to build pressure on governments and worrying trends. These groups have not only gained legitimacy but are also wielding blasphemy as a weapon to target others. The lynching of the Sri Lankan manager of the Rajco Factory, Sialkot is a dangerous manifestation of such tendencies. Even the highest courts have utilised ambiguous Shariat criteria, like non-compliance to 'Sadiq and Ameen' (truthful and honest) norms, to disqualify and unseat PM Nawaz Sharif.

Zia's Decade and Rise of ISI

This dangerous course had been defined by Zia's decade of 1978 to 1988, which catalysed the Pakistan Army's Shariasation, committing itself to *Nizam-e-Mustafa* (rule of the Prophet) and taking upon itself the guardianship of the ideological frontiers. The traditional motto of '*ittehad, yaqeen, tanzeem*' (unity, faith, discipline) was changed to '*iman, taqwa, jihad fi sabilillah*' (faith, piety, holy war in the path of Allah). How do minorities reconcile to such exhortation? Zia also made '*The Quranic Concept of War*' by Brigadier SK Malik, which legitimises the use of terror, a mandatory text for the forces. An interesting quote from the Pakistan Army's official website (reading like the objective of extremist groups) states, 'The mission and aim of a

Momin is martyrdom.' American compulsions of tackling the Afghan imbroglio gave Pakistan an opportunity to emerge as the vanguard in this misplaced campaign, which was legitimised as a theological necessity. Since then, turmoil in the Middle East and plans of a caliphate with Khorasan, which includes India, has enabled Pakistan's terror assembly line to remain active. **A radicalised army in control of the nation and its foreign and security policies, including nuclear weapons, is, indeed, a dangerous warning for the neighbourhood. ISI and ISPR remain two key catalysts in this diabolic game.**

Kartarpur Challenge

The ISI, having probably realised that Kashmir is proving to be a case of diminishing marginal returns, has come up with the diabolic K2 plan to exploit the latent sub-nationalism of the Sikhs. The timing of the Kartarpur Corridor and the initial offer by General Bajwa are indicative of the Pakistan Army's ownership of this move. Apart from this, the anchoring of the construction by the Field Works Organisation and Utiming with SFJ 2020 are all ominous indicators of the shape of things to come. While nobody doubts the loyalty of the Sikhs, fringe groups can be potential prey. It is also pertinent that the Punjabis defeated extremism and are cognisant of the state being put back by a couple of decades. Nobody is even remotely suggesting that the Sikhs are so naive that they will be brainwashed by a couple of posters and the display of remains of a bombshell with a provocative placard blaming India for attacking a gurudwara. Yet, it does open up possibilities for profiling and long-drawn psychological warfare. Combating the Pakistan-aided Drugistan designs remains a major challenge for the Punjabis. While the proxy war in Kashmir may be on a lower level, there are attempts by the ISI to fish for trouble spots and establish linkages with splinter groups in the hinterland to foment trouble. This has been coupled with attempts to raise the Kashmir issue at various international bodies, notably the United Nations, including the Security Council. While these efforts have not found much traction, the efforts continue and are likely to intensify basically to discredit India, especially on the handling of Kashmir. China, as a declared ally, has been anchoring these efforts, and Indian diplomacy has to remain vigilant to counter them.

Conclusion

The near complete disregard of the Kashmir rhetoric by the ummah has resulted in Pakistan blaming fellow international bodies and especially the Islamic nations for giving market-driven compulsions preference over the ummah and religious issues. **The crying need for inter-faith diplomacy is a collective endeavour for theological correction to evolve a moderate religion. Concurrently, Pakistan needs to demonstrate sincerity by dismantling export-oriented *fassadi* assembly lines and detoxifying its army.** India has no choice but to keep its guard up against Pakistan's designs. As the nation with the second largest Muslim population, India also needs to promote Sufi and moderate Islam to preserve its diversity and secular traditions.

Pak Army – In Need of Corrective Surgery

(Written in June 2018)

Pakistan is preparing for general elections, which ironically are turning out to be 'Generals' Elections'. Nawaz Sharif, who has been disqualified by the judiciary in collusion with ISI on specious grounds of not being 'sadiq' (truthful) and 'amin' (honest), has labelled his detractors as 'umpires' and 'khalai-mahalook' (aliens). Army generals are setting the stage for elections by culling uncomfortable elements.

The process was initiated by General Raheel Sharif, who decided to render Altaf Hussain irrelevant in Mohajir politics. He engineered a split in the Muttahida Qaumi Movement (MQM), a powerful regional party in Sind and Karachi. Farooq Sattar was dramatically rescued by the rangers from abductors and catapulted to the helm in MQM, with Altaf left holding a rump in exile. General Bajwa followed it up by arranging an officially sponsored merger of MQM with the Pak Sarzameen Party.

General Bajwa, initially hailed as an apolitical general, has proved to be a committed proponent of the deep state. He surprised seasoned observers by midwifing talks with Tehreek-e-Labaik Ya Rasool Allah (TLYRA) goons, who had taken over roads leading to the capital for three weeks, forcing the change in oath for parliamentarians. The party formed in the wake of the hanging of Mumtaz Qadri, the assassin of Governor Salman Taseer, runs on the fuel of competitive religious extremism and questionable interpretation of blasphemy. Why would an army known for its brutal tactics in Karachi and Swat adopt a kid-glove approach with known rabble-rousers? Was this another foray into marginalising Nawaz, even by propping dangerous dispensation?

It is apparent that the establishment has not learnt any lessons from the huge costs that the nation bears by mollycoddling such snakes. The army chief has promulgated the famous 'Bajwa doctrine', partly to assuage the ruffled feathers of Western powers, who have put Pakistan on the terror watch list.

More ominously, he chose to question the decade-old 18th Amendment to the Constitution, which devolves additional powers to provinces. This enabling provision strengthens federalism and is necessary for balancing disparate sub-nationalisms of Balochs, Pashtuns, Sindhis, Kashmiris, Baltis, besides Punjabis. **Protests and cries of 'Da Sanga Azadi Da' – "What sort of freedom is this?" by the Pashtun Tahafuz (protection) Movement bring back memories of 'Joy Bangla', army repression, and refusal to share power with Bengalis.**

Ishrat Hussain, former governor of the State Bank of Pakistan, in his recent book, *Governing the Ungovernable,* has flagged the Garrison State Syndrome and the nexus between the military and corporates as two biggest stumbling blocks. The private 'Khakhi wealth' approximates 25 billion dollars; concurrently, the army continues to splurge, defying the international benchmark of 3% of GDP.

Pakistan, which in the 90s seemed to be outperforming India, now totters towards an imminent IMF bailout and is rapidly becoming a Chinese dependency. The semantics of failed or failing state apart, the situation in Pakistan is indeed critical.

In this chaos, the Pak army, the institution that should be held accountable, surprisingly retains the highest approval rating of 76% and burgeoning wealth. This despite losing Bangladesh and the surrender of 93,000 soldiers. Repeated misadventures in 1947, 1965, and Kargil seem to have only increased its TRP.

The obvious reason is the crafty manoeuvre of Zia-ul-Haq making the army self-appointed guardians of ideological frontiers. It has also retained the right to interfere in internal affairs with the unique law of necessity, which allows it to impose martial law at will. The current scorecard reads four times, including the constitutional coup in 1953, totalling 38 years out of 71 years of existence. More importantly, it retains a veto in all critical affairs, like nuclear weapons, defence, relations with neighbours, and even overseeing elections.

Ideological frontiers are a very questionable and dangerous concept for an ideology that promotes the Caliphate (junking Westphalian model), Fassad (mischievously referred to as Jihad), and terror as legitimate instruments of war. Hamid Gul's generation served the American purpose but continues to manifest through Lieutenant General Shahid Gul, who recently died fighting for ISIS in Syria. Long years of responsibility (CGS and DGMO) and professional education in the USA could not moderate this general. The rabid tendency at lower ranks is too scary to even contemplate. **Former chiefs, Aslam Beg and Musharaff, are already facing court-monitored actions.** Mercenary skills find ready takers with General Raheel Sharif heading the Sunni coalition, also referred to as the Islamic Military Alliance. There are reports of the deployment of a beefed-up composite brigade in Saudi Arabia besides troops protecting the royal family. The training expertise of retirees is being misused by extremists like the Taliban and Daesh, while ISI continues to deploy them as strategic assets.

The idea, 'prima-facie', may appear utopian, but the Pakistan Army definitely needs externally monitored structured correctives. The UN currently runs security sector reform programmes in more than 15 countries, mostly in Africa. Reforms were earlier implemented in Nepal, Iraq, CAR, and Afghanistan. Support from China will be a pre-requisite and an example of President Xi's successful reforms to rein in the PLA; concerns about Xinjiang and CPEC may help.

Most Pakistani generals have properties, interests, and relatives abroad, and publishing their assets will be enough to show them the 'sadiq' and 'amin' mirror; after all, what applies to politicians is equally applicable to real rulers. Macro reforms should address ideological baggage, commit armed forces to constitutional limits, and privatise foundations like Fauji, Shaheen, and Bahria. Policing, internal security, border guarding, and army responsibilities need to be separated. **An army that derails democracy and development and keeps the neighbourhood in a state of perpetual turmoil is indeed a fit case for corrective surgery.**

Pak's First National Security Policy Doesn't Spell Out Cogent Road Map

(Written in February 2022)

Pakistan has announced its first-ever and much-touted National Security Policy (NSP). The document spells out the national security vision with vague guidelines described as goals. It has been projected as a citizen-centric initiative, and the document is liberally peppered with phraseology like — whole of nation, inclusive national dialogue, unity in diversity, normalisation, pluralistic anti-terror strategy, etc. One typical statement is, "Pakistan safeguards its sovereignty by ensuring national cohesion and harmony, preserving territorial integrity, enhancing economic independence, and ensuring the writ of the state."

The document is laid out in eight sections, spanning 110 pages. However, the public version has 48 pages, hiding more than what it reveals, even in quantitative terms. The NSP has been prepared after a seven-year-long, supposedly consultative effort, reportedly with inputs from 600-odd security analysts and research scholars toiling under the National Security Division (NSD). The document has a five-year currency from 2022 to 2027, subject to revisions/updating.

It was approved by the cabinet on December 28, 2021, and the public version was released on January 14. The endeavour was initiated by erstwhile NSA Sartaj Aziz in the Nawaz Sharif regime and finished by the Moeed Yusuf and Imran Khan duo.

The operating environment (both geo-strategic and geo-economic) for Pakistan has changed drastically, in the interim. America has been replaced by China, the iron brother, and the USA barely finds mention in the document. The policy is skewed in focus towards China, India, and Afghanistan. In sum, critical catalysts of the **three A's (Allah, Army, and America (sic)) have been replaced by ABC (Allah, Bajwa, and China)**. The general is already into the sixth year of his tenure, and the clamour for another extension after November 22 is again growing. The document carries the stamp of the Bajwa Doctrine, mandating a shift towards geo-economics and avoiding hostilities for 100 years. Of course, the proxy war is an unstated, acceptable variant!

Pakistan has been subjected to the ignominy of being placed on the grey list, just short of being blacklisted, thanks to the Chinese veto. Its economy is in the doldrums, and ironically, on the day of release, the State Bank of Pakistan, under the IMF diktat, was placed under restricted autonomy, limiting profligate tendencies. The moot question is: Will it impact the defence budget, and by how much? Pakistan's fiscal crisis is accentuated by the marked loss of support from traditional bailout benefactors — Saudi Arabia and the UAE.

The only constant has been the unrelenting Modi regime.

Economic security is projected as the core objective, seeking to raise the populace to middle-income status. It makes lofty claims – the desire to make economic bases and not military ones. This fits in with yearnings for Imran's 'Naya Pakistan'. The problem is modelling on the ideal of 'Riyasat-e-Madina'. The most serious challenge and inherent contradictions of reining in fassadi, extremist elements, anti-blasphemy warriors like Tehreek-e-Labbaik Pakistan and avoiding the repetition of Sialkot-type lynching incidents are not even addressed.

The nub and relevant part of the policy from our perspective is the fifth section, dealing with conventional military threats, maritime competition, deterrence in the South Asian region, and space and cyber security issues. **India appears 14 times in the document, and the Indian Ocean appears thrice. Barring a single expression of the desire to improve relations with India, all other mentions are negative.** It perceives the expansion of India's nuclear triad and investment in modern technologies as triggers for disturbing the regional balance. It pointedly refers to India seeking to join the Nuclear Suppliers Group without signing the Nuclear Non-Proliferation Treaty.

The policy also highlights the growing asymmetry in conventional forces. **Interestingly, it states that "the possibility of use of force by the adversary, as a deliberate policy choice, cannot be ruled out." This seems to be driven by the continued hangover effect of surgical strikes.** The NSP prescribes focus to be maintained on the LoC and working boundary. Kashmir remains central to its security matrix, and Pakistan blames India for unilateral alterations in the constitutional framework. India is projected to harbour "hegemonic designs" and is held responsible for frozen bilateral ties.

The NSP outlines three major challenges, i.e., external imbalance, vertical inequalities among classes, and horizontal inequalities

between regions. It seeks to prioritise national security objectives by mapping traditional as well as non-conventional threats. **Surprisingly, it introduces the concept of irreconcilable challenges, alluding to the Balochi insurgency.** The NSP remains in denial mode on Pashtun separatism and problems of managing the Durand Line region. Afghanistan is projected as a strategic gateway. However, strategic depth compulsion and proxy warriors as strategic assets are probably hidden in the classified version.

The China-Pakistan Economic Corridor and connectivity are projected as silver bullets, yet zero access to India remains the dominant narrative. The document gives undue weightage to central geographical location and its potential. The NSP reinforces Pakistan as an insecure state seeking parity with India. Anti-Indian culture seems to be raison d'etre for its existence. It has compounded its problems by including the protection of faith as a self-imposed additional frontier, forcing it to punch above its weight.

In sum, the NSP is a compilation of a rhetorical wish list and reminds us of the NDC dissertation days. The document does not spell out a cogent road map. Most importantly, it fails to indicate a commitment to transformational changes to achieve the lofty objectives. **Notwithstanding contradictions and unrealistic projections, it indicates a sobering realisation of economic problems.** It is also evident that the clamour for sanity is gathering traction. It will be somewhat reassuring if Pakistan applies itself to NSP and geo-economics, giving India space to tackle the wolf-warrior on the northern borders.

It is recommended that India should also finalise its NSP. The current reliance on ambiguity makes defence planning difficult. Without clear-cut goals, we deny ourselves the benefits of accountability and net assessment, which contribute to strategic deterrence.

Gen Bajwa's Legacy and Pak Army's New Chief

(Written in November 2022)

Pakistan is staring at an abyss and imploding chaos in the long term, but in the near term, next week is certainly likely to define the course of the nation's travails. Former Prime Minister Imran Khan's Azadi March concluded on November 26 in Islamabad; Lieutenant General Asim Munir, COAS designate, was to retire on November 27, two days before the date of the superannuation of General Javed Qamar Bajwa but got the endorsement of President Arif Alvi on Thursday for all important and coveted assignment of COAS, according to news reports.

In the run-up to this all-important appointment, there were many possibilities and projections regarding the nomination of the next COAS, larger-than-life personae, driving foreign and national security narratives. Shahbaz Sharif rushed to London to consult his exiled elder brother, Nawaz Sharif, and President Alvi consulted his party president, Imran Khan, thereby driving another nail in the coffin of the crumbling democracy. Many options, like the following, were under consideration:

- **The first option being discussed was an extension to General Bajwa, at least till the next national assembly elections due in October-November 2023.** Azadi March, with former PM Imran on the streets, demands the dissolution of the assembly and early elections.

- Couched with this agitation was **the desire to promote his favourite, Lieutenant General Faiz Hameed, former DG-ISI and Peshawar Corps Commander, currently commanding low-profile Bahawalpur Corps.** His case was pushed by President (Imran Khan appointee0. It would also ensure that his bete-noire, Lieutenant General Asim Munir, who exposed the unsavoury antics of Imran, is kept out of reckoning, leveraging technical issues of his retirement date. With the deadline approaching, President Alvi can still upset the apple cart, though it appears that back-room consultations have advised wiser counsel of respecting constitutional proprietary rather than party loyalty.

- **The third option was to select 'apna-banda' by the Sharif clan. This would have meant a violation of seniority and choosing compliant ones like Nauman Mehmood** or even the only non-infantry empanelled one, General Mohammed Amir.
- **Having burnt their fingers in previous nominations, Sharifs have possibly revived the seniority principle of an apolitical army. The seniormost, Lieutenant General Asim Munir, has been recommended for COAS, and next on the panel, Lieutenant General Sahir Shamshad Mirza, notwithstanding his notable track record, has been given a four-star low-profile JCSC assignment.** General Mirza and next in seniority, Azhar Abbas have both been Rawalpindi Corps Commanders and CGS.

Chief Designate Lieutenant General Munir is currently Quarter Master General and has commanded the low-profile Gujranwala Corps, though he has been Force Command Northern Areas (FCNA) Commander, sword arm of Rawalpindi Corps. He has also been DG military intelligence and DG-ISI. His ISI stint was cut short to nine months due to his run-in with Imran. **He is Shia and Hafiz-e-Quran**, a religious course done as a Colonel, he can recite the holy text. He is reputed to be a 'straight arrow', plain-speaking professional, religious, and from a humble background. He is also an OTS, Mangla alumnus, and short service officer, unlike more powerful and well-knit direct entry ones from Pakistan Military Academy, Abbottabad. General Musa Khan, the chief following Ayub, General Zia, and General Arif, VCOAS, who ran the army for General Zia, have been short-service inductees rising to the apex hierarchy. **The biggest worry is: Will General Munir try to emulate Zia, who, despite his St**

Stephen background, altered the very character of the army, giving it ideological and theological frontiers to guard?

The problem is that when in the quiver, most aspirants are straight arrows, but after launch (installation), they become autonomous and acquire a trajectory of their own. Starting with generals Ayub, Yahya, Zia, and Pervez Musharraf, they have subjected Pakistan to decades of recurring military regimes with no real differences or reforms. Meanwhile, **Imran, in his Azadi March, has unleashed a volley of diatribes tarnishing the army's image. He has highlighted oft-repeated issues of corruption, nepotism, and meddling in politics, but, most importantly, exposed the senior vs junior divide.** This alleged hiatus, with Imran claiming that junior officers hero-worship him, is unverified and part of Imran's narcissistic tendencies. Leveraging an anti-establishment streak has the potential to expose a festering fault line promoting insubordination in an otherwise disciplined force. Recent leaks of General Bajwa's tax records indicate another despicable trend. An objective appraisal of Imran's tenure establishes that Pakistan's economy has languished into a financial mess, and the promised 'game changer', the China-Pakistan Economic Corridor (CPEC), has failed to take off. The country continued to be in the Financial Action Task Force (FATF) grey listing with Imran's cosmetic corrections. He annoyed traditional backers, the Chinese, with enquiries into the CPEC. The Organisation of Islamic Cooperation (OIC) nations, particularly Saudis, were also riled by his ill-advised move to bolster Turkey, Malaysia, and Iran as alternate Islamic axis. Imran, presently, is riding unprecedented popularity and anti-America waves without realising that the Dragon embrace may be more dangerous. His own squeaky-clean image was tarnished by gift-gate scandals, the naming of his advisors in the CPEC investigation, and many stories of Bibi Bushra.

General Bajwa leaves behind an equally controversial legacy, topped by the recent exposure of wealth-amassing scandals, otherwise normal in Pakistan Miltestablishment. His advocacy for an apolitical character for the army has been watered down and is essentially a hypocritical version of General Kayani's hands-off approach. **Pragmatically, 'apolitical' in Pakistan's lexicon means civilian rulers being allowed to flounder through, albeit under guidance. He installed Lieutenant General Asim Bajwa as head of the CPEC authority and remote-controlled all-important apex appointments like the Locust Control Agency.** He was leading the diplomatic manoeuvres to revive contact with the USA and Western nations to make Pakistan a 'balancer'. The 'Bajwa doctrine' entailed an internal focus on the economy and stability with geo-political amity. He did foster re-negotiations for a continued ceasefire on the LoC. However, diabolic designs like K2, proxy war, and narco-terrorism have found traction. It seems that General Bajwa leaves a lot to be done with tensions on both the LoC and Durand Line besides the economy in serious distress.

Pak – Descent Into Chaos

Pakistan Stands at Crossroads

(Written in April 2022)

The geo-strategic environment around India has indeed become very murky and chaotic. Pakistan, Sri Lanka, Nepal, Myanmar, and Afghanistan are embroiled in flux and turbulence. The Lankan imbroglio has a geo-economic dimension, with China being the main catalyst for the fiscal abyss and the looming humanitarian crisis. Kathmandu is headed for elections under a court-mandated caretaker government. Naypyidaw is still grappling with multiple insurgencies and the shock of the military usurping power after dismissing the democratically elected government. Kabul continues under an unrecognised Taliban dispensation with a medieval mindset, defying definition.

India remains an island of stability in a turbulent maelstrom, yet at the outset, it will be appropriate to state that an unstable neighbourhood can have a dangerous fallout through socio-political osmosis. Tamil refugees have already started landing on the Tamil Nadu coast. An old African proverb states that "malaise like locusts does not devour only your neighbour's field". It is only the Chinese who believe in "looting the house on fire". India, like a responsible neighbour, has rushed wheat to Afghanistan and diesel and rice to Sri Lanka, along with a financial bailout package.

Imran Khan has unleashed an unprecedented political crisis, orchestrating Act-1 (first round)of the sordid drama in the Pakistani parliament. **His game plan is to divert attention from accumulated anti-incumbency and financial distress generated by three-and-a-half years of misrule. Imran has failed to deliver the promised 'Naya Pakistan' and 'Riyasat-e-Madina'.** The noted cricketer has chosen the 'gully cricket' format by taking the issue to the public by organising huge rallies and frequent televised addresses. His recipe for popular connect is based on allegations of conspiracy theory and a foreign hand (America) to unseat him. The allegation is based on top-secret diplomatic communication (coded cable in cypher), referring to the US bureaucrat's advocacy for regime change. Imran is displaying irrationality in threatening the table of the top-secret cable in parliament. The holier-than-thou attitude toward external influence definitely ranks as hypocrisy in a debt-dependent nation known for the 3As (Amerika-Army-Allah), till it became ABC (Allah-Bajwa-China) with the dependence on China. The CPEC is also described as the 'Colonization of Pak Economically by China'.

His populist strategy is beginning to resonate as Imran is drawing huge crowds, and his party, PTI, reaped success in the recent local elections in KPK. Street power has become a defining trend, as witnessed in TYPL's frequent debilitating blockades. Anti-Americanism in Pakistan is a heady brew that readily blends with the fassadi propaganda and anti-corruption crusades. The foreign hand invariably shapes anti-India mobilisation. While those baying for imploding the country may exult, uncontrolled chaos in neighbourhoods can have unpleasant surprises and ripple effects.

In this drama, the second round belonged to Pakistan's Supreme Court, with CJI Umar Ata Bandial emerging as the man of the match. However, the CJI is a known Imran acolyte with a distinct bias against the Sharifs. The court, in a unanimous verdict, rightly set aside the proceedings conducted by the Deputy Speaker of Parliament. In sum, the dissolution of parliament and ordering early elections were held ultra vires. By implication, the actions of Pakistan's president amounted to rubber stamping without due application of mind.

It is heartening that the court seemed to combine urgency with due deliberation and promote inclusive consultations with the election commission. The strengthening of institutions, as well as checks and balances on the legislature, can be welcome, stabilising trends. **All this must be taken with a pinch of salt as different actors, including even the CJI, have their own vested and covert motives.**

The Pakistani Army and its chief, General Qamar Javed Bajwa, have also decided to project an image of strengthening constitutional norms by remaining in the shadows, at least for the time being. The ISI chief, Lieutenant General Nadeem Anjum, went an extra length to downplay his presence in a meeting with Bill Gates in February. It is very difficult to believe that the khaki will yield control, but it is trying to build up the image or façade of being apolitical. Even a façade is better than nothing, especially with China on a rampage. **It is also heartening that the ceasefire on the LoC has been holding for 14 months. It will be interesting to decipher if the Army is indeed serious about the 'Bajwa doctrine', focusing on rapprochement and trade. It could well be a temporary mutation of stripes by General Bajwa to earn another extension of tenure in November or a different role.**

Like all discredited rulers, Imran is shifting focus to external geopolitics from failure in domestic governance. Surprisingly, Indian strategic autonomy is being praised and used to reinforce Pakistan's yearning for parity syndrome, a desire to punch much above her weight. In sheer desperation, he is even using self-flagellation, stating that Pakistan is being used in a 'use and throw' mode like tissue paper. **Imran, who has been isolated by annoying traditional allies—Saudi Arabia and the Gulf countries—has only himself to blame for his woes.** The US is rightly peeved with him because it is under his watch that General Faiz Hameed, former ISI chief, shredded semblance of a face-saving exit from Afghanistan. He was in Kabul to oversee Haqqani edging out Mullah Baradar, a lynchpin of the US's hopes for continued relevance. A recent Russian visit was another diplomatic hara-kiri of sorts.

China, hyperactive in manipulating domestic politics in Nepal, Sri Lanka, and Myanmar, is surprisingly keeping a low profile in Pakistan. Beijing may prefer Shabaz Sharif, with his track record as a better administrator and strong proponent of the CPEC. Pakistan's desire to repair ties with America is also driven by growing disenchantment with Chinese weapons. Efficacy apart, their serviceability is causing considerable concern. If Pakistan aspires to strategic autonomy, it will be axiomatic to reduce dependence on Beijing and recast the CPEC to avoid a repeat of the Sri Lanka type of fiasco.

In future and ongoing Round 3, filibustering and other antics can further damage Pakistan's credibility and reputation. Geopolitical flux and turbulence are natural, but the management of chaos and keeping it below the threshold in a nuclear-armed neighbourhood is non-negotiable. It requires maturity and strengthening of constitutional institutions coupled with deft diplomacy.

Anarchy & Imploding Institutions in Pak

(Written in November 2022)

Former Prime Minister Imran Khan has resumed his Haqiqi-Azadi (real freedom) March — the second edition from Lahore to Islamabad — after a week-long suspension. The pause was forced by an attack on Imran on November 7, at Wazirabad (Punjab), by a deranged maverick. The march launched on October 28 has paralysed Pakistan's civic life. The fact that Imran survived with only some bullet fragments in his leg indicates that it was a 'lone wolf' amateur effort. Agencies execute attacks like the assassination of Benazir Bhutto and the recent killing of TV anchor Arshad Sharif in Kenya in a professional, albeit cruel manner. They leave no traces of their involvement or smoking guns. The fact that the attack happened in Punjab ruled by Imran's PTI under Chief Minister Pervez Elahi, raises serious questions about the state of law and order in the so-called most settled province.

The first edition of the ill-fated Haqiqi-Azadi March was launched on May 25 from Peshawar, the capital of his native KPK, to Islamabad. It was called off the very next day in the face of resolute police action. In the intervening period, the PML-N government in

Punjab, led by his bête noire, Hamza Sharif, was replaced. Imran has been asking Shahbaz Sharif's government to resign and call early elections. The current term of the national assembly expires in August next year, and elections have to be held by October 2023.

Imran was catapulted into power by hidden forces described by Nawaz Sharif as 'Khalai Makhlooq' (invisible ghosts) in August 2018. His victory as 'selected PM' was managed by the army.

This indeed was ironic, as Nawaz Sharif had appointed General Qamar Javed Bajwa, overlooking the campaign against him alleging Ahmadiyya affiliations in his family. General Bajwa has been even-handed as he has not spared his choice in orchestrated elections, Imran, who granted him an extension, albeit reluctantly. **Imran, in a lacklustre, boat-burning tenure, first antagonised the Chinese with an indifferent and critical approach to the CPEC, coupled with investigations to fix the CPEC's mentor, Nawaz Sharif.**

Next, he annoyed Saudi Arabia by promoting Turkey and Malaysia as alternate OIC power centres. His visit to Moscow just before Putin's Ukrainian misadventure riled the USA. The foremost on his current hit list is America, accused by him of a conspiracy to remove him. His current diatribe is also against the army, allegedly for multiple assassination plots and corruption.

Notwithstanding all this, Imran is riding an unprecedented popularity wave, tapping discontent. His move to fight six out of seven by-elections added another twist to theatrics, laced with narcissism. While he won five seats, narrow margins of victory and poor voter turn-out took some shine off. **Most importantly, it is a sad commentary on the gullibility of the Pakistan Awaam (populace), which keeps crafting 'zero to hero' stories. Abiding affliction with conspiracies, coupled with a love-hate relationship with Amerika (sic), drive the narrative shaping by Imran's cabal.**

He has accused PM Shahbaz, Interior Minister Rana Sanaullah, and Major General Faisal Naseer, DG ISI as key conspirators. He is already discussing the second attempt and threatening to expose those involved. His demand to include those named by him in the FIR is audacious, as it includes serving as head of ISI. It required intervention by the Supreme Court to lodge an FIR against the apprehended attacker. Courts have been part of an imbroglio with flip-flop rulings in the Hamza-Elahi drama in the Punjab assembly and the disqualification of Imran. **Imran has been making unverified claims about dissent in middle and junior army ranks. His speeches tread the thin line between incitement and insubordination. It bears reiteration that the six-year tenure of General Bajwa has created a class of dissenting veterans. It is rumoured that 20-odd generals were denied progression. The demonstrations in front of Lahore and Peshawar Corps Commanders' fortress-like residences and tanks in Nov 2022 are reminiscent of the Tiananmen Square moment.** The army, which remains the only "stabilising" institution, is under unprecedented attacks, denting its Teflon-coated image. There are demands for winding up the propaganda arm, Inter-Services Public Relations (ISPR). DG-ISI was forced to hold a press conference to clarify the killing of a TV anchor.

Long marches are the new coercive tools in Pakistan's political lexicon. They breed anarchy, chaos, and lone-wolf mavericks. Last year, religious fanatics of Tehrik-e-Labbaik Pakistan (TLP) laid siege to communication arteries, utilising the ubiquitous blasphemy card, making ludicrous demands like the sacking of a French ambassador. The ISI has been hob nabbing self-appointed crusaders of anti-blasphemy forces led by the deceased Khadim Rizvi and his son Saad Rizvi of TLP.

Imran's attacker, Naved Basher, is reportedly a self-confessed TLP activist reading Imran's promised Riyasat-e-Medina as blasphemous. General Bajwa has been reiterating his oft-repeated claims on the army remaining apolitical. His intervention for IMF aid and meetings with the US establishment are certainly transgressions beyond his charter, though well-intentioned. **Bajwa's Sandhurst trip and supply of 122m shells to Ukraine through Britain have restored Pakistan's acceptability in the West to some extent.**

The return of Sharif and Bajwa's endeavours has helped to repair relations with the US and secure the F-16 sustenance package.

Pakistan has been taken off the Financial Action Task Force (FATF) grey listing even without meaningful compliance. Imran has accused the army of interfering in the choice of chief minister in Punjab.

With discredited leaders and crumbling institutions, does Pakistan have any alternatives?

The timing of Azadi March, soon after devastating floods and with the economy literally on a ventilator, is most irresponsible. Imran probably timed it to retain relevance and influence the choice of the next Chief of Army Staff (COAS). It appears that the back channel has forced Imran to belatedly clarify that the PM has the authority to make all important appointments. Meanwhile, more skeletons may tumble out of Imran's closet at the army's behest to silence him through litigations.

Pakistan 2023: Caught in Maelstrom of Crises

(Written in January 2023)

The 'awaam' (populace) of Pakistan is grappling with unprecedented headwinds and unrelenting chaos. **While 2022 was a year that they would like to forget, 2023 may prove equally challenging, if not worse.** Pakistan is still reeling from the devastation caused by floods that killed as many as 1,739 people and caused damage amounting to $3.3 trillion. Most severely affected were 35 lakh poor and rendered homeless, with reconstruction costs estimated at $30 billion, or 10% of GDP. The disaster exposed serious deficiencies in the response mechanisms, delivering a rude reality check on the looming dangers of climate change.

The deluge was caused by very heavy rainfall—740% in Baluchistan, coupled with the melting of glaciers. Floods impacted peripheral areas like Baluchistan KPK, GB, Sindh, and Southern Punjab. **Inadequate infrastructure in these areas has been further battered, and tardy relief is magnifying the existing sense of alienation.**

Pakistan is also currently being jolted by TTP blowback as Tehrik has declared Jihad against Pakistani authorities and the army. TTP has carried out 262 terror attacks, including 14 Fedayeen varieties, with one in Islamabad. These attacks accounted for 500 lives and 750 injured. In comparison, in J&K, only 26 personnel and 29 civilians lost their lives in 2022. Concurrently, 172 terrorists, including 42 foreign ones, were neutralised, along with 20 apprehensions. The return of the Taliban in Kabul and the virulent yearnings of fassadis for new hunting grounds have catalysed the resurgence of TTP. The frontier culture has returned to large parts of KPK, with state-yielding authority to TTP. Balochi rebels issued diktat to foreigners (implying Chinese) to leave Gwadar. Pakistan is becoming a quagmire of imploding fault lines. Interior Minister Rana Sanaullah's threat of targeting TTP sanctuaries in Afghanistan has provoked Afghan deputy PM Ahmed Yasser to tweet the Pakistani Army's Dhaka surrender visual. It was accompanied by the dreaded "graveyard of empires" warning. **Pakistan's fancy notion of strategic depth through subservient Afghanistan under the Taliban now lies in tatters. In this uneasy triad of Pakistan, Taliban, and TTP, dangers of consolidation of the Pashtuns on both sides of the Durand line, with fatal consequences for Pakistan, are imminent.** The line itself, cutting across tribal agencies, has never been accepted by the Pashtun tribes. In zero-sum, socio-political contestation, Islamabad losing depth to Kabul can be another possible disturbing scenario for Pakistan. Pakistan's economy is in serious trouble, characterised by frequent desperate pleas for financial bailout packages. It has also brought home other associated complications as the IMF and other lenders, justifiably enough, want to ensure that their funds are not diverted to clear Chinese loans.

Pakistan is requesting grants, but most creditors are only agreeable to giving loans. As a corollary, Pakistan is seeking low-interest loans, which entail protracted negotiations. In all this, Pakistan has realised that the promised ummah (brotherhood) hype is moderated by national interests and fiscal considerations. **The current challenge is**

to raise $9 billion to avoid default. The CPEC has failed to spur the economy. It has landed Pakistan in an unmanageable debt trap and a distinct possibility of Gwadar becoming another Hambantota. The only positive accretion in power generation due to the new CPEC power generation units has also come with the double whammy of dirty coal-dependent power and increasing dependence on costly imports. It cannot be even optimally harnessed and supplied on crumbling transmission and distribution systems, as the CPEC has not addressed this critical prerequisite. Fiscal distress has resulted in the imposition of power cuts. It is now fairly evident that the promised 'game changer', the CPEC, is designed for the Chinese getting a walk over to Gwadar. Pakistan is facing galloping inflation, which is consequent to the failure of crops. **There have been riots for basic commodities like flour. The main employment-generating crop, cotton, has also floundered. Pakistan is scouting for import options.** India seems a natural choice, but like last time, when Imran Khan scuttled his own proposal for the import of sugar and cotton, it is unlikely to fructify. **The worst crisis is the collapse of all the institutions of governance with constant slug fests. Imran Khan has proved to be the unquestioned man (villain) of the match with his futile long march and open incitement of junior officers, yet he retains popular support and has built a strong support base.** The revelation by journalist Javed Chaudhary, close to General Qamar Bajwa, claimed that India and Pakistan were on a rapprochement trajectory in 2021. As per him, both were agreeable to putting the Kashmir issue on the back burner for 20 years. His assertions fit into the template of General Bajwa's statement about the geo-economic pivot during the Islamabad Security Dialogue in March 2021. This was immediately after the ceasefire agreement on the LoC from February 25, 2021. He has claimed that Imran Khan chickened out at the very last minute, misguided by the motivated advice of Shah Mahmood Qureshi.

The obvious question is: Can there be another foray to repair relations, especially when Pakistan is literally on the ropes with the economy on a ventilator? It doesn't seem likely in a country where there is jostling for irrationality to grab attention. Impressed by the popularity of Imran Khan, young Bilawal Bhutto has decided to follow the India-baiting path. **It is fairly evident that the election schedule in Pakistan in October 2023 and India in the first half of 2024 preclude any progress in improvements in relations. Politicians in both countries are likely to leverage rhetoric to garner support.** While it is easy to label Pakistan as a failing and even a failed state, it remains geo-strategically relevant and has started gaining some support. Pakistan has to remain useful to the USA despite iron-brother tangos with China and the Taliban. This, coupled with Punjabi resilience and dexterity, will help them to flounder through and remain a thorn in our Amrit-Kaal journey.

Fiscal Implosion in Pakistan Economy and Impact on Defence Spending

(Written in March 2023)

Key Takeaways

- **While the dollar pipeline is shut, the ill effects of profligate expenditure induced by a rentier mindset have crippled the economy.**
- The IMF and even traditional allies like the Gulf countries are insisting on deep-rooted fiscal reforms.
- **Defence spending may witness cosmetic and nominal reduction.**

Pakistan has landed itself in a fiscal maelstrom due to its profligate, rentier mindset. The country's economy is on the ventilator and is literally gasping for external bailouts. The talks with the IMF remain inconclusive, and the only lifeline has been China announcing a $700 million loan to redress immediate forex emergency. The country's foreign currency reserves had dipped to an all-time low of $3.2 billion, barely enough to cover three weeks of imports. Chinese loans will boost forex reserves by 20%. Pakistan's forex funds are derived from foreign loans and the inflow of remittances, as the country's exports are rather insignificant. Manufacturing is dependent, in most cases, on imported raw materials, creating a vicious cycle of dependency on forex.

Pakistan, lulled by her geo-strategic location, had forged alliances with CENTO/SEATO and iron brother format ties with China. It has also ascribed to herself a larger-than-life role of the guardian of faith, trying to be the leader of OIC. **It will be appropriate to recall the quest for Islamic bomb, where ZA Bhutto stated, "We shall eat grass but make nuclear bomb."** The ISI also set up terrorist assembly lines to further the US agenda in Afghanistan. Pak blatantly milked security funding and managed to double-time the USA by concurrently playing along with the Taliban. The dollar pipeline was shut off with the withdrawal of the US troops from Afghanistan. A **rentier and extractive, manipulative mindset has led to profligate expenditure and failure to build the economy. The belief that the ummah (brotherhood) will ultimately bail out the awaam (populace) lies in tatters as Saudi Arabia and the UAE want the IMF process to be concluded first to obviate profligate spending.**

The major share of the contracts and benefits were cornered by military establishments through their foundations like Fauji, Shaheen, Baharia, FWO, and SCO. The details of this mega empire are chronicled by noted Pakistani expert Ayesha Siddiqa in her book, 'Crossed Swords'. **Nawaz Sharif's plan of adding geo-economic heft by the so-called game changer, the CPEC, has met a similar fate due to inefficiency and corruption. Lieutenant General Asim Bajwa and army-affiliated entities once again cornered their share in the CPEC, making it a failing project.** The oligarchic mindset transcends beyond khaki into the civilian domain. As per Ishrat Hussain, in his widely acclaimed book, 'The Economy of an Elitist State', 1% of the population constitutes the elitist oligarchy. The resultant inequality has reduced very large segments to abject poverty and penury. The recent floods in 2022 and the widespread destruction in their wake have added to fiscal distress.

China accounts for the largest share, i.e., 30% of the total debt, which is more than twice the combined borrowings from the World Bank and the Asian Development Bank. It is approximately three times larger than the loans advanced by the IMF. **The total debt had reached 77.8% of GDP in 2022. Pakistan, as per Topline Securities in a report in the Wall Street Journal, is required to repay $73 billion by 2025. The IMF has been negotiating a rescue package amounting to $6.5 billion with an initial tranche of $1.1 billion.** The significance of these rather tough negotiations by the IMF is that they will trigger the unlocking of other promised packages like $7 billion by Saudi Arabia and the UAE. Iran has also promised to boost bilateral trade from $2 billion to $5 billion by revamping border markets. Uzbekistan has also promised a similar boost in border trade.

The IMF negotiations have remained inconclusive as the IMF would like to ensure that its funds do not get diverted to pay the largest creditor, China, and are invested in economic revival. The IMF diktat stipulates paring subsidies and limiting these to only the needy sections of the populace. They also want higher taxation on the ultra-rich and bring privileged sections into the taxation net. Pak tops the chart with 25 projects under IMF scrutiny. Murtaza Syed, former deputy governor of the State Bank of Pakistan, laconically confessed, "In fact, we are the IMF's most loyal customer." Desperation is such that radicals are making outlandish suggestions of monetising nuclear know-how.

While Pakistan looks for external largesse, it has to revisit the age-old wisdom of – 'charity begins at home'. An objective advice to Pakistanis is, make no mistake, it is an implosion triggered by internal catalysts like predatory corruption, bordering on organised plunder and populist freebie culture, breeding a sense of entitlement to subsidies, particularly in petroleum prices and electricity tariffs. **Imran Khan, who is currently topping the popularity charts, would have to take a large part of the blame for mismanagement besides**

burning bridges with traditional allies like the USA, Saudi Arabia, and the UAE. Unlike India, Pakistan blew up its chances of cheap petrochemical imports from Russia by supplying munitions to Ukraine. This was a self-serving initiative anchored by General Qamar Bajwa to garner US support.

Pak Defence Minister Khawaja Asif, in an event in Sialkot, confessed that the country has already defaulted on financial commitments and is already bankrupt. He blamed the establishment, bureaucracy, and politicians for this mess. The desperation is such that rabid elements have been touting outlandish ideas like selling nuclear know-how. The runway inflation has touched nearly 40% with riot-like conditions for basic commodities like wheat flour (atta). Pushed by the IMF, Shahbaz Sharif's government has launched a major austerity drive. A slew of new taxes being dubbed as mini budget has been announced to raise PKR 170 billion.

He also opined that the IMF or any other external agency cannot redress the situation. He unequivocally stated that the solution lies within. He made a startling revelation that one-fourth of the debt could be paid off if only two golf clubs built on government land are sold off. Former Army Chief General Bajwa and now General Asim Munir have taken the mantle of loan negotiation without much traction. **The Pak Army budget has traditionally been pegged at 2.8% of GDP, which was pared down to 2.2%. In contrast, India has been limiting her spending to around 2% and in the current budget, it is projected at 1.87% of GDP. Pak has earmarked 17.5% of total government expenditure, which is an increase of 11.16% from last year. Comparatively, Indian spending is only 13.18%.** There has been considerable opacity in defence spending, particularly with regard to the allocations made to the ISI and ISPR. Pak has treated terrorists as strategic assets and has been funding them through counterfeit and drug economy. Both have come under increasing scrutiny, including international agencies like FATF.

The moot question is how will this impact defence spending and the deep state? Few demonstrative cuts, like the disposing of

diplomatic properties, are taking place. However, the deep state is unlikely to jettison its dalliance with terrorism. It may temporarily pause, but Pakistan is likely to remain invested in core projects like the K2 cell of the ISI. The deep state is already voicing its demands for additional funds and stating that funds are not even adequate to feed troops. It will be pragmatic to remain vigilant about desperate measures that may be adopted by Pakistan. While it may give us some temporary comfort due to fiscal distress but, in the long run, it will be pragmatic if the nuclear-armed Pakistan is put on leashed IMF-monitored economic recovery.

Implications of Institutional Implosion in Pakistan

(Written in May 2023)

Pakistan is witnessing probably the most dangerous implosion of institutions triggered by a new maverick, Imran Khan. Notwithstanding his being equally guilty of having contributed to the chaos and fiscal distress, the stark reality is that currently, he is the most popular leader. He defiantly won five out of seven by-elections to the National Assembly, and mobs are out on a rampage following his call.

Mobocracy, promoted as an instrument of coercion by the ISI and ISPR through Tehreek-e-Labbaik Pakistan during the October 2021 Rawalpindi siege, is now like the proverbial rogue genie, refusing to be capped.

Social media (SM) posts of marauding mobs at the Corps Commander's residence in Lahore and the reported torching of the iconic F-16 throw up serious apprehensions about the security of the nuclear arsenal. Are we witnessing another spring or colour revolution triggered by the ill-informed awaam (populace)? The sinking economy, natural disasters (devastating floods), and uncontrolled inflation, accentuated by the reticent IMF, have added to desperation.

The government has been forced to apply strict fiscal correctives like the withdrawal of subsidies, multiplying their unpopularity. Does Imran realize that the anti-establishment wave is easy to unleash but difficult to harness? Will it devour him next, for he has no magical wand to rebuild the economy? Imran, the propped-up creation of khaki generals, was installed as the PM in August 2018 after getting rid of Nawaz Sharif by judicial disqualification. The elections, as per the Sharif brothers, were hijacked by khalai makhlooq (unseen ghosts), in an apparent reference to the hidden khaki hands. In less than four years, in April 2022, the army got rid of Imran, who had taken the ultimate risk of breaking free of their stranglehold. He also tried to drive an internal wedge and cultivate a younger lot of officers.

Imran even named an ISI general, labelling him 'Dirty Harry'. He has skillfully leveraged SM to build the narrative of being the only honest leader capable of ushering the much-touted Riyasat-e-Medina. **He has mastered the art of serving the theological chimera and playing the victimization card by releasing videos, including pre-recorded ones. His partner, Bushara Begum ('Pirni'), is reported to enjoy mystical powers, being a part of the makeover from a playboy to Taliban Khan.**

A leader with no real grassroots support or organization was hoisted by the army in the form of Tehreek-e-Insaf. In his tenure, Imran has a dubious track record of destroying ties with traditional allies like Saudi Arabia, the Gulf countries, and the USA. He even launched an ill-advised foray to create an alternate Islamic axis with Turkiye and Malaysia, annoying Saudi Arabia. China and Iran are wary of his grandstanding. He did nothing significant to stem or redress the financial mess, leading to Pakistan becoming a basket case for IMF bailout.

The ruling rag-tag coalition cobbled up by the army has Pakistan Muslim League-Nawaz (PML-N), Pakistan People's Party (PPP), and Jammat-e-Islami (JI). The Sharif faction had been branded corrupt, at the army's behest, by the National Accountability

Bureau (NAB) and the Supreme Court. Consequently, PML has ex-PM Nawaz remote control the government with the current PM Shehbaz Sharif and his daughter Maryam, frequently rushing to London. Zardari Bhutto dominates the other coalition partner, PPP. Asif Zardari, notorious for corruption, is again in remote control mode and the immature Bilawal Bhutto in the cabinet. **In effect, the entire political class is being discredited, and Pakistan has no real credible options.**

President Arif Alvi, Imran's appointee, has been accused of seeking directions from his party. In this crumbling edifice of institutions, the judiciary has increasingly taken conflicting and blatantly partisan stances. CJI Umar Ata Bandial has been accused of displaying pro-Imran tilt, pushing for early elections and granting him bail. The **judiciary had used questionable theological criteria of 'sadiq and ameen' (truthful and trustworthy) to impose lifelong disqualification on Nawaz in April 2018, citing the Panama Gate scandal. Yet, the same stringent parameters have not been applied to Imran and others.**

The anti-corruption watchdog and quasi-judicial body, NAB, is currently headed by Lieutenant General Nazir Ahmed Butt. After fixing Nawaz during the Imran regime, it has now turned against Imran and is out to arrest him. The apparent agenda is to book Imran in Al-Qadir, Toshakhana, and other cases, including treason, to disqualify him from fighting elections.

As Pakistan lurches towards chaos, one can exult, but the task is cut out for the strategic community.

- **First, keep up the vigil as desperate elements often resort to irrational and suicidal recourse.**

- **Second, engage with the international community to build better safeguards for Pak's nuclear arsenal to rule out the spectre of fassadi (jihadi) and dirty bombs.**

- **Third, the humiliated Pakistan Army after 1971 devised a 'thousand-cuts' strategy. In the long term, our challenges remain**

formidable. China, in collusive mode, seeks to revive the CPEC, roping in Afghanistan.

- **Most importantly, the Army and the deep state, though temporarily down, are unlikely to be permanently out.**

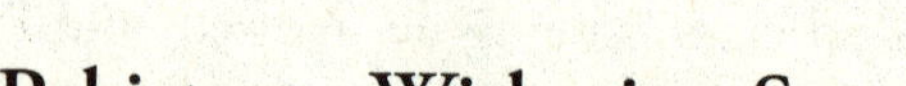

Pakistan – Withering State

PA (Written in May 2023)

Introduction

Pakistan is witnessing probably the most dangerous implosion of institutions triggered by Imran Khan and his followers. Citadels and symbols of army supremacy, residences of corps commanders, HQs, and even the Mianwali airbase were plundered by crowds. Social media (SM) posts of mobs marauding through the residence of the corps commander (4 Corps) in Lahore and the reported torching of the iconic F-16 throw up serious apprehensions on the security of the nuclear arsenal. The constitutional crisis comes at a time when the country is facing a grave economic crisis after defaulting on its fiscal obligations. The obvious conclusions are being drawn on Pakistan being a failing and withering state. The issues and criteria that merit discussion are as follows:

- **Constitutional and Institutional Crisis.**
- **Fiscal Emergency and Economic Distress.**
- **Internal Security and Ethnic Fault Lines.**
- **Unresolved Borders.**

The scope of this discussion is focused on the current evolving situation, largely on the institutional crisis. The other issues are flagged very briefly.

Constitutional and Institutional Crisis

Pakistan, impacted by frequent martial law regimes and the partition of Eastern Pakistan, currently has the third variant of the constitution, which was adopted in 1973. Even this version has witnessed fundamental flip-flop changes with the adoption of the presidential system and later shifting back to the parliamentary one. **Political parties, the judiciary, and the army are the main players in this troika, with the army seeking to retain supremacy and overriding control.** The other instruments, bureaucracy and media, are marginalized as insignificant elements. The country has witnessed the assassination of the first PM, Liaqat Ali Khan, the hanging of PM Zulfikar Ali Bhutto, another assassination of Benazir Bhutto, and the mysterious death of General Zia-ul-Haq. Apart from this, Parvez Musharraf and Nawaz Sharif had to seek exile.

Unseating of Governments

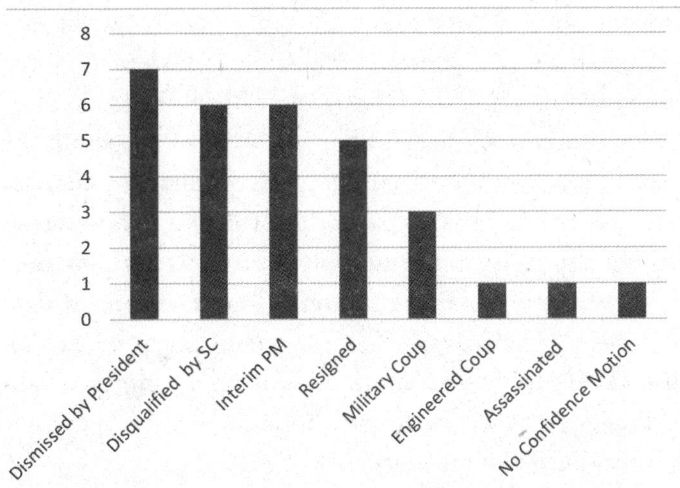

Political Parties

Imran Khan and Tehreek-e-Insaf (PTI). Imran Khan, the propped-up creation of khaki generals, was installed as PM in Aug 2018 after getting rid of Nawaz Sharif by a questionable judicial disqualification. **He was essentially a leader with no real grassroots support or organization and was hoisted by the army in the form of PTI. The elections, as per the Sharif brothers, were hijacked by khalai makhlooq (unseen ghosts) in an apparent reference to a hidden khaki hand.** In less than four years, in Apr 2022, the army got rid of Imran, who had taken the ultimate risk of trying to break free of the army stranglehold. Imran has also tried to drive an internal wedge and cultivate a younger lot of officers. He even recently named an ISI general, labelling him 'Dirty Harry'. He has skilfully leveraged social media to build the narrative of being the only honest leader capable of ushering the much-touted ***Riyasat-e-Madina***. Imran has mastered the art of serving theological chimera and playing the victimization card by releasing videos, including pre-recorded ones. **His partner, Bushara Begum ('Pirni'), is reported to enjoy mystical powers, being part of a makeover from a playboy to Taliban Khan.**

Track Record: In his tenure, Imran has a dubious track record of destroying ties with traditional allies like Saudi Arabia, the Gulf countries, and the USA. He even launched an ill-advised foray to create an alternate Islamic axis with Türkiye and Malaysia, annoying Saudi Arabia. Iron brothers, China and Iran, are wary of his grandstanding. He did nothing significant to stem or redress the financial mess, leading to Pakistan becoming a basket case for IMF bailout. **Notwithstanding his being equally guilty of having contributed to the chaos and fiscal distress, the stark reality is that currently, he is the one of the most popular leader.** He defiantly won six out of seven by-elections to the National Assembly, and mobs are out on a rampage, following his call. President Arif Alvi, Imran's appointee, has been accused of seeking directions from his party.

Sharif Brothers and Ruling Coalition: The ruling rag-tag coalition, Pakistan Democratic Movement (PDM), cobbled up by the army has Pakistan Muslim League-Nawaz (PML-N), Pakistan People's Party (PPP), and Jammat-e-Islami (JI). Sharif's faction had been branded corrupt at the army's behest by the National

Accountability Bureau (NAB) and the Supreme Court. Consequently, PML-N has Nawaz, ex-PM, exiled in London, remotely controlling the government with Shahbaz, the current PM, and Mariyam, his daughter, frequently rushing to London. Zardari-Bhutto dominates the other coalition partner, PPP. Asif Zardari, notorious for corruption, is again in remote control mode, and the "immature" Bilawal Bhutto is in the cabinet. In effect, the entire political class is being discredited, and Pakistan has no real credible options. The main demand of Imran Khan is for early elections to tap his popularity. **The ruling party wants to delay elections till October 2023, when the president and the chief justice would have retired.**

Judiciary

In this crumbling edifice of institutions, the judiciary has increasingly taken a conflicting and blatantly partisan stance. The CJI, Umar Ata Bandial, has been accused of displaying a pro-Imran tilt, pushing for early elections and granting him bail. The judiciary had used questionable theological criteria of 'sadiq and ameen' (truthful and trustworthy) to impose lifelong disqualification on Nawaz Sharif in April 2018, citing the Panama-gate papers. Yet, the same stringent parameters have not been applied to Imran and others. The Anti-corruption watchdog and quasi-judicial body NAB is currently headed by Lieutenant General Nazir Ahmed Butt. **After fixing Nawaz Sharif during Imran's regime, the body has now turned against Imran and is out to arrest him. The apparent agenda is to book Imran in Al-Qadir, Toshakhana, and other cases, including treason, to disqualify him from fighting elections.**

Army

The Pak Army, despite serious blunders and unchecked plunder through Fauji Welfare, Shaheen, and Baharia foundations, has retained a pivotal position in the power matrix. The army has a pervading presence in major projects with General Asim Bajwa, who headed the CPEC Authority till his removal. Both the COAS, General Qamar Bajwa and Asim Bajwa, have been accused of large-scale corruption. Mobocracy has been promoted as an instrument of coercion by the ISI and ISPR through the dubious Tahreek-e-Labbaik Pakistan (TLP) during the siege of Rawalpindi in Oct 2021. It is now like the proverbial rogue genie, refusing to get capped. **The Pak populace has always suppressed angst against the luxurious lifestyle and draconian measures adopted by the Army. The present situation is unprecedented in the scope and audacity of mobs.**

Former COAS had promulgated his Bajwa doctrine, stipulating the army to stay out of politics. Notwithstanding this, General Bajwa had a major role in the sacking of Nawaz Sharif and later Imran, as well as the installation of Imran in 2018 and Shahbaz recently. The tenure of the current Chief (Bajwa protégé) was truncated in Imran's instance. The senior hierarchy is divided and retains contact with political lobbies. Imran's favourite general was retired Lieutenant General Faiz Hameed, whose tenure was cut short by General Bajwa. There are credible reports of three corps commanders not being on the same page as the COAS. There is also increasing talk of General Shamshad Mirza, CJCSC, replacing COAS General Asim Munir. **The air is thick with conspiracy theories, and the use of Rangers in arresting Imran was essentially an immature ploy to circumvent the Bajwa doctrine.**

Fiscal Emergency and Economic Distress

Pakistan is witnessing another spring or colour revolution triggered by corrupt governments and desperate, ill-informed awaam (populace) provoked by Imran. A sinking economy, natural disasters (devastating floods), and uncontrolled inflation, accentuated by the reticent IMF, have added to desperation. As per some reports, **Pakistan has external liabilities amounting to approximately US $80 billion and needs emergency relief of US $8 billion.** The much-promised game-changer, the CPEC, seems to be floundering. The government has been forced to apply strict fiscal correctives like the withdrawal of subsidies, multiplying their unpopularity. Does Imran realize that the anti-establishment wave is easy to unleash but difficult to harness? Will it devour him next, for he has no magic wand to rebuild the economy? The basic problems of Pakistan are food, energy (electricity), water, employment, and education (skilling). **A demographic dividend is threatening to turn into a demographic disaster. Cities like Karachi are becoming urban nightmares with ghettoization into ethnic pockets like Mohajirs, Pashtuns, Sindhis, and Punjabis with gang lords and mafia.** It may be worthwhile to create an economic revival task force under a proven economist like Mehbub ul Haq and empower him.

Internal Security and Ethnic Fault Lines

The chaos has the potential to **accentuate problems of unresolved ethnic fault lines like Baloch, Pashtun, Jiye Sindh, Mohajir, Kashmir, Shia, Ahmadiyya, and Baltis.** Coupled with this is the incessant threat posed by the resurgent TTP and ISIS-KP. The subject requires separate and detailed analysis, but the way forward is genuine devolution of power and grant of autonomy. It is axiomatic that Punjabi domination is reduced for inclusive development.

Unresolved Borders

Pak's dream of strategic depth is eroding with the Taliban refusing to accept the Durand Line. Pak has been forced to start fencing and strengthening border posts like Torkham. However, cross-border raids have increased. The border with Iran also has serious issues relating to a Sunni insurgency in the Sistan province of Shia-dominated Iran. Mercifully, the ceasefire on the LoC, sigfvfvvvvned with India in 2021, is still holding, but the Pak-engineered proxy war continues, raising the possibility of surgical raids and even strikes like Balakot.

Way Forward

Indian strategic thinkers have unsuccessfully tried to discredit the military establishment, attempting to trigger psychological collapse and implosion. Imran seems to have unwittingly grabbed the baton on his own and is engaged in destroying the image of the army. **After General Zia-ul-Haq, who had put the Pak Army on a dangerous Islamist course, destroyed its professional ethos, Imran will go down in history for destroying internal cohesion and also the external invincibility of the army. The Pak Army will have to work overtime to regain its internal cohesion and repair its image.**

As Pakistan lurches towards chaos, initially, one can exult, but the task is cut out for the strategic community as **Pakistan has displayed resilience in the past. Its geo-strategic location keeps it relevant for the major powers, and they are likely to bail it out for their own great game.**

- **First, keep up the vigil, as disparate elements often resort to irrational and suicidal recourse.**
- **Second, ensure that the ceasefire holds, as opening another front with China in belligerent mode is avoidable.**
- **Third, any significant dialogue is unlikely until elections in both countries are over.**
- **Fourth, engage with the international community to build better safeguards for Pakistan's nuclear arsenal to rule out the spectre of fassadi (jihadi) and dirty bombs.**
- **Fifth, the humiliated Pak Army, after 1971, devised a 'thousand-cuts' strategy; hence, in the long term, our challenges are likely to remain formidable. China, in collusive mode, seeks to revive the CPEC and the BRI by roping in Afghanistan and even Iran.**
- **Most importantly, the army and Deep state, though temporarily down, are unlikely to be permanently out and are likely to regroup.**

Resetting Templates in Pak

(Written in November 2023)

The return of Nawaz Sharif after a four-year exile in London adds yet another twist to the tragi-comedy charade of proxy democracy in Pakistan. Nawaz, in his three non-consecutive tenures, has been unseated four times. He has logged nine years, starting from November 1990, the maximum among the neighbouring country's prime ministers. The moot question is: will Nawaz, an avid cricket aficionado, play another innings by beating Imran? More importantly, will the ultimate survivor rescue the nation and its economy, which faces an impending disaster, like its cricket team in the ongoing World Cup?

Sharif: The Comeback Artist

Nawaz's first removal in April 1993 was orchestrated by his mentor (during the Zia-ul-Haq dictatorship), President Ghulam Ishaq Khan. This was Khan's second such high-handed action of removing an elected PM. The first to be dismissed was Benazir Bhutto, paving the way for Nawaz to get elected in November 1990. Nawaz was reinstated by Pakistan's Supreme Court after five weeks, but the reprieve was brief. He was forced to resign, ironically, by his own COAS, General Abdul Waheed Kakar, in July 1993, barely six months into his tenure. In Nawaz's second innings, Pakistan tested a nuclear bomb in May 1998, which Nawaz continues to tout as his major achievement. Buoyed by the nuclear euphoria, Nawaz sacked General Jehangir Karamat, a Benazir appointee, in October 1998.

General Karamat was the kind of army chief Pakistan really needs—erudite and apolitical. After the Kargil fiasco, on October 12, 1999, General Khwaja Ziauddin was sworn in as the chief during General Pervez Musharraf's foreign visit and passed orders to deny a landing to the returning aircraft. In a parallel coup, General Ziauddin was bundled off in less than six hours by Musharraf loyalists. Musharraf not only removed Nawaz but forced him into a seven-year-long exile in Saudi Arabia. Musharraf, ironically, had been preferred by Nawaz, superseding two seniors.

Nawaz's third tenure started in June 2013, after an orchestrated victory in elections, forced by the assassination of Benazir Bhutto, allegedly at the ISI's behest. Once again, in July 2017, he was forced to resign after the famous Supreme Court verdict in the Panama Papers case, declaring him to have failed the specious criteria of 'sadiq and ameen' (being faithful and trustworthy). **Nawaz was eased out, and Imran Khan was hoisted as PM by the mysterious khaki 'khalai makhlooq' (unseen ghosts of the ISI and ISPR) through manipulated elections.** Indicted in multiple cases, Nawaz was banned from political office for life. The sordid drama was masterminded by a Sharif appointee, General Qamar Javed Bajwa, who, like Musharraf, was made chief by superseding seniors and overlooking his alleged familial links to the Ahmadiyya sect of Islam. It is now being rumoured that General Bajwa did help Nawaz with falsified medical reports to proceed to London, purportedly for treatment, which Nawaz converted into an exile by refusing to return.

Deep State Keeps Control

In this unending tale, Nawaz has been given a legal breather by the new chief justice of Pakistan, Qazi Faiz Isa, who is known to harbour a grudge against Imran for ordering investigations against him and stalling his appointment. The clock of favouritism and reprisals seems to have come full circle, as the previous incumbent, Umar Ata Bandial, was not only an Imran appointee but also a known Sharif family baiter. The current kingmaker, General Asim Munir, has many scores to settle with Imran, most notably his unceremonious removal as DG-ISI and declaring opposition to his elevation.

The adage "the more things change, the more they stay the same" applies, at least in Pakistan. Three key inferences are as follows:

- **One, the deep state (miltestablishment) is bent upon a proxy rule by its appointees.**
- **The Pakistan Army is manipulating presidents and even the judiciary to further its agenda.**
- **Three, those who exhibit defiance, like the father-daughter duo of Zulfikar Ali Bhutto and Benazir, were eliminated. Others have been banished either into exile, like Nawaz, or lodged in Adila jail, like Imran, notwithstanding their immense popularity. Chief Justice Isa's tenure could be leveraged to sound the judicial death knell for Imran by barring him from contesting elections**

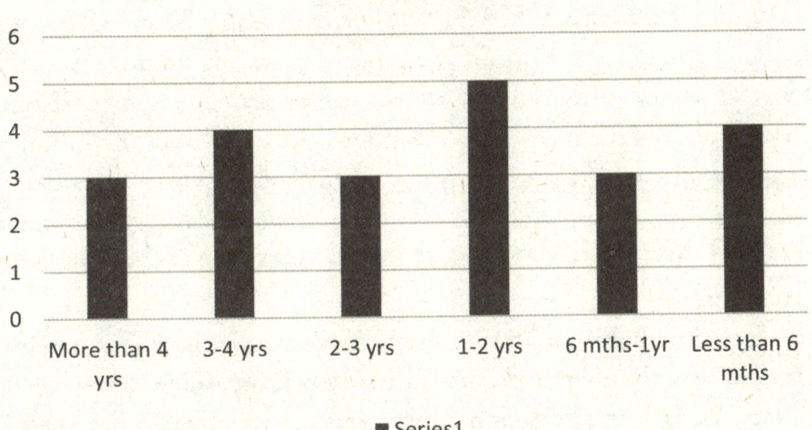

Resetting Templates

Pakistan is grappling with resetting its economic and socio-political templates.

The army cleverly manipulated America (sic) and misused religion (packaged as jihad) to create a dubious model of extractive, rentier economy. **The American exit from Afghanistan and the failure of**

the so-called game-changing China-Pakistan Economic Corridor (CPEC) have reduced Pakistan, literally, to an 'on ventilator' status.

The usual reasons, like corruption and misgovernance by politicians, are being cited. Imran did play his part by burning bridges with the USA with his populist anti-American rants and an ill-timed visit to Moscow. To make matters worse, he riled Saudi Arabia and the UAE by attempting to forge an alternative Islamic grouping of Turkey, Malaysia, and Pakistan.

General Bajwa's rear-guard action in supplying munitions to Ukraine was a desperate action to retrieve the situation. Both Nawaz and General Munir enjoy a much better relationship with the Gulf nations. The return of Nawaz may be a part of an attempted re-opening of the ummah (Islamic brotherhood) pipeline.

However, like the IMF aid, assistance is likely to come with conditions and strings attached. China has also become reticent about further funding the CPEC. With impending elections in both countries, Indo-Pak relations are unlikely to see any improvement till next year, notwithstanding Nawaz's professed inclination to restore trade ties. **The most obvious question is: why not hold the military accountable, which rules by proxy and has intertwined its entities, like the Fauji Foundation, in all key economic activities? Lieutenant General Asim Bajwa's two years with the CPEC were mired in corruption.**

It is time Pakistan and its supporters, especially Gulf countries, realize that the Triple-A's should be Awaam (genuine democracy), Aman (zero terrorism), and Araam (retreat to barracks for khaki), and not America, Allah, and Army, which has been the norm.

The elections in January 2023 threw up interesting trends; major ones are enumerated:

- The stage was set for the exclusion of Imran by getting him convicted and jailed. His party, the **PTI, was also denied its symbol of a cricket bat, and resultantly, candidates were forced to contest as independents.**

- The public defied the army by voting for proxy candidates of Imran's PTI, contesting as independents. However, the Army managed to roll back the verdict and install Shahbaz Sharif as PM, Maryam Sharif as CM Punjab, and Asif Ali Zardari as President.

Update – July 24

- Shabaz Sharif led government flounders along in **crisis management mode without any long-term visionary plan.**
- Imaran Khan retains considerable popularity leveraging pan-Islamism, Muslim exceptionalism, anti-India nationalism and anti-Khaki (army) angst.
- Sharif Government rocked by large scale terror attacks by tanzeems lint TTP has launched country wide Azm-e-Istehkam (Resolve for Stability) in June 2024.

Pakistan – Clashes on Western Border and the Terrorism Inferno Within

(Written in Apr 2024)

Pakistan already battling grave and debilitating fiscal emergency is now getting mired in internal chaos and escalating tension on her Western border. Military-establishment has been utilising Eastern border with India to prosecute its diabolic K-2 (Kashmir and Khalistan) agenda coupled with deadly drug and drone combo. It has been leveraged as a tool to mislead and rally Awaam (populace), ensuring liberal funding and unbridled control in management of security policy. Deep state has touted "strategic depth" dream, with Afghanistan as surrogate/puppet state. It has also claimed peace and tranquility with "ummah (Islamic brotherhood)" states on Eastern border, in contrast to Western one, with India. The much-cherished dreams are in tatters

with repeated skirmishes, aerial attacks and artillery duels with both Afghanistan and Iran. Most importantly, Pak is known for terrorist breeding madarsas and treating them as "strategic assets", primed to be vectored against others. Hillary Clinton in her famous warning to Khaki Generals had warned them that "Snakes in your backyard, will not just bite the neighbours". Ironically, it is now battling them within. Coupled with border clashes are- escalating Baluchi and Pushtun secessionist movements and raging inferno of terrorist attacks.

Af-Pak Border

Durand Line, negotiated in 1893, after 2nd Anglo-Afghan war between defines the border. It was negotiated between Mortimer Durand, British bureaucrat and Afghan Emir, Abdur Rehman Khan. The border traverses treacherous, mountainous terrain and unilaterally divides tribal homeland of Pushtun tribes like Mehsuds, Afridis and others. This line has never been recognized by tribal bodies (Shuras) and even governments in Kabul. Hamid Karzai asserted that Afghans will never recognize it. Aimal Faizi, spokesman for the President, stated in October 2012 that the Durand Line is "an issue of historical importance for Afghanistan. The Afghan people, not the government, can take a final decision on it." Pakistani attempts of fencing it have met with fierce opposition. Notwithstanding resistance, Pak claims to have completed it with just 50 odd km remaining. It is also seeking to reinforce it with ditches and berms as also create 338 crossing points. Notwithstanding these endeavours', its efficacy is highly suspect. This border has witnessed uneasy peace disrupted by artillery duels, aerial strikes and cross border raids. After negotiations, there have been no aerial strikes for two years, since Apr 22.

The recent heightened tension was triggered by a massive truck bomb attack on 16 Mar on Mir-Ali Border-post in North Waziristan by six fedayeens. It accounted for Lt Col (probably CO), Capt and five Frontier Corps (FC) soldiers. Relatively obscure group, Jaish-e-Fursan-e-Muhammad, with links to Tehrik-i-Taliban (TTP) claimed

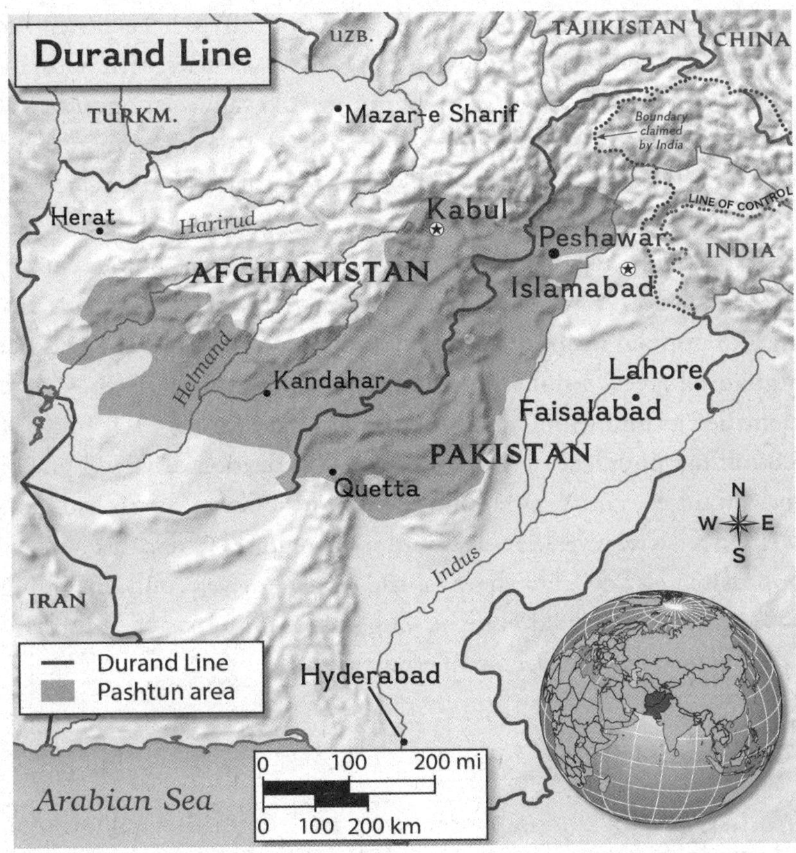

(Map Credit- National Geographic Maps)

responsibility. Pak authorities blamed Hafiz Gul-Bahadur faction and retaliated, on 18 Mar with aerial strikes in two adjoining provinces of Paktika and Khost. Afghan authorities severely criticized violation of territorial sovereignty and killing of eight women and children. However, ISPR claimed that perpetrator of attack, Sehra alias Janan was eliminated. Afghan Government responded with retaliatory Mortar strikes on Pak border posts, killing and injuring more civilians. On 23rd Mar, troop convoy in Dera Ismail Khan was subjected to another fedayeen attack, killing two and injuring 22 soldiers.

Pakistan blames Afghan Government for providing sanctuary and freedom to Tehrik-i-Taliban Pakistan (TTP), ISIS-K to target Pakistani targets. **As per Security analysts, last year (2023), there were as many as 789 attacks, accounting for 1,524 casualties with Security Forces, bearing the major share of brunt.** Pakistan has sought to deal with terrorism by multi-pronged approach. This includes ruthless counter-terrorism operations like Raad-ul-Fassad, characterized by disproportionate use of force and heavy calibre weapons like gunships, tanks and artillery. Fencing of Durand Line, border closure and pressure on Afghan Government are other measures applied. **The most unpopular measure has been directive on 01 Nov 2023 to expel Afghan refugees, numbering approximately 1.7 million. They were identified as undocumented refugees, after preliminary screening of 3.8 million populace of Afghan origin.** Sanitization drive in Karachi and around security establishment pockets like Malir Cantt and Mehran air-base revealed collaboration by refugees in terrorist attacks. Approximately, 4 lakhs have already been driven out, including 80% women and children. This ongoing exercise portends to drive permanent wedge between two ethnicities.

Pak-Iran Border

Pakistan has 909 km long border with Iran, decided in colonial era, spanning hilly and rugged terrain and sparsely populated areas from Taftan to Mand. Iran is building an elaborate barrier system with 3 ft (91.4 cm) thick and 10 ft (3.05 m) high concrete wall, fortified with steel rods, reinforced with ditches and embankments. Concurrently, Pak has also fenced 80% of the border on her side. This border divides Baluchi (Sunni) tribal population, on both sides- Sistan in Shia dominated Iran and Baluchistan, traditionally neglected by Punjabi dominated Pakistan. Both provinces have festering secessionist movements demanding a unified Baluchi homeland.

The uneasy peace on border was broken, when Iran launched missile and drone strikes on 16th Jan in Kohe-Sabz area. It targeted Jaish-al-Adl group (repackaged version of Jundallah), holding it responsible for killing of 11 Iranian Police personnel in Sistan province, in Dec

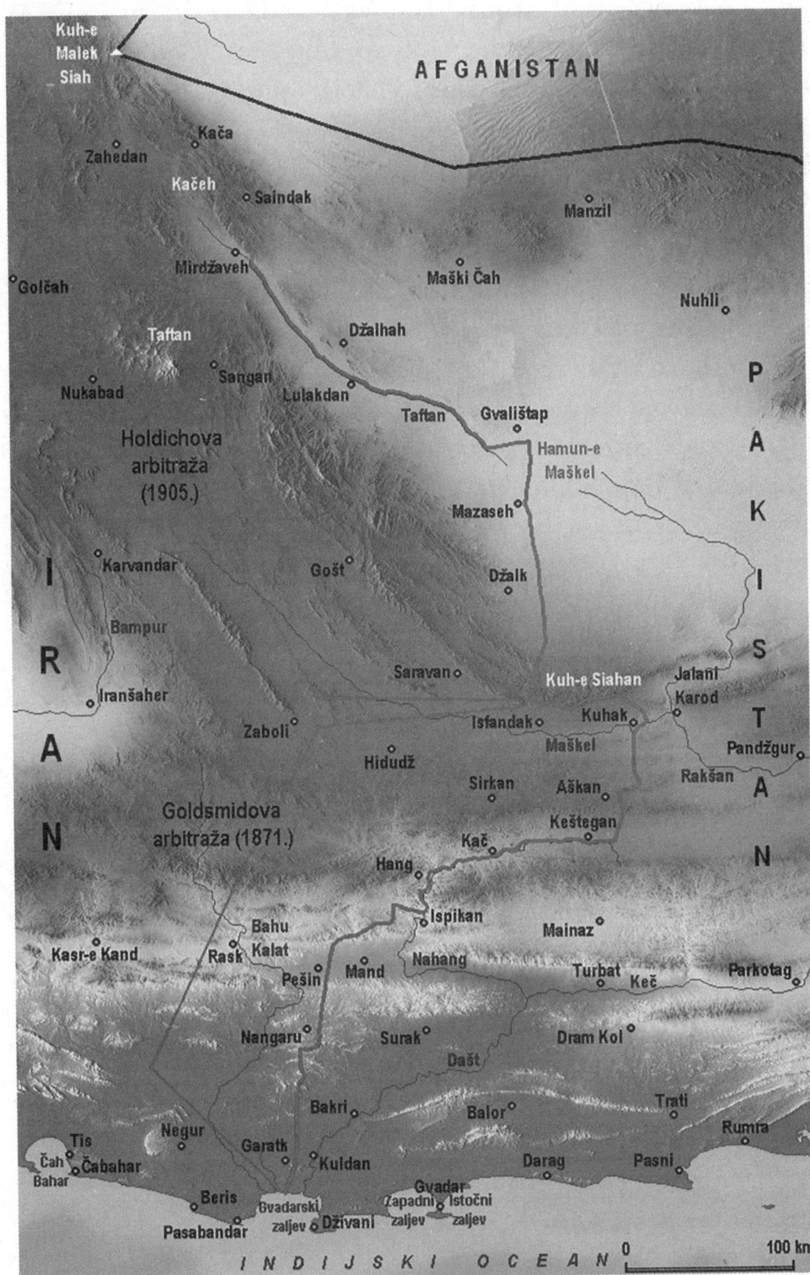

(Map Credit- Wikipedia maps)

2023. Pak retaliated, two days later with multiple drones strikes in Sistan. Unfortunately, both attacks accounted for dozen odd civilian casualties, including women and children. Eleven days later, nine Pak workers perished in another terrorist attack in bordering town in Sistan. Attacks were part of Iranian attacks on targets in Kurd areas and Syria. Viewed in context of ongoing Gaza imbroglio and Houthi raids, the specter of widening arc of conflict in Middle East was very real. The attacks were fueled by mutual suspicion and Iranian apprehensions of US using Pak to unsettle her. It required flurry of visits by diplomats supplemented by brokering by Chinese minister to restore uneasy and fragile sanity on border. **Stakes for China for de-escalation are indeed high with Chinese companies engaged in Gwadar and Saindak Copper and Gold mining projects in NW Baluchistan.**

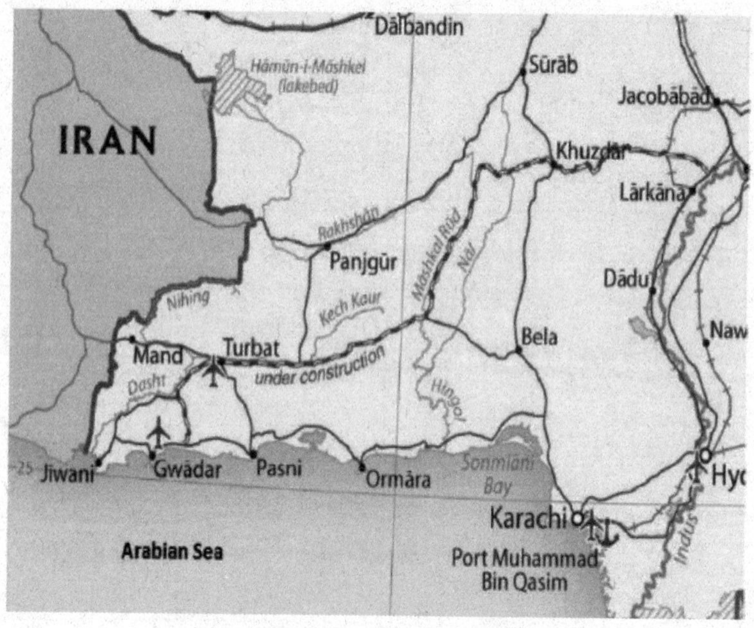

(Map Credit- Research Gate)

Ramzan and Mayhem Cycle

Sanctity and traditional peace of holy month of Ramzan in Pakistan has been bloodied by relentless terrorist attacks. Recently, elected

President Asif Zardari and Gen Aseem Munir, Army Chief attended the funeral of Frontier Corps Lt Col, killed in terrorist attack and vowed revenge. The new government, cobbled after Feb election and considerable manipulation is under intense pressure to show results.

The Mayhem cycle stretching for ten days (from 16th to 26th Mar 2024), included five different attacks, three in Khyber Pakhtunkhwa (KP) province and two in Baluchistan, resulting in the deaths of at least 18 people. All five attacks were fedayeen (suicide) bombings. 12 military personnel, five Chinese nationals and few Afghans and Pak civilians were collateral casualties. Baluchistan Liberation Army (BLA) claimed responsibility for attacks in Baluchistan. Some obscure splinter groups claimed orchestration of two attacks in KP. Nobody has owned-up for attack on Chinese engineers.

China Pak Economic Corridor (CPEC) – New Faultline

On 24th Mar, eight fedayeens of BLA tried to storm Gwadar port complex. While the attack was thwarted, there were conflicting claims on casualties and damages. Pak acknowledges losing two security personnel and eliminating all attackers. In vicinity and two days later, four fedayeens of Majeed Brigade targeted, second largest Naval aviation base, PNS Siddique at Turbat on 26th Mar. Amongst conflicting claims, authorities claimed elimination of all fedayeens and losing only one Frontier Corps personnel. **Turbat base is strategically located 150 odd km North of Gwadar and supports Pak Naval bases of Jiwani and Pasni, both in close proximity (100 km on either side of Gawadar).**

The most significant attack happened on 25th at Besham, near upcoming Dasu dam, on Indus River in Kohistan (KP), killing five Chinese engineers and Pak civilian bus driver. The attack reminded of Jul 21 incident, wherein nine Chinese engineers were killed in similar attack. TTP has denied any role in attack and there is much speculation on possibility of involvement of ISIS-K, Tehrik-e-Jihad- Pakistan (TJP), East Turkmenistan Independence Movement (ETIM) or unidentified

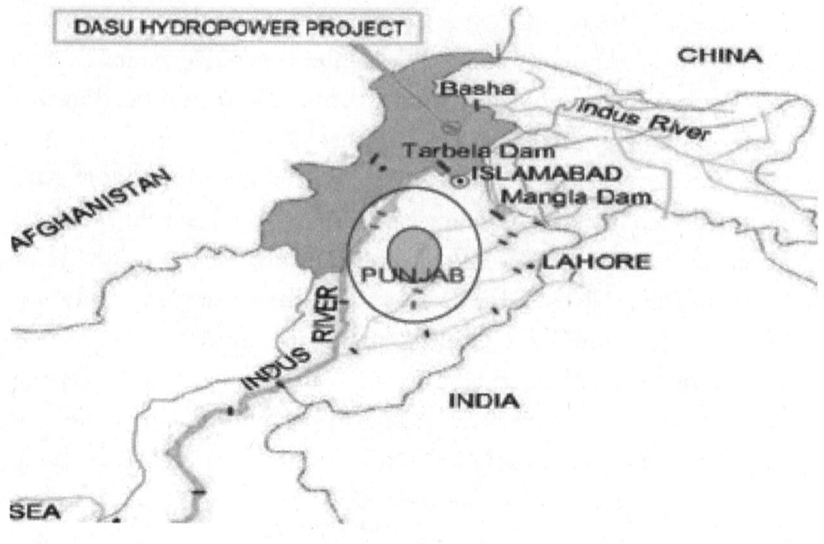

(Map Credit- Research Gate)

groups. Chinese assets on CPEC have literally opened new array of high-profile targets and internal fault-line for terrorist tanzeems. Karachi stock-exchange, Chinese Consulate, Confucius Centre have all been targeted. After recent attacks, Chinese companies (with approximately 2,000 Chinese workforce) have suspended work on not only Dasu (4,320 mw) but also Dimer-Basha (4,800 mw) and Tarbela extension (1,400 mw) projects. Work is going on, only on Mohmand dam (740 mw). Work was stalled for nearly two years after the last attack and could be resumed only on payment of hefty compensation of 30 million dollars. **Pakistan has raisd two specialized divisions, funded out of CPEC funds, yet attacks continue unabated, exposing vulnerability of CPEC, due to fragile internal security environment and more importantly, lack of acceptance by Awaam (local populace).**

Uneasy and Bleak Future

Despite desire to designate Pakistan as a failed or failing state, it's geo-strategic location and large young population, still helps her to retain relevance. The recent communication and assurances by US

President Joe Biden to PM Shahbaz Sharif reinforce this inference. The challenge for Pak policy makers and her international facilitators is to undertake meaningful and holistic reforms instead of cosmetic, quick-fix measures. Genuine reforms like dismantling milt-establishment, terrorist infrastructure, accommodation of genuine Baluchi and Pashtun regional aspirations are long overdue. For Pakistani Awaam (populace), Robert Frost's poem, is most relevant, albeit rephrased (with due apologies), as- **"Woods infested with Tanzeems, are indeed dark and deep, and miles to march, Khaki back to barracks, before we sleep."**

Western Front – Countering Pak

Pulwama: Our Response and Retribution Need to Be Served Cold

(Written after the Pulwama Terrorist Attack in February 2019)

The nation is in a state of deep outrage and anger, consequent to the martyrdom of more than 40 CRPF soldiers in a dastardly attack on an administrative convoy at Pulwama. Pakistan-based Jaish-e-Muhammad (JeM) brazenly claimed responsibility and even released a video announcing the details of the fedayeen (suicide) bomber. This portends ominous trends, the return of home-grown fedayeen and explosive-laden vehicle bombs after two decades, coupled with an unabated radicalisation of the local youth becoming 'fassadis'. **I choose not to name such cowards masquerading as fedayeen and refuse to conspire in the misuse of 'jihad' for reprehensible acts; 'fassad' has to be called out as such.**

Many well-meaning and angry people want revenge. Social media is abuzz with demands ranging from naval blockades to the employment of integrated battle groups (IBGs) and, of course, "surgical strikes". **One is reminded of the famous quote of Desiderius Erasmus, "War is delightful to those who have had no experience of it."** Many a twitter yodha, fresh after seeing Uri, feel that it is as simple as rustling up two-minute noodles. They even outline the attack plan, take a briefing from babus in South Block, get magical Garuda to vector commandos to the JeM hideout of Masood Azhar and after bang-bang, have dinner on Raisina Hill. Our well-meaning public deserves to be educated better. **Concurrently, overexposure to the Armed Forces daily and 'josh' without 'hosh' are counterproductive.**

Options like the withdrawal of the Most Favoured Nation (MFN) status, revoking the Indus Water Treaty (IWT), declaring Pakistan a terrorist state, and breaking diplomatic ties are mentioned as add-ons. Each of these has complications and, of course, limitations, especially in payoffs.

Our response and retribution need to be served cold and at a place and time of our own choosing. Leo Tolstoy has summed it up most appropriately: "The two most powerful warriors are patience and time." Let operational commanders look at contingencies and apply them after detailed analyses. **The hype on revenge induces needless hurry and recklessness. The government seems to be following the sane path by giving the Armed Forces a free hand.**

It is time for politicians to display statesmanship; all parties should affirm solidarity with the government and the forces. It is a distant hope, but nations strive for optimism and well-intentioned initiatives. Can a few statesmen (though they are a dying breed), like Pranab Da, Manmohan Ji, and Advani Sahib, step forward and articulate the national will and formulate guidelines on the politicisation of security matters? These ombudsmen can indeed deliver a message of national consensus to Pindi generals, infusing some sense.

The government has already withdrawn the unilateral MFN status accorded to Pakistan, but it has only limited signalling value because bilateral trade is already at its lowest ebb. The isolation of Pakistan is a long haul, as geography combined with the CPEC and its new role as China's proxy has bestowed it with enviable advantages.

Short of war, leverages are indeed limited. Revoking IWT without having reservoirs and dams to absorb additional water is pointless. We require nearly a decade to construct planned infrastructure. It will also give China an upper riparian status on Brahmaputra and Sutlej, an avoidable precedence. The obvious lesson is: within treaty norms, build on recent welcome initiatives on Ravi and Chenab with time-bound task force orientation and expand the scope to Jhelum and Indus.

Pragmatically, considering our current state of equipment and ammunition inventory, we seem to lack the decisive edge and the

requisite force asymmetry for a full-scale conventional war. Localised grab action is possible, but the resultant stalemate is not worth the effort. The biggest challenge is keeping it below the much-touted threshold for tactical nuclear weapons. This government seems to have the political will to call off the nuclear bluff, but the Armed Forces need time to prepare and augment the conventional arsenal. India, aspiring to become a net security provider, should maintain more than one option, including the conventional domain with a decisive edge. This requires sustained investment backed up with a vibrant defence manufacturing eco-system and functional procurement policies, none of which seem to have been on the priority agenda.

The foremost requirements are objective investigation and follow-up. Despite the much-acclaimed NIA, we have not been able to nail local collaborators to achieve full closure in earlier incidents. Such an operation would have required preparation and an extensive support network, but once again, there was a lack of specific intelligence. The reported usage of approximately 300 kg of explosives indicates a porous monitoring mechanism. The move of such a large convoy with 80-odd vehicles and more than 2,000 personnel defies logic. **The relevant SOPs need to be updated, and safeguards against the emerging threat of vehicle bombs need to be factored in.**

The only viable option seems to be trans-border surgical raids, but they have already become subject to the law of diminishing marginal returns. The need is to invest in more lethal and precise delivery means like drones and stand-off missiles. This, coupled with surveillance and gunships, will make them surgical and lethal to the extent that they have a deterrence effect. Currently, aerial and stand-off attacks seem to be the most discussed option, but they require deliberate planning with a careful selection of targets based on accurate intelligence. **Targeting proven terrorist hubs should be justifiable, provided there is minimal collateral civilian damage and international opinion is sensitised; Americans are already nodding approval.** While the need is for kinetic retribution, a full-spectrum response should include internal dialogue, socio-political measures, and theological correctives, including counter-radicalisation entailing smart soft power. Anger and anguish are understandable, but arson amounts to furthering the agenda of 'fassadis' to exploit fault lines in society.

When the Threshold of Tolerance Is Breached: Balakot

(Written after the Balakot Air Strike in March 2019)

India and Pakistan, the nuclear-armed nations, are in a state of undeclared war. The whole world, with powerful nations leading from the front, is trying to broker de-escalation. The worrying questions are: Where do we go from here? And what happens to the proxy war in Kashmir?

The Balakot aerial strike is indeed a historic and defining milestone in India's strategic calculus and escalation matrix. It qualifies to be classified as a "real surgical strike", meeting the criteria of targeting in-depth and application of aerial/stand-off means. The strike, spearheaded by Mirages, took Pakistan by complete surprise. It also exposed the chinks in the famed formidable Air Defence umbrella. The emphasis on 'real' is intentional because the surgical strikes after Uri, though bold, were technically "synergised shallow trans-border raids".

The aerial capability has existed and been considered but, unfortunately, never exercised. It is to the credit of the government that they displayed political will with attendant risks—political and operational. In this hour of national crisis warranting consensus, the situation has been vitiated due to the impending elections and misplaced politicisation. Surgical strikes are likely to become the new normal in the quiver of options and strategic calculus. It will now be difficult for successive governments to ignore this option.

Bhawalpur, a hub of JeM, the obvious choice, was vacated and risky to engage. On the other hand, the Taleem-ul-Quran seminary at Balakot, managed by Azhar Yousuf, brother-in-law of Masood

Azhar, is situated beyond Pak-occupied Kashmir, where strikes can't be explained away as within Indian (de-jure) or disputed territory. It was a bold and apt messaging choice, with a historic connection to the early manifestation of fassad (mischievously referred to as jihad) during Maharaja Ranjit Singh's period. These theological linkages have been misused to brainwash recruits with the 18th-century exploits of Syed Ahmad Barelvi and Shah Ismail (ironically, natives of Rae Bareli). It is in Pakistan PM, Imran's native Khyber-Pakhtunkhwa province, which hosts a large number of terrorist training camps.

India's focus was on strategic messaging to convey that the Pulwama terrorist attack had indeed breached the threshold of tolerance. More importantly, we have the capacity, skill, and, above all, the political will to strike. The anger and desire for retribution (bordering on revenge) define an angry and impatient 'Naya Bharat'. **It would also be pragmatic to note that, notwithstanding public pressure and media hype, the government carefully selected terrorist facilities away from the population centre for targeting.** The clamour by some 'doubting Thomases' for proof of dead bodies and Pakistan's ploy to describe it as eco-terrorism is literally missing the wood (message) for a few pine trees. The implied message is, 'If you don't act, we will be forced to.'

India nuanced its articulation by initially utilising civilian spokespersons and describing it as a non-military target. The elaborate rationale of explaining it as pre-emptive action for self-defence against elements being trained for a proxy war in Kashmir was spelt out. Overall, India offered a viable window for de-escalation, provided the proxy war was rolled back.

Imran Khan, despite shouting about 'Naya Pakistan', failed to decipher strategic signalling. Driven by public pressure, miltestablishment, and parity syndrome, it decided to take the dangerous escalation course, that too, the very next day, by targeting military installations. It was a double whammy, firstly missing the targets and then losing F-16 to MIG-21. This engagement proved fortuitous for Pakistan; they suddenly had an Indian pilot in their custody. In a comedy of errors, Pakistan refused to accept its casualties and even used F-16s, amounting to a violation of contractual obligations. Imran and the voluble DGISPR kept on trotting conflicting claims, starting with two MIGs and three pilots. International pressure forced Pakistan to hand over the Indian pilot but after considerable drama. Till the very last moment, attempts were made to leverage it for de-escalation and resumption of dialogue.

Wing Commander Abhinandan has emerged as the real hero, who refused to let go of the 'missile lock', risked his life, and created a record of shooting down an F-16 with a MIG-21. His conduct as a prisoner was commendable, and he will remain a role model for generations. Gnats outsmarting Sabres, Centurions outgunning Pattons, MIG downing F-16, mercifully, we have redoubtable crews despite a deja-vu freeze.

The Indian strike and counter by Pakistan have debunked the nuclear bluff, and the nuclear bogey seems hollow. Two aerial engagements have reinforced considerable space below the much-touted yet ambiguous nuclear red lines. The logical corollary is, how much more leeway can be crafted, and can there be more aerial strikes/exchanges?

Pakistan's desire is to settle for a temporary pause on the proxy war with cosmetic actions. Our dilemma is that stalemate amounts to a victory of sorts for Pakistan. Escalation is 'heady' but must be carefully calibrated after giving a chance to Imran to act on his assurances. Pakistan's actions must be verified and are time-bound. War on terrorism is likely to be lonely, as the isolation of Pakistan can only be transient. **It will be a long haul, requiring a range of measures, both internal and external. The ongoing crisis is just a punctuation and certainly not a period.**

Security stabilisation is an essential pre-requisite, yet it has to be complemented with internal healing and de-radicalisation. We need to rein in the warmongering media and educate the public as losses are occupational hazards. **There is a need to forge the national Kashmir policy after the elections. It is also axiomatic to build a range of options, including conventional domains, besides cyber and surgical**

ones. There is an urgent need to address hollowness, especially in air defence and ammunition, through empowered mechanisms with fast-track, liberalised procurement procedures.

On Belling the Cat: Diplomatic Engagements with Pakistan

(Written in June 2019)

India and Pakistan, two nuclear 'frenemies', are locked in a series of senseless confrontations, distracting them from the more relevant and pressing war on the socio-economic front. Surgical strikes, Balakot, and the proxy war in Kashmir drain the exchequer and prevent the optimization of traction and trajectories of economies. The debilitating effect on the sinking economy of Pakistan, which is currently seeking doles and bailout packages, is more serious. **It is for the first time that the Pindi top brass has decided to take voluntary budgetary cuts. In all likelihood, it may turn out to be just an exercise in tokenism with no effect on force ratios, yet it highlights the magnitude of the crisis and a reluctant acceptance that the Pakistan Army is being overfunded.**

The clinching issue in the recent Indian parliamentary elections was national security, which really implies dealing with Pakistan. There are a few major derivatives — firstly, the government has publicly committed to a hard line, which means that terror and talks can't mix. Consequently, it will be well neighing impossible for the ruling dispensation to backtrack in a hurry and without commensurate payoffs. The impending assembly elections will further postpone any such possibility. Hopefully, the establishment across the country would have picked up the sense of national muscular resolve. Analysts in the deep state should also link it with the real message of Balakot that terrorists will be targeted without self-imposed limitation of the Line of Control (LoC) and with the most effective means of delivery. Some more nuanced space has been discovered below the nuclear threshold, and Pakistan may be less inclined to flaunt tactical nukes. They would have also read the writing on the wall: it is 'Naya Bharat'— a five-year mandate with a stable, hard-line government.

On the other side, Imran Khan has four-odd years. Unfortunately, his mandate is a fabricated one, and the real control of 'Naya Pakistan' rests with the generals. With the economy in shambles and the additional challenge of managing the western frontier, the only silver lining is the lap dance with China. The Dragon's indulgence comes with riders, and the security of the China-Pakistan Economic Corridor is the foremost. The moot question is, will China realize the strategic reality and coerce Pakistan to tackle the terror assembly line within? **Pakistan has tried to generate positive signals on the Kartarpur Corridor by restricting the activities of Muhammad Saeed of Lashkar-e-Taiba during recent Eid prayers. There is also a flurry of invitations and offers to revive dialogue on all issues.**

Under immense international pressure, Pakistan sees the commencement of diplomatic engagement with India as the immediate objective. Notwithstanding positive signals, it is indeed very difficult to trust Pakistan, and the bottom line is that all engagements should proceed with abundant caution and after verification. From Zulfikar Ali Bhutto to Muhammad Zia-ul-Haq, extending to Pervez Musharraf and General Qamar Javed Bajwa, it has been an uninterrupted nightmare of doublespeak and treachery, punctuated by a spate of terrorist attacks. Expectations must be pegged down and conditioned on meaningful progress on issues of proxy war, peace on the LoC, and the circumscribing terror dons like Hafiz Saeed, Masood Azhar, and Dawood Ibrahim. The new Lok Sabha should consider adopting a unanimous resolution on national security to strengthen the hands of the government and reinforce messaging for elements across.

Official diplomatic channels can maintain contacts through National Security Agencies (hopefully, Pakistan will appoint one) and casual meetings on the sidelines of multilateral exchanges. In the interim, we should explore the utility of the back channel and track two dialogues. We have had some success with envoys like RK Mishra in the Vajpayee era and Satinder Lambah for the United Progressive Alliance. Even informal contacts like Sajjan Jindal leveraging links with the Sharif family had limited utility. **The government could nominate seasoned domain experts to act as designated back-channel interlocutors. It will serve to fend off the mounting pressure to start diplomatic engagement as a concern in the global community on heightened tension between two nuclear nations, which is natural.**

International pressure to resume negotiations should be managed with the Chinese strategy implying, 'Hurry but slowly and only when it suits you'. The recommended approach is to keep engaging informally till the other party yields on our core national interests. Concrete measures to improve atmospherics like overland transit corridor to Afghanistan, Most Favoured Nation status, and liberalization of trade can be considered but only when reciprocated with commensurate benefits. **Being large-hearted and sentimental must be replaced with a business-like transactional approach accompanied by verification.** The resumption of trade must be preceded by a multi-spectrum solution backed by technological aids like full-body scanners to stymie Pakistan's propensity to misuse it for smuggling drugs, explosives, and counterfeit currency.

There is limited space for track two, which got a fillip with the revival of Neemrana dialogue, the oldest in this genre. Anchored by seasoned diplomats Vivek Katju and Rakesh Sood, it has informal official acceptance. It will be a good idea to continue to vector such dialogue with official briefings, especially on red lines and debriefing after every round. Expectations from such parleys must be realistic, and they should remain discreet. **The proliferation of these exchanges without official concurrence should be discouraged, as they build avoidable pressure on the government. A relevant case in point is Navjot Sidhu's foray on the Kartarpur Corridor, where General Bajwa seems to have outsmarted him.**

It is learnt that the Pakistan Army has expressed the desire to engage with Indian counterparts. Traditionally, our diplomats have discouraged this, probably wanting to reinforce democratic forces across and imaginary fears of contacting coup virus. **They are wrong on both counts, as the Pakistan Army is not yielding ground in a hurry, and the democratic DNA of our faujis is made of Teflon. It is time veterans play a rightful role on this front and are utilised as effective channel for diplomacy.**

Vacation of PoK: The New Dimension in Strategic Matrix

(Written in September 2019)

The resurgence of demand for the vacation of Pakistan-occupied Kashmir (PoK) is a new milestone in the Indo-Pakistan strategic exchange. Though earlier rubbished as mere rhetoric, it is now being discussed as a likely possibility. Bilawal Bhutto, heir apparent of the Pakistan People's Party (PPP), has been asking Prime Minister Imran Khan to stop fretting about Article 370 and focus on saving PoK. It is indeed like forcing a reckless batsman onto the back foot. Pakistan, since partition, has taken a revanchist line, aiming to gain control of the entire state of Jammu and Kashmir (J&K). The malevolent line of thinking was fuelled primarily by parity (getting more than even with India) fixation, self-appointed guardianship of faith (ideological frontiers) syndrome, and above all, the gross under-estimation of Indian capabilities, notably a belief that India lacks the willpower and intent to take on Pakistan.

Khakhi generals have repeatedly been leveraging the first-mover advantage combined with a nuanced and cultivated facade of irrationality to gain control of the escalation matrix in strategic exchanges and retain the initiative. **The narrative of Kabayali Lashkars in 1947, infiltrator task forces with provocative names like Babur, Khilzi, and Ghaznavi in 1965, Razakars in East Pakistan, Mujahids**

in Kargil, and the ongoing proxy war in J&K has continued unabated. The horror story has been punctuated with the inciting and supporting rebels in the North East and Khalistan terrorists. In keeping with our forgiving nature, the new generation of Indians, obsessed with the present situation in the valley, has little idea of the now-forgotten links between erstwhile Pakistan and militant groups in the North-Eastern states dating back to 1952. Utilizing East Pakistan as a staging post, sanctuary, weapons, and training, including Chinese assistance, was funnelled to the Naga militants.

This misadventure continued till the '90s, with the scope extended under the complicit military rulers of Bangladesh to include many other groups, notably the United Liberation Front of Assam. The entire story has been documented by Hein G Kiessling in the highly acclaimed book "Faith, Unity, Discipline: The ISI of Pakistan".

India, in contrast, has been tentative, reactive, and defensive and was able to grab control of strategic interplay only temporarily for brief periods during the liberation of Bangladesh and Operation Meghdoot in Siachen. **This appears to be changing now with Balakot surgical strikes and the revocation of Article 370. India seems to have called off the nuclear bluff, discovered new strategic space below nuclear sabre rattling, and even injected a sense of shock and awe in Rawalpindi General Headquarters. It is indeed heartening to note that, for once, we are in control of the escalation matrix and are living up to the name of 'fox land', used by Pakistan to describe us in their war games.**

The call for re-integration of POK is not all about being wily or clever but fits in with our concept of 'Dharma Yudh' or struggling for the right cause. The vast stretches of occupied territory originally included Gilgit-Baltistan (GB), the Shakshgam Valley, and even Aksai Chin. Even if Pakistan is given the benefit of the doubt on Aksai Chin, illegally seized by China in the '50s while India slept, it cannot be absolved of the criminal act of gifting away 6,993 sq. km of strategically important Shakshgam to the Chinese in 1963. Even worse was a diabolic plot of engineering a secret Karachi pact on April 29,

1949, with forged signatures of the founder president of PoK, Sardar Ibrahim Khan and the chief of J&K Muslim Conference, Ghulam Abbas. The pseudo-agreement separated and legitimized the forcible occupation of 72,971 sq. km of GB to some extent, notwithstanding reservations by India.

The entire occupied territory was technically in 'standstill' mode, and the act was executed without consultation with the local populace of India and was not even reported in the media. By this act, Pakistan took direct control of GB. The sordid plot was kept secret for 59 long years till revealed in the court proceedings of the high court of PoK in the 1990s and later included in the so-called Constitution of PoK in 2008.

Shia soldiers of the Northern Light Infantry were misused as cannon fodder in Kargil, and their sacrifices and mortal remains were not even acknowledged by the ungrateful Pakistan Army. With their leaders in exile, 18 lakh Shias in GB face increasing persecution. **The entire region is being subjected to demographic and cultural inversion on the lines of the Hanisation of Xinjiang. Their natural resources, like gold mines, have been handed over to Chinese companies.**

The vast hydrographic potential of this region is planned to be tapped as part of the China-Pakistan Economic Corridor. It is ironic that GB is being subjected to ecological plundering with the submergence of large tracts of territory. In one case, the reservoir is planned to be situated in GB and the powerhouse in Khyber Pakhtunkhwa, thereby giving royalty benefits to the latter.

Residual PoK, which is only 13,297 sq. km and one-sixth of GB with a population of 40 lakh, is facing increasing marginalization of local Kashmiris and Mirpuris by Punjabi Pothoharis and Pashtuns. The province has a sham democracy with no voice in the parliament, and parties demanding freedom are not even allowed to contest in local elections. All dissent in GB and PoK is suppressed brutally under Schedule IV of the notorious Control of Terrorism Act. On the other hand, an earthquake of 2005 was utilized by Hafiz Saeed and Jamaat-ud-Dawah affiliated NGO Falah-e-Insaniyat to proliferate madrassas and radicalism, creating terror launch pads.

The liberation of PoK, or at least strategic stretches vital for our security, is likely to be a long, tedious, and tough struggle entailing the building up of the required niche capabilities and asymmetries besides a tacit nod or at least acquiescing the stance of relevant powers. In the interim, it is good bargaining leverage to retain initiative on the strategic matrix.

Review of Challenges on Western Front

Key Takeaways

- Chinese aggressive forays have forced India to undertake a review and strategic rebalancing.
- Despite the Northern Front being designated as the primary one, challenges on the Western Front remain in both proxy war and conventional domains.
- India, with the Balakot strike and surgical raids, has crafted space for conventional strikes/war below the dreaded nuclear threshold. Conflict resolution in J&K and the creation of integrated theatre commands coupled with modernisation are recommended.

The Western Command, the pivotal command on the Western Front, celebrated its platinum jubilee on 15 September 2022. It is an opportune time to look beyond nostalgia and ceremonials to take stock of operational dynamics and emerging challenges on the Western Front. The review is also warranted because we have belatedly chosen to discard our obsessive affliction for the Western Front. **Jolted by Chinese actions in Doklam and Ladakh, the Northern Front has been belatedly designated as the primary front. Consequently, there has been a shift of forces from the Western to Northern borders as part of the rebalancing.**

It is presumed that we intend to upgrade from a dissuasive to a credible deterrence posture against China. Concurrently, we have also planned to graduate from credible to punitive deterrence against Pakistan. **The obvious questions are – will we be able to maintain punitive or decisive deterrence on the Western Front, or is there a recalibration in the deterrence ladder?** Most importantly, it is imperative to avoid getting trapped in a collusive two-and-a-half-front imbroglio.

This review is structured on four key parameters, i.e., border determination, topography, strategy, and operational strategy.

Border Determination

The border is based on the hurriedly crafted Radcliffe line (approximately 3323 km). Its sanctity was challenged by Pakistan in October 1947. After the UN mediation, the Cease Fire (CF) was enforced in January 1948, and the Karachi Agreement was signed in July 1949. It re-designated the 830-km border in erstwhile J&K as the Cease Fire Line (CFL).

In April 1965, Pakistan launched an offensive in Rann of Kutch, resulting in another round of British and UN mediation. The Sir Creek dispute covers 93 km of unresolved maritime border. The Shimla Agreement in 1972 converted the CFL to a more defined Line of Control (LoC), measuring 740 km, starting from Sangam (near Akhnur) and extending towards the north. Pakistan continues to dispute the settled portion **covering the Jammu, Samba, and Kathua districts (193 km), terming it as the 'Working Boundary' to keep alive the bogey of the entire state being disputed. To this end, there is the constant attempt to extend the arc of proxy war up to Samba-Kathua.** The northern stretch beyond NJ 9842, spanning the Siachen Glacier (approximately 110 km), became the Actual Ground Position Line (AGPL) in 1984 after pre-emptive Indian deployment.

Approximately 2000 km of the International Boundary (IB) has been properly fenced as part of the phased programme, starting from the '80s. The system, besides tiered fencing, has surveillance towers, patrolling tracks, and a lighting system. In addition, after the CF agreement on the LoC in 2003, the LoC was also fenced with an ad-hoc system. Notwithstanding fencing, riverine and hilly terrain provide ample avenues for infiltration. In addition, Pakistan has been utilizing tunnels and increasingly using drones for fomenting narco-terrorism. The legitimacy of the LAC was enhanced by India choosing to confine operations in Kargil (1999) in the LoC sector. More recently, the CF agreement on the LAC was again reiterated by both sides on 24 February 2021. **However, the right to respond and target terrorist infrastructure was reiterated during coordinated cross-border raids after the Uri attack. More importantly, the Balakot surgical strikes reinforced this assertion, as the target was beyond even the disputed Pakistan-occupied Kashmir (PoK) and Khyber Pakhtunkhwa (KPK).**

Topography

The next parameter is topography, which has undergone significant changes. Pakistan utilized the Indus Water Treaty (IWT) award to build new irrigation channels. Canals, salinity, and flood control projects were designed to boost the defensive layout. Similarly, canals on the Indian side, like the Indira Gandhi Canal have enhanced obstacle potential. After the 1965 war, both sides added an array of Ditch cum Bundh (DCB) systems to bolster defence potential further. The net result is that space for manoeuvre and application of large formations in the heartland of Punjab has been restricted. The flank of decision has been pushed to the desert. Conflicts in the developed sector are likely to be like slug fests with shallow objectives akin to the current unresolved imbroglio in Ukraine stretching beyond six months, with no end in sight. In our context, Kargil stretched to only 11 weeks, and the rest ranged from two to seven weeks.

Operational Strategy

Thirdly, taking stock of operational strategy. **Pakistan has been driven by a relentless revanchist approach.** It has been matched by reactionary but more than resilient response by India. Pakistan's recklessness is fueled by the 'parity-fixation' and the self-ascribed role of guardian of ideological frontiers of the Islamic world. It manifested in Kabayali raiders in 1947 and the failed Op Gibraltar infiltration as a prelude to the 1965 operations. The defeat in Bangladesh and the initial success of the USA-funded Mujahideen assembly lines in the '80s resulted in Pakistan opting for proxy war as the preferred tool. Kargil was a repeat episode of a failed infiltration plot.

Pakistan projects a façade of cultivated irrationality, posing the threat of nuclear war to preclude the conventional one and yet keep bleeding India with a thousand cuts. India seeks to apply agile Integrated Battle Groups (IBGs) as the refinement of the cold-war strategy. **Decisive victory with the destruction of strategic reserves seems unlikely with the current force levels, and punitive deterrence is more pragmatic for India. Objectives will have to be shallow and limited, with built-in exit options, in case of stalemate. It bears reiteration that with the Balakot strike and surgical raids, India has partially debunked the much-touted Pak nuclear bluff and carved out nuanced space for conventional war/strike below the nuclear threshold. In the long run, coercive leverage as the upper riparian state needs to be developed. The endeavour to build disruptive capabilities in cyber and other emerging domains is warranted as a counter to proxy war.**

Force Levels

Finally, a brief analysis of force levels and organizational structures. **India didn't really anticipate any serious threat from Pakistan and opted for the ad-hoc and temporary Delhi and East Punjab (DEP) Command after partition.** The DEP Command was designated as the Western Command after the unprovoked J&K conflict. The operational responsibility was from J&K to Bikaner (Rajasthan). Operations in 1947–48, 1965, 1971, and even the Ladakh sector in 1962 were primarily orchestrated by the Western Command. The Southern Command was in a supporting role. The 1971 war highlighted the complexities of the span of control, setting the stage for the raising of the Northern Command. Later, the South-West Command was carved out in 2005, five years after the Air Force had raised theirs. The proxy war in Kashmir has been raging since the '90s; the Siachen, Kargil, and Ladakh conflicts have validated this pragmatic step. In fact, the arc of terrorism in the Western Command is limited upto the Samba-Pathankot-Gurdaspur belt.

The primary instruments of operational articulation are the Corps, especially the Strike Corps. 1 Corps was raised in April 1965 and saw action within months. 2 Corps was raised for Bangladesh operations. However, after the war, it was retained and shifted to the west. 21 Corps came up in 1990. New pivot Corps – 12 (1987), 14 (after Kargil in 1999), and 9 (2005), added to force levels. Pakistan has managed to maintain force parity to match force levels. It is now reported that 1 Corps and a few other formations have been affiliated with the Northern Front. However, all three armoured divisions remain on the Western Front. **The focus should be shifting from quantitative to qualitative asymmetry as Pakistan manages to juggle up numbers with Mujahids and Rangers. The thrust has to be on agile Integrated Battle Groups (IBGs).**

The proxy war has created two distinct response paradigms against Pakistan. The Northern Command is engaged in tackling challenges of terrorism, while the other forces on the Western Front, and even the Northern Command, to an extent, are geared up for conventional warfare. In the proxy-war-impacted regions, the objective is to work towards conflict termination and, in the interim, maintain a security environment to run functional elected governments. It is supplemented by the capability to execute punitive surgical strikes. The latter requires intelligence and political willpower backed by differentiated and specialized capabilities.

Way Forward

The natural corollary is, do we require a huge investment in conventional war capabilities? The notion that hybrid wars will spell the death knell for conventional ones is being discarded after the Ukranian war. It bears reiteration that the opening of the Punjab front in the 1965 war helped India to upset Pakistan's plan to localize conflict in J&K. We need to retain options in the conventional domain. Both India and Pakistan use tanks as primary platforms and have large fleets. The challenge lies in retrofitting and imaginative dispersed employment to reduce vulnerability against top attacks by drones. Answers lie in agile platforms and disruptive technologies, as well as leveraging drones and cyber warfare.

The way forward is speedy conflict termination in J&K, backed up by effective punitive surgical strike capability. In the conventional domain, an integrated theatre command subsuming Western, South-Western, and Southern Commands of the Army and Western and South-Western of the Air Force to generate synergy and create options is overdue. The revamping of surveillance, modernization, disruptive technologies, and cognitive warfare remain key challenges in this transformation.

Af-Pak and Taliban

A Virus Incubating Across the Durand Line

(Written in April 2020)

India seems poised to manage the current pandemic triggered by the Wuhan Virus, but another equally deadly pathogen of religious extremism is being incubated across the Durand Line in Afghanistan. This has ominous implications for India, as evidenced by the **recent ISIS-K attack on 25 March 2020 on a 200-strong religious congregation in the historical Gurdwara Hari Rai Sahib in Kabul. 25 Sikhs, including an infant, were brutally killed in the ghastly attack** lasting six hours.

Sikhs, approximating two lakhs in the '80s (in the pre-Mujahideen era), were tolerated due to their belief in the holy book rather than idol worship. Sikhs and other minorities, as well as their religious places, have come under increasing attacks, with the current numbers dwindling to barely 700.

(Map source-https://www.cia.gov/library/publications/the-world-factbook/geos/af.html)

Last July, a prominent Sikh leader Awtar Singh Khalsa, the only non-Muslim voice in Loya Jirga (Afghan parliament), was killed with 20 others in a suicide attack at Jalalabad. In yet another attack in March this year, 32 Shias were brutally killed. The attack in Kabul was followed up the very next day with a remotely activated blast in the vicinity of funeral rites, as cremations are abhorred by Islamists and crematoriums are being shut forcibly.

In the aftermath of the attacks, the minuscule Sikh and Hindu populations of Afghanistan have been trying to migrate to other countries, even temporarily coalescing in Jalalabad or across Khyber. US Congressman Jim Costa has asked his government to give refuge to the persecuted communities.

The overwhelming desire is to get back to India. It has thrown up a tricky dilemma, as evacuation will be tantamount to a vote of no-confidence in the current regime of Ashraf Ghani. **Will it ultimately result in the destruction of the Afghan connection with Guru Nanak's legacy after the senseless plundering of Bamiyan Buddhas? These obviously fit into the ISIS and Taliban monotheistic template of Khorasan Wilayat.**

The mastermind of the Kabul attack, Abdullah Orakzai, a Pakistan national known as Aslam Farooqi, has been nabbed by the National Directorate of Security (NDS). He has a dubious background, having operated with the TTP and other groups. Having been recently anointed as leader, he was involved in petty intra-group rivalry.

The attack has a sinister implied message for India, as ISIS claimed that the terror squad included Abu Khalid al-Hindi, originally Mohammed Muhsin (28), a resident of Kasargod in Kerala. If verified, this would make him the second ISIS suicide bomber, after Abu Yusuf al-Hindi or Shafi Armar, who was eliminated in Aug 2015. Doubts have arisen, as some reports point out, that Muhsin was killed in a drone strike in June 2019. It may be an attempt to utilise the Indian connection as another diabolic, divisive propaganda ploy.

Prima facie, it is difficult to believe that the attack in Kabul could have been orchestrated without ISI facilitation and complicity. It appears to be part of Pak's design to prop up the acceptable Taliban and use ISIS for dirty tricks.

The NIA has joined investigations, and it is hoped that the plot will get unravelled, with the NDS showing initial determination. As per intelligence analysts – SITE and other researchers, nearly 40% of IS-K leaders in Afghanistan and Pakistan have cross affiliations with other groups. The recent discovery of three joint Mustaqils (camps) of Taliban and Jaish-e-Muhammad in the Nangarhar province, where Indian ISIS recruits were also operating, points to sterner challenges for us. As per the alarm raised by Castelium.ai, an American technology regulatory agency, Pakistan has utilised the Covid-19 crisis to halve its terror watch list from 7,600 to 3,800, omitting even the dreaded Zakiur-Rehman Lakhvi.

Afghanistan is hurtling towards catastrophic disaster, as the USA has decided to abandon the Afghan government. The problem has been outsourced to Pakistan and the Taliban. The vague agreement with the Taliban of February 29 seeks to abandon the legally constituted government and much-needed endeavour of building a democratic and tolerant society. The most ironic element is concessions amounting to abdication without the government even being made a party to deliberations. **There are no verifiable parameters and obligations expected from the Taliban except a reduction in violence duly sweetened by the release of prisoners.**

Bluntly, a new American policy is — Afghans, you are on your own, and we are off! **This is after sinking more than $3 trillion and, most importantly, losing more than 4,000 lives, including civilian contractors.** During my interaction with the passing out Afghan cadets at the IMA in Dec 2014, despite repeated attempts to establish their regional ethnicities, the resounding reply was — we are Afghans. The much-cherished dream of evolving a more moderate theological model and society, backed by unified security forces utilising collaborative Western influences with Saudi and Jordanian royalties, lies in tatters.

The Taliban is gaining increased ascendency against some resistance by the Afghan National Defence and Security Forces with dwindling assistance from the remnants of NATO and Resolute Support Mission; it is a new extremist great game unleashed. Al-Qaeda, Taliban, ISIS, TTP, IMU, and multiple competing Shuras like Quetta and Miran Shah are vying to scale newer heights of Salafism. The game has multifarious ethnic indigenous players—Pashtuns, Tajiks, Uzbeks, and Hazaras, with international performers—Uyghurs, Turks, Kazakhs, and other nationalities. **The old proverb that Afghan warlords can agree on only one thing—to continue quarrelling—has added another sinister dimension: competitive demonstrated extremism. A bleak future awaits future generations of Afghans, particularly women.**

As the world combats the Covid-19 pandemic, it will be apt to recall that Henry Kissinger's secret trip to China was routed through and facilitated by Pakistan. The ongoing, ill-advised midwifing foray in Afghanistan is likely to sprout deadlier contagions. **George Santana famously remarked: "Those who cannot remember the past are condemned to repeat it." Will we ever learn from history?**

(Map source-https://www.researchgate.net/figure/Afghanistan-Rivers-and-geography-UNEP-2002_fig2_328664534)

Retaining Relevance in Afghan Imbroglio

(Written in August 2021)

Afghanistan is in turmoil; the Taliban, combined with assorted desperate factions, is battling the Afghan National Security Forces (ANSF) in a violent struggle to take over the coveted and pivotal geo-strategic space. **The salience is drawn from its "buffer state" location on the confluence of Han, Persian, Turkish (Xinjiang and Turkmenistan), Arabic, Central Asian (connected to Russian), and Indian civilizations.**

The British, after unsuccessful forays, were forced to endure this unruly territory as an autonomous bulwark against the Soviets. In the great game in the '80s, the Western-backed Mujahideen were pitted against the Soviets in a proxy war, finally driving the Russians out. Yet, another edition of a great game witnessed Americans edging out the Taliban in the Global War on Terror (GWOT), targeting Al-Qaeda and later ISIS after the 9/11 attack in 2001.

The turbulent frontier has always defied conventional governance parameters and norms with an assortment of autonomous tribal ethnicities. The Af-Pak region, astride the Durand Line, has been traditionally administered through seven autonomous agencies like Waziristan, Bajaur, and tribal assemblies or Shuras of tribes like Mehsuds. These Shuras hold 'Loya Jirgas', the grand assemblies entailing tortuous and lengthy confabulations, ending with 'khap' type of diktats. **The codified traditions and edicts, like 'Pashtunwali', override all other laws, including Sharia and Hadith.**

Outwardly, seeming united, the Taliban is, in effect, a complex conglomeration of disparate groups like the TTP. Many are described with appendages of the Shura that they owe allegiance to, like Quetta, Peshawar, Jalalabad, etc. **The fractious nature of the Afghan society is best summed up in the famous words of the noted scholar Ahmed Rashid after a Loya Jirga, "Afghans have only agreed to disagree amongst themselves".**

In the current context, Taliban factions have a consensus on getting rid of Americans and the Western forces, as well as the recently anointed President Ashraf Ghani. The atmosphere after the recent American exit from the Bagram base is accompanied by a sense of euphoria of once again forcing out another external power. The tally now includes the UK, the USSR, and the USA with a pertinent question: will China be the next one, provided it decides to intervene with the PLA?

US forces are finally pulling out from Afghanistan after two decades. **Many describe it as a sort of abandonment after having sunk more than $2.26 trillion and losing 2,442 Braveheart's and 800 private security contractors. In addition, the toll includes 1,144 soldiers of the 36-nation ISAF (NATO) coalition, 72 journalists, and 444 aid workers of NGOs.** Ironically, the British, with the enviable tradition of the Commonwealth War Graves Commission, is unable to give appropriate honour to its 450 Braveheart's in Afghanistan.

The Soviet Union lost 14,400 soldiers in the decade of 1979–89 in American-organised, Saudi allies-funded, Pakistan-orchestrated, fassadi (packaged and justified as jihadi), Taliban-executed mayhem. Afghan casualties at the most conservative scale were approximately 70,000 odd combatants of various militias, 47,000 civilians, and 10 million refugees, including the internally displaced populace.

Americans had some justification for the initial intervention. It could be termed overreach, but it lost the plot in execution. **General Dave Miller, former head of Army Training and Doctrine Command, most aptly remarked, "Believe me, it's a lot easier to invade a country than to leave it in an ordinary manner."**

The Taliban was created through contrived midwifery, wherein the Mujahideen (religious fighters) were given a semblance of respectability. The Mujahideen, having acquired considerable notoriety in the civil war, ISI chose to fix it by inducting Madrasa graduates with a more acceptable name of Talibs (students in Pashto).

Taliban 1.0 was a bunch of compliant, self-obsessed fighters led by the late Mohammad 'Mullah' Omar, willing to dance to the ISI's

tunes. He chose to usurp Mehdi-like powers for himself by wearing the Prophet's spiritual cloak of Khirqa-e-Mubarak at Kandahar. This act, borrowed from Sufi mystical practices, itself doesn't meet the Wahhabi or Salafi criteria. They rose like phoenix in 1994 and, after consolidation in 1996, ruled till 2001. The ISI's puppetry often drew the lighthearted comment that the Taliban were functioning, in effect, more like Shagirdan (followers).

Taliban 2.0, in comparison, comprises more politically aware and confident leaders. They are likely to be more autonomous. Pakistan has been most surprisingly trusted once again to exercise its influence on the Taliban to salvage some sort of face-saving exit for the USA. Having assessed altered dynamics, Pakistan has already reiterated that it is only a facilitator and not the guarantor in the peace process. Is Pakistan looking for risk mitigation before another spell of civil war?

The proposed solution seeks to avoid a unilateral, 'winner takes it all' solution in favour of the Taliban. It promotes an inclusive solution that gives due representation to all segments of society. The Western world wants a fair share for women in education and employment. It also hopes that the new regime will not allow the resurgence of Al-Qaeda and ISIS. In essence, it doesn't want the re-establishment of the Emirate of the Taliban.

It is important to remember that Pashtuns constitute roughly 40% share, followed by Tajiks – 25%, Hazaras – 10%, and many other smaller tribes – Uzbeks, Nuristanis, etc. The North-South fault line has existed from the times of the late Ahmad Shah Massoud (Lion of Panjshir) and Rashid Dostum. This apart, the Herat province bordering Iran, under Ismail Khan, is also arrayed against the Pashtuns. The Taliban has taken care to induct non-Pashtuns and Haji Furqan, and Uyghur key commander who led the recent offensive in the North. It is learnt that China wants his role to be circumscribed. In this age of hypocrisy, it is likely that the Taliban will follow Pakistan and jettison Uyghurs and the Ummah (Islamic brotherhood).

Taliban, in a psy-war offensive aided by Pakistan, has been proclaiming that it has gained control of 85% of the territory, key border crossings, and major districts. **Reliable demographic experts opine that 75% of the population is currently huddled in cities, with 25% in Kabul's capital region alone.** It will be more appropriate to accept that the Taliban retains contested and shifting control in 45–50% of the area, over 25–30% of the populace and one-third of 421 districts. Key districts remain under government authority.

The real control of Afghanistan is through its population centres – Kabul, Herat, Jalalabad, Kandahar, Mazar-e-Sharif, Kunduz, strategic communications, and border checkposts. The USA, despite reservations, has agreed to allow Turkey, part of the NATO mission, to guard Kabul airport, providing an airhead for diplomatic presence that is vital for the peace process. Turkish Forces have the wherewithal and expertise to execute this mission. It is very likely that Turkey may develop leverage and stake in the peace process, though currently, the Taliban doesn't approve of their presence.

The Pakistan-aided Taliban propaganda has triggered waves of migration and exodus. It is important to remember that conflicts in Afghanistan are characterized less by fair play and more in terms of shifting loyalties, treachery, and Bakshish (bribery) combined with propaganda. The ANSF, with approximately 3.5 lakh strength, has been limited to Counter Insurgency force format. Its officer cadre and junior leadership trained by India have shown remarkable resilience and are currently contesting a complete Taliban takeover.

Update: Most surprisingly, the entire Afghan National Army capitulated and did not show any cohesion or resilience.

Pakistan's insistence and Indian reticence have resulted in the ANSF being devoid of air power, guns, and tanks. India has provided only eight refurbished MI-35 gunships but could have done much more. American promised 'over the horizon' air support remains critical for the ANSF, as evidenced by the recent Kandahar raid and in Balkh, where the Taliban suffered considerable casualties.

The challenge for the USA is to generate actionable intelligence and find a suitable base, preferably in proximity, for such operations. The option of a Shamsi base in Baluchistan (on lease with the UAE for hunting) is no longer feasible, as the lease has expired. This apart, Chinese presence in Gwadar and hostile public sentiment precludes it. The USA is looking at options for bases in Uzbekistan and Tajikistan, though the latter with a pro-Soviet tilt is less likely. Russia has scheduled exercises with Tajik and Uzbek forces as part of the Collective Security Treaty Organization (CSTO) at the Harb-Maidon training ground, close to the Afghan border, from 05 to 10 Aug 2020. **The underlying message is that everyone wants a stake in the great game.**

The Doha peace process is making slow progress. Concurrently, Russia, with the USA and China, has activated a troika, which has been extended by inviting Pakistan. Some analysts, including the Soviet FM Sergey Lavrov, have mooted the idea of the inclusion of Iran and India in the extended troika. Surprisingly, Zamir Kabulov, designated representative, countered this with his dampener, "India can't join because it has no real influence with the Taliban." This is strange, for the Taliban barely represents 45%. The Pakistan and Ghani regimes are constantly sniping at each other, and Islamabad enjoys very little trust amongst non-Pashtun ethnicities.

Mullah Abdul Ghani Baradar, leading the Doha delegation, is assiduously creating a facade to garner better acceptability. The Taliban realizes that to manage Afghanistan, they need external funding and support for the economy, employment, and reconstruction. Once again, Pakistan has facilitated a connection with China. In the early '70s, it was Kissinger and Nixon who were the conduits to Beijing. This time, it was Mullah Baradar travelling to Tianjin. Ready assurances have been given to China on the curtailing activities of ETIM, security for Chinese economic activities, like Aynak copper mines, and peace in Xinjiang. Sources indicate that the Taliban is willing to give similar guarantees to India for Kashmir.

Objectively analyzing, assurances on security, women empowerment, and inclusive solutions are like manifesto promises. Once the new regime is installed, it may become a game of competitive Salafism, leading to a revival of Khorasan, ISIS, and even ETIM. These trends were seen in the attacks on Sikhs and their shrines. The Taliban denied their role, leaving ISIS as the most likely culprit. China needs to learn appropriate lessons from the recent casualties of nine engineers at Dasu despite funding two light special security divisions (34 and 44) tasked with the protection of the CPEC assets and workforce.

Analysts are waiting to unravel the Chinese enigma and riddles. Firstly, will China show real commitment and put boots on the ground? The second option is, will Beijing utilise a combination of outsourcing to Pakistan and buy its way out through funding? Most countries want China to get bogged down in Afghanistan as a logical sequel to its aggressive rising China policy. **However, China is likely to prefer the second option of relying on Pakistan and leveraging its deep pockets. Like all historical misadventures, these are, in all probability, likely to backfire in the unscrupulous killing fields of Afghanistan. The question is: how soon?**

Indian prime concerns are protecting the infrastructure assets created, safeguarding the interests of our traditional allies (Northern Alliance), and retaining goodwill generated through education and assistance in health and equipment serviceability. India has twin macro challenges of maintaining discreet channels with the Taliban yet building the capability to provide aid to friends. India needs to retain its traditional domain awareness through intelligence networks in the region.

Concurrently, India should seek to convince the CAR nations to allow India to join their efforts in providing regional security. Uzbekistan and Tajikistan, where medical and other assistance teams were stationed at Ayani, are most relevant. Revival or partnership in such endeavours can be major enablers for us. India also needs to work with both the Soviet Union and the USA to seek participation in their regional initiatives. One such recently announced endeavour is the US-promoted 'Afghan Quad' with Pakistan, Uzbekistan, and Afghanistan.

While India shouldn't put boots on the ground, it should build its relevance through astute diplomacy and networking with all players. It will be in India's interest to contribute wholeheartedly towards an inclusive and tolerant regime in Kabul.

Seeking Clarity on Taliban 2.0 and the Afghan-Pakistan Situation

(Written in August 2021)

The great game in Afghanistan is an addictive affliction, having engineered the ignominious defeat of most external forces except Maharaja Ranjit Singh. In Higher Command (2001–02), my dissertation was 'Containment of Jihadi Fundamentalism in Afghanistan'. The prescriptive initiatives included forging strategic linkages with Iran and (central Asian regions) CAR, backed up with connectivity's. Chah Bahar, rail/road links, air bases in CAR, and connecting with ethnic groups, especially Pashtuns, were other main recommendations. They remain relevant.

The driving factor was needed to outflank the Turkmenistan-Afghanistan-Pakistan-India (TAPI) pipeline, with Taliban-1.0 clamouring to act as pipeline police. With the ascendancy of Taliban-2.0, the China-Pakistan Economic Corridor (CPEC) becoming 'Afghan-Pakistan'-EC is an ominous possibility. The next great game could be the colonisation of 'Afghan-Pakistan' economically by China.

In 2008, I studied the same subject at the macro level at National Defence College (NDC), with the initial assigned topic, 'Combating Jihadi Fundamentalism with Soft Power'. During my one-year-long study, I forced four refinements in the objective, settling on managing Islamist extremism with smart power. Another column can be written on refinements, but only relevant aspects are enumerated.

- Firstly, **the most important prerequisite is defining the correct**

end state. Americans obviously chose and stuck to the wrong one, finally abandoning it.

- Secondly, the **Afghan situation mandated inclusive regional management. The USA failed to exhibit flexibility and, notwithstanding its dubious record, outsourced it to Pakistan.**
- Thirdly, **smart power dictates customising localised solutions. The USA, on the contrary, tried imposing its own models of governance and security on tribal society.**
- Fourthly, **management requires a long-term commitment. The least President Biden could have done is to time the US exit in winter when the tempo of Taliban operations would have been slower.** It should have fulfilled its commitment to 'over the horizon' (OTH), air and drone cover to Afghan National Defense and Security Forces (ANDSF).

Answers to the sudden collapse of ANSDF lie in a 120-page, US Congress-mandated report in 2015 by the Special Inspector General for Afghanistan (SIGAR). This report gives enough clues on the ghost army and police, propped up on bloated payrolls, cornering $300 million in salaries. It highlights many dubious deals like the junking of 20 G222 Italian cargo aircraft costing $549 million for a mere $40,257, with no real flying, indicating a vicious stranglehold of contractor lobbies. Most commentators underestimated the potential of bribery (Bakshish) and deal-making, overriding instruments in the Afghan model of warfighting.

The emerging situation has triggered discussion on the following two sensitive issues:

- The **first one is on the training imparted by India to around 1,000 Afghan officers.** Pragmatic analysis, after having both trained with and instructing many foreign students, is that they are trained on persuasive and liberal terms. Learning is directly proportional to their self-motivation. The IMA recently witnessed fracas triggered by Tajik cadets.

- The **second one relates to the possibility of influencing IMA-trained Sher Mohammad Stanikzai. A similar hype was generated on General Bajwa's association with Indian peacekeepers in Congo.** Stanikzai, known for his strident criticism of India, reached out, albeit belatedly, requesting India to retain its diplomatic presence in Kabul. On balance, the acceptance of his suggestion would have only enhanced the Taliban's legitimacy. **The bottom line is that he has to survive in the Taliban hierarchy, where loyalty to its ideology is the key determinant.**

In the evolving maelstrom of fassadi brouhaha, Madrasa-trained soldiers are in the vanguard. Hence, it is difficult to trust the guarantees given at Doha and Kandahar. Even the overarching 'Rawalpindi Shura' run by ISI may be in for a few surprises. The much-touted exploitation and monetising of $3 billion mineral resources is subject to establishing a security regime free from the protection money culture of warlords. Some semblances of resistance led by VP Amrullah Saleh, backed by Ahmad Massoud (Jr) and Rashid Dostum, are emerging. The Panjshir group can gain traction only with meaningful external support, especially from Iran and Russia. The biggest challenges are the narco-terrorism-funded economy and the possibility of prolonged localised civil war. Currently, all financial reserves are frozen, and that remains the only viable leverage to promote inclusive solutions and a check on terrorism.

Update: Resistance by Northern Alliance has failed to gain any appreciable traction.

There is mounting apprehension about the shape of the government being proposed. Taliban spokesman Zabihullah Mujahid has touted the Islamic Emirate model with Hibatullah Akhundzada as temporal head, like the Iranian Ayatollah and messianic Mullah Omar. Akhundzada has the dubious distinction of securing the allegiance of Al-Qaeda head Ayman al-Zawahiri to be Emir-ul-Momin. He proposes to run the administration through Naib (No. 2). Mullah Abdul Ghani Baradar, a contemporary of Mullah Omar, the founding father, is likely to assume this role. He could be assisted by Mullah Yaqoob (Omar's son), the current military head, and Sirajuddin Haqqani. Meanwhile, according to rumours, Akhundzada is in ISI custody, like Baradar, before his release in 2016. The apex structure would include a nominated council — Rehbari Shura, which defies all democratic models. The Taliban's continued disapproval of even adopting Islamic Majlis (assembly), a guided democracy model like Iran, remains a major stumbling block. Concurrently, Hamid Karzai, Abdullah Abdullah, and Gulbuddin Hekmatyar are attempting to secure representation for non-Taliban elements. Iran is also looking for a role for Shia leader Ismail Khan.

Though reprehensible, it is important to remember that a certain amount of violence and even torture is endemic across Khyber. Bedouin societies accept war booty (ghanimah) after ghazw (raid), with the leader retaining 1/4th and the balance being divided among the raiders. Kabul is witnessing Talibs living their fantasies of childish pranks in amusement parks after commandeering embassy vehicles.

The real danger of the Taliban is firing the imagination of more dangerous mutations, promoting Khorasan and Ghazwa. After all, the Taliban is not merely a group but a dangerous, virulent idea that needs to be managed with smart power. Even original promoters—Saudi Arabia and UAE—on the transition path to moderate Islam are scouting for antidotes

Afghanistan Is Turning into a Horror Show

(Written in September 2021)

The recent 21st Shanghai Cooperation Organization (SCO) summit meeting in Dushanbe has once again brought to the fore the unresolved imbroglio in Afghanistan. Prime Minister Narendra Modi, in his short but focused virtual address, flagged the challenges of terrorism and the need for theological correctives to promote a moderate and inclusive regime. **Notwithstanding these very relevant concerns, the great game unfolding in the Afghanistan-Pakistan region is degrading into a horror show of sorts. The neighbours, including traditional supporters of the Taliban like Iran and a new breed of backers, Russia and even China, are worried and apprehensive.**

It is literally a triple-whammy, as there were widespread expectations that the Taliban in its 2.0 avatar would be inclusive and moderate. As a corollary, expectations were that the regime would be more tolerant towards women and minorities. It was categorically assured that terrorism will neither be allowed within nor proliferated across borders. In a country with the highest density of warlords, competitive extremism, Tora-Bora-type caves, and Panjshir-like valleys, such assurance amounts to chasing the ever-elusive mirage.

The planned Taliban makeover projected Mullah Abdul Ghani Baradar, with the Doha group, as the brand ambassador. It was also rumoured that diverse strands of opinion, represented by Abdullah Abdullah, Hamid Karzai, Ismail Khan, and Hekmatyar, may be included to garner acceptability. The initial draft wish list included Hibatullah Akhundzada as Emir-ul-Momin, temporal head, and Baradar, heading the executive Rehbar council.

The optimists didn't cater for the bull-run by the Pindi Shura, operating from ISI HQ at Aabpara. Leading the charge, General Faiz Hameed made sure that the Haqqanis and their lackeys ruled the roost. It was a repeat of sorts of 2001, when another ISI general, Mahmood Ahmed, and Mufti Shamzai of the Binori mosque encouraged Mullah Omar to initiate jihad against the USA. The Taliban, who were veering around to hand over Osama bin Laden, were incited to set in motion a catastrophic chain of events and go back on that commitment.

The ISI-compliant Taliban regime has 17 internationally designated terrorists like Sirajuddin Haqqani and a notorious band of five with a Guantanamo track record, described as Gitmo-5. **The ISI, in its obsession with strategic depth, has**

forced the Taliban into retrograde 1.1 formulation, with a barely notional representation of non-Pashtun tribes. Even among the Pashtuns, the ISI has cherry-picked, leaving out Iran-backed Abdul Qayyum Zakir. Iran has already articulated its angst and asked for investigations of Pakistan's role in the Panjshir operations. The dispensation described as the acting arrangement is headed by low-profile Mullah Hassan Akhund, notorious for the destruction of the Bamiyan heritage site.

Hibatullah, the supreme leader, has surprisingly vanished, like Mullah Omar, whose death was announced years later. Similarly, Deputy Prime Minister Baradar was missing during the recent visit of the deputy PM of Qatar. He has sent an audio message and a handwritten note and even made a brief TV appearance, but the mystery is getting murkier. Is he injured and recovering in a safe sanctuary after the reported clash with the new Haqqani, enfant terrible in Kabul, Khalil? In this round, the Haqqani clan has outsmarted Kandahar and other shuras. **Sirajuddin, notorious for earning an endorsement by the Al-Qaeda (AQ) leader Zawahiri, has emerged as the de facto power centre. Many of these leaders carry the baggage of linkages with groups like AQ and IS-KP, and a notable one in this ilk is Qari Fasihuddin, the army chief, with sympathies to East Turkestan Islamic Movement, Beijing's bête noire.**

China has made the right noises in the SCO, even calling for the release of seized foreign funds. Yet, it remains cautious on recognition. The influential think-tank, the Chinese Academy of Trade and International Cooperation (CATIC) has sounded a note of caution on the much-vaunted mineral wealth. It feels that, except for iron ore, **it may require 8–10 years of stability to commercially exploit minerals, subject to initial estimates proving good.** It also said the projected Afghan leg of the CPEC may be an additional drain on the already financially stressed venture.

China has committed a modest $31 million but is unlikely to put boots on the ground. Staring at the food crisis, it has limitations in immediate food grain criticalities. The new joke in Darra Adam

Khel arms bazaar is – after American burgers, it's time for Chinese chow-mien.

President Biden continues to convey his annoyance by refusing to call up Imran, and Blinken flagged Pakistan's duplicitous behaviour, suggesting a reworking of relations. Now that the USA is no longer dependent on Pakistan's logistics bridgehead, concrete measures are required to rein in Pakistan mavericks. Immediately, non-NATO, strategic ally status should be revoked, personalised sanctions against Pakistan generals and the endeavour to downgrade Pakistan to the FATF blacklist are warranted.

The ISI euphoria may not last long, as there are signs of disquiet all over. The Panjshir resistance, though presently quelled, may erupt after the winter pause, consolidation, and, more importantly, backing by Iran and Tajikistan. The TTP faction under Noor Wali Mehsud has been reinforced with leaders like Faqir Mohammed released by the Taliban. The Pakistan Army is already bearing the brunt of increased attacks. Nationalist Taliban factions under Baradar, Zakir, and Sadr are regrouping to minimise Pakistan interference.

Some sections of civil society have stood up for the Afghan flag and currency. Two decades of education and development have unleashed some green shoots of yearning for peace, at least in urban areas. Afghanistan faces a humanitarian crisis, and international bailout and diplomatic recognition should be coordinated and linked with the conditionality of inclusiveness, human rights, and the role of women.

For Taliban supporters, some traditional tribal wisdom: "Pusht-e har teppe, yek padishah neshast" (Behind every hillock there sits an emperor). **In Afghanistan, the seminal truth is "Har saray Khan deh" (Every man is a Khan). Pakistan will be well advised to drop fancy notions of controlling the destiny of Khans across Khyber and focus on domestic Pashtun and Baloch separatism.**

Regaining a Sense of Relevance in the Afghanistan Maelstrom

(Written in November 2021)

Afghanistan is reeling under the ever-worsening humanitarian maelstrom with harsh winter, pandemic, and famine. The disaster is compounded by the inept Taliban government, struggling to find even basic international acceptance. The stark reality festers in the form of the plight of a significant number of refugees in the Western and Gulf countries. It has also triggered in Europe a feeling of being let down by the unilateral US pullout, as also guilt pangs on the current plight of the Afghan populace, particularly refugees, minorities, women, and children.

Growing differences in perceptions is a diplomatic opportunity that Pakistan and China seek to exploit by giving humanitarian crisis overriding importance and relegating other critical issues to the background. **There is concerted orchestration by Pakistan to magnify projections of crisis to secure the release of frozen funds, amounting to approximately $9.5 billion, thereby whittling down minimal leverages still retained by Western nations.** Pakistan organised an international seminar to coincide with the Troika Plus meeting to hype up its pro-Taliban agenda.

It will be worthwhile to reiterate red lines — inclusivity and pluralism; zero tolerance on terrorism, including the proliferation of narcotics and arms; ensuring basic human rights, especially for women, children, and minorities. Humanitarian relief under the regime, where minorities like Shias and Sikhs are being targeted and women terrorised, mandates the incorporation of safeguards to enable just coverage to include marginalised sections. India, as a likely major donor of wheat, needs to ensure international monitoring.

Chinks in collective resolve to link diplomatic recognition with compliance with red lines are already manifesting. Taliban appointees have taken over embassies and consulates in Pakistan.

The same may happen in China and later in Russia. The need is for collective action to retain leverage and incentivise compliance with internationally agreed objectives.

The collapse of the Doha process has sprouted alternative mechanisms like Troika Plus (Russia initiated with the USA, China plus – currently, Pakistan and Iran), the Moscow format (enlarged regional formulation, including India), and the recent Delhi dialogue, amongst others. India is literally at the margins, struggling to regain relevance. We are paying a heavy price for supporting a duly elected regime and not opening parallel channels with the Taliban.

The US, on its part, has tried to initiate regional dialogue concurrently aimed at countering China through Quad variants. The Central Asian one, announced before the Taliban takeover, is unlikely to take off. The USA, Afghanistan, Uzbekistan, and Pakistan are the members of this one. The Middle Eastern variant has the USA, Israel, the UAE, and India. Ironically, Israel and the UAE have long-standing security cooperation arrangements with China, including technology exchanges.

In these confusing times of plurilateralism, the Indian initiative with Russia, Iran, and all five Central Asian countries is a very timely endeavour. Unfortunately, Pakistan stayed away and even influenced China to do likewise. India has very difficult and complicated choices, starting with the need to accept fait accompli and 'real politick' of dealing with the Taliban. Between inactivity, dubbed as strategic patience, and smart engagement, the latter is a pragmatic option. **The harsh reality is that the transition has been outsourced to Pakistan, yet India must forge a consensus to preclude Pindi from hijacking the plot completely.**

The challenge can be outlined as regaining relevance, cementing consensus to nudge the Taliban towards responsible governance, in effect, retaining leverages till compliance. More importantly, explore shared concerns and safeguard them. In the Delhi dialogue, notwithstanding the Russian participation, some back-tracking by Moscow on the Delhi consensus has been reported. The need is to be wary of the stance of Zamir Kabulov, Russian interlocutor, in the Troika Plus dialogue and his alleged pro-Pindi leaning. Is Russia utilising Nikolai Patrushev and Kabulov to remain engaged with two differing approaches?

Indian opportunities lie with Iran and its ire at the continuing marginalising of Shia, Hazaras, and Ismailis. Insurgency in Sistan and the growing number of refugees from Afghanistan have heightened concerns in Tehran. **It is an opportunity to re-energise connectivity projects like Chabahar and Zaranj-Delaram as part of the North-South corridor.** Sidestepping US antagonism towards Iran and sanctions are the key challenges. Though seemingly tough, India needs to keep chipping at the possibilities of reviving a stake in the Ayni air base in Tajikistan. **This is especially critical as China has reportedly secured the go-ahead for a policing and surveillance facility, essentially a benign euphemism for a military base.** Our forays and efforts should include the Fergana Valley in Uzbekistan, which is supposedly more autonomous.

It may seem non-Kosher, but it will be worthwhile to tie up with Americans, including the utilisation of the operating base, for OTH surveillance of possible areas of operation of ISIS and variants. It can have spin-offs in capability building, technology exchanges, and messaging to ward off Chinese designs in Gilgit-Baltistan. It is time the USA woke up to a mess created due to over-dependence on Pakistan and built redundancies through India.

Euphoria in Pakistan over the Taliban victory is having a blow-back effect. The government there caved into self-appointed, anti-blasphemy warriors of the TLP by accepting its unreasonable demands. It has resulted in main streaming and virtual carte blanche to the extremist party, whose cadres fired at and killed security personnel. In another incident, Pakistan's Prime Minister **Imran Khan had to appear before the Supreme Court to explain amnesty to the TTP, perpetrators of the massacre of APS Peshawar. The growing perception is that the military has virtually capitulated in the Sirajuddin Haqqani-brokered agreement.**

Repeated assurances that ISIS and TTP are under control are not even worth the value of the rapidly sinking Afghani currency. It is time the world woke up to the triggering of the domino effect of competitive extremism by the legitimisation of the TLP and TTP. The malevolence needs to be capped before we confront new variants of ISIS, IMU, ETIM, and more radical offshoots of the Taliban. **The answer lies in keeping the focus on red lines and ensuring zero tolerance for terrorism, especially its proliferation in the neighbourhood.**

Re-Engaging with the Taliban

(Written in June 2022)

The dastardly attack on Gurdwara Karte Parwan in Kabul on 25 May 2022 virtually sounded the death knell for the multi-cultural character of Afghanistan. Another historic shrine, Gurdwara Har Rai Sahib, was targeted in an even more ghastly attack exactly two years back, accounting for 25 deaths. While the recent attack had only one Sikh casualty, structural damage to the only functional shrine was extensive. The same gurdwara has been subjected to periodic encroachments under the pretext of road widening. In 2018, an attack on the historic Gurdwara Nanak Sahib in Jalalabad had left 18 dead.

Sikhs numbering 2–5 lakhs (2–5%) in the '70s have dwindled to less than 500. The community was spread across Kabul, Jalalabad, Kandahar, Ghazani, Khost, and other cities. As traders, money lenders, Unani, and herbal medicine practitioners, they had endeared themselves to society. More than a dozen gurdwaras have been destroyed in the civil war. The obvious question is — after the obliteration of the Bamiyan Buddhist relics, are Sikhism and its shrines next on target?

These attacks have been projected as retaliation for unconnected events in India, like J&K and the blasphemous remarks controversy. The offer by the ruling dispensation to repair and protect gurdwaras needs to be backed up by actions on the ground. The Sikh diaspora across the Durand Line has also been facing sporadic attacks. While e-visas were granted by Delhi, the lament that these could have been accorded earlier has been articulated. E-visas for 3,000-odd Afghan students also require priority handling.

Terrorist attacks have been owned up by various factions of the ISIS. Perpetrators are recycled inductees from various tanzeems with multiple affiliations. The 2020 attack was executed by the Indian-origin ISIS-Levant Khorasan cadres, Abu Khalid al-Hindi and Murshid Mohammed TKJ from Kerala. However, the mastermind was Abdullah Orakzai alias Aslam Farooqi, having affiliations with Lashkar-e-Taiba and Haqqani factions. He was amongst the prisoners released by the current Afghan regime upon taking over. The latest attack has been owned by the ISIS-Khorasan Province faction. The suicide bomber had his roots in Jaish-e-**Muhammad. It bears recalling that Masood Azhar was amongst the first to visit Kandahar, the spiritual capital, to pay obeisance to the new regime.**

In the complex bevy of multiple groups enjoying sanctuary in remote areas on the Af-Pak border—Nangarhar and Kunar—exacerbated by the internal tussle between Taliban Shuras and factions, it is difficult to resolve the 'who and why' of attacks. Behind the cover of IS, many pursue diabolic agendas. **It will be safe to assume that Peshawar Corps Commander Faiz Hameed may know the real answers. With the impending nomination of the all-powerful Army chief, it could be his way of staking relevance.**

There has been a significant move forward in engaging with the Taliban regime, who have been inviting India to reopen the embassy. The assessment team, led by the joint secretary, visited Kabul, including mission premises. It appears that Indian aid has been well received, and assets like the embassy have not been vandalised. Dr Abdullah Abdullah returned to Kabul after a 44-day visit to India. The visit, although described as personal, included extensive interactions with the Indian establishment and diplomats from the US and France. It is also relevant that Hamid Karzai, the former president, unlike Ashraf Ghani and others, remained in Kabul through the turbulent phase of transition.

There is speculation that the attack could have been orchestrated by the ISI to stymie normalisation of relations. The saga of India—from being the hot favourite with Afghans to being completely left out and now struggling to regain relevance—is indeed interesting. Relations hit the nadir in 1996–99 with the proliferation of Mujahideen terrorists in the valley, defined by the sordid hijacking drama at Kandahar in 1999. In this period of internal strife, India chose to support the Northern Alliance and non-Pashtun leaders like Tajik, Ahmad Shah Massoud (Lion of Panjshir), and Uzbek Rashid Dostum. Another rude jolt was the attack on the Indian embassy in Kabul in 2008; casualties included my NDC coursemate, Brigadier RD Mehta, press attaché, and two ITBP officials.

While officially treating the Taliban as a pariah, the UPA re-established back-channel links in 2011. Mullah Abdul Salam Zaeef, the Taliban envoy in Islamabad, despite Guantanamo Bay prison track record, reportedly made numerous visits to India. He was seen at a Goa literary event in Nov 2013 with then FM Chidambaram. Repeat mistake of siding with Ashraf Ghani in the face of the imminent US pullout and zero-contact with the Taliban completely marginalised India in the Afghan reconciliation process. India was quick to pull out of Kabul in Aug 2021, but Pakistan, Russia, and China maintained their presence. **Ten months down the line, 15 countries now have missions, and the number is likely to grow. In the recent SCO dialogue, India was conspicuous as the lone ranger.** In the interim, many of our core concerns, including democracy, women empowerment, and links with terrorist groups, have not been addressed. Yet, there is a realisation that Panjshir's resistance has not gathered traction. The Taliban, unified as fighters, appear faction-ridden in governance. There are openings with moderates like IMA-educated Sher Mohammad Stanikzai, currently deputy FM. Russia originally worked hard to keep India out, but after the Ukrainian crisis, it seems more chastened.

Afghanistan was jolted by a massive earthquake, with the epicentre in Southern Khost province. **While diplomatic recognition by India is not in the offing, India has rightly responded to signal commitment and reach out to Afghan society by sending a technical team.** It is good that motivated distractions like the gurdwara attack have not been allowed to deride long overdue corrective steps. The physical presence of even a small team is likely to generate multiple benefits, including better security for the diaspora. Concurrently, the Taliban needs to do much more to protect minorities and address Indian concerns.

Taliban 2.0 May Just Be Floundering Along

(Written in March 2023)

As Pakistan gasps for a fiscal bailout and external assistance from a reluctant IMF, neighbouring Afghanistan has been witnessing much worse. The promised version of Taliban 2.0, after America's hurried exit in August 2021, is yet to find acceptability with continued denial of official recognition to the regime. Only China, Iran, Pakistan, Russia, Turkiye, Turkmenistan, and Qatar have extended accreditation to Taliban diplomats. India has a non-diplomatic presence in Kabul to coordinate relief assistance. The Islamic Emirate of Afghanistan, in its 19th month, is still working with only an interim cabinet, lurching towards theocratic autocracy. Foreign reserves of $7 billion left by the Ashraf Ghani regime remain frozen, with half of the amount, $3. 5 billion, re-appropriated in trust for damages and rehabilitation of 9/11 victims.

The USA, in the tortuous **Doha dialogue, visualised the new regime to ensure three fundamental objectives — quelling terrorism, basic human rights, particularly for women, and stability in governance. Pakistan had taken on the role of guarantor.** There was an informal understanding with the US to install Ghani and other moderates at the helm. In keeping with his perfidious nature, erstwhile ISI boss Lieutenant General Faiz Hameed was in Kabul to oversee the installation of the Pakistani nominees.

Power Struggle

Consequently, Mullah Abdul Ghani was not only sidelined but subjected to physical manhandling by the Haqqani clan. Fisticuff governance was again witnessed last week when the minister of higher education fractured his arm, courtesy of a senior functionary, resorting literally to 'arm-twisting' during a meeting.

The present Amir-ul-Momineen (a title that means commander of the faithful), Hibatullah Akhundzada, initially dismissed as a reclusive theocratic leader, is proving to be the toughest obscurantist. As per sources, he has stymied efforts towards the transition to the Rahbari Shura (a steering high council) for collective leadership. He is being blamed for the denial of secondary and university education to women, as well as employment.

Talking Democracy

Stability, one of the key desired objectives, should include both rudimentary democracy and inclusivity. Democracy in the form of jirgas/shuras, collective decision-making tribal bodies, remains a non-starter, with Akhundzada in Peshawar acquiring an Ayatollah-like veto power. The other metric of inclusivity, which is a critical prerequisite in the diverse Afghan ethnic society, is being only notionally applied. Abdul Salam Hanafi, an Uzbek, has been appointed as the second deputy PM with a peripheral role. Tajiks, the second largest ethnic group, find representation through Qari Fasihuddin as head of the Afghan Army. The Hazaras (Shias) have Abdul Latif Nazari as a mere deputy minister.

The real power centres are Sirajuddin Haqqani, the all-powerful interior minister, and Defence Minister Mullah Yaqoob, who is

Taliban founder Mullah Omar's son. The Haqqani clan has grabbed control of the Kabul Capital Region, where 25% of the country's population is huddled.

There is an Indian connection, too, in the form of IMA-trained Sher Mohammad Stanikzai, the spokesman of the high-profile Doha Dialogue, who has been relegated to deputy foreign minister. The Western desire to accommodate former President Hamid Karzai and Dr Abdullah Abdullah is unlikely to fructify, notwithstanding their continued presence in Kabul.

The major factor aiding the continuity of the Taliban is the inability of the Panjshir Valley-based National Resistance Front (a morphed version of the late Ahmad Shah Massoud's Northern Front) to find traction and support. The Taliban's declaration of zero tolerance to terrorism sounds hollow in the light of Al-Qaeda head Ayman al-Zawahiri being sheltered in the personal property of the Haqqani clan till his elimination by an American drone. The Taliban government is half-heartedly battling the Islamic State Khorasan Province (ISKP), which orchestrated attacks on Gurdwara Karte Parwan in Kabul and has now shifted focus to Chinese and Russian entities to embarrass the regime.

The Taliban has promised to prevent the export of terrorism to neighbouring countries by controlling Xinjiang-focused East Turkestan Islamic Movement (ETIM), Islamic Movement of Uzbekistan (IMU), IS-KP, Jaish-e-Muhammad (JeM), and Lashkar-e-Taiba (LeT). The calibration of control and sanctuary to these groups act as significant leverages for the Taliban, especially in China.

The TTP Factor

The most complex and sensitive element is in dealing with Tehrik-e-Taliban Pakistan (TTP), which has an avowed aim to install a Sharia-compliant regime in Pakistan. It also promises an autonomous homeland for Pashtuns, extending on both sides of the Durand Line. **Having been partners in crime for decades, the Taliban has obvious**

limitations in checking TTP, which has significant tribal support in frontier provinces on both sides.

There have been an increasing number of cross-border clashes and raids. TTP has increased the targeting of Pakistani personnel, like the recent suicide attack on a police congregation in a Peshawar mosque.

Efforts by the Taliban to broker and extend a ceasefire between Pakistan and TTP have not found success. Pakistan has started fencing and fortifying the Durand Line and border posts, notably the Torkham crossing. **The ISI's dream of strategic depth lies in tatters. China, having burnt its hands in the CPEC, remains a reticent player, refusing to get directly involved.** Beijing's current interests are the control of ETIM and shepherding commercial mining interests, like the Aynak copper mine, for exploitation after stabilisation.

The Taliban's survival is currently based on the financial drip being administered through international relief agencies. Cash doles amounting to $20 million are being injected periodically to prevent starvation and abject penury. The misery and plight of the populace is another diabolic leverage of sorts, ensuring some succour.

Distribution has become a victim of the recent diktat to female aid workers to wear hijab. The measure has since been reviewed, particularly for medical and health workers. The only bright spot in the Taliban report card is a comparative reduction in corruption.

India was kept out of the reconciliation process on Pakistan's insistence and complicity by the USA and even Russia. India is now increasingly being courted by the Taliban. **The current Indian focus is on disaster relief and inclusive capability building with local tribal ownership. However, Taliban assurances cannot be taken merely at face value. The way forward is caution and trust after due verification.**

Taliban at the Helm but Situation Fluid in Kabul

(Written in August 2022)

The Doha accord had sought zero-tolerance on terrorism, especially providing sanctuary to Al-Qaeda and ISIS. It also expected inclusiveness in society, with a fair representation of non-Pashtun ethnic groups. There was optimism about basic human rights. The elimination in Aug 2022 of al-Zawahiri in Kabul and in a safe house provided by the Haqqani clan exposes the hollowness of the Taliban regime on the most critical parameter.

August 15 was declared a holiday in the Islamic Emirate of Afghanistan (IEA) to mark one year of Taliban rule. **There was little cause for celebration as the Taliban, which promised to transform to a 2.0 avatar, has, at best, crawled to 1.1.** The country continues to languish as a pariah state with recognition from only China, Pakistan, and Russia. Humanitarian crises in the form of refugees and famine have reduced it to a basket case. Aid is being pumped in by UN agencies and NGOs. **India made considerable contributions to disaster relief during the recent earthquake and famine with wheat shipments. India has even restored the presence of officials in its embassy, terming it a non-diplomatic presence.** Similar ad-hoc set-ups have been instituted by many other countries, primarily to coordinate relief and retain contact with a larger populace. To be fair to the new regime, the overall level of violence has indeed diminished, though it is because the prime perpetrators are now in the seat of power.

In order to attempt an objective appraisal, it is important to start with the Doha process and its major thrust areas. Even the Taliban regime, after a drone attack on Ayman al-Zawahiri, accused the USA of violating it. Doha accord had sought zero-tolerance on terrorism, especially providing sanctuary to Al-Qaeda and ISIS. It also expected inclusiveness in society, with fair representation of non-Pashtun ethnic groups. There was optimism about basic human rights, particularly women's education and employment, coupled with fair justice without reprisals.

The elimination of al-Zawahiri, the so-called Emir of Al-Qaeda in Kabul and in a safe house provided by the Haqqani clan exposes the hollowness of the Taliban regime on the most critical parameter. This apart, recent frequent terrorist attacks in the capital, traced to ISIS-KP, validate the presumption that the Taliban is either complicit or not in full control. As per some experts, it may even be orchestrating calibrated attacks by fringe groups. Most terrorist elements have shifted allegiance, driven less by ideology and more by egos, petty personal rivalries, and the urge to control revenue-generating sources like narco-terrorism and protection money for transit. How else can a sudden resurgence of the ISIS-KP faction be explained?

It is important to reiterate that the Taliban has many factions and Shuras, depending on tribal affinities. Mullah Hibatullah Akhundzada, the Emir, is confined to the spiritual capital, Kandahar, like Mullah Mohammad Omar. He is the temporal head only, with writ limited to the interpretation and enforcement of Sharia. In the tussle between Shuras, the Haqqani clan, headed by Sirajuddin Haqqani, has cornered most spoils and portfolios. Mullah Hasan Akhund, PM, remains in outer orbit. Kabul's capital territory, the scene of al-Zawahiri elimination and dastardly Gurdwara attacks, is controlled by the Haqqanis, indicating serious failure in governance. **The state of the security situation is so tenuous that even the Haqqanis rushed to their cave shelters in Paktika after the drone attack.**

The other Shuras and their leaders, like two Deputy PMs, Mullah Abdul Ghani Baradar and Mawlawi Abdul Salami Hanafi, Uzbek (the most significant non-Pashtun face), are all nationally represented. The alternate power centre in the Rahbari Shura is Defence Minister Mullah Yaqoob (Mullah Omar's son). From the Indian and global perspective, the Doha group, anchored by Mullah Baradar and moderates like the IMA-trained Sher Mohammad Stanikzai, remain on the margins.

In the Afghan game of thrones, the ultimate arbiter, the Peshawar Shura (based in HQ 11 Corps), has seen a major shake-up. **The master manipulator and Imran acolyte, Lieutenant General Faiz Hameed, ex-ISI chief, has been consigned to the defensive formation, 33 Corps, at Bahawalpur. He has been replaced by Bajwa loyalist Lieutenant General Sardar Hassan. Pakistan, despite protracted talks and mediations by a group of clerics led by Muhammad Taqi Usmani, has failed to work out an acceptable deal with the TTP.** There are frequent clashes on the Iran-Afghan border and on the Durand Line. Despite fencing, the TTP continues to operate on both sides. The situation is likely to get vitiated in the run-up to polls in October.

The National Resistance Front, which had been hibernating in the Panjshir Valley and waiting for an operationally conducive summer, has not found much traction. Consequently, Tajiks, Uzbeks, Hazaras, and Ismailis remain largely unrepresented. The only hope for inclusiveness simmers in the continued presence in Kabul of former President Hamid Karzai and Abdullah Abdullah, but that is subject to the Taliban hierarchy paying some heed to them. The human rights record remains abysmal, with women pushed out of education and employment into veil and mandatory male escorts. Notwithstanding window dressing, flogging and reprisals are back in Taliban Kangaroo courts.

Acting Foreign Minister Amir Khan Muttaqi has been shuttling to Gulf capitals to push for recognition of the IEA. India, with investments of US $2 billion, is under pressure to restart work on development projects like the Shahtoot (Salma) dam. The situation has become more complex with China seeking to include India in the Afghan resolution process, notwithstanding the fact that the China-Pak-Russia troika spared no effort to keep India out of the Doha process, Quadrilateral Coordination Group (QCG), Ankara dialogue, and even regional initiatives. **Viewing from the Indian perspective, from total abhorrence to the reopening of informal contacts with the Taliban, is a major and welcome step in keeping with altered realities.**

India has opportunities due to a groundswell of popular acceptance, yet we can proceed only with caution and after due diligence.

Update: July 2024

- **The Taliban continues to be in power, having completed over two years, and in 1.1 mode. It has failed to implement three conditions of stable and inclusive democracy—zero tolerance to terrorism, basic human rights, especially for women and children, and no reprisals.**
- **The Taliban--affiliated staff has taken over the Afghan embassy in New Delhi, and India maintains a non-diplomatic presence in Kabul.**
- **Pakistan continues to grapple with the TTP and has lost a significant part of its leverage. Pakistan and Taliban regime appear to be at loggerhead with cross border strikes by Pakistan and clashes on border.**

Indus Water Treaty

Leveraging Indus Water Treaty (IWT): A Realistic Appraisal

(Written in July 2017)

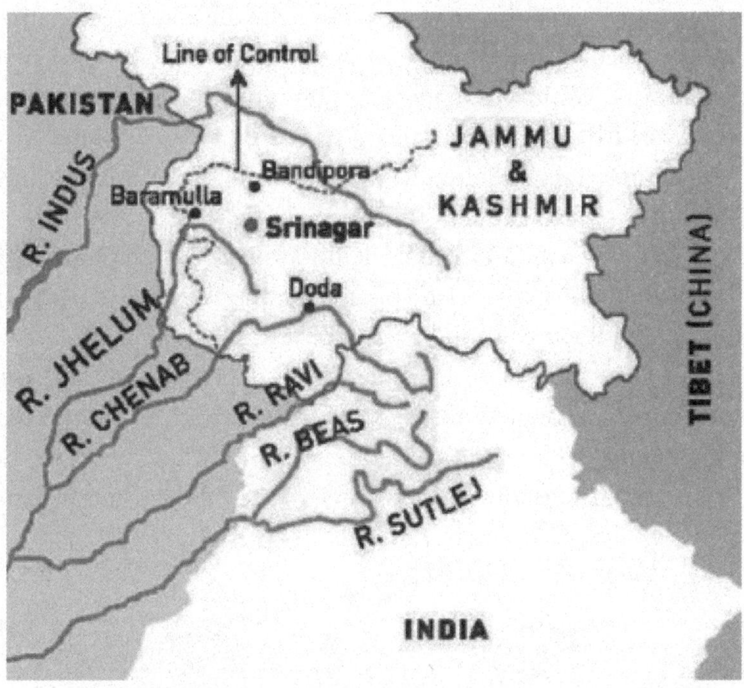

(Map source-https://images.app.goo.gl/rBy78BtqEfUS6)

For some time, India has been trying a firmer approach with Pakistan in an attempt to increase the cost it must bear for supporting cross-border terrorism. The surgical strikes, heavier retaliation to cross-border firing, and such activities are a manifestation of the hard-line adopted at New Delhi. However, it doesn't seem to have the desired effect on Pakistan.

The Indus Water Treaty (IWT) has been under much debate and is being touted as an ultimate leverage to choke Pakistan, setting the stage for a call for the use of water as a weapon. **Former Pakistani President Pervez Musharraf, in his thesis at RCDS, had identified water as the most likely flash point between India and Pakistan. More than the potential and morality of water as a weapon, it is the attendant capability in terms of dams and storage that needs to be realistically appraised.** The question that begs an answer is, even if we want to, can we do it? Any renegotiation of the IWT is likely to bring in China and Afghanistan, as well as new issues like climate control. The answer lies in an ancient Chinese proverb- "hide your shine-bide your time", implying work within the treaty norms but utilise in-built provisions.

The World Bank brokered treaty signed in 1960, allocated rivers in two groups, i.e., Eastern: Ravi, Beas, and Sutlej amounting to 33 million acre-feet (MAF), entirely to India, and Western: Indus, Jhelum, and Chenab, 135 MAF, mainly to Pakistan. India has rights on the western rivers in terms of 'run of the river' power projects, irrigation, and flood control upto specified limits, which are shown in the tables. While our share, prima facie, may appear skewed, utilisation is even more worrying. With a less water-intensive horticulture-based economy in the Kashmir valley, the potential really lies in hydro-power and inter-basin transfer to quench water-stressed Punjab and Haryana.

Share: Western Rivers

River	Storage**	Power**	Flood Control**	Total**
Indus	0.25	0.15	Nil	0.40
Jhelum	0.50	0.25	0.75	1.50
Chenab	0.50	1.20	Nil	1.70
Total	1.25	1.60	0.75	3.60

*(** All figures in MAF)*

Power Utilisation: Western Rivers

Executed**	Under Construction**	Planned**	Total Allocated **	Total Utilised and Planned**
3034	2526	5046	18600	11406 (61.33%)

(**All figures in MW*)

Analysis of eastern rivers reveals that every year, nearly a million acre-feet of water flows out from the Ravi to Pakistani Punjab and 1000 cusecs (0.0019 MAF) from the Sutlej at Husainiwala. It is important that we build the physical wherewithal in terms of storage for positive control as a strategic capability. This has been grossly lacking because of interstate disputes, and it is to the credit of the central government that, in March 2017, it pushed the contending parties into an agreement. Dispute on the Ravi has been regarding the Shahpur Kandi Dam since 1999. Punjab and J&K governments have not been able to resolve issues of compensation, power, and water distribution. **In a welcome development, the project has been designated as a centrally monitored one with 90% funding by the centre. Punjab has agreed to provide 180 MW of power at ₹3.50 per unit to J&K. In addition, the Jammu region will get 1150 cusecs of water, boosting irrigation and enhancing the defence potential of the Upper Tawi link canal.** Armed with a positive nod from the new Punjab Government, the centre needs to ensure fast-track and time-bound execution. We should take this forward by harnessing minor rivers like Degh (Basantar), Ujh, Tarnah, and Bein as water increases obstacle potential in the strategically important Shakargarh Bulge and aids infiltration into the r corridor.

The Sutlej is not a major problem, with reasons for water flowing to Pakistan being leakage because of the lack of maintenance of antiquated sluice gates at Husainiwala and the silting of the Harike reservoir. Once again, the central government has brokered a much-delayed agreement, and now Rajasthan and Punjab have agreed to fund their respective shares. This must be followed up with de-weeding Hycinth from Harike, which has gobbled up approximately 80% of the storage capacity. Repairs of head works and de-silting of all reservoirs—Gobind Sagar (Bhakra), Maharana Pratap Sagar (Pong), and Ranjit Sagar (Thein)—are overdue. There is a strong case for the raising of Ecology (Dredging) TA battalions for de-silting to augment storage, which can be utilised for inter-basin transfer and flood control. It may be relevant to mention that the push forward on clearances has been assisted by the army, flagging the issue repeatedly and providing impartial data with evidence.

The western rivers, for us, are mainly the Chenab and the Jhelum, as the Indus has only limited potential, yet it needs to be optimally harnessed. Dynamism manifesting in recent clearances to Sawalkot, Pakal Dul, and Bursar on the Chenab should lead to a mission mode approach. The 'go-ahead' to fill the Kishanganga storage is another welcome move and is an appropriate message to the Chinese engaged in competitive hydrographic counter action at the Neelum Valley project for Pakistan. It's time we accelerate the Tulbul project on the Jhelum for flood control and navigation, building on the only issue of convergence amongst opinion makers in the valley. There is a need to improve the silt disposal of the existing reservoirs on Chenab, Salal, Baglihar, and Dulhasti, especially Salal, because of a sub-optimal design agreement.

Mercifully, our hydrographers have catered to such an upgrade. Envisaged projects are well within our allocated share, and we should continue to execute our plans, disregarding the delaying tactics by Pakistan. **Despite huge technological challenges, it is time to examine the possibility of inter-basin transfer of some of our balance share (approximately 20,000 cusecs or 0.04 MAF) from the Chenab to Ravi-Beas through tunnels to avert a looming water crisis in the Northern region. India, with 17% of the world population, has only 4% water share and storage of barely 90 days compared to two years in some countries.**

A popular Pakistani folk ditty describes the centrality of water in Pak Punjab, "*Ravi vichon waghan teen naharan, do sukiyan, teh teeji waghe hi nah* (From Ravi flow three canals, two are dry and third one doesn't even flow)". In a water-stressed economy with groundwater receding to alarming levels, we need to build our capability on a war footing to include dams and reservoirs and also maintain the existing ones to harness a legitimate share of water to exercise positive control. While dams are not in sync with new ecological narratives, they have strategic relevance as China is planning a bouquet of three dams on the Indus for Pakistan as part of the CPEC. **In times to come, to keep its canals flowing, Pakistan should be forced to introspect and improve its relations with its upper riparian neighbour.**

Reappraisal of the Indus Water Treaty (IWT)

(Written in May 2021)

Update:

- **The IWT meetings and consultation, which had recommenced in March 2020, got suspended again in 2023. Meetings were held in 2021 and 2022 (22–23 March in New Delhi). The suspension happened after Pakistan insisted on invoking the Permanent Court of Arbitration, Hague, even when the concurrent mechanism of neutral expert was initiated. India termed it as a dilatory tactic by Pakistan and has boycotted it.**
- **India issued a notice to Pakistan on 25 January 2023 that it intends to modify the existing IWT as per Article XII (3). India asserted that Pakistan has refused to resolve the Kishanganga and Ratle projects for the last five years.**
- **UN neutral experts accompanied by Pak delegates visited**

sites on Chenab along with Indian counterparts in last week of Jun 24. This implies that process under neutral experts in underway, while India continues to boycott court of arbitration proceedings.

India and Pakistan resumed periodic consultations on the Indus Water Treaty (IWT) after a gap of nearly eighteen months. The last meeting was held on 30–31 August 2018 in Lahore. This gap was officially ascribed to the COVID pandemic. Notwithstanding this explanation, the hiatus was consequent to the Balakot strikes of February 2019, the abrogation of Article 370, and the recall of High Commissioners by both sides. The 116th meeting of the Permanent Indus Commission anchored by Indus Commissioners of both nations met in New Delhi on 23–24 Mar 2020 and held consultations.

The main item on the agenda was planned by India on the Chenab River and its tributaries. The focus in the last two meetings has been on designs of Pakal Dul (1000 MW) and Lower Kalnai (48 MW). These talks followed the agreement on a ceasefire on the LAC between both sides on 04 March 2020. The obvious question is: Is this part of a larger rapprochement or at least recalibration after relations had touched the very 'nadir'?

The specific issues related to IWT merit detailed analysis. Can there ever be a 'win-win' formulation under this treaty originally slanted in favour of a lower riparian state? Alternatively, driven by looming water scarcity in India, which has the lowest per capita water availability, will it become a more potent instrument, in the quiver of leverages, for the upper riparian nation? It is relevant to draw attention to the thesis submitted by Brigadier (later General) Pervez Musharraf during a course at the Royal College of Defence Studies (RCDS), which surmised that water would indeed be the primary 'casus belli' for the next round of Indo-Pak conflict.

Mature and compliant Indian response to the IWT needs to be contrasted with reports of Chinese plans to construct a 1,100-km channel linking Yarlung Tsangpo (Brahmaputra) with the

Taklamatan Desert. As an upper riparian state, China has set a very poor example in the Mekong River projects, thereby starving downstream delta countries. China is also anchoring mega hydel projects on the Indus, like Daimer-Basha and Kohala on the Jhelum, as part of the China-Pak Economic Corridor (CPEC).

The Chinese quest for clean water in Shaksgam for proposed silicon chip projects has been cited, among other possible reasons, for the recent incursion in Ladakh. There was also hype on the river manipulation project in Galwan. India had already been administered periodic jolts of Chinese high-handedness as upper riparian during the Pare-Chu deluge in the Sutlej in 2000 and, more recently, the Brahmaputra floods, even after express agreement and funding on the sharing of hydrological data. After opacity and denials, China seems to be revealing its intentions for a water war with India.

The Indus Water Treaty (IWT) has survived three and a half wars and an unabated proxy war, logging more than 50 years of uneasy existence. Brokered by the World Bank, supporters of the treaty describe it as "uninterrupted and uninterruptible". Like many relics of the Nehruvian era, steeped in liberalism, it was an era when water wars were not even thought of.

The IWT is a complex bundle of paradoxes. Despite the Kashmir war of 1947–1948 and Pakistan's dalliance with Naga rebels (Phizo escaping to London through East Pakistan in December 1956), the treaty invested in hope, magnanimity, and development to cement relations. **The IWT enabled the construction of the Bhakra, Pong, and Ranjit Sagar dams and the Rajasthan Canal. It triggered the green revolution, helping India overcome 'ship to mouth' and PL-480's existence.** How can we forget the Monday fast in the '60s when the nation had a serious food crisis?

Critics blame the Indian hierarchy for not leveraging upper riparian status and bartering away rights of three western rivers (Indus, Jhelum, and Chenab) in lieu of exclusive rights of three eastern rivers (Ravi, Beas, and Sutlej). In effect, it amounted to 135 MAF — million-acre feet — (80.2%) share to Pakistan, compared with 33 MAF (less than 20%)

for us. India also agreed to contribute 83 crores (in pounds sterling) towards the construction of dams and replacement canals in Pakistan.

Ironically, in Pakistan, surviving on a Punjab-centric, agrarian economy, there were prolonged protests describing the treaty as a complete sell-out. Considering the non-water intensive, horticulture-based economy in Kashmir, coupled with the challenges of tapping western rivers upstream, it was probably logical to tap western rivers through Tarbela and other dams in Pakistan and construct canals to link Marala to Ravi and Balloki barrage to Suleimanki. Counter viewpoint, to some extent, is driven by hindsight, which comes with a 20×20 vision.

Riled by Pakistan's engineered fassadi agenda and consternation due to the lack of dissuasive measures, there have been desperate demands for the abrogation of the treaty and sloganeering like "terror and water should not be allowed to flow together". There is a demand for the revocation of the treaty and choking Pak Punjab of much needed water. **A mini trailer was flashed in 2008 with a filling of the Baglihar reservoir on the Chenab. Though well within the treaty norms, as per Pak media, it resulted in an estimated 30% crop losses. We may discount it as Pak hype, but it is beginning to pinch, and Sawalkote and other dams may really hurt.** The Indian position is justified by floods in Pakistan and a large amount of water running off through the Indus basin to the Arabian Sea, primarily due to poor basin management. In any case, in a highly skewed treaty, we are entitled to optimise our allocations.

The reality check on emotive exhortations throws up a few interesting pointers on the need for calibration and well-considered actions. The following need careful consideration-

- **Firstly, the treaty has no exit clause and the only remedy lies in invoking the most rarely utilised provisions of the law of treaties under the Vienna Convention.**

- **Second, any attempt to renegotiate requires a bipartisan agreement. Pakistan would draw in China and probably even Afghanistan (Taliban controlled) as co-riparian states. The China**

factor is already manifesting in the CPEC Hydel projects in the Indus and Jhelum in GB and POK.

- **Thirdly, it is elementary that stopping water without building reservoirs can only be an unmitigated disaster. Building capacities in the challenging terrain of the Indus basin, especially the western rivers, is both a time and resource-intensive exercise.**
- **Fourthly, hydel dams had literally gone out of fashion after the Tehri Dam and other such disasters.**

The most important and harsh truth is that we have failed to utilise the full potential of the legitimately allocated eastern rivers and allowed annually approximately 5 MAF of precious water to flow downstream to Pakistan due to inter-state bickering. **However, the saving grace is that the central government has stepped in and worked on a much-delayed balancing reservoir at Shahpur Kandi on Ravi, which has gathered pace and is nearly 60% complete.** It is hoped that the project will be functional by 2023.

Update: The project has missed another deadline, and it appears that it may be completed by mid-2024 only.

It is also heartening that satellite projects on smaller rivers like the Basantar (Degh) and Tarnah are being given a much-needed push. Long overdue repairs of the regulator mechanism on Hussainiwala Headworks are nearing completion. Hopefully, more water from the Sutlej will reach legitimate recipients—farmers in Rajasthan—rather than being wasted across. In a welcome departure, the centre has not only given impetus but also assumed ownership through funding.

Our record on western rivers remains uninspiring, primarily due to repeated obstacles created by Pakistan through IWT, coupled with a lack of concerted action by us. The IWT permits India to create storage on the western rivers of 1.25, 1.60, and 0.75 MAF (million-acre feet) for general, power, and flood storages, respectively, amounting to a total permissible storage of 3.6 MAF. It does not stipulate that India delivers assured quantities of water to Pakistan, and instead, it requires India to allow flow to Pakistan the water available in these rivers, excluding the limited use permitted to India by the treaty. There are no quantitative limits to the hydro-power generation, utilising the western rivers, nor any limit to the number of run-of-the-river projects upstream. For general, power, and flood storage, amounting to a total permissible storage of 3.6 MAF, India has built no storage and has yet to utilise its entitlement, even partially. Further, of the 1.34 million acres permitted for irrigation, India is using only 0.792 million acres. Out of an assessed potential of 18,653 MW, projects worth only 3,264 MW have been commissioned so far.

The Salal project near Reasi on the Chenab has serious silting-related issues due to Pak obduracy in design formulation, and it is likely to manifest in Baglihar also. Faced with a similar challenge, the iron brother of Pakistan, China, has carried out blasts in the Sanmenxia Dam to flush out silt. Notwithstanding Pak's obscurantist behaviour, our hydrographic designers have incorporated de-silting plugs in even vintage dams like Salal, which will hopefully be activated in the future to drain the silt.

The IWT, in its conception, while outlining differing perspectives, mandated the need for sound, economical, and efficient designs, even in an era when issues like climate change, de-silting, livelihood, and non-consumptive usage were not critical. These issues of navigation and livelihood have been highlighted in the stalled Wullar barrage (Tulbul navigation project) for minimum draught in the Jhelum. Notwithstanding Pakistan's delaying tactics and leveraging dispute resolution mechanisms—arbitration and even ICJ, it has only managed some minor tweaking on run-of-river projects like Kishanganga. In almost all cases, the Indian stand has been upheld; however, it has caused considerable time and attendant cost escalation penalties. **We need to push ahead with Pakal Dul, Lower Kalnai, Sawalkot, Ratle, and Bursar, as even with these projects, total utilisation,**

out of a potential 18,600 MW of power, will only be enhanced to approximately 62%. Concurrently, India has utilised a very small portion of the agreed storage of 3.6 MAF.

India, with 17% of the global population, has barely 4% freshwater reserves. Even by optimistic projections, we have only 90 days of reserves compared to many countries boasting of two years' worth of pounded reserves. Reports of Chinese plans to construct a 1,100-km channel linking Yarlung Tsangpo (Brahmaputra) with the Taklamatan Desert should inspire us to take on the Chandrabhaga tunnel project for inter-basin transfer from the Chenab. It will be fair to surmise that the IWT, though suboptimal, can be better harnessed to optimise benefits through sustained focus. In sum, we should discard emotive distractions and focus on building hydrological infrastructure to tap our legitimate share of allocations under the IWT. The central government has taken appropriate initiatives, and they must be followed through.

Shahpur Kandi: Inching Towards Indo-Pak Water Wars

(Written in May 2024)

Media reports built great hype on the completion of the Shahpur Kandi Project (SKP) with the catchy headline of India stopping the flow of waters of the Ravi River to Pakistan. Pak newspaper Dawn had reported that the filling up of the reservoir for the Baglihar Dam (on the Chenab) in 2008 had resulted in 30% crop losses in Pakistan. For Pakistan, the Ravi is the River of Punjab and Lahore. The famous ghazal by Pak singer Sajjad Ali sums it up poignantly, "*Jeh Ravi which Pani koi na, teh apni kahani koi na*", meaning, if there is no water in the Ravi, we have no story to tell. The obvious question is: Are we heading towards Indo-Pak water wars?

SKP Project

Objective assessment indicates that 98% of the work is complete. The filling of the reservoir has commenced, and it will take two to three months to fill up the reservoir for the projected water level for power generation requirements. Recently constructed dams and reservoirs have been the missing parts of the Ranjit Sagar Dam (RSD) at Thein. RSD was commissioned in 2001, after the inter-state agreement in 1979. The scheme was upgraded to a national project in 2008, but work commenced in 2013, only to get stalled in 2014. The centre had to step in 2018 to resolve the festering dispute between Punjab and J&K.

Balancing reservoirs in large dam systems is an essential prerequisite for exercising positive control of water flowing downstream. SKP, 11 km from Thein, is a multipurpose project and includes two hydel projects (55.5 m height) with an installed capacity of 206 MW. It seeks to check the uncontrolled flow of water (approximately 2 MAF) to Pakistan and harness it for irrigation. It is projected to supply 1,150 cusecs of water for irrigating 32,173 hectares in the Kandi belt of Kathua and Samba through the Main Ravi Canal. The earlier tedious method of lifting water into the Tawi Lift Canal will be simplified with gravity feed. **Regulated water supply in canals will bolster the defence potential of the vulnerable Kathua-Samba Corridor.** J&K will also get a 20% share of power. Punjab, besides getting 80% power, will draw water to irrigate an additional 5,000 hectares. Balancing the reservoir will also optimise the water supply to the Upper Bari Doab Canal (UBDC), which was erratic and inefficient, conditioned by power generation considerations.

Ravi River – Water Utilisation

The Indus Water Treaty (IWT) allows India to utilise the waters of three western rivers—Ravi, Beas, and Sutlej. As per some estimates, 95% of the water would get utilised, but some of the water, especially in the rainy season, would still flow to Pakistan. The Ravi basin includes many tributaries like the Ujh, which join after transiting through the Shakargarh bulge in Pakistan. A follow-up project at Makaura Pattan in Gurdaspur is nvisaged to further impound approximately 600 cusecs of water for irrigation and drinking water supply. Punjab had asked for central funding of 412 crore in 2019. Haryana has even pitched for an ambitious link canal like SYL from the proposed dam to Harike to boost the water supply downstream.

The Ravi is a trans-border river, defining 70 km of the Indo-Pak border and is notorious for shifting its course. It is resuscitated in Pakistan by link canals transferring water from the Marala Dam on the Chenab. It also provides a number of enclaves on both sides. These can be utilised as launch pads as they obviate the need to fight tricky river-crossing operations. Defences are supplemented with Ditch cum Bundhs (DCBs). **Hydrological control of Ravi definitely aids operational plans.**

Criticality of Water Management

India has the lowest per-capita freshwater availability, with barely 4% freshwater reserves for 17% of the global population, creating severe water stress. Even by optimistic projections, we have only 90 days of reserves compared to many countries boasting of two years' worth of pounded reserves. Freshwater is becoming a much sought-after resource, as it is required in large quantities for silicon chip fabrication. **Chinese aggressive forays to control the 'Water Table of Asia' in Tibet are ascribed to looming water stress and ambitious plans for chip manufacturing.**

China enjoys upper riparian leverages on our major rivers like Indus, Sutlej, and Brahmaputra. The Dragon has a very dubious record of opacity and refusal to share even mandated data. **It was accused of triggering the Pare Chu deluge in the Sutlej in 2000 and the Brahmaputra floods in 2020.** It is reportedly building the Yarlung

Zangbo Dam on the Tsangpo (Brahmaputra) with plans to build a 1,100-km-long channel to the Taklamakan Desert.

Climate change-induced melting of glaciers is further curtailing the availability of water. Parvez Musharaff, in his RCDS course thesis, had inferred that water would be the next trigger for an Indo-Pak conflict. Both countries face unresolved domestic inter-state water disputes like Cauvery and SYL in India and Kalabagh and Kohala in Pakistan. The abysmal track record of water management in Pakistan is reflected in periodic floods, most notably the debilitating deluge in 2022 and the build-up of salinity in the Indus basin.

Dysfunctional IWT

The IWT mandated an 85% share of the Indus basin to Pakistan, with a near total share of three western rivers—Indus, Jhelum, and Chenab. **Notwithstanding the pronounced tilt towards Pakistan, mercifully, it allows India to build storage for run-of-river projects for power generation and livelihood issues like the Tulbul Navigation project (Wullar Barrage) on the Jhelum, flood control, etc.** India can build storage of 3.6 MAF and has the potential to generate 18,653 MW of power, whereas our current utilisation is barely 0.75 MAF (31%) storage and 3,264 MW (17%) hydro-power. Pak obduracy is resulting in delays in de-silting operations in existing IWT dams, notably Salal (Reasi) on Chenab.

Belated Indian efforts like the Kishanganga Project and the Ratle Dam on the Chenab have been dragged by Pakistan concurrently to the Court of Arbitration and neutral experts. India has refused to be a party to such filibustering and concurrent dispute-resolution mechanisms. Resultantly, the annual meetings of the IWT Commission have become irregular since the Uri (2016) and Pulwama (2019) attacks with demands that the IWT should be scrapped. The last IWT meeting was held in May 2022. In January 2023, India gave notice for modification of the treaty. **The key requirement is**

to convince Pak to allow India to harness its agreed potential on western rivers. India has a number of projects on the Chenab, like Ratle, Pakal Dul, Kiru, and Bursar, in the pipeline. **The even bigger challenge is to convince China to behave as a responsible upper-riparian state.** It is time China treats the water table as a Global or Asian common and shares it equitably.

Proxy War in J&K

(Map source-https://www.mapsofindia.com/mapinnews/encounter-in-sopore/)

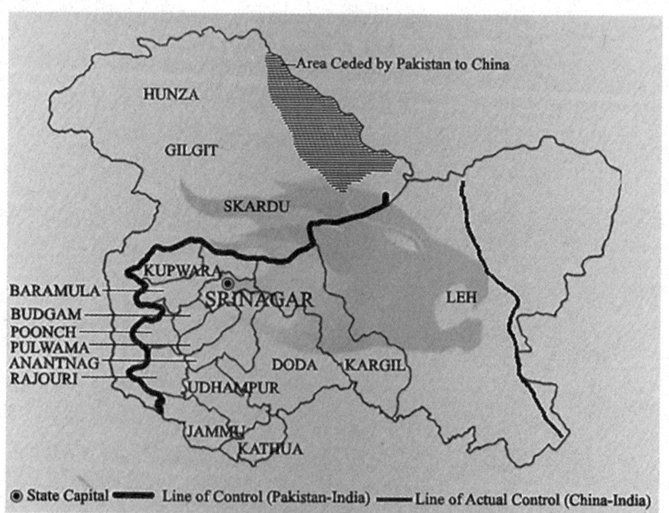

(Map source-https://www.satp.org/satporgtp/publication/faultlines/volume16/article1.htm)

KEY STATISTICAL DATA

Terrorist Attacks

An attempt has been made to tabulate and plot certain compiled data from authentic and reliable sources to aid analysis. These have also been plotted graphically to establish important trends.

Year	Incidents-Killings	Civilians	Security Forces	Terrorists/ Collaborators	Not Specified	Total
2000**	1910	1260	573	2260	28	4121
2001	2802	1508	883	3005	108	5504
2002	2329	1255	721	2454	181	4611
2003	2321	1280	524	2328	216	4348
2004	1679	849	531	1466	134	2980
2005	1750	1105	439	1584	111	3239
2006	1376	966	400	1283	146	2795
2007	1290	932	439	1219	113	2703
2008	1122	915	366	1232	92	2605
2009	1158	685	435	1112	31	2263
2010	864	757	359	747	21	1884
2011	555	393	199	465	02	1059
2012	539	274	132	429	02	837
2013	442	308	177	386	02	873
2014	523	400	167	441	04	1012
2015	437	176	152	398	03	729
2016	492	204	178	525	00	907
2017	443	202	172	437	01	812
2018	478	217	183	540	00	940
2019	332	159	132	330	00	621
2020	299	100	106	385	00	591
2021	314	116	104	365	00	585
2022	281	100	47	266	01	414
2023	277	150	82	228	06	466
2024££	158	86	39	227	00	352
Total	24191	14397	7540	24112	1202	47251

***- From Mar 2000* *££- up to 22 July 2024*

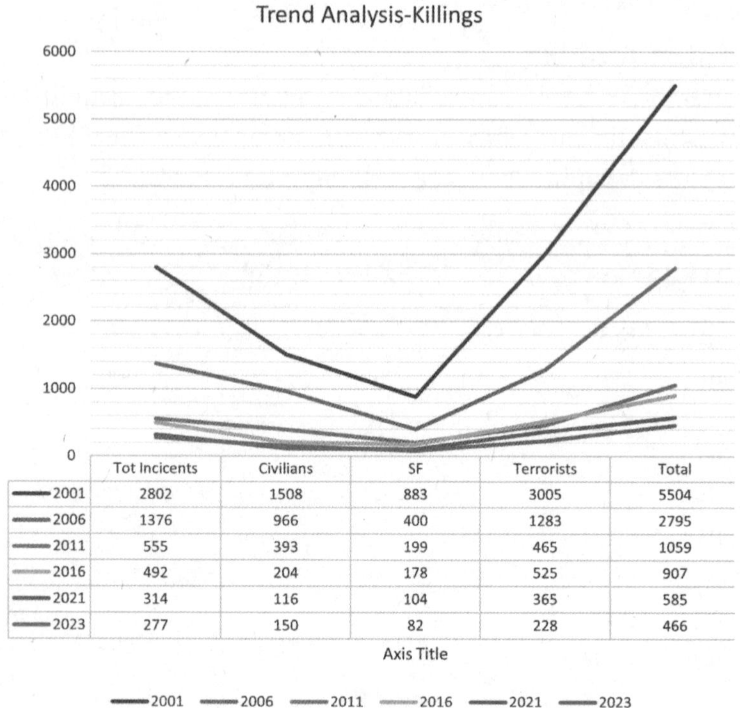

	Tot Incicents	Civilians	SF	Terrorists	Total
2001	2802	1508	883	3005	5504
2006	1376	966	400	1283	2795
2011	555	393	199	465	1059
2016	492	204	178	525	907
2021	314	116	104	365	585
2023	277	150	82	228	466

(Source: Information compiled from open media sources)

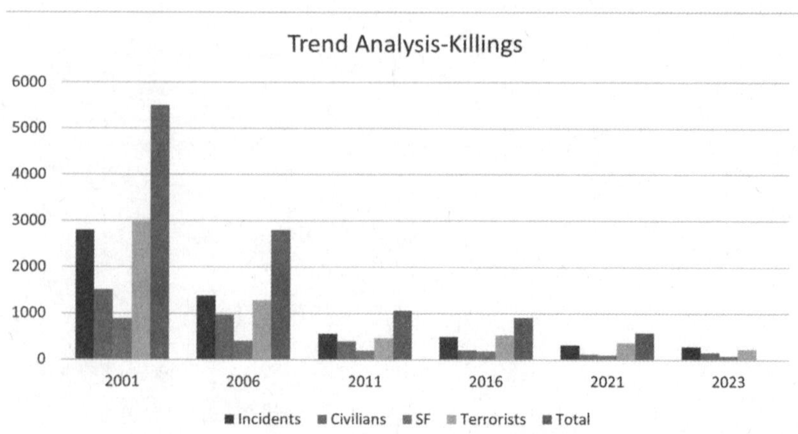

Major Fedayeen Attacks on Armed Forces Establishments in J&K – 2013–16

Date	Location	Establish-ment-Type	Casualties	Terrorist-Casualties
26-09-2013	Samba	Armoured Regiment	01-Offr,02-Jawans, 04-Police, 02-Civilians	03
28-03-2014	Janglot	Artillery Regiment	01-Jawan	03
27-11-2014	Kathar, Arnia	Engaged during transit near DCB	03-Jawans, 04-Civilians	04
05-12-2014	Mohra, Uri	Artillery Unit	01-Officer, 07-Jawans	06
20-03-2015	Rajbagh, Kathua	Police Station	03-Police, 02-Civilians	02
21-03-2015	Samba	Armoured Regiment	Nil	02
27-07-2015	Dinanagar	Police Station	04-Police, 03-Civilians	03
02 to 05-01-2016	Pathankot	Airfield	01-Officer, 06-Jawans, 01-Civilian	04
11-09-2016	Poonch	Brigade HQ	01-Police	03
18-09-2016	Uri	Brigade HQ	17-Jawans	04
06-10-2016	Langte	RR Battalion HQ	Nil	03
29-11-2016	Nagrota	Artillery Unit	02-Officers, 05-Jawans	03

Major Fedayeen/terrorist Attacks – 2016 onwards

Date	Location	Terrorist Group	Casualties Terrorists	Casualties-SF
18-09-2016	Brigade HQ, Uri	JeM	04-neutralised later	19-fatal, 50-injured
27-04-2017	Panzgam Camp, Chowkibal, Kupwara	JeM	03	01-Officer & 02-Jawans-fatal. 07-injured
10-02-2018	Sanjuwan Base (Jammu) Over 24 h gun battle	JeM	03, attack synchronized with Afzal Guru's death anniversary	06-Jawans, 01-Civilian-fatal. 20-injured
11-08-2022	Dhangri Camp (Rajouri)	LeT	02	04-Jawans-fatal,01-injured.
01-01-2023	Dhangri village, Rajouri	LeT	03-neutralised later	07 civilians, including children-03
22-11-2023	Dera Ki Gali-Rajouri- ambush on two vehicles	Let-JeM	Probably neutralised later	05-including two Captains-fatal, 02-injured
21-12-2023	Dhatyar Mor-Surankot—Rajouri ambush on army vehicles	**	@@	04 soldiers killed
05-01-2024	Search operation in Shopian	LeT	01	Nil
12-01-2024	Firing on convoy-Poonch	**	Nil	Nil
18-01-2024	Land mine-LoC-Nowshera	-	Nil	01 killed, 02 injured
05-04-2024	Infiltration bid-Baramulla	**	01 killed	Nil

11-04-2024	Search operation-Pulwama	LeT	01 killed	Nil
04-05-2024	Poonch district-attack on IAF vehicles	**	@@	01 IAF soldier killed, 05 injured
08-05-2024	Encounter-Kulgam	LeT	02 neutralised	Nil
03-06-2024	Cordon and search-Pulwama	LeT	02 killed	Nil
9-06-2024	Reasi district-attack on bus with pilgrims	**	@@	09-civilians killed, 33 injured
11-06-1024	Arnia, Kathua border	**	02 terrorists neutralized	01 CRPF personnel
12-06-2024	Attacks on Gandoh and Chattargala check points/Army Transit Operating Bases	**	@@	07 security personnel injured
06-07-2024	Cordon and search-Kulgam district	**	06 neutralised	02 soldiers killed
08-07-2024	Attack on military convoy, Bani-Machedi-Kathua district	**	@@	05 Army personnel killed, 05-injured
16-07-2024	Attack on search operation in Doda district	**	@@	04 Army personnel killed
19-06-2024	Cordon and search-Watergam-Baramulla		02 killed	02 injured
23-07-2024	LoC post Poonch district	**	@@	01 Army personnel

** Claimed by The Resistance Front (TRF)-affiliate of LeT. Concurrently, Kashmir Tigers, extension of JeM also claimed responsibility. These could also be coordinated and joint attacks. Reports also circulate are reports that a group of 60 SSG trained or SSG personnel have infiltrated for these terrorist attacks.

@@ Terrorists being well trained, unlike fedayeens break contact. Most are accounted for in subsequent combing and search operations.

No Quick-fix Solution to the Kashmir Issue

(Written in December 2017)

As a colonel in the North-East, I had the privilege to accompany a new and dynamic corps commander for his meetings with two very wise governors. The general, in his exuberance, spelt out his plans to eliminate all ultras in one year. Both governors opined that such complex problems cannot be viewed in a tenure-centric time frame. More importantly, they asked him to spare moderate ones (extremist leaders) so that there is someone to engage with, as a permanent solution needs to be locally engineered. As we attempt the new approach in J&K, it is apparent that there can be no quick fix 'jugaad' type of solution. The essence of smart power is an optimum mix of a complex bevy of hard and soft power instruments. Valley experts may turn around and ask, 'After all, we have been doing this in our famed "Iron fist in velvet glove" policy. So, what is new in this jargon?' Well, the short answer is that smart power does not advocate different and new elements but seeks to apply existing elements differently in a dynamic manner with long-term commitment. It is the choice between multi-stage reconstructive surgery and incremental homeopathic doses.

Once again, security forces have brought the overall security situation in J&K under control. But it is also the oft-repeated 'deja vu' moment, for such missed opportunities have been created earlier and squandered for want of follow-up in socio-political domains. We seem to have temporarily strayed from our focus on the 'awaam' (people) as the centre of gravity. Driven by armchair strategists and TV warriors, the buzz was to sort out the terrorist groups and stonepelters. The post-mortem of frequent attacks on camps inevitably triggered a frenzy to first convert camps into impregnable fortresses.

The PM's call on Independence Day for engagement instead of gun and abuse, followed by the appointment of an interlocutor, is indeed reassuring, for we seem to be rediscovering our 'mojo' of a people-centric approach. This has been acknowledged globally. In keeping with the ongoing inclusive dialogue, contact with all segments, including Hurriyat, needs to be taken to a meaningful conclusion. Large-heartedness, particularly towards young first-time offenders, is called for. Instead of dropping charges against stone pelters, temporary suspension of charges coupled with probation for a specified period is recommended.

There is a call to tone down army deployment and bring the police to the fore. While this model succeeded in Punjab, it is unlikely to work at this stage in the valley despite the demonstrated competence of the J&K police. **On balance, it may be better to follow the ancient Japanese wisdom of 'hurrying slowly' and not losing sight of the consequences of premature thinning out from South Kashmir, which resulted in an alarming degradation in the security situation.** In all security matrices, RR should remain the key enabler as it has acquired an enviable domain competence and track record. The only lament is that despite multiple tenures, very few officers acquire cultural and linguistic competence. Most officers and JCOs on the field have a superficial knowledge of Kashmiryat to engage in any meaningful dialogue with opinion makers. The Indus Water Treaty is another element where we have considerable leverages within the existing treaty; however, these have yet to be applied. It is time to get our act together and execute projects in a time-bound manner. The current water crisis in the valley can be utilized to forge consensus and push the Tulbul navigation project.

Soft power has to be applied concurrently on a long-term basis and not in a 'zero-sum' format. The current norm seems to be to mix hard and soft power on a reciprocal formula. As an obligation to citizens, minimum necessary soft power must be dispensed, especially in disturbed and remote areas where civil administration is conspicuous by its absence or makes a transient appearance. Consequently, military and civic action is an inseparable component of the security grid. It is time to refine and experiment with posting young and competent IAS officers as civic affairs coordinators in the sector and Force HQs of RR. Instead of being in sceptic mode, the state should invest in 'Sadbhavana' on an institutional basis.

Soft power, by its nature, is slow acting, yet strong cultures like ours should have confidence in the cooperative effect of our beliefs and not turn off the tap at minor provocations. Hence, medical succour, sports meets, music/cultural/film/media exchanges, track two, and people-to-people contact should continue. Already, the Pak populace compares their model with ours; such exchanges will only lead to greater introspection and strengthening of moderate elements. The recent Saudi initiative by Crown Prince Mohammed bin Salman (MBS) in reforming Islam needs to be supported by a theological collaboration of a moderate strand of Indian ulema, who have considerable influence on both Deobandi and Barelvi schools. It is ironic that Kashmiris, who invoke Article 35 A to safeguard their property, have allowed Salafis and Wahhabis to plunder cultural terrain, making Kashmiryat an endangered species. Is it time to emulate MBS and attempt basic theological correctives? As the country comes out of Permanently in Election Mode (PIEM) after the Gujarat and HP elections, it will be a good idea to engage with political parties to share interim feedback and build consensus around smart national response.

Mediators Need to be Experts Sans Govt Links

(Written in November 2017)

The journey of Indian nationhood has been tumultuous, punctuated by many internal conflicts. The Naga insurgency erupted in the '50s, followed by equally violent movements in the entire North-East. The Naga movement has the dubious distinction of being a perpetually festering problem, which, despite 67 years and three agreements, is still to find closure. The ongoing proxy war in Kashmir is the most severe challenge, keeping the nation literally on edge with frequent skirmishes in the valley and daily TV encounters. Separatist elements in peripheral areas leverage centrifugal forces generated by alienation and ethnic as well as theological fault lines. They draw ready sustenance and support from Pakistan and China. Sporadic incidents of Islamist terrorism and the still simmering left-wing extremism have kept even the hinterland in a state of turmoil. **In this maze of multiple insurgencies, the success rate in terms of conflict resolution remains very poor, and the only notable positives have been Mizoram and Punjab. Putting Laldenga insurgent leader in charge as CM was an imaginative stratagem.**

In Punjab, security forces, especially the Punjab Police, were given a free hand. But regardless of the recent success in Sri Lanka, the hard power-centric model is an extreme option. It is difficult to analyse various conflicts to prescribe a common template for resolution, yet there is a need to have a discussion on an indicative model. Though neither discreet nor well-defined, most conflicts tend to follow stages like initiation, escalation, stabilisation, recession, resolution, and closure. These phases get complicated as they often overlap and stage a comeback, like the painful relapse after sickness.

Well-synergised security agencies, when given operational freedom, invariably stabilise the situation and put it in a recession loop. The timespan varies as per the complexity and severity of the conflict and operational parameters. The frustrating reality is that response to conflict meanders along without a clear-cut road map, especially in the socio-political domain. Often, it is a story of missed opportunities and 'deja vu'. Invariably, after appreciable improvement in the security situation, premature relaxations and lack of political process led to crises like South Kashmir and North Nagaland, reigniting the escalatory cycle.

The only redeeming feature is that after twenty-odd years of ceasefire in Nagaland, people have become addicted to peace, but the drift of two decades has entailed huge opportunity costs. While Nagaland has seen the demise of two leaders (Isak Swu and Khaplang), out of the original trio, with only Muivah holding the torch, yet with every death, new challenges spring up. There is a case for replacing the 'drift and tire out' approach with a dynamic conflict resolution model.

Critical enablers are mediators/interlocutors and the time of initiation of dialogue. It would be ideal for keeping the mediation window open right from the very beginning. The ideal resident interlocutor can be the governor, hence the need for an expert with domain competence, no previous baggage, and a father figure image. When I was a colonel in Nagaland, the army had a very meaningful relationship with Shyamal Datta, who was probably the most dedicated and clued-up governor, yet Naga leaders could never trust him because of his IB pedigree. Unfortunately, all parties are now using gubernatorial appointments as a sinecure or dumping ground for retired politicians, politically aligned bureaucrats, and security officials. It is axiomatic that in trouble-prone states, merit takes precedence over political affiliation.

Starting with the Naga groups, a number of monitoring mechanisms have been set up to supervise agreements with ultras. Initially, with two NSCN factions, these were termed as ceasefire agreements, thereby giving needless legitimacy to the demand for a Naga nationhood. These bodies, if leveraged properly, have the potential to provide additional channels for negotiations. While we have refined their nomenclature, there has been inadequate analysis and feedback to evolve effective mechanisms.

Initially, retired army generals headed such bodies, but of late, the police have usurped this space, and unfortunately, some appointees have very limited domain knowledge based on an odd tenure, sometimes of dated vintage and in much junior capacity. Objectivity demands a mention that not all army incumbents measure up to expectations, hence the need for stringent selection.

Last in the negotiation chain are designated interlocutors; the most important ones are handling Nagaland and Kashmir, who, despite their enviable credentials, have an IB tag. The first two interlocutors in the Naga peace process were IAS officials and were opposites of each other, underlining the lack of set guidelines for such appointments.

The first preferred Bangkok and visited Nagaland only when forced to accompany Swu and Muviah. The second had been the chief secretary and spoke fluent Nagamese. An interesting, though failed experiment was a three-member team in Kashmir during the UPA regime to balance intellectual, bureaucratic, and theological connections. It is difficult to prescribe a model, especially when 'horses for courses' is being replaced by 'jockeys for seasons' depending on the party in power, yet it is an important subject that requires research and refinement and a national consensus.

Kashmir – Need for Full-Spectrum Approach

(Written in April 2018)

Last month has seen very intense exchanges, including artillery duels, across the LoC. It has indeed been one of the bloodiest chapters, with considerable damage to civilian lives and property. While uneasy calm prevails, it appears that we have hit the law of diminishing marginal returns in our much-touted strategy of 'Hot LoC' and raising the costs of proxy war. However, in the hinterland, security forces had unprecedented success, accounting for 13 terrorists at three different locations.

Every summer, 'mischief diviners' of the ISI roll out new strategies with ploys like stone pelting (replication of the intifada) coupled with spreading the arc of terrorism to newer areas like South Kashmir and Jammu-Kathua-Samba. **Though rather early, this year, a new element is manifesting in the stoning of tourists. This misguided tactic amounts to economic harakiri and a reprehensible form of fedayeenism, dealing a twin blow to the tourism-based economy and the culture of Kashmiriyat.**

Just before the onset of summer, our think tanks indulge in intellectual 'manthan' (brainstorming) to anticipate and work out options to combat these challenges. In keeping with our reactive character, a full-spectrum, proactive approach is seldom discussed.

The Panjab University (PU) organised a national-level seminar attended by the director of the Vivekanand International Foundation, the finance minister of Punjab, two army commanders, veterans, and a large number of academicians. This was followed by serious deliberations by a collegium of very senior veterans of tri-city from all three services. I found myself as a 'first termer', an army jargon to describe the juniormost, and was asked to project their collective wisdom appropriately, hence this jotting.

There was a unanimous view that the security situation was getting under control. However, significant improvement can only happen if the problem is addressed at its centre of gravity, which is the 'awaam', the people of Kashmir; hence, it requires a socio-political approach. While there is a clamour to revive our past glories and legendary heroes, we seem to be missing out on eternal wisdom propounded by Kautilya. Chanakya Neeti has specified *saam* (negotiations), *daam* (bribe), *dand* (punishment), and *bhed* (intrigue) as four essentials.

Chanakya also implied that force or dand is applied selectively by designated functionaries like the *dandpal* (adjutant). Kings and statesmen are supposed to be more known for *daan* (largess) and *khasma* (pardon). It appears that everyone has become a victim of a competitive masochistic urge to punish, and our responses, even for serious issues of conflict resolution, are becoming hostage to the TRP factor.

Arthshastra has suggested that, ideally, all instruments should be applied concurrently, and different players should play their varied roles. The optimum solution is like a complex new recipe that requires skill, experience, and a fair degree of intuitive decision-making. We have overestimated the efficacy of our 'stick' as surgical strikes and fire assaults seem to be losing their deterrent value.

It is also relevant that at the other end is an obstinate Punjabi Musalman, who is a mirror image of our Punjabis, even bearing common surnames, with an additional theological underpinning, which only adds shades of fanaticism to his character.

An important spin-off from the recent seminar was the realisation of the imperative to study the contemporary realities of the populace. We need to build our linguistic skills, especially Shahmukhi, without which it is impossible to understand the dynamics of regional and vernacular dialogue across the Radcliffe Line.

There is also a worrying concern with regard to our fortress mentality in protecting our camps and security establishments. While some hardening is desirable, the key lies with the 'awaam', who live around these camps. Fortified by a liberal dose of Vitamin 'N' (Nationalism), the gullible public demands 'zero infiltration', losing sight of the age-old maxim that no defence line can ever stop the determined terrorists of the fedayeen genre.

Incorporation of technology in camp security is most desirable as it reduces the load on already harassed troops, yet it is not a panacea, as gadgets have limitations. A solution based on physical hardening, surveillance, and involvement of police and the public coupled with quick reaction teams is recommended.

Other so-called leverages have only limited efficacy. The withdrawal of the Most Favoured Nation (MFN) status and the designation of Pak as a terrorist state are cosmetic measures that are unlikely to yield any tangible benefits. **The threat of the revocation of the Indus Water Treaty (IWT) really amounts to playing to the gallery, as we must first create reservoirs to store water.** The recent policy initiative of a time-bound approach to push our projects, especially on the Ravi (Shahpur Kandi dam), and repair the leaking Hussainiwala Barrage should be implemented relentlessly. In the interim, it is good to keep Pak engaged through the IWT to get clearances for our plans for live storage on the Chenab (Sawalkote, Pakal Dul, and Bursar dams) and the Tulbul Navigation project on the Jhelum River.

It is high time we applied benign and constructive '*bhed*' (intrigue) combined with '*daam*' (money) to help rightly-inclined grassroots politicians to resuscitate themselves, as there is a dangerous vacuum apportioned by anti-national elements. Cyber warfare and covert intelligence operations require long-term commitment and imaginative orchestration.

In the long run, we have to further refine our surgical strike capability to make it more lethal, precise, and remote. There is also an inescapable requirement to address 'hollowness' to regain a punitive edge in conventional forces to resuscitate the proactive (cold start) strategy. A full spectrum approach with concurrent options is indeed long overdue in J&K.

Jammu & Kashmir Highlights Paradigm Shift in Conflict Resolution

(Written in October 2019)

Key Takeaway:

- Most acceptable conflict resolution models entail a five-step process –Stabilisation, Engagement, Package Proposal, Negotiation, and Accord, also referred to as SEPNA.

The recent hard-line endeavours in Jammu and Kashmir (J&K) have thrown up pertinent questions on a possible paradigm shift in the application of conflict resolution models. Will a security-centric approach be the new normal? The formation of Nagaland in 1963 literally unleashed a 'domino effect', resulting in the splintering of Assam into the seven sisters, including the grant of statehood to Union Territories (UT) like Arunachal and North-East Frontier Agency. The standard prescription to address regionalism was to create states and a plethora of autonomous regional councils – Bodo, Kachari, Kuki, etc. **Historic amendments in Articles 370 and 35-A, coupled with the downgrading of J&K to a UT, amount to jettisoning the earlier trend of pandering to sub-national aspirations.** While each conflict has its own set of unique challenges, precluding templated solutions, there are a few common parameters that need to be flagged. **Conventional conflict**

resolution models have been characterised by steps like stabilising the security environment, engaging with groups, proposing solution packages, negotiations (often prolonged ones) and, finally, accord – summed up into the acronym SEPNA.

The Naga insurgency erupted in the '50s, followed by equally violent movements in almost the entire North-East (NE). The Naga movement has the dubious distinction of being a perpetually festering problem. Notwithstanding many agreements – like the 16-point agreement of 1960, the Shillong accord in 1965, and the recent framework agreement in 2014 – it is still to find closure. While violence in the NE simmered down, the proxy war in Kashmir emerged as the most complex challenge, having kept the nation on edge for three decades with frequent terrorist attacks in the valley, followed by daily court-martial on TV and Twitter. Separatist elements leveraged centrifugal forces generated by alienation and ethnic/theological fault lines, drawing ready sustenance and sanctuary from external forces like Pakistan and China. Special credit must be given to current governments in Bangladesh and Myanmar for denying bases and flushing out ultras.

Simmering left-wing extremism combined with the looming threat of the fedayeen have kept even the hinterland in a state of uneasy calm. In this maze of multiple insurgencies, the success rate in terms of conflict resolution remains poor, and the only notable positives have been Mizoram and Punjab. An imaginative stratagem of installing Laldenga at the helm catalysed the solving of the Mizo problem. Punjab has been the only successful, hard power-enabled solution wherein security forces, especially the Punjab Police, were given a free hand. Despite success against the Liberation Tigers of Tamil Eelam in Sri Lanka, the use of force remains an extreme option. Its recent application in Kashmir is due to prolonged cumulative frustration built up due to Pakistan stymieing all other options like Sadbhavana. Yet, this model is restrained and, unlike the heavy-handed approach prevalent in the American and Pakistan armies, where gunships and heavy weapons are used freely.

Security agencies led by the army, given operational freedom and synergy, invariably stabilise the situation and put insurgency in a recession loop, as evidenced repeatedly in J&K and NE. The frustrating reality is that response strategy lacks a clear-cut road map, especially in the socio-political domain. More often than not, it is a story of missed opportunities and 'deja vu'. Flare-ups in south Kashmir and northern Nagaland are recent examples. The oft-repeated cliché of 'prevention is better than cure' needs to be adopted by creating a separate specialist administrative cadre dealing with national security, which is also endorsed by former governor NN Vohra. It can be a contemporary version of the erstwhile Indian Frontier Administrative Services. More importantly, Central Armed Police Forces have proved unequal to the task, forcing the army to step in; they need to take up this challenge.

The only redeeming feature in Nagaland is that after 20-odd years of standstill, the populace has become addicted to peace, and this acts as a restraining influence on insurgents. Drift is also relished by agencies and forces, as it gives them relevance and unaudited funds. However, the status quo needs to be broken by innovative initiatives. The impasse of two decades has imposed huge opportunity costs, reducing the 'Act East' policy to a mere paper exercise. The National Socialist Council of Nagaland remains obdurate, insisting on a separate constitution and flag. The biggest challenge is to address these aspirations and yet extend a nuanced interpretation of 'one nation, one constitution' to the NE. Financial inclusion, dismantling of the extortion regime, and enabling genuine economic liberation are key challenges. There is definitely a strong case for replacing the 'drift and tiring out' approach with dynamic conflict resolution initiatives. It will be interesting to see if groups in the NE draw any lessons from the new hard-line approach in Kashmir.

Critical enablers are mediators/interlocutors and initiation of dialogue. It would be ideal to keep the mediation window open, allowing moderates to come on board. Nagaland also has a formal monitoring mechanism headed by an army general. The mechanism has the most inappropriate nomenclature of the Cease Fire Monitoring Group, giving additional legitimacy to separatists as cease fire is normally between sovereign nations. Ideally, the nominated mediator should operate from the state concerned. The Naga peace process, in earlier years, was steered by a former bureaucrat who preferred Bangkok, rarely visiting the NE. The transition from non-resident Indian to a resident mediator, RN Ravi, in his new role as governor, is very welcome. J&K witnessed a failed experiment of a group of interlocutors headed by Dileep Padgaonkar, aided by Radha Kumar and MM Ansari. The current interlocutor, Dineshwar Sharma, seems to have yielded ground to the governor and the National Security Advisor. Over-reliance on former intelligence operatives requires review and balancing.

The government, in all likelihood, has an action plan, which is yet to be shared as ambiguity seems to be the current flavour. The transparency and involvement of domain experts will not only result in value additions but will also inject a certain amount of peer review and accountability.

Change in Terror Template

(Written in May 2020)

Key Takeaway:

- Pakistan seeks to take the war into the 'non-kinetic' domain.

As summer sets in the Kashmir valley, Pakistan has revived its proxy war, upping the ante. The current summer, the first after the altered constitutional status of J&K, is likely to be a defining one. There is discernible desperation on the part of the ISI to alter the 'terror scape' in terms of the organisation of tanzeems (terror groups). Concurrently, agencies across seek to tweak the template of waging the Kashmiri struggle. The picture is further bloodied by a chain of incidents in the Af-Pak region, with Indian connect and obvious serious ramifications for us. At this evolving stage, we can only forecast emerging likely scenarios that need rigorous monitoring to shape our response strategies.

The broad contours of underlying macro trends can be gauged from the Pakistan Army's recent publication, Green Book 2020, although such manuals are often also used as part propaganda, serving as a smokescreen. Unmitigated hostility to India and Kashmir centricity is evident. There is the realisation of strategic milestones of Balakot and revocation of Article 370 and Section 35-A, coupled with India's hardened stance. General Bajwa, in his foreword, emphasises that 'These will have a lasting imprint on the geopolitics of the region'. It chases the dream of getting India bogged down in the Kashmir quagmire. As postulated by Farzana Shah, Pakistan seeks to take the war into a 'non-kinetic domain' — characterised by information, cyber, and psychological operations. The book recommends that the struggle should incorporate all these influences and be given indigenous character, exploiting 'misinformation'.

The first indication of the reordering of structures was provided by Castellium AI, a US-based regulatory company. The internationally monitored terrorist list was halved, from 7,600 to 3,800, without any explanation by Pakistan, in April. Surprisingly, downsizing is yet to be flagged by the FATF. The listing excludes Zakiur Rehman (Lakhvi), the mastermind of the 2008 Mumbai attack. Pakistan could utilise the pandemic or other ISI ploys to account for some of them before the mandated FATF review in June, postponed to September.

The ill-advised US hurry to abandon the elected government under Ashraf Ghani and hand over Afghanistan to the Taliban has opened a few other possibilities for the ISI. The most worrying is the sudden emergence of the Islamic State-Khorasan (IS-K), manifested through the dastardly attack on the historic Guru Har Rai Gurdwara in Kabul on March 25. It was orchestrated by the newly anointed Amir, Aslam Farooqi Akhundzada, a Pakistan national and a recycled LeT operative. The terror squad purportedly included Abu Khalid al-Hindi, originally Muhammad Muhsin (28), a resident of Kasaragod in

Kerala. If verified, this would make him the second Indian IS suicide bomber after Abu Yusuf al-Hindi or Shafi Armar, eliminated in 2015.

Doubts have arisen because the media had reported that Muhsin was killed in a drone strike in 2019. It could be mischievous attempts to portray the Indian connection as part of the misinformation campaign. The interrogation of the mastermind, Farooqi, was followed by the nabbing of the elusive Kashmiri recruiter, Aijaz Aihangar, presumed to be dead for two decades. The reported concentration of 50-odd Indian-origin IS operatives in the Nangarhar province and the hyperactivity of its surrogate, Islamic State Hind Province, on social media is indicative of a plan to proliferate the extremist contagion of Wilayat (IS province) to include India, harking back to Gazwa-e-Hind.

The diabolical attack in Kabul, killing 25 members of Nanak Naam Lewa sangat, has thrown up disturbing questions regarding the status of the K-2 project, linking Kashmir with Khalistan, through the Pak Army-orchestrated Kartarpur Sahib project. The lukewarm response of the pilgrims and the Covid crisis has acted as a dampener. The SFJ-2020 referendum has failed to find traction. Another development has been the damage to all five domes of the gurdwara due to severe storms. It reinforces the perception of tearing hurry, lack of planning, and non-adherence to Rehat Maryada by the FWO when fixing flimsy fibre-glass contraptions.

The ISI controls most events in Kabul and attempts to explain the attack as a rogue action that defies logic. Many unexplained possibilities of developing IS-K as a counterweight to the Taliban, and even the addition of Khorasan in K-2, making it K-3, need monitoring. Attempts to revive militancy and smuggling of drugs and weapons using innovative delivery means are likely to continue, notwithstanding the recent nabbing of KLF associate Billa Mandiala with a cache of weapons.

LeT has been renamed The Resistance Front (TRF) to meet the twin objectives of escaping FATF scrutiny and delinking from fassadi roots. The use of 'fassadi' (strife creator) instead of jihadi is well-considered, as Pakistan has termed its counterterrorist operation as Radd-ul-Fasaad.

The incorporation of the term 'resistance' in the TRF is designed to evoke sympathy and repackage as it localised struggle. The inspiration is probably derived from Palestine, on the lines of stone pelting and 'intifada'. Earlier, the JeM had renamed itself Majlis Wurasa-e-Shuhuda Jammu wa Kashmir (gathering of descendants of martyrs of J&K) for similar reasons. **Later, JeM created the new formulation of the People's Anti-Fascist Front (PAFF).**

A distinct spurt in attacks in North Kashmir, under the banner of the TRF, can be understood as a new tactic to revive insurgency in an otherwise stabilised region. It may indicate plans to activate other dormant areas like Doda and Kathua. The morale of the security forces has been boosted by the elimination of Riyaz Naikoo, commander of the Hizbul Mujahideen. As terror activities in the valley gather pace, **it will be imperative to remain agile to shifting paradigms of the proxy war. It calls for a better use of technology, information operations, and relentless targeting of key commanders. Concurrently, the socio-political push for conflict resolution is axiomatic.**

Choose 'Smart' over 'Smart Alec' for Conflict Resolution Strategies

(Written in January 2022)

Key Takeaways:

- Nagaland remains the Gordian Knot, defying solution; at present, insurgents are enjoying de facto powers with rampant extortion.

India is gearing up for the Amrit Mahotsava, but notwithstanding celebratory fervour, many conflicts within remain unresolved. The dominant mood being self-laudatory, honest introspection is hardly the flavour of the season. Even the United States of America, despite 245 years of independence, faces a new set of challenges. So, it would be appropriate for India to take an objective reality check and formulate requisite conflict resolution templates.

Conflict resolution is conceptualised as a combination of methods, structures, and processes involved in the peaceful ending of a conflict. The common strategies recommended are: firstly, in the hard power domain, avoidance (back burner approach) and quelling; secondly, in the soft power realm, yielding, conciliation, cooperation, and competitive coexistence. My recommendation is for a smart power strategy, entailing focused minimal application of hard power combined with soft power. The foremost requirement is to craft a 'win-win' strategy based on building long-term trust. Unfortunately, most often, parties to the conflict, notably insurgent groups and governments (through interlocutors), try the 'smart alec' approach, derailing the entire process.

India, despite 'Bharatvarsha' and 'Akhand-Bharat' projections, suffered constraints caused by prolonged colonial 'divide and rule' regimes. It will be appropriate to reiterate the remarks of National Security Advisor Ajit Doval, "India has always lost due to treachery and enemies within." The sheer range of diversities and lack of linguistic glue generate fissiparous and centrifugal tendencies. According to accepted classification norms, India can, at best, be designated as a 'nation-state' or 'cultural state"

Hence, the first challenge after independence was to integrate 520-odd princely states. Despite considerable obduracy on the part of many dominions, all four elements of *saam* (negotiations), *daam* (inducements), *dand* (punching), and *bhed* (intrigue) were utilised by relatively inexperienced rulers. While it has become fashionable to indulge in ruler bashing, aided by hindsight, the Plebiscite in Junagadh, Operation Polo (Hyderabad-1948), and the merger of Puducherry and Goa operations (1960) are shining examples of conflict resolution. It is also important to remember that efforts to project only Sardar Patel need to be rationalised with the fact that Patel passed away in December 1950, within 40 months of independence.

Despite the resistance from the government, linguistic states had to be accepted, which nurtured seeds of conflicts. The decades of the '60s and '70s were dominated by external conflicts of 1962, '65, and '71. These conflicts and skilful leveraging by Shastri and Indira Gandhi with slogans like 'Jai Jawan Jai Kisan' transformed them into people's wars. They played a significant cementing role in our troubled journey of forging nationhood.

Two festering fault lines, Left Wing Extremism (LWE) and Naga insurgency, owe their origin to this period. LWE started in 1967 in Naxalbari and, despite being quelled by the army, kept simmering to manifest again in the '90s. Proxy war, often understood to be synonymous with Kashmir and Khalistan, in fact, was initiated with China and East Pakistan, providing sanctuary to Naga rebels in the late '50s.

Notable silver linings are the resolution of the Mizo and Punjab insurgencies. The former was a classic application of the smart power of co-option by putting Laldenga in charge. The same has been tried in less critical situations, like the Gorkhaland and All Assam Students' Union movements, where Subash Ghising and Prafulla Mahanta were mainstreamed. Ironically, all such leaders, when placed at the helm, have failed to fulfil aspirations, getting consigned to oblivion. Nagaland remains the Gordian Knot, defying solution despite the passing away of two (Khaplang and Isak Swu) out of three musketeers, as Muivah continues to hold out. De jure mainstreaming of the National Socialist Council of Nagaland (Isak-Muivah) remains key. Currently, insurgents are enjoying de facto powers with rampant extortion.

Punjab is the only example of a hard power solution, albeit combined with the support of society. It is also unique because, unlike other problems, state police were empowered, and the army remained in the background. It is a pity that despite the massive expansion of the Central Armed Police Forces and the state police, including specialised battalions and intelligence agencies, we remain hesitant to empower khaki, heavily relying on the Armed Forces.

The unfortunate reality is that everyone loves simmering insurgency. It ensures the flow of funds (many non-audited), rewards, and allowances for forces and agencies. Even insurgents are happy with extortion. Resolution can be expedited if normalcy is incentivised.

It would be appropriate that across the state, the application of the Disturbed Area Act (DAA) is stopped. In each designated disturbed district, the state government should yield control on the posting of deputy commissioner, senior superintendent of police, and other functionaries to the joint consultative mechanism and special audit of funds by the centre. The army should review its statistical (kills-based) citation award process in favour of normalcy parameters.

The role of society has been critical in Punjab, Mizoram, and, to a certain extent, even in Nagaland, where no rebel group can take up arms readily, as the populace has literally got addicted to the cease fire regime since 1997. It will be prudent to avoid the replication of divisive strategies for narrow and immediate political gains. Trust and normative power of societies like Punjabis should be consolidated and harnessed.

The creation of states with the splitting of Assam and even an unmanageable number of autonomous councils has, to a limited extent, satisfied the aspirations of tribal satraps. However, the permanent solution lies in economic development and skill building. The North-East, with collective tribal ownership, reserve forests, and pressure on unexploited resources, is witnessing frequent armed clashes. It is imperative that issues of inter-state borders are upfront and a priority, as "good fences make good borders".

The functioning of the Ministry of Development of North-Eastern Region (DoNER) and NE Council need to be reviewed, with bottom-up planning and genuine autonomy. The North-East Frontier Agency was managed by the Ministry of External Affairs till the '60s. We experimented with the internal security division in the Ministry of Home Affairs (MHA) in the '80s. Is there a need to reorganise the MHA to facilitate conflict resolution? We should also consider designating the right kind of interlocutors, as over-reliance on intelligence background is not working.

Protection of Bases

Of Army Camps, Fortresses, Scapegoats, and Accountability

(Written in July 2019)

Ancient scriptures articulated realistic wisdom, Veer Bhogya Vasundhara, implying that brave soldiers will enjoy the privileges of the universe. Chanakya, the wise sage, counselled rulers to look after their armies in billeting, emoluments, and privileges. Britishers, abiding by this logic, created quaint but very habitable cantonments like Mhow and Deolali with microclimates of their own, facilitating training and recuperation. The issue of military camps and their security has become relevant due to a reported move by the Defence Ministry to compulsorily retire some camp commanders to fix exemplary responsibility consequent to terrorist attacks.

After independence, a new set of 'paper tigers' emerged from files and decided to abandon seminal wisdom, pushing forces to peripheral areas. Consequently, the three largest post-independence military stations, Bathinda, Hisar, and Binnaguri, defy all planning parameters. They have extreme climate and debilitating humidity, and the largest one figures in the old Punjabi expression, 'via Bathinda'. The land allocated to the army had to be reclaimed to make it even buildable. Unfortunately, after cantonments have been developed as islands of excellence, the desire now is to grab them and push the army to the wilderness.

Most camps came up in the pre-insurgency era when security was an elementary and routine function. Our military stations have rudimentary protection in terms of cattle fencing, without even boundary walls. Apart from this, they lack a perimeter patrolling track for surveillance and quick reaction. The scenario is grave in stations located in insurgency-affected areas. Army camps are in penny packets, posing challenges in providing separate stand-alone security grids for each pocket. In Jammu, the army is in eight pockets with highways passing through them. The ill-advised settlement of Rohingyas in the proximity of Sanjuwan was flagged but dismissed. Unfortunately, it served as a probable launch pad for a terrorist raid two years later.

Air Force stations are comparatively better off with basic boundary walls and Defence Security Corps (DSC) pickets to protect them. The main problem is encroachments, violating the statutory "no construction" buffer zone with high-rise constructions overlooking these vital stations. Influential parties with the right connections have stymied efforts to remove such encroachments.

A few important **parameters for camp security** are:

- First, **no camp can be impregnable, as history bears testimony to the repeated breaching of even the most formidable Berlin Wall.** According to official records, more than 1,00,000 people attempted to breach the legendary wall; 5,000 succeeded, and nearly 150 lost their lives.

- Second, **security requires a multi-spectrum response with a combination of technical surveillance and human elements, the latter including designated security and access control elements as well as the proactive involvement of all inmates.**

- Third, **surveillance requires networking with the civilian populace, police, and intelligence agencies. The biggest deterrence is a quick reaction and assured neutralization, which has an exponential effect.** It is best to have layered security and, ideally, neutralize nefarious elements even before they reach their target.

- Finally, **guard against fortress mentality,** which ties down troops in tiring repetitive activity, thereby deflecting them from core functions of the domination of environment and training. Such diversion furthers terrorists' design.

The crux of camp security is an inclusive, people-centric approach, which, at the macro level, translates into the involvement of all agencies and people. The socio-political elements must address the Kashmir problem at its core. In all hybrid war scenarios, the centre of gravity or focus must be on the people, but we seem to be getting caught in the quagmire of fortress mentality, shifting from a proactive to a defensive approach. Border guarding needs major revamping but requires complementing with multi-tiered deployment and participation of all agencies.

As army commander, I had to take up special drives to put together the basic semblance of perimeter security. We had depots and installations swamped by jungles. **These exercises were called Paridhi Suraksha (perimeter security) and Swacch Paridhi (clean perimeter). It simply implies keeping the perimeter clean, developing a patrolling track, dominating the periphery with training, and maintaining quick response teams.** The onerous responsibility of camp security has to be handled in 'mission mode' with all hands on board yet not allowing it to overtake core functions. Theoretical studies with ambitious budgetary projections and skewed over-reliance on gizmos must be supplemented with short-term jugaad solutions in the current environment of budgetary choke. At best, technical solutions can only be provided in an incremental manner, and these have gestation delays. **Smart fences are effective but certainly not a panacea. They suffer degradation due to weather and require manning by trained personnel.** The need is to motivate Jagruk Hindustanis (citizen warriors) like the carpenter who detected the presence of terrorists much before Samba and vectored army reaction, disregarding personal safety.

Armed forces, unlike most other agencies, have very rigorous norms of accountability, where justice is quick and punishment severe. In the army, the mere court of enquiry is enough to jeopardize well-honed careers and destroy reputations. Ironically, punishment is invariably diluted or set aside by Armed Forces Tribunals and courts, who give the benefit of the doubt to the accused. **Those at the helm must fix incorrigible ones, but more importantly, they must**

nurture a climate to build leaders and guard against the 'zero-error syndrome'. Responsibility in these cases is diffused and shared with elements outside the army with differential levels of accountability. Enough and more has already been meted out to camp commanders in terms of entry in their profiles, which is likely to impact career progression. Those advocating scapegoating may like to read the story of Colonel Megh Singh, creator of 'Meghdoot Force', the forerunner of Special Forces. Despite his court-martial, General Harbaksh gave him responsibility and later promotion on the execution of successful raids. It is hoped that wiser counsel will prevail, and the issue will be left to the discretion of the services.

Not Just Fences and Walls

(Written in December 2016)

Alongside technical measures to secure defence bases, a quick-reaction and a people-centric approach (involving people) is vital. There is growing concern about increasingly frequent attacks on our defence bases, especially the breaching of perimeters. While the concern is genuine, it should be tempered with a better understanding of the challenges faced by base commanders. Most breaches entail some failures at a tactical level, but all slip-ups are subjected to rigorous post-mortems, defaulters taken to task, and appropriate lessons learnt. Yet, defences are never perfect as attackers keep innovating; hence, simply guarding bases is a repetitive activity which leads to complacency.

Our defence camps are from a pre-insurgency era. Their location is a function of land availability. Otherwise, why should an armoured division get sited in Hisar, where the first challenge is extreme weather? Many of our defence installations are hemmed in within civilian areas; some have highways passing through them. In outlying areas, some installations have become real estate destinations despite initially being in barren or water-logged areas. As a result, there have been rampant encroachments, making a mockery of mandatory safety distances.

Besides free access, our bases have structures in their vicinity that provide a platform for reconnaissance, infiltration, and even stand-off attacks. With every incident, there is renewed focus on these, but little is done to remove them. Momentary concern subsides, and new encroachments spring up.

Recently, there has been talk of a study considered a panacea or a "silver bullet" to counter attacks on our bases. The study maps major problem areas in security infrastructure, manning patterns and response mechanisms. **However, recommendations for hardening security entail huge expenditures and long gestation periods.** While we can release more funds and simplify procedures, we must decide on prioritisation and optimum security levels as attackers now switch from Uri on the LoC to Nagrota deeper in. No defence line is impregnable; a determined attacker will find chinks and, if aided by fifth columnists, can be vectored into target locations. There is a clamour for technical surveillance, but the human element is relevant.

It is a harsh reality that in most attacks like Mumbai (26/11), Pathankot, Uri, and Nagrota, there was considerable evidence of local help. Yet, we have not been able to book such elements. There is no closure on follow-up investigations. In some cases, technical evidence like GPS has been mishandled, resulting in the obliteration of vital data. The detention of many apparently mentally deranged persons in the vicinity of our bases is another aspect for analysis. However, our current system allows such detainees to be released after perfunctory screening.

While we look at long-term measures, the basics remain relevant. Recent helpful initiatives include "Swacch Paridhi" and maintenance of perimeters, which includes the relocation of trees that provide a Tarzan-like entry. Another exercise is "Paridhi Suraksha", the development of perimeter patrolling tracks and better surveillance with activities like riding. While Pathankot had a security wall, most bases only have a basic fence. Security hardening must go with layered surveillance, warning, and response mechanisms.

Alongside, an example of the human element is shown in the story of a "Jagruk Hindustani", a simple carpenter at Arnia, who, on April 15, alerted the army and took a soldier on his own bike to point out four trained terrorists waiting to move to Samba. The ensuing encounter led to the elimination of all the terrorists. The villager was honoured with a commendation and is a soldier now. Another such incident was near Udhampur, where two civilians overpowered a terrorist, earning a police job and richly deserved gallantry awards. Border areas are nefarious for smuggling narcotics, arms, and even cattle. This is worrying. These areas deserve the best administration and police; currently, very few IAS and IPS officers are posted there. Almost all attacks have seen terrorists travelling, taking lifts in civilian vehicles, and even spending a night near a camp to strike at dawn. **While hardening bases is important, for security, we must encourage a "Jagruk Hindustani" approach as well.**

(Map source-https://mapsofindia.com)

No Installation Can be a Fortress

(Written in February 2018)

The recent terrorist attack on the Sunjuwan Army camp on February 10, in which seven persons were killed, was the second on the same camp, albeit after a gap of 15 years. It brought back painful memories as well as a flood of calls, offers for articles, and TV appearances. My plea has been to let the heat and dust settle to enable a meaningful analysis. During my tenure as Western Army Commander in 2015–16, we faced two attacks on Armed Forces installations (Samba and Pathankot) and two police stations (Kathua and Dinanagar). Each of these had lessons. The most abiding lesson came from Arnia, where a carpenter alerted the army to eliminate four dreaded terrorists in the intermediate tier well before they reached their intended target at Samba.

The Jammu-Samba-Kathua (JSK) belt along the National Highway (referred to as the terror highway) provides ample opportunities for infiltration due to riverine stretches and the proximity of targets with high TRP value. It keeps alive the Pak bogey of an unsettled Working Boundary (WB) stretching from Akhnoor to Kathua (termed by us as International Border or IB), thereby seeking to project the entire J&K as disputed.

However, the attempts at the extension of the arc of terror with attacks on Dinanagar and Pathankot in the settled IB sector were most perplexing. The Pakistani establishment tried to explain the Pathankot attack as a rogue action, and that possibly enabled a visit by a Pakistan investigation team to this air base. A lull of nearly two years seemed to indicate that the plan to extend JSK to Pathankot and Gurdaspur may have been rolled back. Now, an open boast by the Jaish chief portends terror returning to JSK and adjoining areas under tacit ISI patronage. The obvious question is, has Pakistan decided to jettison the previous understanding?

There are numerous small camps in this belt, initially based on the availability of land dating back to the pre-insurgency era. Most camps have been overtaken by civilian habitations and communication arteries, flouting mandatory safety distances even in the case of sensitive air bases like Pathankot. Jammu itself has seven such camps, including Sanjuwan and Kaluchak, previously targeted in the second biggest attack after the recent one on the Uri camp.

In proximity, there have been attempts on Janglot and multiple ones on Samba, a favourite target for the fedayeen, who describe it as Maheshwar camp, referring to the temple in the vicinity. While the army has pragmatically yielded land in Jammu for the expansion of the airport and university, response from civilian agencies has been tardy; hence, the relocation of civilian pockets and consolidation of camps is unlikely.

The harsh reality of security is that no installation can be turned into an impregnable fortress. The formidable defence lines of Maginot and Barlev were breached. As per official records, more than one lakh people attempted to breach the legendary Berlin Wall, with 5,000 succeeding and nearly 150 losing their lives. Security has two essential and interconnected dimensions: infrastructure and people. **Our committees and armchair experts tend to focus only on the security apparatus and recommend converting every camp into a mini fortress with high-tech gadgetry and drones.**

While surveillance and anti-intrusion devices enhance security appreciably, they are not magical silver bullets. The recent release of funds for enhancing security is most welcome, but its application on the ground is bedevilled with numerous obstacles like cumbersome procedures, limited availability of expertise, gestation period, and ever-lurking auditors.

The crux of camp security is a people-centric approach, which, at the macro level, translates into the involvement of all agencies and instruments of the state. As a first step, socio-political elements have to address the Kashmir problem at its core. In all hybrid war scenarios, the centre of gravity or focus has to be on people, but we seem to be getting caught in the quagmire of the fortress mentality, which furthers the aim of proxy warriors, making us defensive and tying down troops.

Border guarding needs to be reinforced further. **It has to be supplemented by multi-tiered deployment and the participation of 'Jagruk Hindustanis' (citizen warriors)** like the carpenter from Arnia. Early indicators, such as taxi driver Ikagar's mushrooming mansion, have to be dealt with, and SPs of the Salwinder variety cannot be allowed to run riots in sensitive border districts.

It is believed that most such attacks have a vectoring element and insider support. How else can intruders enter an air base at its most deserted corner with non-functional lights and overhanging trees enabling an easy entry? **The unfortunate part is that the investigation loop is never completed due to petty and parochial interests and, above all, vested political links combined with the '*chalta hai*' attitude.** To add to our woes is inept forensics and 'jugaad' by the state police in handling GPS and such devices seen after the Dinanagar incident, resulting in the loss of valuable evidence.

While it may sound pedantic, more attention needs to be given to ensure secure parameters with a track for patrolling and quick reaction. Jungles and nullahs around our military camps have a contributory role in intrusions, as seen in Nagrota and now Sanjuwan. The security routine is repetitive and strenuous. We tried programmes like 'Swacch Paridhi' (clean perimeter) and 'Paridhi Suraksha' (perimeter security) to make the activity more imaginative.

Attacks certainly need to be minimised, and response in each case must be efficiently backed up by thorough investigation to identify the insiders and deal with them like Israelis do, closing the loop.

Approach Towards the Protection of Military Installations

Proxy war manifests in various actions designed to spread terror in the form of kidnapping, hostage taking, hijacking, attacking, and ambushing convoys, planting Improvised Explosive Devices (IEDs), etc. The most audacious form, often involving the application of the fedayeen (suicide bombers), is the attack on military installations. These nefarious attacks have been occurring as a global trend, and India has also witnessed a large number of such attacks. The challenge is in preventing them and, on occurrence, minimising their effect, followed by a credible response.

Scope and Terminologies

Strategy Vis-à-vis Approach: The article attempts to discuss an approach rather than a concrete strategy, as each military base or installation has its own peculiarities, and it is difficult to stipulate a universal strategy or even a template like a one-size-fits-all. However, an approach is more flexible, wherein indicative guidelines can be utilised to evolve a specific action plan or Standard Operating Procedure (SOP) customised to the relevant base.

Base and Installation: The term installation or even base is flexible to cater to small, medium, and large bases or installations, which, in different Armed Forces jargon, are described as Vulnerable Area (VA) and Vulnerable Point (VP). The categorisation of VAs and VPs is customised to targeting parameters, especially for aerial attacks. Consequently, they also help to deduce connected requirements for defenders like air defence cover, the size of the protection party, and preliminary or reserved demolition plan in the event of an imminent attack. For the attacker, they help to prioritise targets, explosive load, and other targeting parameters.

Focus: Terrorists choose their target based on an entirely different set of factors, such as possible visibility or Targeted Attack Protection (TAP) or media value of the attack, the chance of success, local support, etc. Repeated attacks in the Samba belt of the Jammu-Pathankot Sector are driven by these visibility factors: the ease of infiltration, proximity to the national highway, and the main communication link to the erstwhile state of Jammu and Kashmir. The focus of this article is tuned to terrorist attacks in the Indian context. However, relevant inferences have been drawn from global and regional scans to devise a recommended approach.

Macro Trends for Protection

Bottom Line Reality: The urge for safety and protection has witnessed the development of fortresses, moats, and barriers in the form of formidable defensive lines and walls. The Great Wall of China, the Berlin Wall, the Maginot Line, and the Barlev Line are relevant examples. As per official records, more than 1,00,000 persons attempted to breach the legendary Berlin Wall; 5,000-odd succeeded, and 150 lost their lives in the process. The famed multi-layered Barlev defences across the Suez, linking the Sinai Peninsula, were a hybrid of multiple layers of physical and technical means. Though described as impregnable, the Arabs breached them in the Yom Kippur War of 1973 using rudimentary and basic techniques. Defensive barriers are increasingly incorporating technical means like surveillance cameras, CCTV, smart fences, and now, surveillance drones integrated into automated warning and alarm systems. On balance, technology aids, but it is neither the silver bullet nor panacea for assured impregnability. The bottom line and seminal reality are that no wall or fence can stop a determined attacker, especially when aided by collaborators.

Evolving Trends: While defensive means have evolved, concurrently, attackers have kept pace in their tactics, even adopting fedayeen tactics. In certain ways, it is a cat-and-mouse game. The very idea of attacking a protected military camp is based on audacity, regardless of near-certain death, but this generates very high visibility. Often, it is timed to commemorate certain notable events in Tanzeem's (terrorist group) calendar, like the death anniversary of a terrorist, wherein the security personnel are aware of a higher probability of attack, yet the attacker chooses a suicidal approach. Desperation or determination has been evidenced in the Germans storming the Belgian fortress of Eben Emael in 1940 with gliders. Drones currently reflect a nuanced progression in the aerial domain in the current context, both for attacks like the Jammu air base intrusion by mini drones and for defensive surveillance.

Dynamic Nature of Threats: Starting with the ancient Greek Trojan Horse perfidy in the city of Troy, the threat has now morphed into cyber bugs, also referred to as malware or Trojans. Closer home and in our context, tunnelling is being resorted to by terrorist groups for infiltration, especially in the Jammu-Kathua-Samba Sector. Hence, there is a constant need to analyse the dynamics and evolving trends both in the threat matrix and in protection measures. Terrorists keep varying their pattern of targeting like heightened attacks in the Jammu-Pathankot belt in 2013–16—three years, Samba (twice), Kathua, Arnia (foiled attempt aimed at Samba), Janglot, Dinanagar, and Pathankot. These have now petered off with the current focus in the last two years (2022–23) in Poonch-Rajouri. It seems like going back to Hill Kaka, Operation Sarp Vinash, and the tumultuous period of 2003. Terrorists also have a choice to shift periodically to attacking convoys and ambush. In this dynamic flux of varying areas of attack and its methodology, security forces tend to slacken down in out-of-focus areas, treating them as routine, often violating the basic SOPs, resulting in setbacks like the recent ones in the Poonch-Rajouri sector.

Mapping of Threats in the Indian Context. Tabulated data is appended:

Year	Incidents-Killings	Civilians	Security Forces	Terrorists/ Collaborators	Not Specified	Total
2000**	1910	1260	573	2260	28	4121
2001	2802	1508	883	3005	108	5504
2002	2329	1255	721	2454	181	4611
2003	2321	1280	524	2328	216	4348
2004	1679	849	531	1466	134	2980
2005	1750	1105	439	1584	111	3239
2006	1376	966	400	1283	146	2795
2007	1290	932	439	1219	113	2703
2008	1122	915	366	1232	92	2605
2009	1158	685	435	1112	31	2263
2010	864	757	359	747	21	1884
2011	555	393	199	465	02	1059
2012	539	274	132	429	02	837
2013	442	308	177	386	02	873
2014	523	400	167	441	04	1012
2015	437	176	152	398	03	729
2016	492	204	178	525	00	907
2017	443	202	172	437	01	812
2018	478	217	183	540	00	940
2019	332	159	132	330	00	621
2020	299	100	106	385	00	591
2021	314	116	104	365	00	585
2022	281	100	47	266	01	414
2023	277	150	82	228	06	466
2024££	158	86	39	227	00	352
Total	24191	14397	7540	24112	1202	47251

***From Mar 2000 ££up to 22 July 2024*

(Source-https://www.satp.org/datasheet-terrorist-attack/fatalities/india)

Recent Terrorist Attacks: The information on the number of recent terrorist attacks was provided in the Lok Sabha by Shripad Naik, the Rajya Raksha Mantri, in a written reply in July 2019, however, it is dated as it is more than five years old. It had details of Terrorist Initiated Incidents (TIIs) in the erstwhile state of Jammu and Kashmir and the North-East. These include all kinds of incidents, such as attacks on camps, as well as ambushes and contact incidents. The details tabled in the Parliament are as follows:

Year	J&K	NE	Total
2016	09	06	15
2017	23	10	33
2018	54	11	65
Up to July 2019	13	05	18
Total	99	32	131

Statistical data is further validated by the tabulated analyses of relevant aspects of incidents from 2013 to 2016, including mapping dates, locations, and their type, as well as their own and terrorist casualties. This tabulation is limited to the fedayeen on bases and military camps. The information is sourced from the Policy Brief on Fedayeen Attacks prepared by Colonel Vivek Chadha from the Institute of Defence Studies in December 2016.

The table below analyses fedayeen attacks for three years (2013-2016), including in areas such as J&K. This is the period when most such attacks had taken place.

Date	Location	Establishment-Type	Casualties	Terrorist-Casualties
26-09-2013	Samba	Armoured Regiment	01-0ffr,02-Jawans, 04-Police, 02-Civilians	03
28-03-2014	Janglot	Artillery Regiment	01-Jawan	03
27-11-2014	Kathar, Arnia	Engaged during transit near DCB	03-Jawans, 04-Civilians	04
05-12-2014	Mohra, Uri	Artillery Unit	01-Officer, 07-Jawans	06
20-03-2015	Rajbagh, Kathua	Police Station	03-Police, 02-Civilians	02
21-03-2015	Samba	Armoured Regiment	Nil	02
27-07-2015	Dinanagar	Police Station	04-Police, 03-Civilians	03
02 to 05-01-2016	Pathankot	Airfield	01-Officer, 06-Jawans, 01-Civilian	04
11-09-2016	Poonch	Brigade HQ	01-Police	03
18-09-2016	Uri	Brigade HQ	17-Jawans	04
06-10-2016	Langte	RR Battalion HQ	Nil	03
29-11-2016	Nagrota	Artillery Unit	02-Officers, 05-Jawans	03

Major Fedayeen Attacks on Armed Forces Establishments in J&K

(Source: Information compiled from open media sources.)

The relevant details of the period from 2016 onwards are tabulated further.

Date	Location	Terrorist Group	Casualties Terrorists	Casualties-SF
18-09-2016	Brigade HQ, Uri	JeM	04-neutralised later	19-fatal, 50-injured
27-04-2017	Panzgam Camp, Chowkibal, Kupwara	JeM	03	01-Officer & 02-Jawans-fatal. 07-injured
10-02-2018	Sanjuwan Base (Jammu) Over 24 h gun battle	JeM	03, attack synchronized with Afzal Guru's death anniversary	06-Jawans, 01-Civilian-fatal. 20-injured
11-08-2022	Dhangri Camp (Rajouri)	LeT	02	04-Jawans-fatal,01-injured.
01-01-2023	Dhangri village, Rajouri	LeT	03-neutralised later	07 civilians, including children-03
22-11-2023	Dera Ki Gali-Rajouri-ambush on two vehicles	Let-JeM	Probably neutralised later	05-including two Captains-fatal, 02-injured
21-12-2023	Dhatyar Mor-Surankot—Rajouri ambush on army vehicles	**	@@	04 soldiers killed
05-01-2024	Search operation in Shopian	LeT	01	Nil
12-01-2024	Firing on convoy-Poonch	**	Nil	Nil

18-01-2024	Land mine-LoC-Nowshera	-	Nil	01 killed, 02 injured
05-04-2024	Infiltration bid-Baramulla	**	01 killed	Nil
11-04-2024	Search operation-Pulwama	LeT	01 killed	Nil
04-05-2024	Poonch district-attack on IAF vehicles	**	@@	01 IAF soldier killed, 05 injured
08-05-2024	Encounter-Kulgam	LeT	02 neutralised	Nil
03-06-2024	Cordon and search-Pulwama	LeT	02 killed	Nil
9-06-2024	Reasi district-attack on bus with pilgrims	**	@@	09-civilians killed, 33 injured
11-06-1024	Arnia, Kathua border	**	02 terrorists neutralized	01 CRPF personnel
12-06-2024	Attacks on Gandoh and Chattargala check points/ Army Transit Operating Bases	**	@@	07 security personnel injured
06-07-2024	Cordon and search-Kulgam district	**	06 neutralised	02 soldiers killed

08-07-2024	Attack on military convoy, Bani-Machedi-Kathua district	**	@@	05 Army personnel killed, 05-injured
16-07-2024	Attack on search operation in Doda district	**	@@	04 Army personnel killed
19-06-2024	Cordon and search-Watergam-Baramulla		02 killed	02 injured
23-07-2024	LoC post Poonch district	**	@@	01 Army personnel

*** Claimed by The Resistance Front (TRF)-affiliate of LeT*
Concurrently, Kashmir Tigers, extension of JeM also claimed responsibility. These could also be coordinated and joint attacks. Reports also circulate are reports that a group of 60 SSG trained or SSG personnel have infiltrated for these terrorist attacks.

@@ Terrorists being well trained, unlike fedayeens break contact. Most are accounted for in subsequent combing and search operations.

An analysis of the two tables shows that attacks in the Samba-Pathankot belt, which was the focus in 2013–16, have reduced from 2017 onwards. These attacks don't consider ambushes like Lethpura (Pulwama) on 14 February 2019 on the Central Reserve Police Force (CRPF) convoy, wherein a lone JeM suicide bomber caused 40 fatal casualties. More recently, on 21 April 2023, five soldiers were killed and one injured in an ambush on a Rashtriya Rifles vehicle by JeM near Bhimber Gali (Poonch). Another dastardly improvised explosive attack was on the District Reserve Guard, the auxiliary force of Chattisgarh police, by Left Wing Extremists (LWE) leading to the fatalities of ten jawans and a civilian driver. Fratricide incidents like the recent one in Bathinda military base on 12 April 2023, leading to four fatalities, are not discussed as they are of different categories and require separate correctives and mitigation measures. **Terrorists have shifted their focus to Poonch-Rajouri since mid-2022. Later, form June 2024, they widened the arc to include Reasi-Kathua-Doda area.**

Challenges in Camp Security

Locational Challenges: The British planned the first set of cantonments away from population centres, often in climatically suitable hill stations. Hence, stations like Wellington, Simla, Kasauli, Yol, Panchgani, Mhow, Deolali, etc., came up. Even in cities, cantonment areas were sited at the periphery with a clear demarcation of civilian and military pockets. After independence, the land was allotted, often on political consideration, in places like Bathinda, Hisar, and Binnaguri. The primary threat being conventional wars in the proximity of borders, terrorist threats were not given due importance. Hence, local protection considerations got watered down. This unplanned urbanisation has resulted in the following challenges:

- Civilian pockets, encroachments, and residential areas sprout along the periphery of bases.
- In some cases, encroachments have taken place in buffer or no construction zones of sensitive installations like ammunition dumps, air bases, and HQs.
- Highways and communication arteries have been constructed through military areas, providing easy access and observation.
- Dominating high-rise structures have come up in proximity to vital institutions.

Internal Layout of Bases: Most army bases still have only cattle fences and lack perimeter walls provided for air bases and major depots. Uri and Samba camps had only basic cattle fences when they were first attacked in 2016 and 2013, respectively. After the attacks, some attempts were made to harden fences with Corrugated Galvanised Iron (CGI) sheets and other contraptions. Bases are very green spaces; some are like biodiversity parks. They often have nullahs, rivulets, and micro-forests, which are exploited by terrorists to hide, like in the Pathankot and Sanjuwan attacks. Very few bases have continuous and clear perimeter patrolling tracks. Some have overhanging trees, providing Tarzan-like entry over the wall or fence, as evidenced in the entry at the Pathankot air base in 2016.

Satellite and Isolated Pockets: Constraints of land availability have forced the creation of isolated and satellite pockets. As an example, Jammu has as many as eight pockets; each one requires its own security, surveillance, and response mechanisms, imposing huge financial costs and human deployment penalties. Three outlying pockets—Sanjuwan, Kaluchak, and Ratnuchak—have borne the brunt of terrorist attacks. Many of these, due to unplanned urban mushrooming, are in stand-alone mode with little mutual support from other pockets. In some cases, highways further divide these pockets into sectors like Patiala and Bathinda stations.

Night and Bad Visibility Challenges: Almost all bases and perimeters lack night and low visibility surveillance devices like thermal imaging. Some bases even lack basic flood lighting, and even where provided, they may be unserviceable, as in the case of the Pathankot air base.

Proximity to Borders: Bases and military posts in the proximity of borders provide terrorists with an opportunity to infiltrate, strike, and ex-filtrate without elaborate logistics support. They also provide opportunities for reconnaissance to detect vulnerabilities.

Criminal Ecosystem in Border Belt: Criminals often find shelter and operate in border areas due to difficult terrain and lax law enforcement systems. These areas have shady gangs indulging in human and cattle smuggling, particularly on the Indo-Bangladesh border. Other activities include narco-trafficking, arms smuggling, counterfeit, and illegal mining. An informal media survey in 2016 established that very few all-India cadre officers from the IAS and the IPS are posted in such areas. It will be apt to quote examples of sacked SP Salwinder Singh in Pathankot and Inspector Devinder Singh in the Srinagar Airport in this regard.

Repetitive Routine: Security duties entail long tenures of duty, which are repetitive and mundane, causing fatigue.

Coordination: Base security is handled by multiple agencies, which often work in silos, creating issues of coordination and accountability.

Lack of Skilling: Troops employed on security-related duties like the DSC and Territorial Army are treated as auxiliary forces, which are sub-optimally equipped. They have human resource-related problems with age profile, a lack of initiative, and sub-optimal periodic refresher training. These troops seldom get recognition and lack motivation.

High Cost of Modernisation: Technological surveillance and modernisation of equipment entail very heavy expenditure and dictate prioritisation.

Long Gestation: The construction of perimeter and surveillance systems takes time and entails gestation periods.

Foreign Origin of Equipment: Dependence on foreign-origin equipment, especially Chinese cameras, creates vulnerabilities. There is a need to develop indigenous manufacturing and avoid foreign systems.

Collaborators: It is a considered opinion that most attacks are supported or even vectored by local or in-house collaborators. However, in most cases, these collaborators escape investigation and legal action.

Demographic Pockets: Interested parties have allowed the settlement of vulnerable sections of the population in the proximity of military camps. Rohingya pockets have come up adjoining the Sanjuwan Base and Gujjar settlements in the Samba belt, which are in close proximity to the installations. These have been utilised by attackers for reconnaissance and logistics, including the staging of their attacks. Mazars and such religious shrines have also been misused for access and reconnaissance.

Investigation and Forensic Backup: It has been seen that investigation is often tardy and slow, and the forensic support is inadequate. Evidence, even when available, gets mishandled. For example, the GPS recovered in the Dinanagar attack (on the police post) was mishandled due to tinkering by local jugaad (improvisation) experts in Mohali.

Symbolic Scapegoating Approach: The investigation loop, after most incidents, fails to fix full accountability, identify and book collaborators, and often lapses into symbolic scapegoating with the fixing of one odd person in the chain, like the base commander and two lower officials after the Pathankot incident. In this incident, no seniors of police and CAPFs, or even collaborators, were identified and held accountable.

Lack of Transparency and Peer Review in Follow-up: Most investigation reports are classified, and even non-redacted portions are not put in the open domain. There is total absence of peer review. It is indicative of a fire brigade response and failure to learn long-term lessons for genuine security audits of bases.

Policy Approaches for Protection

Operational: There could be various macro-operational approaches for the protection of bases and installations, like the following:

- **Defensive or Reactive Approach:** This methodology focuses on boosting protection in terms of walls, fences, surveillance devices, and such defensive measures.

- **Offensive or Proactive Approach:** This format seeks to identify the potential source of the threat and nip it at the origin, ideally or before it impacts the protected installation. This approach is practised, to a certain extent, by the USA in its Homeland Security of Continental America. It has been used as a justification for the target of terrorist groups like the Taliban, ISIS, and Somalian groups. The concept has obvious limitations—both the selection of the target and even its efficacy. The Twin Tower attacks on the World Trade Center, New York, of 9/11 is a relevant example in this context. After the Uri attack and the Pulwama ambush, surgical raids and the Balakot Surgical Strikes were executed. While they delivered a strong deterrent message and reduced the frequency of attacks, the series of recent incidents in Rajouri reflect a continued threat and the need for a hybrid or combined approach.
- **Hybrid or Combination Approach:** This is also termed offensive defence and is a balanced combination of strong dissuasive protection and an offensive approach articulated in localisation, neutralisation, and targeted punitive response. The Israelis rely on strong, highly automated surveillance and intelligence systems backed with assured offensive surgical response.

Physical vs Technical: Another set of policy choices is about the physical hardening vis-à-vis reliance on technical aids. It is a decision between a physical wall or a smart fence with electronic surveillance, including a CCTV system. Protection, especially surveillance and technical, entails considerable expenditure, as well as considerable gestation. Hence, a cost-benefit analysis and prioritisation are mandatory due to fiscal constraints. In addition, life cycle maintenance and upgradation are due to obsolescence in technology. In sum, both physical and technical could be utilised to complement each other.

Armed Forces Study and Planned Correctives

Armed Forces Study: After the Pathankot air base incident in 2016, the government ordered a tri-service study headed by the former vice chief of the army staff (VCOAS), Lieutenant General Philip Campose. This panel suggested that perimeter security entails three key ingredients, beginning with quality local intelligence gathering, smart technology for fence management, and ensuring a quick response. The report visualised a sort of buffer or no man's land between the boundary and the inner fence. The idea was that in case there was a breach, the response mechanism should be efficient enough to neutralise the intruders in this buffer strip between the first and second layers of the base perimeter.

Financial Dimension: The study made several highly ambitious recommendations, entailing a huge budgetary expenditure. As per media reports and informed sources, the committee had identified a paucity of funds allocated for base security as one of the main reasons for the army's inability to secure its camps by installing high-tech surveillance gadgets, including electrified fences, night vision devices, radars, and CCTVs for effective access-control, perimeter security-cum-intrusion detection systems, and better intelligence response mechanisms. As per reliable estimates, there are more than 600 big and small and isolated camps in Kashmir, and every camp needs at least ₹1–2 crore to upgrade its security to acceptable levels. The media also reported that the army, navy, and IAF, in 2017, had sought more than ₹2,000 crore to strengthen the perimeter security of their prioritised sensitive bases. There are more than 3,000 such installations, including 600 categorised as sensitive by the three services after the Pathankot air base attack in January 2016.

Response Mechanisms: The same study had recommended revamping the designated protection force, DSC, with revamped 20,000 strong, physically fit soldiers. It also recommended arming them with AK-47s instead of 7.62-mm Self-Loading Rifles (SLRs).

The equipment upgrade recommended faster vehicles, bulletproof jackets, and night vision devices.

Follow-up and Implementation of the Study: The report didn't receive an expeditious response, and it was only after the attacks on the Uri Brigade in September 2016, Panzgam in April 2017, and, more importantly, the Sanjuwan base attack on 10 February 2018, that the MOD belatedly approved ₹1,487 crore budgetary allocation on the same day, probably forced by the increasing media and social media pressure.

VCOAS-delegated Powers. In July 2017, the government briefed the media and also built up a narrative that VCOAS have been delegated with substantial financial powers amounting to ₹40,000 crore. It was claimed in July 2018 that out of these allocations, they were allowed to spend up to ₹800 crore annually towards upgrading the perimeter security of sensitive installations. However, the share allocated towards the upgrade of security must be balanced with several critical modernisation requirements like armaments, munitions, and equipment, already with shortfalls in ten types of armament systems and 45 types of munitions.

Recommended Measures

At the macro level, the policy recommended **is a balanced combination of a proactive offensive-defensive approach.**

- There should be efficient intelligence and surveillance systems to predict threats, enable dissuasive measures, and gear up protective barriers.
- Defensive measures should be in layers, starting with a likely point of infiltration to provide depth and reaction time.
- The base should have a well-organised perimeter and an automated protection system manned by requisite well-trained personnel. There should be a perimeter patrolling track acting as a buffer and providing a second layer within the base.

- **The aim should be to expeditiously detect the intrusion, localise it, and neutralise it by Quick Action Teams (QATs). Ideally, this process should be completed in the buffer zone.**

- It is recommended that surgical strike or response capabilities should be built up to deliver a punitive message across borders or LOC by nuanced targeting of the source of the attack.

It is necessary that at the base level, the organisation has to be balanced with an optimised and synergistic utilisation of technology and human resources. In a resource crunch reality, at least on an interim basis, hygiene factors and human resources will remain relevant. The following could be considered:

- **Have a people-centric approach to make the population in proximate areas partners like the Reliance Mitra program, where all vilaged in vicinity of refinery are incorporated as stake holders.** It will be appropriate to recall the contribution of the carpenter in Arnia in 2015 and residents in Udhampur in 2016 in nabbing terrorists.

- Periodic cyber hygiene exercises like Swachh Paridhi should be undertaken to maintain and reinforce the perimeter.

- The presence and domination of the perimeter should be boosted by regular training activities like physical training, riding, and treks. The Western Command had conducted these as Surakshit Paridhi exercises wherein intrusions and response were simulated and tested. Local dogs that have been duly vaccinated can be trained and utilised to boost the alarm system.

- Released Agniveers can be inducted into the DSC for a more youthful profile.

In the long term, municipal and civic authorities should play their part by carrying out the demolition of unauthorised structures. They should also create bypasses to reduce civilian traffic and install view cutters where relocation is not possible. Civil police and intelligence agencies should play a meaningful role in access denial and access control. The government, on its part, should remain committed to upgradation and modernisation by making dedicated budgetary allocations.

Conclusion

Protection of bases will remain a persistent and formidable challenge, which will require modernisation and eternal vigilance. A resource-crunch economy and introduction of technological innovations balanced against an obdurate and desperate set of infiltrators requires a whole-nation approach. The system has to be based on the prioritisation of bases as per sensitivity and a judicious mix of technology and human resources. The bottom line is that bases must be prepared and ready to take on any threat.

References

1. Data compiled till 7 July 2019
2. PIB, Attack on Armed Forces, Ministry of Defence. 17 July 2019
3. Katoch, Prakash, Securing Perimeter of Military Establishments. *Indian Defence Review* (IDR), Quarterly Journal, 12 February 2018, http://www.indiandefencereview.com/news/securing-perimeter-of-military-establishments/
4. Singh, KJ, Not Just Fences And Walls. *The Indian Express*, 9 December 2016, https://indianexpress.com/article/opinion/columns/terrorist-attack-uri-mumbaiattack-indian-army-pakistan-pathankot-nagrota-4417668/
5. Singh, K J, Of Army Camps, Fortresses, Scapegoats and Accountability. *Times of India*, 21 July 2019, https://timesofindia.indiatimes.com/blogs/generalsjottings/124201/

6. Samanta, Pranab Dhal, Lessons from Sunjuwan: Get a Smart, Effective Perimeter Security System at Military Bases. *The Print*, 14 February 2018, https://theprint.in/opinion/state-of-play/lessons-from-sunjuwan-get-a-smart-effectiveperimetersecurity-system-at-military-bases/35497/

7. Sen, Sudhi Ranjan, Pathankot Attack: Commander Faces Show-Cause Notice. *Hindustan Times*, 30 January 2019, https://www.hindustantimes.com/ india-news/pathankot-attack-commander-faces-show-cause-notice/storyvmOBCA1QRy3gP44nHEaAoN.html/

8. Staff, Onmanorama, From Pathankot to Pulwama: Here's a List of the Deadliest Attacks on Indian Military Camps. *Onmanorama*, https://www.onmanorama.com/news/india/2023/04/12/major-military-camp-army-baseattacks-pathankot-pulwama.html/ - Accessed 11 May 2023.

9. Chadha, Vivek, Countering Fidayeen Attacks. Manohar Parrikar Institute for Defence Studies and Analyses, 15 December 2016, https://www.idsa.in/policybrief/countering-fidayeen-attacks_vchadha_151216/

Northeast: Challenges and the Way Forward

Eyes on Manipur: Disturbing Trends and the Way Forward

(Written in May 2023)

The improving situation in the North-East (NE), characterised by a reduction in violence, has been a welcome trend. It had gotten an impetus with the BJP becoming part of ruling coalitions in most states, providing a "double engine" effect in the region.

The role of central agencies has always been catalytic and even overriding in the NE. This gave a much-needed push to policy, which otherwise has gone through only semantic upgrades, like "Look East", "Think East", and "Act East".

It has manifested in enhanced reach to border areas through tunnels, mega bridges, and expansion of road, rail, and air connectivity. Unfortunately, ethnic violence in Manipur and violence leashed in its wake has delivered a reality check, mandating measures to cap the mistrust.

Comprehending North-East

It is axiomatic to reiterate a few critical paradigms of understanding the NE.

- The founding principle is based on an established law of physics of **centrifugal forces. It implies that fissiparous tendencies are natural in peripheral spaces.** These fuel the desire for autonomy and, if not handled well, separatist/secessionist yearnings, as seen in multiple insurgencies like Naga, Mizo, ULFA, etc. The list of all such movements, many unresolved, is indeed long.

- The second principle is that **ethnicity and identity are defining markers.** Identity fixation, manifested in Nagaland separating from Assam on December 1, 1963, unleashed a domino effect, with the region splintering into seven states by 1987, giving it the "one brother, seven sisters" character. These states are complemented by 27 autonomous councils under the Sixth Schedule for Bodos, Dimasas, Karbis, and others. Unfortunately, our approach is largely superficial, wherein we brand them as tribes, often condescendingly.

- Three, **traditional land-holding norms and nomadic lifestyle, compounded by colonial laws like inner-line and forest areas, complicate the fixation of boundaries** of councils and states. Consequently, violent inter-tribe and even inter-state clashes occur.

- Four, **across the Brahmaputra, life moves "lahe-lahe" (easy and slow)**. Impatience needs to be curbed by shifting to a lower gear and understanding better. Having served in the NE, I have imbibed the Zen principle, "even when hurrying, do it slowly".

- Five, as a logical corollary to the first four principles, the **desire for integration and mainstreaming needs to be moderated and customised to local aspirations.**

- Six, a **parallel economy in the region is driven by extortion.** Even government employees/contractors contribute to forced levies, euphemistically described as taxation.

- **Most importantly, there is a seminal principle that insurgency is over only when it is comprehensively resolved.** The Naga movement, the mother of all insurgencies, started in the '50s and continues to fester despite a cease-fire (an inappropriate term) and talks for 23 years. We have numerous suspensions of operations (SOO), a more appropriate term, and ongoing talks with affected groups. The only comprehensive resolution has been Mizoram with the Laldenga model, by putting the rebel leader in the chair.

- **Finally, in the long term, it is worthwhile to build mutual dependencies to make the NE populace realise that India needs them as much as they need India.**

External Drivers

The environment across the Siliguri Corridor is shaped by our neighbours. Unlike the western border with just one inimical Pakistan, **the NE region has one declared adversary, China, a benign Bhutan, and the other three nations in shifting ambivalent orientation.** The common understanding that a proxy war was initiated in the '80s with the Khalistan and Kashmir movements needs to be corrected.

The real watershed was Phizo escaping to erstwhile East Pakistan and Mowu-Angami to China in the '50s. Bangladesh, under Ziaur Rahman, Ershad, and Begum Khaleda Zia, and right till the recent clampdown by Sheikh Hasina, remained a hunting ground for the ISI. It is to the credit of the present regime that Anup Chetia was handed over, and others were driven out. Myanmar has often facilitated transit and temporary camps. Demographic movement and open borders add complexity to the environment. While we mostly discuss the 'Miya' factor, the influx of Bhupalese, Chakmas, and, more recently, Chins has also created problems.

Complexities of Manipur

In a diversified identity mosaic, Manipur is an apt example of hyper-ethnicity, characterised by a skewed demographic distribution and rebel groups from all ethnicities. The state has approximately 53% of the Meitei (Vaishnavite and Sanamahi) population concentrated in the valley, accounting for barely 10% of the area open to all. Sanamahi (8%) is the traditional religion of nature worship and animistic traditions. Sharing space with the Meiteis are Pangals (Muslims), who constitute 8% of the population.

Christians (Nagas and Kukis) account for 39%. Nagas are 23% and reside in the upper hills. Kukis, Chins, and Zomis, residing in the lower hills, make up 16%. The Sixth Schedule protection in the hills bars settlements from outsiders. Kukis reside in southern Manipur but exercise a choke hold on communications to Imphal through Sadar Hills. Apart from the majority of Meitei CMs, Manipur also boasts of having two Naga and one Pangal CM. These CMs, despite tensions, managed complexities with odd aberrations like the Naga-Kuki clashes in 1998.

During peak insurgency, Meitei groups insisted on Meitei-Mayek (script) and traditional dress (the wrap-around Phanek), and Hindi films were banned.

The new disturbances came when SOO, with Kuki groups, was rescinded, and there was an anti-drug and anti-encroachment drive, with Kukis being at the receiving end.

The situation has been exacerbated due to the influx of the Chins from Myanmar into Mizoram and Manipur. The trigger was a high court verdict directing the state government to take up ST status for Meiteis in four months. The environment, unfortunately, was replete with the branding of Kukis as nomadic infiltrators, though some other hill communities like Paites (a Naga tribe) were also targeted. The saving grace has been Assam Rifles and the army providing timely succour and relief. Trust having been severely degraded, Kukis are demanding a separate administration. It will require intervention by the central government, wherein mature handling and better perception management are critical.

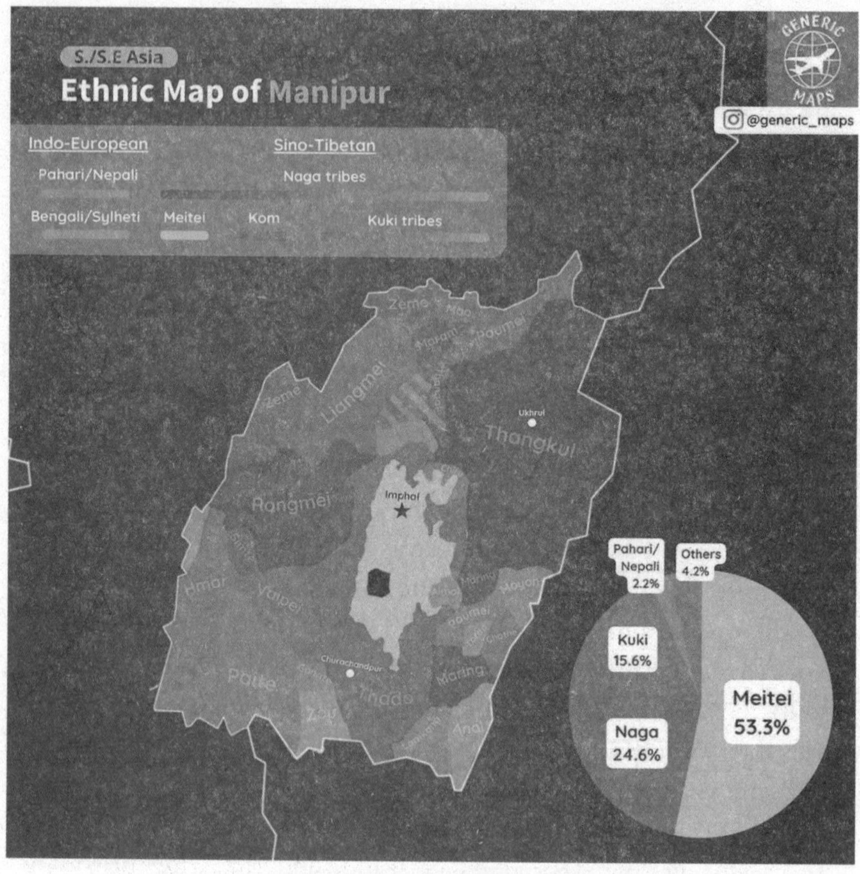

(Map source-https://images.app.goo.gl/1RzkgTN9VqTrNT57)

Manipur: A Chance Slipping in the Northeast

(Written in August 2023)

In 2017, I wrote an article titled, 'Manipur Opportunity High – Lighting the Possibility of Using the State as a "Gateway to the East" and a Catalyst for the Centre's Act East Policy'. Six years later, on May 28, another column was titled, 'Eyes on Manipur: Disturbing Trends and The Way Forward'. It has been 66 days since the manifestation of malfeasance, yet we seem to be still groping for some semblance of a resolution. It appears that fatigue is beginning to set in, and attention is shifting to riots in France and the Khalistani vandalism abroad. Ironic indeed, but we seem to be lapsing into the age-old malady of keeping the North-East (NE) remote and out of focus.

As a measure of gratitude to the wonderful people of the NE and Manipur, this follow-up is another attempt to continue meaningful discussions and seek normalcy. In this scope, it attempts to skirt the all-pervasive 'whodunit' temptation. The present state of a binary divide in communities is such that any attempt to unravel the plot only adds to the schism and blame game. A formal inquiry has been ordered. It is hoped that it will help to move forward in the process of truth, reconciliation, and at least some semblance of justice, although the process inspires little confidence, at least currently.

(Map source-https://images.app.goo.gl EnSX8AvN3J QnoGTa8)

External and Regional Factors

It is indeed ironic that the new US ambassador has strayed into uncharted territory and even offered to help in the Manipur crisis, though he has added the caveat 'if requested for such assistance'. This utterance breaches the established norm of staying clear of domestic issues and is especially jarring in the current Indo-US bromance. Hopefully, the US will stay away from any forays, but it should bring home the stark realisation that the issue is serious and Manipur issue is beginning to find resonance abroad.

In the regional context, even more serious is the Myanmar government's sharp reaction to the Indo-US joint statement calling for the release of all political prisoners and the restoration of democracy. Myanmar's cooperation is critical for the resolution of the Manipur quagmire and kickstarting the 'Act East' Policy. **More importantly, with the ubiquitous presence of China, do we want another collusive manifestation in the east along with the Sino-Pak one in the West? It is imperative that we find ways to assuage the military junta in Tatmadaw on priority.**

Drivers for Reconciliation Process

The process of healing has to start by building on the realisation that we can choose many things but have no choice in our neighbours. Even with the hypothetical scenario of separate administration for Kukis, communities have to co-exist as neighbours. Contentious issues like ST status and forest and land rights need to be put on the back burner till we build inter-community consensus. The root cause of turmoil is fear and uncertainty. **The Meiteis are apprehensive, sandwiched between Greater Nagalim and Kuki-Chin-Zomi homeland demands. The lifelines to the Imphal Valley, NH-2 (from Dimapur-Kohima), and NH-37 (from Silchar) are subjected to regular coercive blockades by hill tribes.**

The menace of rooting out illegal poppy cultivation requires to be tackled with a de novo approach. Combating a narco-terrorist economy (approximately Rs 40,000 crore) and larger than even the state budget requires a multi-dimensional approach. While it is expedient to target small fish (illegal farmers), much more important is to tackle mafias with political connections and linkages with terrorist groups. Concurrently, alternatives in terms of skilling, vocations, and replacement remunerative crops have to be devised. It is equally important that such initiatives are seen to be impartial and that they avoid stereotyping and targeting any particular community.

Security Matrix and Challenges

Columns of the army—Assam Rifles (AR), CRPF, BSF, ITBP, and SSB—numbering approximately 40,000, are deployed to aid the civil authority, besides Manipur Police, as per media reports. These have been put under a coordinating HQ led by a former DGP of CRPF. The initial deployment was more in fire brigade mode. It is now being rationalised to 'one force, one area', with the likelihood of BSF being given charge of the most volatile Bishnupur and Churachandpur. **The focus is to stop inter-gang fights and create buffer zones.**

Security forces face multiple challenges; just to enumerate important ones:

- The first is the absence of the AFSPA regime in the valley, which is used by insurgents as a rest and recuperation base and eventually as a launch pad in connivance with sympathisers.
- Second, **the state has gotten nearly 4,000 weapons looted, many of them having found their way to militants. It would be relevant to quote a Manipuri general: 'In the Kashmir valley, we chased a few hundred, maybe less than 500 weapons; here, numbers are scary.'**
- Third is the open and porous borders in difficult terrain, coupled with inadequate forces and minimal infrastructure for border management and controlling narco-terrorism.

- Fourth is the partisan interference of NGOs, especially Meira Paibis.
- And finally, the issue is the mischievous narrative of painting the Assam Rifles as a pro-Kuki force.

The problem is likely to foster; hence, a unified command and redeployment of forces, preferably a combination of Assam Rifles and CRPF, aided by the army is recommended. The CRPF should even induct three to four *mahila* (women's) battalions to control Meira Paibis. It may appear retrograde, but AFSPA needs to be re-imposed, at least temporarily, in the valley areas. In the long term, border infrastructure, intelligence, and bodies to control narco-terrorism need major revamping. The information vacuum needs to be bridged to counter divisive narratives.

The Way Forward

The idea of imposing the President's Rule has floundered, with the CM orchestrating a melodramatic coup. Concurrently, the peace committee has not found any traction, with Kukis objecting to the CM at the helm. The real status is that communities, including even academia, are pushing divisive narratives. The centre should consider a more proactive intervention with a short-term President's Rule with an unambiguous mandate and authority to recover arms and restore sanity. **Concurrently, much-needed inter-community rapprochement can be initiated by an independent external group of trusted interlocutors to foster bipartisan healing.**

Punjab and Khalistan Problem

Punjab – Seeking the Way Forward in a Simmering Crisis

(Written in June 2023)

Introduction

Role models like Rishi Sunak, PM of the UK, and Ajay Banga, recently appointed President of the World Bank, bolster Punjab's image, giving it a larger-than-life narrative. The community is characterized by an adventurous and industrious spirit, very visible and known to be punching much above its weight classification, notwithstanding small numbers. Unfortunately, back home, Punjab and Punjabis have been in the news, mostly for the wrong reasons. The unending chase of the self-appointed head of Waris-Punjab-De (WPD), Amritpal Singh, turned into a tragi-comic drama and charade, finally leading to his apprehension after more than a month-long, hit-and-miss chase. Punjabis have been spearheading unresolved farmers' agitation, which has been unfairly dubbed as a 'Khalistan' linked movement.

Dominant Narratives

The two dominant narratives are drug addiction ('udta' or delirious Punjab) and the threat of revival of the separatist Khalistan movement. This erodes the image of farmers, sportsmen, and enablers of the green revolution, as also numerous much-acclaimed charity initiatives by organizations like the Khalsa Aid. Even abroad, especially in Canada, some Punjabis are embroiled in drug trade and extortion. The recent shooting of the top UN-designated gangster Amarpal Singh in Canada, attacks on Hindu temples in Australia, and violent protests and attempts to ransack the Indian High Commission in London are ominous trends. The recent report by Colin Bloom, a reputed and independent faith engagement advisor of the UK government, recommended a detailed investigation into pro-Khalistan activists and the application of necessary correctives. Many such maladies have been soft-pedalled in Canada, the UK, and Australia, allegedly due to the compulsion of vote-bank politics. It will be appropriate to examine emerging challenges and flag appropriate coping strategies.

Challenges

Demographic and Theological Environment: Punjabi society has traditionally been syncretic with a tolerant, multi-faith character that lives in harmony. The approximate demographic distribution is – Sikhs (57%), Hindus (38%), Muslims (2%), and a visibly increasing number of Christians (2%). The culture is referred to as Punjabiyat, and the inclusive faith as 'Nanak Naam Lewa', with Sufi influences. **Punjab has approximately 32% Scheduled Caste (SC) Dalit population, divided into Ramdasias, Mazhabis, Kabeer Panthis, Ravidassias, and Adi-Dharmis sects, often jostling among themselves.** This is the highest percentage of SC in a state. Unfortunately, the Sikh religion has been taken over by Gurdwara tussles and competitive extremism and has become intertwined with mainstream politics. This has resulted in the sprouting of deras (seminaries) and sants (spiritual heads), some even with private militias. The overarching religious body, **Shiromani Gurdwara Parbandhak Committee (SGPC)**, has been forced to yield control of Nanded Sahib and Patna Sahib, temporal seats, referred to as takhats. Similarly, DGPC and HGPC have come up in Delhi and Haryana. A new trend is fomenting societal tensions by orchestrating sacrilegious acts (described as beadbi) like the Bargari incident, wherein the holy book was desecrated by mischievous elements. Another notable phenomenon is faith healing camps to convert poor Dalits.

K2 Conundrum: Pakistan is reportedly running a Kashmir-Khalistan (K2) project through the ISI, aimed at reviving the Khalistan movement even when the situation in Kashmir is improving. Many extremist leaders are operating from Pakistan. The recent shooting down of the dreaded and wanted Khalistan Commando Force Chief Paramjit Singh Panjwar in Lahore corroborates this fact. As a corollary, there are regular reports of sightings and shooting down of drones by security agencies. The drone-drug combo is being misused by the narco-terrorism mafia across the border to drop weapons besides drugs, of course in connivance with agencies and Rangers across. **It is fairly apparent that currently, Khalistan and separatism have no real traction within Punjab. The old generation still recalls the difficult period and 'Santaap' (suffering) during the '80s and '90s. The fact that Amritpal and his movement failed to gain traction and he was described as Bhagoda (absconder) amply proves their irrelevance.** However, the movement simmers abroad amongst the diaspora with sporadic, high TRP-grabbing incidents aided by complicit elements in authority.

Agrarian Complexities: Punjab continues to be the granary of the nation with a record-breaking output. The overflowing granaries enabled the free grain scheme, which provided much-needed relief during the COVID-19 pandemic and the Ukrainian conflict, which had disrupted grain supply. **However, the 'rice-wheat' cropping pattern is an irrigation-intensive process, resulting in the water table receding/depleting and creating a spectre of looming water stress.** Burning of crop residue, along with other factors, creates choking environmental pollution in the National Capital Region (NCR). Rampant use of chemical fertilizers and pesticides has poisoned soil and water, leading to a high incidence of health hazards like cancer. Land holdings have become smaller, and farming is done by contracted migrant labour, which is creating demographic challenges.

Socio-political Determinants: The politics are a complex cocktail of theologically inclined parties, like factions of Akali Dal.

The unprecedented majority given to the Aam Admi Party (AAP) was essentially a rejection of established parties. **The Punjabi society is characterized by a few defining peculiarities.** These include –

- First, **an overbearing sense of scepticism.** This also leads to Punjab being perpetually out of step with central authority, manifesting in non-ruling (opposition) parties like AAP at the helm of the state.

- Second, the **youth need persuasion and sensitive handling** as Punjabi nature is described in the seminal quote, *"Pyar naal saadi jaan bhi le lo, Jora-Mardi naal, assi pinde di joon bhi nahi deni"*. It means that with love, you can ask for our life, but with coercion and force, we shall not part with even unwanted lice on our bodies. This is often mistaken as entitlement or bullying, which is avoidable.

- Third, **if convinced about a sense of fair play and the right cause, the very same lot is willing to blindly follow the leader.** The caveat is that leadership has to be earned, as we see in Sikh soldiers and the response of soldiers and rural peasantry in the 1965 and 1971 wars. Most importantly, the Green Revolution, transforming the starving PL-480 dependent, ship-to-mouth national economy into grain exporting one, bears reiteration on this account.

- Fourth, the **Punjabi youth are aspirational and willing to live on the edge, and they increasingly seek greener pastures through migration.** This has resulted in the eulogizing of gangsters, guns, and even drugs. Ironically, even those aspiring to drive trucks prefer to do it in Canada and the USA.

- Most importantly, the **central government has undertaken multiple initiatives, including emotive ones like recognizing the martyrdom of Sahebzadas (sons of Guru Gobind Singh), yet it requires more efforts to overcome persistent scepticism amongst society.**

The Way Forward

The **solution to Punjab's woes mandates multi-dimensional and focused long-term commitment.** It is high time that the law-and-order mechanism in the border state is sorted out. Pakistan is hell-bent on prosecuting the K2; it is axiomatic that the police and central agencies should be synergistic, stay focused on operations, and keep out of partisan politics. The reality is that state administrative and police cadres are divided along political affiliations with incessant inter and intra-cadre tussles. Supreme Court-mandated reforms, outlined in the Prakash Singh Committee report, need to be applied post-haste.

Externally, hierarchy and diplomats have red-flagged extremist tendencies, and pressure has to be kept up, as these governments tend to pander to vote banks. It is also necessary that those identified as dubious are denied reciprocal citizenship benefits like Overseas Citizens of India (OCI) and Non-Resident Indian (NRI) privileges. The problem has political dimensions, wherein theologically inclined parties are sprouting factions that seek recognition by positioning themselves on the extremist fringes. The established parties owe it to Punjab to forge Punjabiyat and inclusive 'Nanak Naam Lewa' culture. **In the long term, it is all about tackling socio-economic problems, primarily enabling Green-revolution-2.0, skill-building, and building an eco-system for employment to reclaim the lost glory of Punjab.**

The bottom line is that problems, although serious, are manageable and flagged. Given the right catalysts – meaningful leadership, commitment, and central initiatives, Punjabis are self-starters and are blessed with legendary resilience and improvisation (jugaad). They have it in them to rebound. Meanwhile, the diaspora should contribute by anchoring meaningful initiatives back home but, most importantly, desist from supporting malevolent elements and fissiparous tendencies.

Clash of Corridors – BRI, CPEC, and IMEC

Strategic Appraisal of the Belt Road and China-Pak Economic Corridor

Chinese infrastructure and Connectivity projects around the world have an element of "national security" and are less of an economic offer for host countries.

—Mike Pompeo, former US Secretary of State

Introduction

It is now an established and **academically validated conclusion that the building of all-weather roads or transportation corridors by China has catalysed and paved the way for the country's prosperity.** The current Chinese domestic network linking markets to distribution centres acted as a pathway to trade, governance, and unprecedented progress. It was described as a hub and spoke model, along with many other similar names, The proof is in lifting 770 million people out of poverty. President Xi Jinping declared in the CCP Congress that China has achieved the first centennial goal of achieving modest prosperity and banishing poverty. This is also documented in the joint book titled *Four Decades of Poverty Reduction In China: Drivers, Insights for the World, and the Way Ahead*. It is important to reiterate that connectivity has always been relevant in great games in the form of Silk Roads and maritime corridors like spice routes. Many other developing countries are trying to replicate this infrastructure push as a poverty alleviation measure in the form of roads, freight, and maritime corridors as a sort of panacea or silver bullet. **However, the real challenge lies**

in correct initial planning, timely project execution, and, most importantly, corruption-free management.

China, flush with surplus capital and infrastructure-building capacities, embarked on a global initiative in the form of the BRI in 2017. The Chinese outward reach has been propelled by a desire to present an alternate mode of development. It also has historical drivers, as China, driven by the Middle Kingdom Syndrome, perceives it as the pivot. This is also coupled with the desire to redress alleged historical and colonial wrongs to claim her rightful place on the global stage. BRI attracted as many as 120 odd countries, and it seemed that every nation wanted to join what was hailed as the 'project of the century'. This much-heralded initiative seems to be floundering, with many dismissing it as a 'road to nowhere'. It is important to take note of the legendary resilience of China and carry out an objective assessment of BRI to map the likely trends.

History of Silk Roads-Major Inferences

- The Royal Road of the Persian Empire in the fifth century BC, which predates the Chinese Silk Roads, is the earliest known transport corridor.
- The earliest Chinese transportation corridor initiative was the eleventh-century BC Silk Roads of the Han dynasty, spanning approximately 4,000 miles (6,500 km). Chang'an-Tianshan Corridor in China-Kazakhstan-Tajikistan has been accorded a UNESCO heritage site status
- Besides terrestrial connectivity, the Chinese invented the Mariner Compass, a master instrument for seafaring, in 220 CE. Chinese had also constructed dry docks and the capability to make large ships. The Chinese Treasure Fleet under Admiral Zhang earned notoriety for its exploitative voyages.
- **The basic drivers for Chinese outreach are:**

- ▶ **Firstly, the Middle Kingdom orientation or syndrome**
- ▶ **Secondly, the correction of alleged historical wrongs perpetuated by various colonial empires in the 'century of humiliation'**
- ▶ **Thirdly, the desire to build and showcase alternative models of development**
- ▶ **Fourthly, the availability of surplus capital and infrastructure-building capacity**

The Pandemic and the Ukrainian Conflict – Major Lessons

- **Public health is a vital component of CNP**, and well-being can boost gross domestic product (GDP).
- A pandemic, at best, can be tackled with a scientific and evidence-based approach rather than quick-fix solutions like the failed Chinese Zero-Covid policy of lockdown and selective vaccination.
- The sharing of transparent data and statistics enables peer review, which is vital in tackling pandemics.
- **Dependencies in health-related supplies can create strategic vulnerability,** and this was even used as leverage by China.
- **Self-reliance and decoupling of supply chains** are the new trends.
- Health and vaccination corridors are manifesting.
- The increasing frequency of natural disasters dictates **the need for disaster mitigation, relief, and the creation of disaster-resilient infrastructure.**
- Notwithstanding the pandemic, resilience and innovation can help to persist with limited activity, throwing up new possibilities in remote working and Work From Home (WFH). Some of these are being retained even after the return of normalcy due to cheaper costs and flexibility.

- **BRI and the CPEC have been significantly impacted by Covid-19.** The BRI's northern links to Europe through Eurasia have been stymied.
- The Ukrainian war has spurred the development of the International North-South Transport Corridor (INSTC) and the improvisation of the Wheat/Grain Maritime Corridor.
- In sum, pandemics are proliferated by **vectors like viruses and bacteria, which travel along transportation corridors. Hence, it is important to deal with them on a global basis with a cooperative endeavour.**

Appraisal of the Belt and Road Initiative (BRI) – Major Inferences

- The concept of mega connectivity was **first propounded in 2013 as OBOR but later renamed BRI in 2017.**
- **Belt and Road, or '*yidaiyilu*' in Chinese, really implies 'a "belt" of overland routes and a maritime "road" connecting Southeast Asia to Eastern Europe and Africa'.**
- BRI, described as **the 'project of the century' and the '21st Century Silk Road'**, is planned to extend to 65 countries, touch the lives of 62 per cent of the world population, entail an expenditure of 30 per cent of global GDP, and harness 75 per cent of energy reserves.
- BRI summits in 2017 and 2019 were attended by 120 countries, including 29 at the apex level. **India was the most notable absentee.**
- China has a presence in 42 ports in 34 countries with a stated desire to extend to 75 ports as part of the 'String of Pearls' or maritime bases.
- As many as **42 countries are currently trapped in a debt repayment crisis**, termed a 'debt trap'. Despite the pandemic-induced

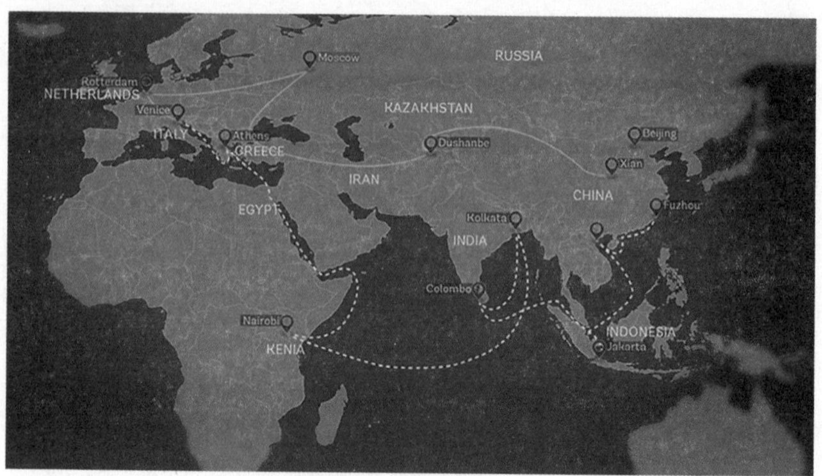

(Source-Official website of BRI-https://eng.yidaiyilu.gov.cn/wap/wap.htm)

humanitarian crisis, China has only agreed to reschedule the debt of the 17 most distressed nations.

- China is attempting to extend her influence and **foster dependencies in cyber and space domains by promoting Digital and Space Silk Roads.**
- **BRI projects are carbon intensive** with large greenhouse gas (GHG) emissions and don't really comply with climate action plan norms.
- BRI projects are encountering multiple challenges, such as debt servicing, corruption, security, inefficient project execution, and opposition from the local populace.
- China has assured and is **attempting to rebrand the initiative as BRI-2.0 after a review.** However, host nations remain largely sceptical. These are being packaged as **Global Development/Security/Cultural Initiatives in 2021,2022 and 2023.**
- **America is attempting belated rear-guard action in the form of B3W**, and similar infrastructure initiatives are proposed by multilateral forums like the Quad.

Manifestations of the Debt Trap

- **Sri Lanka** has been forced to yield control and lease **Hambantota for 99 years.**
- **Pakistan** has also handed over **de-facto control over Gwadar to China by allowing a 43-year management control.** Pakistan has become **a basket case.**
- **Malaysian PM** Mohamad had **cancelled the Railways project** amounting to US $20 billion on the grounds that the country could not afford such exorbitant projects.
- **Tajikistan** had to yield control of **1,158 sq. km of territory to China** in 2010 in lieu of loan waivers. This territory is now being used by **Chinese companies to mine minerals, including gold.**
- **Laos has yielded control of her electricity grid to China for 25 years** as part of debt restructuring.

Analysis of CPEC

- CPEC was **first considered in 2003** and offered to Pervez Musharraf but was not progressed. **Nawaz Sharif in 2013 announced launching of CPEC, describing it as game-changer**, the project got traction in 2015 with signing of MOUs.
- Described as geo-economic oriented project, it is **manifestation of China-Pakistan collusive linkages and is another addition to geo-strategic glue after gifting of Shakasgam Valley.**
- **Project traverses through contested PoK and GB, on which India has de-jure territorial claim.**
- CPEC encompasses **critical strategic spaces like Shaksgam Valley, Khanjureb pass located in confluence of multiple civilizations.**
- Project is situated in **highly volatile KPK and Baluchistan affected by insurgencies and terrorism.** The region is **loosely administered**

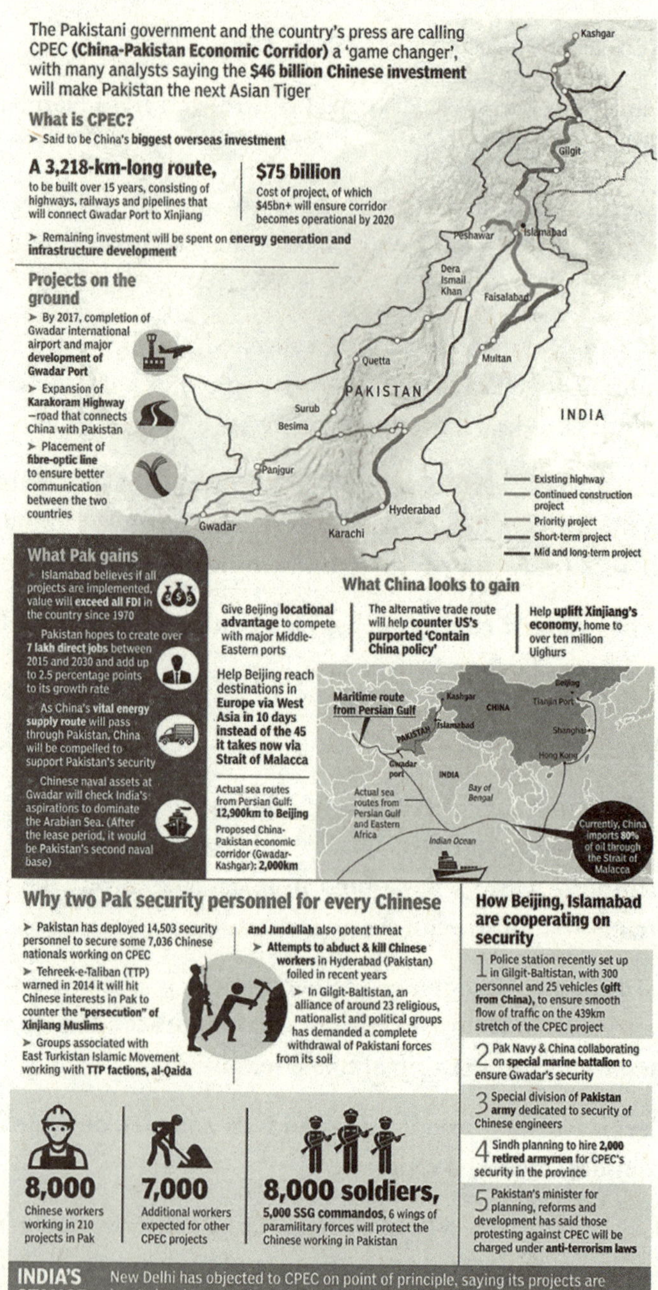

(Graphic Source-Times of India-Rajat Pandit)

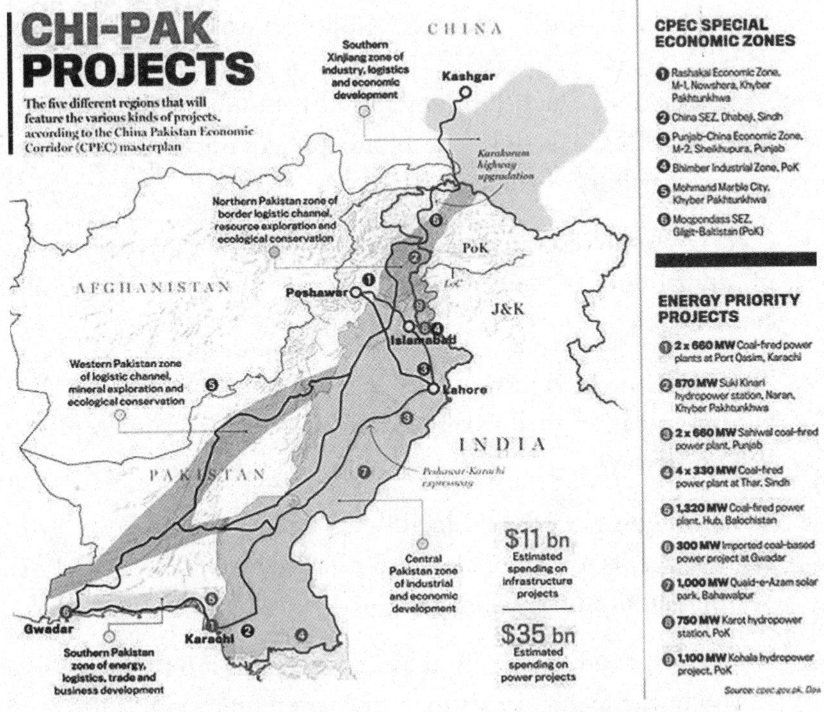

(Source Graphic-India Today-Tanmoy Chakraborty)

with traditional codes and has **large number of warlords or self-styled Emirs.**

- **Gwadar on Makran coast is the pivot with warm water connectivity** and potential to reduce dependencies on sea lanes transiting through **Malacca strait.**
- **Ambitious project includes power generation, road connectivity, port development and FTZs and SEZs as the focus areas.**
- Financial **outlay is pegged at $ 46 billion with possibility of growing to $ 62 billion** and more. Currently, however **it is stalled due to rethink and review** of projects.
- Project in **more than seven years has missed deadlines and has made tardy progress.**

- Major gain has been **addition of approximately 6 GW power generation** out of projected 12-15 GW, making approximately 45% accretion. The **utilisation and distribution of this power is tardy as CPEC has only one minor project on up-gradation of power distribution grid.**
- Most power projects are **coal based with GHG and have problems of availability of coal.** Three hydel projects are still under construction.
- There have been **improvements in 3218 km long road corridor** but **up-gradation to all weather capability at Khnanjureb pass is still underway.**
- While **ongoing Orange Line Metro project bundled as early harvest has been commissioned but other project like ML-1 are pending on funding challenges.**
- **Gwadar** has been **notionally activated and lacks infrastructure** like captive power plant, water supply and communications. Overall, it is **underutilized and yet to find traction.**
- Security threat to Chinese workforce and **repeated terrorist attacks has created major concerns.**
- Pakistan has **added two light Divisions equipped with sophisticated equipment and other dual use capabilities** in the garb of CPEC.
- Pakistan is caught in **debt trap and economic crisis leading to spectre of Hambantota type of situation and even talk of economic colonisation.**
- Project has potential to **escalate regional tension and added to strategic challenges for India.**
- **India needs to be prepared to face long term threat posed by China and Pakistan in collusive mode.**

Recommended Indian Response Matrix

- **China is increasing its presence and influence in Indian Ocean** using bases like Djibouti, in conjunction with Gwadar, Hambantota and other bases as part of its **Maritime Silk Road (erstwhile string of pearls) and two oceans strategy.**
- Chinese attempt to secure role in Chabahar after launching Gwadar as also Kyaukphyu in Myanmar in relation to Indian venture of Sittwe, is **indicative of desire to stymie Indian connectivity initiatives.** It doesn't fit into **propaganda narrative of shared prosperity and regional co-operation.** On the contrary, it is more appropriate to read it in the context of Chinese maxim, "**One mountain cannot take two tigers**".
- **China** though a **late entrant** is utilising its fiscal clout and port development leverages to **set up forums to counter already established ones.**

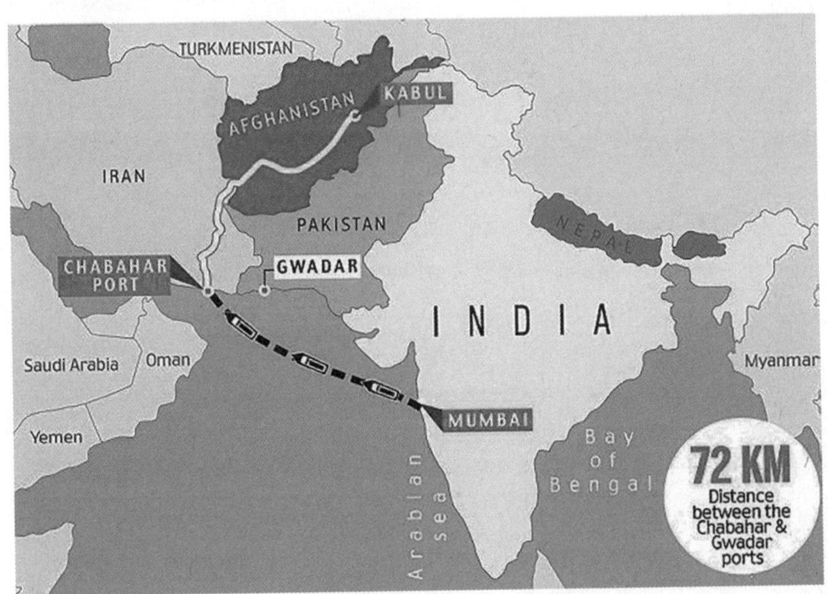

(Source Graphic-ORF report on Chabahar port)

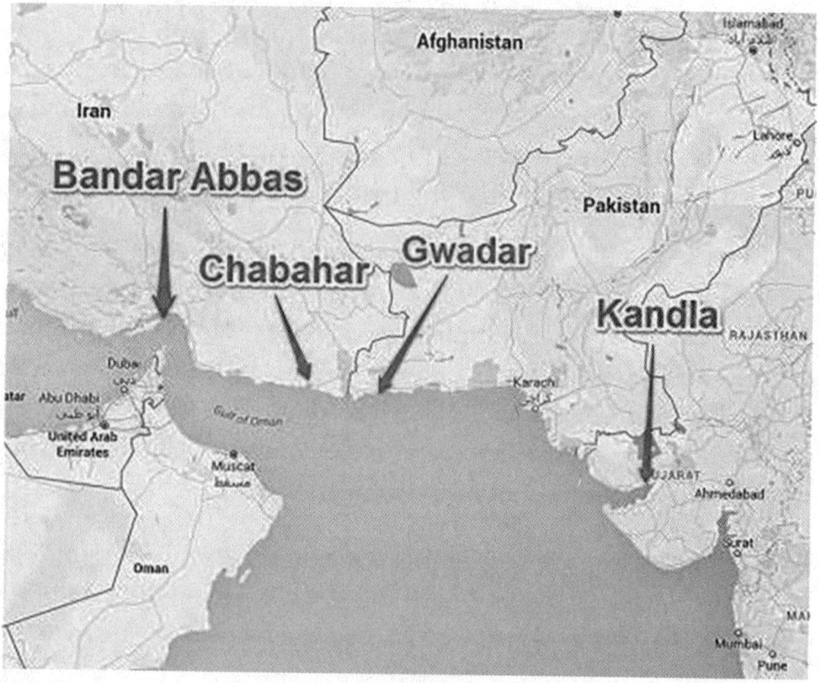

(Source-Levina, The Chanakya Forum)

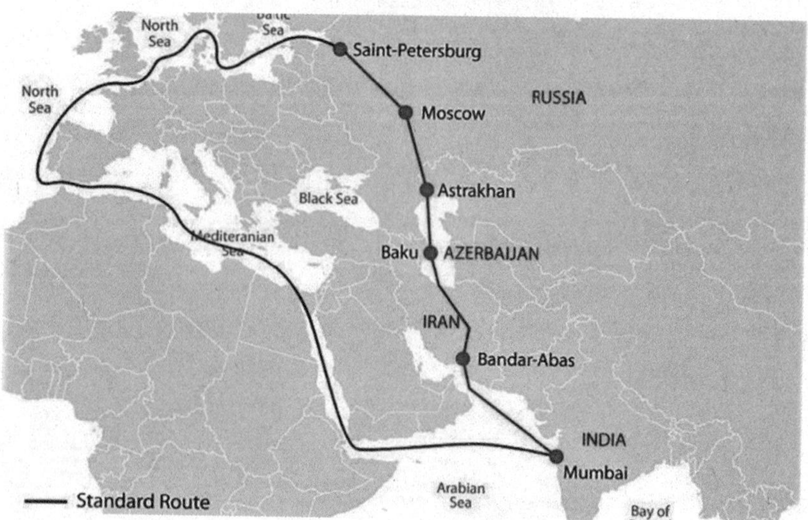

INST-(Source-Levina, The Chanakya Forum)

- Indian Ocean and Indo-Pacific are becoming **increasingly contested spaces with maritime strategic power games.**

- Chinese threat must be **viewed in collusive format with Pakistan and can manifest in various domains-land, air, cyber besides maritime. CPEC could contribute to this as a flank of application, launch pad and for logistics.**

- India is looking at **holistic response** based on alternate connectivity, increased co-operation, tie-ups for access to more bases and strategic up gradation.

- **India has an indifferent record in its regional connectivity projects and needs to review its project management strategy.**

- **INSTC has the potential to negate salience of CPEC and bypass Gwadar** maritime choke being attempted by China.

- **Alliances like QUAD have only limited utility as partners are reluctant to physically apply forces. India may have to face its threats largely on its own.**

- **Adopt whole of nation approach to cope up with China.**

India at a defining stage in journey of its development in '**Amrit-Kaal**' (75 to 100 years) is faced with **complex challenges of balancing its resources-**

- Between development and defence-'**guns vs butter**' dilemma.

- Apportioning between **land-based threat and maritime domains.**

- Resolution of tech asymmetry-**current vs future.**

Concluding Inferences

- Transportation corridors or **connectivities will enjoy seminal relevance and will continue to 'proliferate influence'.**

- There are serious concerns about **the lack of compliance with climate action goals** in most BRI projects. Their carbon audit is warranted.

- China has been forced to review and repackage the BRI and even the CPEC, but **it is unlikely to pull out or foreclose in the short term.**

- The CPEC is currently in stagnant mode and has made only a marginal difference to the life of Pakistan's population. Pakistan is caught in a fiscal emergency, debt trap, and high inflation. The power situation remains grim.

- **Gwadar, with its strategic location, has major utility for China's Indian Ocean push but is also a very serious security challenge for India**

- The success of corridors is conditioned by **'bottom-up' planning based on local aspirations and the environment in a 'win-win' format**, most importantly, in a corruption-free, efficient, and timely project execution.

- The crux is inclusive planning and customisation to enable and trigger economic activity for debt servicing. The CPEC is a prime example of sinking more than $40 billion spread over nearly a decade, yet Pakistan is caught in a fiscal emergency, food riots, inflation, and a power crisis.

- Projects should **build local competencies and the stake of communities.** They should up-skill and empower the population of host countries.

- Planning, execution, and funding of projects should be transparent and compliant with international norms, including auditing.

IMEC – Ramping-up for the Connectivity Game

(Written in November 2023)

The real icing of the G20 summit was on the sidelines, in the declaration of the new India-Middle East-Europe-Economic Corridor (IMEC). This initiative, projected as pathbreaking, has the potential to develop a more efficient connectivity ecosystem.

It may also checkmate China's Belt and Road Initiative (BRI) and, more specifically, the China-Pakistan Economic Corridor (CPEC), which have a direct bearing on India. It may sound a bit discordant, but many such lofty projects have floundered after launch, and our track record in the infrastructure realm has been rather uninspiring. It is a must to analyse the issue objectively to ensure that it does not end up as another missed opportunity.

Update: The **project is currently stalled due to the ongoing Israeli offensive in Gaza and only planning and preparatory work is underway.**

Salience of Connectivity Corridors

The salience of connectivity corridors since ancient times, like the 5-BCE dated Royal Road of the Persian Empire and the Chinese Silk Roads, have served to bind empires, spanning nations. The alignment of the proposed IMEC links India through a maritime route to Red Sea ports, a freight corridor through the Arabian Peninsula to Israel, and going on to Europe. It brings the focus back to the Middle East or West Asia as a competitive connectivity hub. Iran and Turkiye are already pitching for the revival of a tweaked version of the ancient Persian Empire's alignment, linking present-day Iran, Iraq, Syria, and Turkiye.

These highways and maritime corridors have served multiple purposes as part of geo-strategic powerplay. Objectives have included: first, geo-economics for trade, starting with barter for silk and spices; second, geo-theological for proselytization and proliferation of religions; and third, geo-political for tax collection, law enforcement, and alliances. On the downside, there is the spread of pandemics, like smallpox in the 6th CE and then the Black Plague. In present times, Covid-19 proliferated along these pathways and aerial corridors. Looting and plunder by Mongol and Mughal hordes were also executed through these routes.

BRI and CPEC

Chinese, flush with surplus funds and infrastructure-building expertise, launched the One Belt One Road (OBOR) in 2013. Stung by criticism, they had to repackage it as BRI in 2017 to make it sound more inclusive.

However, as it happens in translated Mandarin terminologies, 'belt' is terrestrial/surface link and 'road' is a maritime corridor spanning oceans, with a covert aim to have a presence in 95 odd ports.

Chinese, as per internationally verified estimates, claim to have lifted approximately 700 million people above the poverty line by linking manufacturing hubs with markets. The Chinese model is being replicated in India with projects like the Golden Quadrilateral corridor and freight corridors.

The crucial challenge is time-bound execution, ensuring quality and minimising corruption. Climate change has inducted requirements of disaster resilience and green corridors. In our context, collapsing highways in Himachal Pradesh and Uttarakhand are a stark warning signal. China has also curated newer variants like the Digital Silk Road and space and health roads. Notwithstanding failed projects like Hambantota and a debilitating debt trap, the Chinese footprint is ominous across Africa.

Indian Track Record

Forays in connectivity corridors can be traced back to the stalled Kaladan multi-modal project linking Sittwe in Myanmar to the Zokhawthar border town in Mizoram. Even the India-Myanmar-Thailand trilateral highway has been impacted by the disturbed internal situation in Myanmar. In contrast, China has operationalised the Kyaukphyu project and the China-Myanmar corridor with connectivity and a pipeline to Yunan. China has also muscled its entry into the Chabahar port project in Iran. It is likely to take over a rail link to Hajigak in Afghanistan, usurping the old border road project of Zaranj-Delaram. Another much-acclaimed project, the International North-South Corridor (INST), linking Mumbai to St Petersburg through Bandar Abbas and the Caspian Sea, has become a casualty of power politics. **In sum, tardy project implementation coupled with instability in the extended neighbourhoods has made it a litany of languishing, sub-optimal projects.**

The Way Forward

IMEC is the somewhat belated outcome of the Build Back Better World (B3W) plan announced by US President Biden in 2020. It has leveraged initiatives of the Abraham accord, I2U2 (India-Israel-USA-UAE) and India-USA-Saudi Arabia negotiations to put together this project. The transit time from Mumbai to Port Suez, using the clogged Suez route, is approximately 11 days. IMEC is likely to take six days to reach the Dammam/Jebel Ali Red Sea ports. Added with one-two days of transhipment and rail freight to Haifa, **it saves three-four days in transit and 20–25% in cost.**

The big advantage is that major building blocks of Indian and European legs (from Port Piraeus in Greece) are already in place. The main requirements are a rail link in Jordan, connecting it with the Saudi rail corridor (currently under modernisation) and Israel on the other end. The rail corridor is based on uniform standard gauge, obviating transhipment. Saudi Arabia has committed $20 billion, and the rest should be possible through a multilateral lending forum. India has already acquired a presence in the Haifa port and has shown interest in Port Piraeus, especially in keeping the Chinese out.

Various stakeholders have their own interests, such as the USA wanting to promote decoupling from the Chinese supply chain. India will have to step up its manufacturing base. Considering our domain competence, we should also bid for a role in rail infrastructure creation. Saudi and Israeli interests include the resolution of the Palestinian issue. Saudi Arabia also seeks guarantees against Iranian nuclear bombs. Concurrently, China has been actively promoting rapprochement between Iran and the Gulf states. In this age of multi-polarity, Gulf countries are playing a balancing game by joining BRICS with China and OPEC, plus with Russia besides IMEC. The challenge is to keep focus on our interests in this new complex game. For India, Russia, Iran, and Central Asia remain strategically relevant. **In our plurilateral template, it is not a zero-sum game of corridors but a multiplicity of connectivity and redundancies, which is important to cater for strategic flux.**

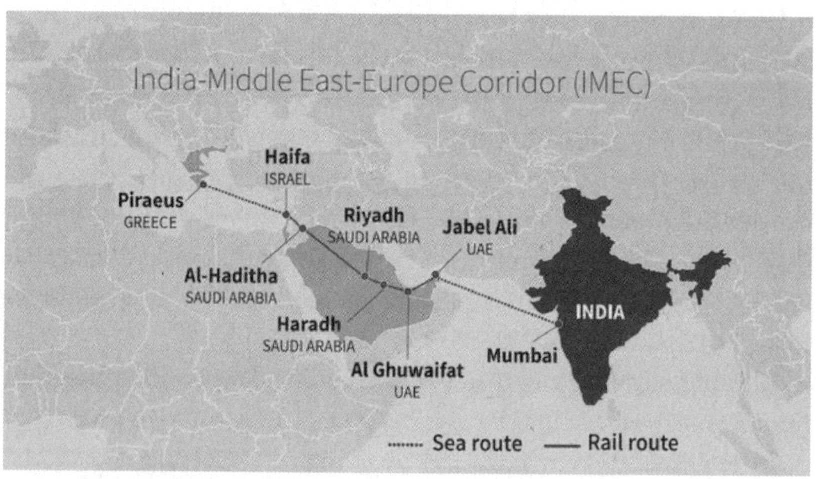

Jottings: An Abiding Narrative

The first part of Jottings covers important contemporary issues, yet there are many more waiting to be discussed. These include subjects like transformation, HR policies, ceremonial, CPEC-BRI, North East and many more.

Depending on your feedback, we will follow-up with more books. It will be good idea if you, dear readers, share your valuable perspectives through e-mail (singhkayjay3363@gmail.com) or even social media (X-@kayjay34350; LinkedIn or Facebook).

The ultimate joy for an author is not only in readers buying and reading the book but in their imbibing the Mantra of LED-PAL: Location, Economics, Demographics, Past Narratives, Alliances and Adversaries and Leaders to make sense of dynamic flux in the strategic environment. National Security mandates a 'whole of nation' approach and participation by all Citizen Warriors as we face the challenges of the emerging BANI (Brittle, Anxious, Non-linear and Incomprehensible) environment.